'A broad and important collection of es‥ ‥ing-
ing together the authoritative maj‥ ‥ork
by emerging scholars and analysts. ‥ of
feminist psychoanalytic study, whici ‥r,
than ever.'

Grace ‥*ua, Berkeley*

'One of the fundamental discoveries o ‥*J*analysis was that sexuality is
not simply about intimacy, but is ridden by the social. Social relations are very
much at work in sexuality, which is why shifts in social relations often play out
on the ground of sexuality, as questions of sexuality and its vicissitudes. Contemporary debates are striking evidence of this connection, and this collection
of essays captures, reiterates and reflects on it most impressively.'

Alenka Zupančič, *Institute of Philosophy at the*
Slovenian Academy of Sciences and the Arts

Psychoanalysis, Gender, and Sexualities

Transcending the sex and gender dichotomy, rethinking sexual difference, transgenerational trauma, the decolonization of gender, non-Western identity politics, trans*/feminist debates, embodiment, and queer trans* psychoanalysis, these specially commissioned essays renew our understanding of conventionally held notions of sexual difference.

Looking at the intersections between psychoanalysis, feminism, and transgender discourses, these essays think beyond the normative, bi-gender, Oedipal, and phallic premises of classical psychoanalysis while offering new perspectives on gender, sexuality, and sexual difference. From Freud to Lacan, Kristeva, and Laplanche, from misogyny to the #MeToo movement, this collection brings a timely corrective that historicizes our moment and opens up creative debate.

Written for professionals, scholars, and students alike, this book will also appeal to psychoanalysts, psychologists, and anyone in the fields of literature, film and media studies, gender studies, cultural studies, and social work who wishes to grapple with the theoretical challenges posed by gender, identity, sexual embodiment, and gender politics.

Patricia Gherovici is a psychoanalyst and analytic supervisor. She is a multiple award-winning author who has authored or edited six books, including *Please Select Your Gender* (2010) and *Transgender Psychoanalysis* (2017).

Manya Steinkoler is a psychoanalyst and professor of English BMCC, CUNY. She has co-edited with Jessica Datema, *Revisioning War Trauma in Cinema* (2019), with Vanessa Sinclair, *On Violence and Psychoanalysis* (2019), with Patricia Gherovici, *Lacan, Psychoanalysis and Comedy* (2016), and *Madness Yes You Can't: Lacan on Madness* (2015).

Psychoanalysis, Gender, and Sexualities

From Feminism to Trans*

Edited by Patricia Gherovici and Manya Steinkoler

Routledge
Taylor & Francis Group

LONDON AND NEW YORK

Cover image: Robert Morrissey / EyeEm; Gettyimages

First published 2023
by Routledge
4 Park Square, Milton Park, Abingdon, Oxon OX14 4RN

and by Routledge
605 Third Avenue, New York, NY 10158

Routledge is an imprint of the Taylor & Francis Group, an informa business

British Library Cataloguing-in-Publication Data
A catalogue record for this book is available from the British Library

Library of Congress Cataloging-in-Publication Data
Names: Gherovici, Patricia, editor. | Steinkoler, Manya, editor.
Title: Psychoanalysis, gender, and sexualities: from feminism to
Trans* / edited by Patricia Gherovici and Manya Steinkoler.
Description: Abingdon, Oxon; New York, NY: Routledge, 2023. |
Includes bibliographical references and index. | Identifiers:
LCCN 2022020865 (print) | LCCN 2022020866 (ebook) |
ISBN 9781032257587 (hbk) | ISBN 9781032257600 (pbk) |
ISBN 9781003284888 (ebk)
Subjects: LCSH: Transgender people. | Sex differences. | Sex. |
Psychoanalysis.
Classification: LCC HQ77.9 .P79 2023 (print) | LCC HQ77.9
(ebook) | DDC 306.76/8—dc23/eng/20220613
LC record available at https://lccn.loc.gov/2022020865
LC ebook record available at https://lccn.loc.gov/2022020866

ISBN: 9781032257587 (hbk)
ISBN: 9781032257600 (pbk)
ISBN: 9781003284888 (ebk)

DOI: 10.4324/9781003284888

Typeset in Garamond
by codeMantra

Contents

Contributors

Dina Al-Kassim, Professor of English and Chair, Graduate Studies, Institute for Social Justice 2014–2020, Affiliate, Institute for Social Justice, Associate, Peter Wall Institute of Advanced Studies, University of British Columbia, Vancouver, is a critical theorist who works on political subjectivation, sexuality and aesthetics in transnational modernist and contemporary postcolonial cultures, including the Middle East, Africa, Europe and the United States. She is the author of *On Pain of Speech: Fantasies of the First Order and the Literary Rant* (2010). Al-Kassim's publications have appeared in *Grey Room, International Journal of Middle East Women's Studies, Public Culture, Cultural Dynamics,* and the volume *Islamicate Sexualities.*

Sheila L. Cavanagh is a professor at York University, Toronto. She is the past chair of the Sexuality Studies Association (Canada) and the former co-editor of *Somatechnics* Journal. Her research is in queer theory, transgender studies, and psychoanalysis. Cavanagh edited a special double issue of *Transgender Studies Quarterly on Psychoanalysis* (2017), co-edited *Skin, Culture and Psychoanalysis* (2013), and is co-editing a special issue of *Psychoanalysis, Culture & Society* on the psychoanalysis of Bracha L. Ettinger. She is completing her third book monograph titled *Transgender and the Other Sexual Difference: An Ettingerian Approach.* She published *Sexing the Teacher* (2007) and *Queering Bathrooms* (2010) and is a GLBT Indie Book Award finalist and recipient of the CWSA/ACEF Outstanding Scholarship Prize Honourable Mention (2012). Her scholarship has been published in a wide range of psychoanalytic, gender, and sexuality studies journals.

Marcus Coelen is a psychoanalyst and psychoanalytic supervisor practicing in Berlin and New York. He has published on Freud, Lacan, Proust, Blanchot, Bataille and other authors, is the co-editor of the book series *Neue Subjektile* with Turia+Kant in Vienna as well as of the journal *RISS,* Berlin. He teaches at Columbia University, New York and Munich University and is a member of *Das Unbehagen.*

Elena Comay del Junco is a writer and assistant professor of philosophy at the University of Connecticut. Her research in the history of philosophy spans ancient Greek and Roman philosophy as well as the Islamo-Arabic tradition. She also works on political philosophy and feminism. Her essays and criticism have appeared in *The Point, The Los Angeles Review of Books, The New Inquiry, The Chicago Tribune*, and other publications.

Monique David-Ménard is a professor of philosophy and director of research at the University Paris-Diderot. She is the former director of the Centre d'étude du vivant (2005–2011) where she created the program "Gender and Sexuality." She is an associate member at ICI-Berlin (International Center for Inquiry). As a practicing psychoanalyst in Paris, she is a member of the Société de Psychanalyse Freudienne. She is also the co-founder of the ISPP (International Society for Philosophy and Psychoanalysis) and a member of the International Network of Women Philosophers at the UNESCO. Her most recent books include *Tout le plaisir est pour moi* (2001); *Deleuze et la psychanalyse: l'altercation* (2005); *Les constructions de l'universel, psychanalyse, philosophie* (2009); *Éloge des hasards dans la vie sexuelle* (2011); *Corps et langage en psychanalyse* (2016); *La Vie sociale des choses. L'animisme et les objets* (2020).

Tim Dean is the James M. Benson Professor in English at the University of Illinois, Urbana-Champaign, USA. Widely published in the areas of queer sexuality and psychoanalysis, he is the author or editor of *Beyond Sexuality* (2000), *Homosexuality and Psychoanalysis* (2001), *A Time for the Humanities* (2008), *Unlimited Intimacy: Reflections on the Subculture of Barebacking* (2009), and *Porn Archives* (2014). His new book, authored with Oliver Davis, is *Hatred of Sex* (2022).

Patricia Gherovici is a psychoanalyst, analytic supervisor and Sigourney Award recipient for her clinical and scholarly work with Latinx and gender-variant communities. She is the co-founder and director of the Philadelphia Lacan Group and Associate Faculty, Psychoanalytic Studies Minor, University of Pennsylvania (PSYS), Honorary Member at IPTAR the Institute for Psychoanalytic Training and Research in New York City, and Founding Member of Das Unbehagen. Her books include *The Puerto Rican Syndrome* (2003, Gradiva Award and Boyer Prize); *Please Select Your Gender: From the Invention of Hysteria to the Democratizing of Transgenderism* (2010) and *Transgender Psychoanalysis: A Lacanian Perspective on Sexual Difference* (2017). She has published two edited volumes (both with Manya Steinkoler) *Lacan on Madness: Madness Yes You Can't* (2015) and *Lacan, Psychoanalysis and Comedy* (2016). Most recently, she published a *collection* (with Christopher Christian) *Psychoanalysis in the Barrios: Race, Class, and the Unconscious* (2019, Gradiva Award and American Board and Academy of Psychoanalysis Book Prize).

Oren Gozlan is a clinical psychologist and psychoanalyst. He is the chair of the Scientific Committee, and faculty at the Toronto Institute of Psychoanalysis and teaches at the Toronto Institute of Contemporary Psychoanalysis and the Canadian Institute for Child and Adolescent Psychoanalytic Psychotherapy. He is a member of the IPA committee for Gender Diversity and Sexuality. His book *Transsexuality and the Art of Transitioning: A Lacanian Approach* won the 2015 American Academy & Board of Psychoanalysis annual book prize. He is the winner of the Symonds Prize for 2016 and the Ralph Roughton Award for 2022. His edited collection titled *Critical Debates in the Transsexual Studies Field: In Transition* was a finalist for the 2019 Gradiva Award.

Darian Leader is a psychoanalyst working in London and a member of the Centre for Freudian Analysis and Research. He is the author of several books, including *Introducing Lacan* (1992); *Why Do Women Write More Letters than They Post?* (1996); *Freud's Footnotes* (2000); *Stealing the Mona Lisa: What Art Stops Us from Seeing* (2002); *Why Do People Get Sick?* (with David Corfield) (2008); *The New Black: Mourning, Melancholia and Depression* (2009); *What Is Madness* (2012); *Strictly Bipolar* (2013); *Hands* (2017) and *Jouissance; Sexuality, Suffering and Satisfaction* (2021).

Juliet Flower MacCannell writes on literature, art, architecture and philosophy as well as psychoanalysis. She is the author of over 90 articles and several books, including *The Hysteric's Guide to the Future Female Subject* (2000); *The Regime of the Brother* (1991); *Figuring Lacan: Criticism & The Cultural Unconscious* (1986 and 2014–reprinted), and the co-author of *The Time of the Sign* with Dean MacCannell (1982). She has edited a number of volumes for the Irvine Humanities Series, including *The Other Perspective in Gender and Culture, Thinking Bodies,* and was the contributing editor for *Critical Dictionary of Feminism and Psychoanalysis,* Oxford: Blackwell (*Elizabeth Wright, General Editor*).

Her most recent publications include essays on "The End(s) of Violence," "The Echo of the Signifier in the Body: Drive at Work Today," "Anxiety: Genuine and Spurious," "Why Culture? A Psychoanalytic Speculation," and "Refashioning Jouissance for the Age of the Imaginary." Her essay re-evaluating her 1991 work, "The Regime of the Brother Today," is to appear (in German translation) in a two-volume collection, *Post-Oedipale Gesellschaft,* ed. Tove Soiland, Marie Frühauf und Anna Hartmann, Vienna: Turia + Kant.

In 2015, she was named the Outstanding Professor Emerita of Comparative Literature and English at UC Irvine, where she taught from 1980 until she retired. She was the co-chair of the California Psychoanalytic Circle from 2000 to 2017, and the editor of its journal *The Journal of Culture and the Unconscious.* She is also the co-creator (with Dean MacCannell) of 22 art installations at SomArts Gallery's curated annual Day of the Dead exhibition (San Francisco: 1998–2020).

Ranjana Khanna is a professor of English, Women's Studies, and the Literature Program at Duke University. She works on Anglo- and Francophone Postcolonial theory and literature, and Film, Psychoanalysis, and Feminist theory. She has published widely on transnational feminism, psychoanalysis, and postcolonial and feminist theory, literature, and film. She is the author of *Dark Continents: Psychoanalysis and Colonialism* (2003); *Algeria Cuts: Women and Representation 1830 to the Present* (2008). She has published in journals like *Differences, Signs, Third Text, Diacritics, Screen, Art History, Positions, SAQ, Feminist Theory,* and *Public Culture*. Her current book manuscripts in progress are called *Asylum: The Concept* and *The Practice and Technologies of Unbelonging*.

Elissa Marder is a professor of French and Comparative Literature at Emory University where she is also affiliated with the Departments of Women's Gender and Sexuality and Philosophy. She is a founding member of the Emory Psychoanalytic Studies Program and served for many years as the director. Her publications include *Dead Time: Temporal Disorders in the Wake of Modernity (Baudelaire and Flaubert)* (2001); *The Mother in the Age of Mechanical Reproduction: Psychoanalysis, Photography, Deconstruction* (2012); *Time for Baudelaire (Poetry, Theory, History),* eds. E.S. Burt, Elissa Marder, Kevin Newmark. *Yale French Studies* vol. 125/126 (Spring, 2014); *Literature and Psychoanalysis: Open Questions,* ed. Elissa Marder. *Paragraph* Volume 40; Issue 3 (November, 2017). Situated at the intersection of psychoanalysis, deconstruction and feminism, her work engages with texts and questions that challenge traditional conceptions of temporality, birth, technology, sexual difference and the limits of the human.

Geneviève Morel is a psychoanalyst in Paris and Lille. She's a member of CRIMIC (Paris-Sorbonne) and CFAR (London), and president of Savoirs et clinique and Collège de Psychanalystes- A.l.e.p.h. She directs a clinical seminar in l'UHSA (CHU-Lille). Her books include *Ambiguïtés sexuelles: Sexuation et psychose* (2000, published in English as *Sexual Ambiguities,* 2011); *Clinique du suicide* (2002); *L'œuvre de Freud. L'invention de la psychanalyse* (2006); *La loi de la mère. Essai sur le sinthome sexuel* (2008, published in German as *Das gesetz der Mutter,* 2017 and in English as *The Law of the Mother,* 2018); *Terroristes: Les raisons intimes d'un fléau global* (2018).

Dany Nobus is a professor of Psychoanalytic Psychology at Brunel University London, founding scholar of the British Psychoanalytic Council, and former chair and fellow of the Freud Museum London. He is the author of numerous books and papers on the history, theory and practice of psychoanalysis, most recently *Critique of Psychoanalytic Reason: Studies in Lacanian Theory and Practice* (2022).

Kelly Oliver is W. Alton Jones Professor of Philosophy at Vanderbilt University. She is a past co-director of the Society for Phenomenology and Existential Philosophy (SPEP), and a founding member of both the Kristeva Circle and philoSOPHIA. She is the author of 16 scholarly books, and the editor of another 13 books, along with over 100 scholarly articles. Her work has been translated into eight languages. She has been interviewed on ABC News, appeared on CSPAN Books, published in the *New York Times* and *Los Angeles Times*, among other appearances and publications in popular media. She is also the author of three award-winning mystery series.

Ray O'Neill is a journalist and psychoanalytic psychotherapist. He lectures at Trinity College Dublin and Dublin City University, and is a research associate with the Centre for Gender and Women Studies at Trinity College Dublin. He co-hosts the RTE television show Then Comes Marriage. He is a member of APPI, Association for Psychoanalysis and Psychotherapy in Ireland, and a member of the College of Psychoanalysis. He is the author of "The Lies, The Wish, and The Wardrobe: Homophobia, Homosexuality and the Closet in Analysis"; *The Letter*, Vol 26, Autumn 2002; "Naming the Loves that Dare Not Speak Their Name: The Politics and Perils of Language and Sexuality," *The Letter*, Vol 28, Summer 2003; "Oedipus dup(e)licated: (Re)Producing children in the postmodern world of Hyperreality," *The Letter*, Vol 36, Spring 2006; "This Sex which is Not One: Luce Irigaray: Sexual Difference, Différance, and (In) Differ(e/a)nce," *The Letter* (forthcoming); "I's Wide Shut: The Traum(a) of the Sexual Relationship" Formation Clinique du Champ Lacanien, Paris (forthcoming).

Manya Steinkoler is a full professor of English at Borough of Manhattan Community College, CUNY and a psychoanalyst in New York. She has published books and articles on psychoanalysis, film and literature. Her recent books include: co-authored with Jessica Datema, *Revisioning War Trauma in Cinema: Uncoming Communities* (2019); edited with Vanessa Sinclair, *Psychoanalysis and Violence: Contemporary Lacanian Perspectives* (2018); edited with Patricia Gherovici, *Lacan, Psychoanalysis and Comedy* (2016) and *Lacan on Madness: Madness, Yes You Can't* (2015). Recent articles have appeared in various scholarly and psychoanalytic journals, including *Division Review* and *La Clinique Lacanienne*. She is the co-organizer of the Psychoanalysis on Ice Conference (Reykjavik 2014, 2017) with Michael Garfinkle, where psychoanalysts from all schools and trainings come together to discuss concepts fundamental to the field, and is the co-chair and originator of the Transitions and Transactions: Literary Pedagogy at the Community College Biannual Conference, that has now become international and is the only conference of its kind, dedicated to meeting the challenges particular to the teaching literary studies at the community college level.

Yannik Thiem is an associate professor of Religion at Columbia University. They specialize in queer and feminist theory, religion and politics, and critical theory. Thiem is the author of *Unbecoming Subjects: Judith Butler, Moral Philosophy, and Critical Responsibility* (2008) and their second book *Ripples of*

Redemptive Time: The Ethics and Politics of Temporality in Hermann Cohen and Walter Benjamin is forthcoming. Currently, Thiem is working on a new project entitled *Queer Nuisances: Race, Religion, Sex and Other Monsters* drawing on queer theory, transfeminism, religious studies, critical race theory, as well as European early modern philosophy. Most of Thiem's work to date was published under their previous name, Annika Thiem, which remains Yannik's official double as far as the government of Yannik's country of origin, Germany, is concerned.

Calvin Thomas is a professor of English at Georgia State University in Atlanta. He is the author of *Male Matters: Masculinity, Anxiety, and the Male Body on the Line* (1996); *Masculinity, Psychoanalysis, Straight Queer Theory: Essays on Abjection in Literature, Mass Culture, and Film* (2008), and *Ten Lessons in Theory: An Introduction to Theoretical Writing* (2013). He is the editor of *Straight with a Twist: Queer Theory and the Subject of Heterosexuality* (2000) and *Adventures in Theory: A Compact Anthology* (2019). Other fairly recent publications include "No Kingdom of the Queer" in *Derrida and Queer Theory* (2017) and "Beckett's Queer Art of Failure" in *The New Samuel Beckett Studies* (2019). He is currently working on the second edition of *Ten Lessons in Theory*.

Eve Watson is a psychoanalytic practitioner, clinical supervisor and academic. She co-edited (with Noreen Giffney) *Clinical Encounters in Sexuality: Psychoanalytic Practice and Queer Theory* (2017). She is the current editor of *Lacunae*, the APPI International Journal for Psychoanalysis, a peer-review journal. Dr Eve Watson (Ph.D.) is a psychoanalytic practitioner working in Dublin, Ireland. She also teaches on undergraduate and graduate programs. She has published in Irish and international journals, and has book chapters in congress proceedings of the Paris Forums du Champ Lacanien (2011, 2009), in *Lacanian Psychoanalysis with Babies, Children and Adolescents* (2017) and *Lacan's Ecrits: A Reader's Guide* (2018). She is a full member of the Association for Psychoanalysis and Psychotherapy in Ireland (APPI).

Jamieson Webster is a psychoanalyst in private practice in New York City. She is the author of *The Life and Death of Psychoanalysis* (2011) and *Conversion Disorder: Listening to the Body in Psychoanalysis* (2018); she also co-wrote, with Simon Critchley, *Stay, Illusion! The Hamlet Doctrine* (2013). She writes regularly for *Art Forum*, *Spike Art Quarterly*, and *The New York Review of Books*. She teaches at the New School for Social Research and is a member of IPTAR and Das Unbehagen.

Introduction

Patricia Gherovici and Manya Steinkoler

More than 30 years ago, with groundbreaking books like *Gender Trouble* (1990) and later *Bodies that Matter* (1993), Judith Butler ignited a new way of thinking about gender that blazed across global academia. They provided a critical reading of psychoanalysis that radically changed the way people talked about sex and gender. They did this quite simply by positing a "performative" concept of gender (meaning that gender is enacted at will) that divorced sexuality from any essentialist foundation. In their unforgettable contention, Butler observed that contemporary feminism had "gotten in trouble" by becoming a "woman's" movement, that is, by assuming that women were a uniform group with shared identities, interests, and goals. The critique of patriarchal culture made on behalf of the presumed universality of "women," they argued, had produced an "unwitting regulation and reification of gender relations" (1990, 5–6). Feminism limited to women would have reinforced a binary view of gender relations, which happened to be the very template from which feminism was trying to break away. Butler argued that any political claim made in the name of all women treated as a seamlessly homogenous category would amount to a self-defeating gesture. Butler's argument calls up Jacques Lacan's formula: "Woman does not exist," which means that, unlike masculinity, which is a universal function founded on the phallic exception of castration, woman is non-universal. Butler would take Lacan to task for his repeated use of the concept of the phallus even though for Lacan, the term functions as a signifier, a holder of meaning, and is not reducible to an anatomical organ.

If gender was socially constructed, as Butler asserted, could it be constructed differently, or did social conditions impose some sort of determinism? Did construction offer the possibility of agency and transformation? Since for Butler the notion of a gendered self, which Robert Stoller (1985) called "gender core" (pp. 11–14), is produced along "culturally established lines of coherence" (Butler, 1990, 24), gender, in this sense, is not simply an attribute that persons are supposed to have (as a humanist feminist position may claim) or a relation (as sustained by social constructivists; p. 10). Butler's proposition was that "being" a sex or gender is fundamentally impossible (p. 19).

DOI: 10.4324/9781003284888-1

Butler's innovation resonated with Luce Irigaray's critique that grammar can never be a true index of gender relations because it presumes a model of gender as a binary relation between two positive and representable terms. Irigaray (1985a) claims that this binary masks the univocal, hegemonic male discourse that silences the feminine as the site of subversive multiplicity. This refers to the impossibility of a grammatically denoted substance that would correspond with a word like "feminine" as defined by grammar: the feminine sex becomes a point of linguistic absence. Then, gender is neither a noun nor is it a set of attributes—gender is always a doing, constituting the identity it is purported to be (Butler, 1990, p. 24–25).

This was one of Butler's most important arguments in their effort to move beyond the binary frame. If gender is always performative, it is not a substance—it is not an attribute, as a humanist feminist position might argue, or a relation, as sustained by social constructionists—it exists only in so far as it is staged in a social scene. Butler's early thinking has had enormous influence on subsequent definitions of gender and sexuality. For them, sexual identification was akin to gender parody; it was an imitation without an original. Thanks to them, the notion of gender lost consistency and was liberated by being pluralized. Whether one complies with the ascribed traditional gender roles or traverses gender boundaries, one would necessarily put on a gender performance. The idea that gender was performative challenged an earlier feminist critique of sex as produced by discourse. It questioned the sex–gender divide and rejected the idea of compulsory heterosexuality. Not only gender but also sex and sexuality became performative.

Butler's impact on feminism was huge and was relayed by a large audience who appreciated their forceful reformulation of the links between bodies and gender, so much so that this new vision exceeded a purely feminist base. However, when the transgender movement became more visible a few years later, one of its most fundamental claims was to challenge the notion that the physical dimension of gender was inconsequential. The trans* postulation foregrounded the aspect of embodiment and reclaimed the body as sexed, rejecting the notion of a simple parody. We have sketched a bare bones history of the early intersections and debates. More than three decades later, we have felt the need to revisit this heated controversy because we believe that psychoanalysis has a key role to play in it; above all, psychoanalysis always positions itself at the intersection between body and discourse. As practicing psychoanalysts, our interest is not to provide an official history of these complex movements. Our main interest, rather, is to propose a hypothesis of cross-pollination of feminism, psychoanalysis, and trans* discourses to launch a conversation without suspicion or exclusion. This is the shared aspiration of the contributors to this collection. The effort to discuss gender and sexuality from a psychoanalytic perspective reveals a foundational interrelatedness that should not be overlooked. In the last 20 years, we believed that we were in the midst of a "post gender," "non-binary," "agender," or "gender-fluid" era. Some even considered that we lived in "post sexuality" times; younger generations were either putting off becoming sexually active or renouncing sex altogether as "asexual"; statistics seemed to confirm a cross-generational "sex recession."

Beginnings

From the very beginnings of psychoanalysis, Sigmund Freud showed that human sexuality was not explained by the reproductive function. Instead, by exploring psychosexual development, Freud realized that sexuality is the result of a complex evolution. His discovery that unconscious libidinal drives are the cause of psychic motivation transformed the way we think about sexuality and gender. Nevertheless, his theories are assumed to have lost relevance, and are often dismissed as symptomatic of bourgeois Victorian sexist prejudices. If such a view were accepted, psychoanalysis would be deemed an outdated relic of the nineteenth century—and we would all be living happily in the post-gender, post-sexuality, and post-psychoanalysis era. But perhaps there was undue haste in the declaration of all these "posts." We can say, paraphrasing Mark Twain, that the reports of the death of sex, gender, and psychoanalysis have been greatly exaggerated.

While the terms "sex" and "gender" may appear commonplace, albeit only superficially understood, their historical connection, evolution, and motley association are worth examining more closely. Freud characterized his discovery of the unconscious in sweeping terms, calling it a humbling milestone in human intellectual development. A blow to "naive self-love," he equated it with the Copernican and Darwinian revolutions: now we would no longer be masters of our own minds, let alone the center of the universe or of creation. When the psychoanalytic revolution dethroned the ego's mastery by way of the unconscious, it linked subjectivity to sexuality for good. Freud showed that human sexuality is problematic because it defies understanding. His theories transformed our conceptions of subjective agency, as well as gender and sex; they reminded us that human sexuality was anything but natural—it has little to do with having babies or biological programming. Often, it has very little to do with pleasure either.

Freud discovered that neurotic symptoms presented an enigma whose answer concealed not just a memory of a traumatic erotic encounter or a primal scene, but a repressed wish. He revealed the unconscious power of something besides pleasure, positing that sex is not just pleasurable, but also traumatic and potentially destructive. Psychic repression is an intrinsically failed system: the sexual drive emerges in the form of a symptom, offering the same subversive satisfaction that occasioned its initial repression. Freud (1953a) observed that the symptoms themselves could be so libidinally invested as to actually come to constitute "the patient's sexual activity" (1901). This accounted for the fact that sexuality was not reproductive but disruptive, always raising its ugly head in symptoms. Any organ in the body could behave in a sexual manner. For Lacan, one of his closest readers, Freud's discovery that sexuality finds satisfaction in a symptom reveals that human sexuality is fundamentally "skewed" (2006, 676). Sexuality is not "straight," but "twisted," even when it is sublimated. As Lacan wryly put it during one of his seminars:

> In other words—for the moment, I am not fucking. I am talking to you. Well! I can have exactly the same satisfaction as if I were fucking. That's what it means. Indeed it raises the question of whether in fact I am not fucking at this moment.
>
> (Lacan, 1981, 165–166)

Lacan shows us that the sexual drive is satisfied both in and out of bed. One may in fact be experiencing just as much erotic enjoyment by writing or reading this paragraph as one does in furthering one's carnal knowledge. In fact, renunciation itself can be sexually satisfying. The point is that even when we manage to get away from sex, we don't get away from sex; abstinence *is* sexual. Lo and behold, sex remains problematic and excessive even when we are not having any.

The perplexing excess can only be alluded to circuitously. Freud explained this excess in human sexuality by differentiating between "instinct" and "drive."[1] The notion of drive lies at the limit of the organic and the inorganic, a liminal concept that accounts for the intersection between organism and psyche, life and death, body and language. The notion of the drive is a limit-concept that also accounts for a fault innate to the pleasure-principle, pointing to its beyond, but also to its linguistic environment.

Language precedes our arrival in the world. A baby is spoken about even before it is conceived. Names, often chosen before birth, inscribed on gravestones or transmitted to future generations, will survive us. The infant (*infans*, Latin, "without speech") becomes a "speaking-being" via its interaction with early caretakers. Needs are never experienced directly but always mediated. Someone conditions and interprets. The defenseless newborn enters a back-and-forth in which crying, gestures, and noises are interpreted by the main caretaker as "messages," thereby constructing meaning. If language impacts the body before birth, it continues to denaturalize any relation to need; it is in this manner that instinct becomes drive. The drive emerges at the intersection of language and flesh, a convergence that Freud detected in the formation of hysterical symptoms. Language carves out the body into erogenous zones, creating a map of forbidden areas. Unlike animals, who do not need sex education and rely on instinct to reproduce, humans lack sexual knowledge; we need to be told stories of birds and bees, storks and cabbages, seeds and eggs. This unknowable kernel at the center of sexuality is the source of our love for knowledge, which is nonetheless always marred by our passion for ignorance. As such, this blind spot serves as an inspiration for queer studies theorists, who against many dismissals of psychoanalysis as dated patriarchal, sexist, and homophobic argue that

Freud's drive theory debunks the binary of heteronormativity and the illusion of sexual normalcy.

Pink Freud?

Is there such thing as a "Pink Freud"? As a matter of fact, in a foundational psychoanalytic text of 1905, *Three Essays on Sexuality*, Freud (1953b) conceives of the sexual drive as fundamentally bisexual and intrinsically queer, as Christopher Lane and Tim Dean (2001) have shown. Philippe Van Haute and Herman Westerink (2017) have demonstrated in a careful textual study that Freud's first edition of the *Three Essays* did not mention the Oedipus complex and in fact promoted a de-heterosexual and polymorphous sexuality. This constitutional queerness of psychoanalysis has been productively developed and elaborated in the work of Judith Butler (1990, 1993, 2002), one of our contributors, Tim Dean (2000, 2004), David Eng (2001), Lee Edelman (2004), and Paul B. Preciado (2013), among others. Using the critical tools of psychoanalysis, queer studies have shown that at the level of the sexual drive, there is no predetermined object or gender, and consequently, no prescriptive norm. This potential freedom of the sexual drive, a freedom which is also its doom, does not sit well with the public, or even with most psychoanalysts. Institutionally, psychoanalysis would often address this reality through the lens of conservative values, going against the grain of psychoanalysis' own foundations, but its theory has nevertheless been at the root of many trenchant critiques of the dominant hetero-patriarchal culture.

While Freud never grappled with gender directly, he problematized human sexuality when he talked about sexual difference as the psychical consequence of the child's discovery of the anatomical distinction between the sexes. Even though Freud's work on infantile sexuality appears to describe a progression from childhood latency to adult sexual activity, he nevertheless proposes a non-linear evolution, as is made clear by even the most cursory reading of the famous case studies. He posits adult sexuality as infantile, perverse, and polymorphous in his amazing vignettes: ironing bank notes, coughing like Daddy does, postponing defecation against one's will, worrying about unpaid debts, hearing a disquieting clicking sound during intercourse, or even just having a headache—all attest to how sex may appear where you least expect it. Freud's point is that even when sex goes nowhere, it still comes back. It is precisely in this non-normative manner that Lacan intervenes in debates about sexual difference by introducing the notion of "sexuation," which is based not on anatomical borders but on modalities of enjoyment. Lacanian psychoanalysis adds a new term to recapture the magnitude and radicality of the Freudian discovery. Even though the sexuation formulae could be read as reinstating a binary, it could also be read as a matrix proposing a set of mobile modes of sexual positioning. Lacan's sexuation, which will be revisited in Darian Leader's Chapter 3, Geneviève Morel's Chapter 5, Ranjana Khanna's Chapter 10, Juliet Flower

MacCannell's Chapter 11, and Sheila L. Cavanagh's Chapter 15, can be interpreted as a fluctuating relation describing the process by which the subject becomes embodied and sexed in the encounter with language, offering an original contribution to feminist, queer, and trans discourses on sex and gender, sexual identity, sexual orientation, and performativity. Picking up where Freud left off, Lacan gives us tools to overcome the deadlock of current debates on gender and sexuality, superseding the binary of sex and gender. Neither sex nor gender fully expresses the radicality of the difference at stake.

Radical Difference

Insofar as it denaturalizes sex in terms of culture and history, and problematizes gender as unstable and conflicted, psychoanalysis forces us to reconsider patriarchal and heterosexist forms of cultural and ideological domination. Furthermore, psychoanalysis goes beyond the gender–sex binary; neither biology nor culture alone can fully account for either sex or gender. Instead, our sexual being results from a combination of the two, with an unruly surplus that exceeds both. This bridging of mind and body, as well as the fact that they are never coterminous, is specific to psychoanalysis, whose theoretical understanding has had long-lasting historical impacts.

Feminist thinking has contributed needed corrections to sexist, patriarchal notions that led psychoanalysis away from its own initial discoveries. Some feminists have rejected psychoanalysis altogether, but many have read psychoanalysis critically and productively to challenge traditional notions of gender and sex. Feminist readers have reinvigorated the power of psychoanalytic theory, and psychoanalysis has offered feminism a theoretical basis for a non-essentialist understanding of gender and sexuality. Psychoanalysis' generalized attack on biological identity that problematized gender, sex, and embodiment energized discourses like queer and trans discourses. The contributions of psychoanalysis have influenced feminism, queer studies, and what Susan Stryker calls its "evil twin," trans* studies (Stryker, 2004). However, the extensive bibliography on gender has rarely addressed the intersections between psychoanalysis, feminism (understood here as a social movement, a theory, and a political discourse against gender oppression), and transgender discourses.

The connection between transgender discourse and psychoanalysis has a contentious history of resistance and acceptance. The link goes back to the very beginning of both movements, when there was a short-lived but close collaboration between Sigmund Freud and the other Einstein of sex, Magnus Hirschfeld. Hirschfeld, a principal figure in the history of the LGBTQIA+ movement, published many of Freud's early articles in his sexological journals and took a serious interest in psychoanalysis. In 1908, at the very beginning of the psychoanalytic movement, Hirschfeld co-founded one of the first psychoanalytic groups along with Karl Abraham, the Berlin Psychoanalytic Society (Gherovici,

2011, 2017). Hirschfeld was openly homosexual and an activist for the rights of sexual minorities. A pioneer sexologist who championed the de-criminalization of homosexuality, he would open the world's first Institute of Sexual Science in 1919. Despite this promising initial alliance between the emerging fields of sexology and psychoanalysis, as a result of unfortunate prejudice on the part of some of the members of Freud's early group, Hirschfeld would come to distance himself from psychoanalysis altogether.

However historically significant this distance may have been, the initial interrelatedness persists and, as Michel Foucault argues in his *History of Sexuality*, a historical deployment of sexuality since the classical age "can serve as an archeology of psychoanalysis" (Foucault, 1990, 130). Foucault, perhaps unwittingly, exposes a connection that, as Dean and Lane (2001) observe, makes it look as if a history of sex "were really all about psychoanalysis" (8). Psychoanalysis has not just played an important role in the history of sexuality, both trans and cis; in fact, this interrelatedness "is not just referential, it is foundational" (Gherovici, 2017, 46). Psychoanalysis is essential not only historically, but also in considering contemporary approaches to gender, sexuality, and the body.

In this regard, Patricia Elliot has mapped out the theoretical terrain and the disputed borders between feminist, queer, and transgender studies. Aware that they inhabit "contested sites," she underlines the critical and creative potential of open debate and dialogue (Elliot, 1998, 2001, 2010, 2014, 2017). Sheila L. Cavanagh (2017) argues for a "transgender turn" in psychoanalysis in her introduction to the special issue of *Transgender Studies Quarterly*. Regarding what she calls "Transpsychoanalytics," she claims that there are more grounds for critical collaboration than there are for opposition. Following this trend, we can locate the work of Gayle Salamon (2004, 2010), Griffin Hansbury (2011, 2018), Avgi Saketopoulou (2014, 2015, 2017), Oren Gozlan (2008, 2010, 2014, 2016, 2018), Jack Pula (2015), Adrienne Harris (2011), Ken Corbett (2016), Shana Carlson (2010, 2014, 2017), Jack Drescher et al. (2010, 2012, 2016), Marco Posadas (2017), Chris Coffman (2010, 2017, 2022), and Tobias B. D. Wiggins (2020a, 2020b). This promising development regards the trans* experience as an invitation to think beyond the normative bi-gender, Oedipal, and phallic landscapes.

We have structured this collection in three sections. (I) The Genealogy of Sex and Gender; (II) Queering Psychoanalysis: Fantasy, Anthropology, and Libidinal Economy; (III) Being and Becoming TRANS*. This organization sets up a progression from foundational discussions to the discourse of queer resistance to normative modes of thinking to current trans* debates. We have chosen to include the asterisk in trans* both as a symbol of multiplication and as a pointer to an annotation or a footnote, and in this context, it is used as a diacritical placeholder for a myriad of gender possibilities. Our aim is not to apply psychoanalysis to trans* studies, rather to encourage mutual transformation and dynamic interaction.

Loaded Words

We have seen that the current language of gender and sexuality studies inherited a psychoanalytic vocabulary. Again, this linguistic proximity is not
just lexical but foundational. "Gender" was central to the feminist movement,
and reappears in current discussions of embodiment, cis and trans*. While
feminism made us aware that gender is a social construct and not an anatomical destiny, most people do not know that the concept of gender is older than
commonly accepted, and has a charged history, as revealed by its etymology.
The term dates to the ancient world, deriving from the Latin *genus* (family, clan,
race, lineage). The Latin word comes from a Greek root which means to give
birth, an original separation; Aristotle used it in his system of classification to
denote difference and similarity. In its current usage, the term retains these
early meanings of belonging, or not, to a group or class.

The contemporary use of gender in English first appeared in 1915, in a publication by Liverpool surgeon William Blair Well. Well described a complex
medical case of what was then described as hermaphroditism, which today
would be called intersexuality. Intersex people are those born with anatomical
structures that defy a binary. While intersex births are rare, they are nevertheless as prevalent as red hair among the global human population. Very seldom
do these "disorders of sex development," as they are described by the medical community, develop into life-threatening consequences. Moreover, intersex
conditions do not constitute a disease. In the past, newborns who presented
some atypical combination of chromosomes, hormones, gonads, or genitals that
made the sex assignment problematic were treated as having a medical emergency prompting immediate surgical intervention. Nowadays, there is growing
consensus not to intervene early in such cases, because as many intersex activists
claim, reassignment without proper consent would constitute "gendercide."

Like the often loaded words "psychoanalysis," "feminism," "trans*," and
"sex," "gender" has histories and diverse meanings that result from the cultural
and linguistic contexts in which it emerged. In 1915, a surgeon was confronted
with a patient whose "true sex" was not evident from the anatomical structure.
Since the case concerned someone described as "an attractive woman, unfortunately with testicles," a word was needed to describe this "aberration": that
word was "gender" (cited in Domurat Dreger, 1998, 166). With the rise in the
early twentieth century of innovative medical technologies, it was possible to
confirm the actual presence of testes and ovaries as indications determinative
of sex. The point here is simple: it was only when technological developments
allowed clinicians to intervene at the level of the flesh that the term sex began
to refer exclusively to anatomy. The advances in medical technology called for
the necessity of a specific term for sexual determination, artificially separating
gender and sex. Historian and bioethicist Alice Dorumat Dreger (1998) contends that the evolution of medical technology allowing for interventions in the
body separated sex from flesh. One type of sex would be considered exclusively

biological; another type of sex, not dependent on the materiality of the body, would be considered the result of interpretation, culture, and social function: that type of sex was called gender.

Let us underline that in this medicalized context, the word gender was used to denote traditional sex roles, as early medical practices were aimed at buttressing the heterosexual couple. Medical discourse reduced the multiplicity of the trans* feminine experiences to a single "official" version, as observed by Emma Heaney (2017). In a similar vein, the 1950s saw a wave of surgeries implicitly aimed at confirming heterosexual identities. The pioneering physicians in the then-emerging sex-change clinics that were first designed for the treatment of intersex cases, such as John Money's at Johns Hopkins, gave currency to the notion of gender as purely psycho-social. John Money (1955) believed that children were born with a neutral, extremely malleable gender, and that only after age two did children consolidate a stable gender identity as a result of socialization supported by anatomical signs. This hypothesis bolstered early interventions to "correct" intersex cases. These medical technologies modeled on normativizing, heterosexist interventions, however, made available the nascent practice of what was then called "sex-change" all the while opening new possibilities for livable embodiments for transgender people.

As the technology became more refined, the psychoanalyst Robert Stoller (1968, 1975), a close collaborator of John Money, proposed the notion of "core gender identity," i.e., the internalized idea of the individual's belonging to a particular sex, a psychic result of embodiment. Stoller made a great contribution to the emerging field of gender reassignment, which would eventually evolve into a separate practice occasionally at odds with intersex rights. In a stark contrast with a recent trend of early gender transitioning for children as young as age two, intersex advocates propose postponing any surgery until adolescence, or when informed consent becomes possible. While intersex and transgender rights appear mutually contradictory, they both use the mechanisms of social and medical gender production to assert the right to choose gender assignment, case by case.

Initially, Stoller's collaboration with Money was focused on intersex conditions, exploring the so-called anomalies of sexual identity before going on to work with transgender people. Stoller distinguished between "those with biological defects of their sexual apparatuses (intersex patients)" and "those, in the absence of demonstrable biological defect, who have a pronounced deviation in their gender identity" (Stoller, 1975, 1). Stoller distinguished "core gender identity," an internal sense of a gendered self, from "sexual identity," which included sexual activities and fantasies. Navigating the treacherous boundary between soma and psyche, Stoller initially supported the notion of a biological force, an organic drive determining gender. But finding himself unable to locate this anatomical bedrock, Stoller later developed an explanation for transgender orientation that appealed to a model with a psychologically simplistic and essentialist explanation. Stoller summed up gender identity in reductive general formulas for "feminized" boys, i.e., "dominant mother, father pushed to the side, infant cuddly and lovable, mother-son too close" (1975, 193). As the reader might surmise, this scenario is not only applicable to feminine boys, but is encountered daily in garden-variety neurotics of any gender orientation.

In cases of male-to-female transsexualism, Stoller proposed a mimetic, essential femininity passed from mother to son: "What his mother feels is femininity; what he feels is femininity" (p. 204). The model was one of imitation: the son copied the mother, and the mother's excessive closeness to the son was considered a negative influence. In keeping with such formulaic and universalizing tendencies, one of Stoller's various prototypes for transgender manifestations was a distant father and a bisexual mother, who was assumed to have had a period of extreme tomboyishness as a child. For Stoller, these were factors contributing to the creation of transsexuality, especially in cases of male to female. For female-to-male transsexuals, Stoller's speculation can be rendered as an absent father and a depressed, needy mother who masculinizes girls who subsequently take on the role of the husband. While Stoller was trying to find a blueprint for cross-gender identification, it is clear that such "fail-safe" formulations apply to many cases that have nothing to do with transgender persons specifically. In addition, he fails to account for many other cases of gender variance.

At the same time, Stoller is a complex figure who is often unfairly dismissed. Both a pioneer and a man of his time, though he was originally a believer in a biological model, he moved toward a psychological one where gender results from a combination of anatomy, assignment at birth, and environmental influences. His idea of gender as an internalized social construction was neither biological nor psychoanalytic. It was Stoller's answer to Freudian considerations about sexual identity, gender difference, fetishism, and sexuality. His position was closer to a social psychological one. Because of this, it has often been refuted by psychoanalysts. Whether accepted by psychoanalysts or not, the notion of gender as related to identity was proposed by Stoller as a way to convey an inner sense of being male or female, a definition which became extremely popular in the 1970s.

In the 1970s, the feminist movement appropriated the word gender from the medical field where it emerged. Gender became politicized as a means of questioning the essentialism of power relations between the sexes. Gayle Rubin (1975), Kate Millet (1971), and Nancy Chodorow (1978) are some of the feminist theorists responsible for this important work. In this context, the word gender took on a purely cultural meaning. Then by the 1980s, for feminism, the term gender had replaced sex altogether as a descriptor for being a man or a woman (MacKinnon, 1989). In the 1980s, gender was increasingly used to denote sexual identity, to the point that by the new millennium, gender would effectively replace sex in everyday language, at least in the United States. The word "sex" became limited to sexual practices that may or may not determine sexual identity.

By the 1990s, the notion of gender and sex as socially constructed was becoming increasingly accepted in wider intellectual and academic circles (Butler, 1990; Fausto-Sterling, 1999). The use of gender by second-wave feminists has been extensively criticized for its universalism, which failed to recognize the diversity of its base. As bell hooks (1981) observed, Betty Friedan's (1963) well-known proposition that women needed to exit the constraints of homemaking and get professional careers was the privilege of white, post-war, middle-class, married women. The essentializing assumptions that presuppose a shared experience that excludes racialized minorities have left deep marks on current identitary debates. As C. Riley Snorton (2017) shows in his study of the racialized production of gender for black trans* people, we need an analysis of the power dynamics that inform and construct group identity, since the dominant logic of identity assumes race and gender to be fixed and knowable. Behind a sense of identity, there is always exclusion; groups are formed by constructing sameness and excluding difference.

Gender is a formation that involves designations of sameness and difference. While gender, as currently understood, is the socially constructed meaning designating difference between the sexes, sexuality is situated closer to the body, a body that is marked by class, race, ethnicity, nationality, and transnational movements. In everyday vernacular, the word "gender" is used to determine whether we experience ourselves as male or female or something else, and is thought to encompass a vast range of identitary possibilities, an evolving conviction about one's self. Indeed, even the word "gender" has been on a trajectory of polysemy and non-arrival. Already in the 1980s, feminist historian Joan Scott (1988, 1996) used gender as a category of analysis and not as an attribute of the body in order to explore forms of power. For instance, Scott analyzed labor and equality, detecting a masculine presumption and bias in valorized modalities of work; gender allowed for a critique of lived reality. More recently, the term gender has been used in debates determining qualificatory participation in competitive sports, showing a shift in social discourse. The mercurial term has shifted from hormone levels to women's rights and back again, from endocrinology to an ethics of difference, from describing identitary diversity to debates about inclusion in athletics.

Even today, when we think of gender, it is often assumed that it means an identity issue, the expression of an inner truth. This usage is a derivation of Stoller's core sense of gender identification, the notion of a self located somewhere on the gender continuum, or even outside of it. In the context of the genealogy of gender, the invention, popularity, and adoption of the term "cisgender" are quite significant. As gender acquired more and more varied meanings, revitalized by the transgender movement, the word "cisgender" made its formal entrance into the English language. "Cis" is from the Latin prefix meaning "on this side of," and is the opposite of "trans*" which means "across" or "on the other side of." The use of "cisgender" is important in many ways. It overcomes the trans*/non-trans* divide, depathologizing gender diversity and sexual nonconformity. The Merriam-Webster dictionary defines cisgender as the condition in which one's "internal sense of gender corresponds with the sex the person was identified as having at birth." In the Oxford English Dictionary, cisgender "designates a person whose sense of personal identity corresponds to the sex and gender assigned [...] at birth."

In both American and English dictionary entries, the notion of an internalized gender identity remains close to Stoller's definition that affirms identity on the basis of an internalized sexual difference.

In the United States in particular, we are expected to declare some sort of identity in order to exist in society, and this identity is often gendered. At the same time, identitary claims that buttress notions of self and social representation often collide with subjective experience. This can be explained by way of the psychoanalytic premise that the subject emerges when identity fails. Here, psychoanalytic theory acts as a corrective to combative identity politics and the use of gender theory to uphold identitary claims. Psychoanalysis contends that the impossibility of the representation of sexuality in the unconscious implicitly challenges the fixity of identity. In this regard, Yannik Thiem's contribution to this collection (Chapter 18) proposes a shift in our construction of gender. Thiem invites us to move away from thinking of gender "as primarily a self-reflexive, even if socially mediated, self-identification" and begin seeing "gender and race as ongoing elaborations of embodied addresses and responses." It is in this sense that gender transition raises the issue of raced embodiment and necessarily interpellates the neglected intersection of gender and race by considering the unspoken status of normative whiteness.

The wish to believe in a stable identity aims to suture the gap that psychoanalysis reveals to be constitutive of subjectivity. While identity promises to be the expression of one's authentic self, and pledges to bequeath meaning, in actuality, psychoanalysis shows that it is constructed by identification with an other; as such, it is structurally and foundationally alienating. With this in mind, we may ask: are identitary claims representative of or useful to the minorities they seek to advocate for? Behind the promise of unity, there is often a discrepancy between social mandates and subjective experience. This disjunction has been studied and considered in a variety of disciplines. It is exemplified in anthropologist David Valentine's (2007) ethnographic research of New York's low-income trans women of color who conceive of gender and sexuality in terms that differ from those used in political activism; many do not even identify with the category of transgender at all. Valentine notes that the use of the term "gender" that underpins "transgender" denotes normative gender privileges for white, middle-class gays and lesbians but erases the experiences of poor, gender-variant persons of color. The supposedly common use of terms can ignore the very populations they claim to represent and support.

While the term "gender" enabled activists to advocate for gender-variant individuals, Valentine (2007) shows that this advocacy carries implicit assumptions about gender and sexuality, thus unwittingly reinforcing racial and class hierarchies that, ironically, negatively impact the most vulnerable transgender-identified people—young, poor people of color. Socially constructed categories of power oppression such as gender, race, and class are mutually constitutive; they are not isolated or distinct and should be addressed as interrelated.[2] For example, a black trans* woman may become a victim of violence as the result of the aggregation of racism, sexism, and transphobia; these systems of oppression combine in an overarching structure of domination (Talia M. Bettcher, 2007).

The academic conception of a sharply defined contrast between gender and sexuality does not necessarily describe how people of varied backgrounds think of themselves. This semantic discordance is often expressed in the issues that bring someone to an analyst's office. For instance, the artificiality of the separation of gender identity and sexual orientation is heard in the worries of some analysands who no longer ask, "Am I a man or a woman?" or "What is a woman?" (ontological questions concerning gender identity) but "Am I straight or bisexual?" In the latter, the uncertainty about their being conflates object-choice with sexual orientation as a marker of identity (Gherovici, 2010). To understand the variegated use of these terms, we need to address the unconscious dimension of sexuality, love, eroticism, fantasy, trauma, and identity, to name a few, at play in the construction of subjectivity and a world that we call "reality."

A Time of Transition: Our Moment in Perspective

For some time, it had appeared that the many waves of feminism had permanently changed the geography of our social and political landscapes. We thought we had become more grounded in an increasingly tolerant, inclusive, egalitarian, and representative democratic society. This trajectory felt linear, participating in Enlightenment notions of social progress. At least in the West, reality was becoming more just; everyone was supposedly becoming "included"; even gender, the oldest human divide, was eroding quickly. Or so it seemed.

By the beginning of the twenty-first century, the social and theoretical advances of feminism in the developed West seemed to be geared to successfully challenge discrimination based on a hierarchal division of gender. They inspired and were often superseded by activism against other forms of oppression (protecting the rights of the vulnerable: children, refugees, displaced minorities, transgender people, and especially transgender persons of color).

At a more global level, in the era of Trump–Putin–Erdoğan–Bolsonaro chauvinistic ethos, tolerance of difference, which is essential and constitutive of democracy, our cherished promise of equality, was threatened, and remains in peril. Same-sex marriage is legal in the United States and in various countries, while globally, we see homophobia on the rise. The transgender movement has been extolled as the new civil rights frontier, while legal protections for transgender persons are being rescinded. Global representation of women in government is at an all-time high, while women's reproductive rights are threatened by a virulent backlash in many locations where those rights had seemed secure and unassailable. The debate regarding sexual difference has resurfaced more urgently. Today more than ever, given our polarized political climate and the need to critique the imaginary impasses underpinning the current regressive volte face, psychoanalysis offers real tools to resolve the stalemate.

For recent generations in the United States—Xs, Ys, Millenials, and Zs—not only is gender identification fluid, but the possibility of moving between genders has put into question the mandate to choose a gender and challenged traditional notions of identity. Indeed, nowadays, the use of gender-neutral pronouns is becoming a widespread practice. At the same time, Freud's observation that the first assertion one makes upon running into a stranger is always a gender classification remains accurate, even when the answer itself defies the gender binary. Gender fluidity renders our most rudimentary means of perception and classification null and void, exposing the imaginary nature of our judgment capacity, revealing the delusions by which we live.

While gender fluidity makes us aware that the wool of identity is being pulled over our eyes, as far as sexuality is concerned, we are completely hoodwinked, as we have seen. The spectrum of gender makes us realize that we cannot assume the gender of the other; sexuality makes us realize that we assume we know ourselves. If, as Paul B. Preciado (2020) claims, our new gender-fluid moment reveals that the old gender binary regime is crumbling, sexuality continues to cause earthquakes. Despite the various sexual upheavals of the past century and the increasing acceptance of non-normative expressions of sexuality, sex continues to scandalize and outrage us. Today, revelations of sexual misconduct explode all around us, confirming that despite the loosening of gender norms and the reported decline in sexual activity, sex remains the gadfly it has always been, and it's worth reflecting on in our moment of a so-called "sexual recession." Social commentators attribute the recent decline in a sexual activity to causes ranging from the internet, to the prevalence of social media, to lack of body positivity, to easily accessible pornography, to fear of disease, to pharmaceutical drug use, or even to the idealization of abstinence. No matter what the purported cause, there has been a definitive change in bedroom habits. And this change has inspired powerful responses. We find ourselves in an ideological morass: gender liberation confronts the new conservatism; the #metoo movement protesting sexual exploitation occasions a tsunami of sexual harassment allegations; in 2016, a majority of US women voted a known misogynist and sexual bully into the White House; social media makes sex available at a swipe, while "asexuality" becomes a popular new identity choice.

Today, we may have forgotten that when Freud announced the primacy of sexuality in human life, his revelations were shocking. Even though Freud was accused of "pansexualism," proposing theories that challenged "civilized" morals, the irony is that the sex that was supposed to be found everywhere is in fact found nowhere. The real scandal revealed by psychoanalysis is the inherent structural impasse, a "nothing" at the core of sexuality. Sexual difference concerns how this obscure, fundamental negativity is expressed. As we have seen, gender and sex are our attempts at dealing with this impasse. As in Plato's famous allegory of the cave where projected shadows are taken for reality, sexual difference can only be represented in a distorted and insufficient way. Sexual difference resists representation because it operates at the level of drives, which are not on the side of meaning but concern the realm Lacan calls the Real, an unfathomable dimension beyond language.

Both sexual orientation and gender identity are approximations for something that cannot be symbolized or imagined. Like God and death, sex belongs to the troika of unrepresentables. Any attempt to represent sexuality directly encounters an impossibility posed by what psychoanalysis calls sexual difference. This concerns a failure of representation at the center of language. Language's failure, however, is its possibility. Language stems from both the impossibility of arriving at full meaning as well as the very excess it produces and cannot account for; sexuality is what we are never done "talking about." As Charles Shepherdson (2000) puts it, language imposes a failed imperative to represent sexuality; yet, words will always fail to represent it. For the Argentine psychoanalyst and critic Oscar Masotta (1991), the unconscious is what doesn't work between sexuality and representation. Sexuality is conflictual and antagonistic; it does not "work." It is the wrench thrown into the smooth functioning of the assembly line. Recently, Alenka Zupančič (2017) has proposed that sexuality is the main philosophical problem posed by psychoanalysis, marking an ontological stalemate that dislocates and transposes the philosophical question of being. For Zupančič, psychoanalysis shows a fundamental negativity that defies completion. This negativity, however, has productive potential insofar as it resists heteronormative political and social mandates, as Lee Edelman and Lauren Berlant (2014) explore in *Sex, or the Unbearable*.

Sexual Apposites

The contemporary notion of gender marks the beginning of an ongoing "terminological and philosophical debate" that is still far from over, as Genevieve Fraisse (2014, 969) notes. The seemingly obvious distinction between gender as cultural and sex as biological implies an opposition between nature and culture that is played out in the relation between the sexes, sustaining the illusion that sex is "natural." Etymologically, sex (from the Latin *secare*, to cut) is a mark of separation. Similarly, "gender" implies a cut distinguishing sexed beings, "men" and "women," from potential "masculine" and "feminine" attributes. "Gender" emerges in this context, as the need to rethink the *difference* between the sexes as a political and philosophical problem. Both gender and sex imply difference, and their definitions are not sufficiently delineated. For example, in Barbara Cassin's *Dictionary of Untranslatables*, it is noteworthy that while there is one extensive entry for "gender," the entry for "sex" devotes most of its pages to a detailed discussion of "gender." To avoid this epistemological and terminological obfuscation, psychoanalysis has approached the problem of sexual difference as a difference that does not entail an affirmation of meaning or a proposition of value but rather an empty determination. Between men and women, between women and women, between men and men, between neither men nor women and neither women nor men, all we have is incommensurable difference.

The intractability of sexual difference has permeated clinical practice, at times even to the surprise of some psychoanalysts who, in the service of adaptation, focus their attention on "emotional maturity" and "ego strength" while discounting erotic life. Long absent, soon forgotten, sex and gender have become misconstrued in many contemporary psychoanalytic practices and theories, and have been considered a natural, desirable, linear destiny. For example, those psychoanalysts who have opted to emphasize early object relationships and attachment neglect their sexual components, avoiding the aggressive, traumatic aspects of the sexual drive. They assume that sexuality is about intimacy and sociability, and disregard the radical dissolution and alterity that sex awakens. Leo Bersani (1987), to the contrary, has eloquently challenged the idea that sex "has anything to do with community or love" (215), highlighting the "self-shattering solipsistic jouissance" brought about by sexual enjoyment; intense sensual sensations invoke a dissolution of the subject's bodily boundaries (222). Following Freud's observation that sexual pleasure occurs when a certain threshold of intensity is traversed, when the organization of the self is momentarily disturbed by sensation, Bersani argues that when we are having sex with another person, we are no longer self-contained subjects. On the contrary, sexual enjoyment is "socially dysfunctional" (222). Bersani praises "the inestimable value of sex as—at least in certain of its ineradicable aspects—anti-communal, anti-egalitarian, anti-nurturing, anti-loving" (215). While sex might be interrelational, it is not redemptive but rather "anti-social," a quality Robert Caserio et al. (2006) ascribed to queerness, and one that we extend to sexuality in general. Sex is the privileged site where optimistic attachment and the hopeful promise of reparativity become undone. Sex has something that cannot be accounted for by capitalistic economy, an idea that Juliet Flower MacCannell discusses in her chapter in this collection; the accounts do not tally for women, as we shall see.

Relational psychoanalytic theorists, however, such as Stephen Mitchell (2002), view sex as an expression of a wish to establish contact and intimacy. For Mitchell, sex is a manifestation of sociability. While in some cases, sex might overlap with tenderness, love and sexuality are often distinct, a theme developed extensively in palliative self-help books such as Esther Perel's *Mating in Captivity* (2014). Even feminist relational psychoanalysts such as Adrienne Harris, Jessica Benjamin, or Muriel Dimen, who made important contributions to gender theory, have not addressed the disruption introduced by the structural non-relationality of sex. While sex may overlap with love, they should not be confused. Lacanian psychoanalysis unmasks the sanitized, romanticized version of sexuality that alienates and stifles desire in the imaginary trappings of social norms. Lacan remarked that while all his analysands talked about was sex, and not just sex, but rather bad sex. Lacan's insight merged with the scientific proof brought about by William Masters and Virginia Johnson whose guide to sexuality was in fact a guide to sexual dysfunction. Its title, *Human Sexual Inadequacy* ([1970] 2010a), meant that what sex amounts to, for humans, was something that was fundamentally inadequate. Let us note that *Human Sexual Inadequacy*, first published in 1970 had a brief run at the top of the best-seller list but went out of print. However, the 1997 reprint was even more comprehensive: it condensed the classic *Human Sexual Response* ([1966] 2010b) and *Human Sexual Inadequacy* but the title was simply *Human Sexuality*.

In our experience, even those analysands who vaunt their sexual enjoyment, whether in normative or transgressive practices, nevertheless affirm that something is amiss. Even when pleasure occurs, where we expect to find the other, we find an absence. As Alain Badiou writes:

> Lacan reminds us, that in sex, each individual is to a large extent, on their own, if I can put it that way. Naturally, the other's body has to be mediated, but at the end of the day, the pleasure will always be your pleasure. Sex separates, doesn't unite. The fact that you're naked and pressing against the other is an imaginary representation. What is real is that pleasure takes you a long way away, very far from the other. What is real is narcissistic; what binds is imaginary. So there is no sexual relationship, concludes Lacan.
>
> (18)

In Lacan's perspective, it is not that love is a compensation or a disguise for "the sexual relation that does not exist," but that love makes that inexistence tolerable. Love concerns the very being of the other. In love, we are not limited by the narcissistic trappings of the images projected on Plato's cave's walls—we accept the loved other in their being; we love them as they are. While there is a release in tension achieved by the sexual act, this discharge evokes emptiness, expressed by Galen's famous *post coitum omne animalium triste est*. After sexual union, the human animal is sad. Loving tenderness after sex concerns the other's subjectivity; it focuses on the other's being. We could say that it is during the post-sex embrace that the discrepancy of the "meeting" of the bodies is unceremoniously unmasked (one's arm falls asleep, one's foot cramps, one is unable to sleep troubled by the snoring of the other). When tolerated, love not only makes up for these awkward moments, but is not perturbed by the disappointment (negativity) encountered at the core of sex.

Since in love one tries to approach the being of the other, one takes the other not as a medium through which to achieve pleasure, as is the case with sex, but in the amorous encounter, the other's existence is taken as it is. The other exists in you, roughness, pimples, warts, and all. Lacan concludes that with regard to love, gender is irrelevant (Lacan, 1998, 25). Sexual desire is triggered by an object that *causes* desire and makes us structurally lacking. This object is partial and not gendered, separating sexuality from heterosexist mandates and constraints. As Dean (2000, 264–268) has noted, Lacan's notion of the object *a* holds a great deal of promise for future theorization in gender studies and sexuality, as it is democratic and ungendered. Love, as we have seen, goes beyond the potentially fetishistic qualities of the object inspiring desire, to address the other's being. In fact, the notion of a fixed gender identity could reify the ego to defend against a potentially shattering sexual encounter, reducing the partner to an image.

Sexuality versus Identity

Let us continue exploring the conundrum of love, desire, and sexual enjoyment to further disturb the commonly held notion of a confluence between sexuality and identity. For psychoanalysis, all the trouble with sex and gender derives from unconscious sexual difference; this crucial difference is neither an affair of nature, nor a historical construction, for in terms of the unconscious, sexual difference belongs to an inaccessible domain. Sexual identity is not determined by innate factors; rather, it is created by the language into which we are born and with which we are spoken of even before our birth. As Jean Laplanche (1992, 2007) argued, the question of gender cannot be reduced to an expression of biological drives separated from culture, because gender touches on the way culture impacts the body, creating what Maurice Merleau-Ponty (2002) called the "body-schema" as a result of translations and negotiations of linguistic inscriptions. Complex dynamics of identifications determine sexual identity and contribute to the process of sexual embodiment.

Apparently, feminism and psychoanalysis should agree on these points: both privilege subjective experience and both highlight the work of society to shape individuals. However, feminism tends to take the sexual body as a given, whereas psychoanalysis, especially in its Lacanian elaboration, insists on the process of sexuation in embodiment. Thus when Juliet Mitchell (1973, 1997) assessed the importance of psychoanalysis for feminism, she pointed to their distance. She felt that she had moved from the mainstream feminist position of the 1970s, a time when feminism decried psychoanalysis, specifically its notion of penis envy, as a servant of patriarchy. Mitchell eschewed the proposed link with biologizing essentialism. Influenced by the Lacanian conception of the phallus as a signifier, she emphasized the cultural and historical construction of power relations in a psychoanalytic critique of patriarchal culture, reclaiming psychoanalysis as useful for feminism both in the academy and in clinical practice.[3] Other feminist critics also influenced by Lacan followed. The "English Speaking Continental Feminists" brought new life to feminist thought. Alongside Mitchell (*Psychoanalysis and Feminism*, 1973) were Jane Gallop (*Reading Lacan*, 1985 and *The Daughter's Seduction*, 1982), Jacqueline Rose (*Sexuality in the Field of Vision*, 1986, 2005 and her influential introduction to the selection *Feminine Sexuality*, 1982), Elizabeth Grosz (*Jacques Lacan: A Feminist Introduction*,

1990), Teresa Brennan (*The Interpretation of the Flesh: Freud and Femininity*, 1995), and Elisabeth Wright (*Feminism and Psychoanalysis: A Critical Dictionary*, 1992). These critics countered earlier feminist dismissals, reclaiming Freud's analyses for feminist purposes.

The early debates in psychoanalysis paved the way for a challenge to essentialist notions of femininity that would be crucial for the development of feminist theory. Further, challenging the centrality of the Oedipus complex and its heterosexist developmental telos, feminism showed that being a woman and being a mother were distinct. Separating these concepts that were often linked in popular understanding would remain controversial as women increasingly took on roles outside the parameters of motherhood. The Anglo-American as well as the continental feminism of the 1970s interrogated the social and political ideas of the mother in her various functions. Many feminist thinkers made use of the psychoanalytic elaboration of the pre-Oedipal mother–child bond by developing the earlier contributions of Melanie Klein, Donald Winnicott, and the British object relations theorists who followed them. Among the authors who developed a psychoanalytically influenced feminist critique, as it concerned both femininity and motherhood, were Nancy Chodorow (*The Reproduction of Mothering*, 1978, and *Feminism and Psychoanalytic Theory*, 1989), Dorothy Dinnerstein (*The Mermaid and the Minotaur*, 1998), Jessica Benjamin (*Bonds of Love*, 1988, and *Like Subjects, Love Objects*, 1995), and Mardy S. Ireland (*Reconceiving Women: Separating Motherhood from Female Identity*, 1993).

While the Anglo-American psychoanalytic feminist tradition emphasized pre-Oedipal sociality and intersubjectivity, focusing on the values of integration, harmony, and more pragmatically, on the psychic effects of power dynamics in the political environment, continental feminism highlighted self-division and the internalized other. Also seeking to disentangle femininity from maternity, the "French Feminist" writers such as Luce Irigaray, Julia Kristeva, Sarah Kofman, Catherine Clement, and Hélène Cixous made use of psychoanalysis, emphasizing feminine subjectivity, language and writing, the unconscious, and the experience of the feminine body. These theorists were closer to psychoanalysis than their "fore-mother" Simone de Beauvoir, who, like Freud, questioned femininity as a given destiny for a girl, famously arguing that one is not born but rather becomes a woman. De Beauvoir was suspicious of psychoanalysis for a variety of reasons, most importantly due to its focus on the phallus and the perpetuation of masculinist prejudices. She directly critiqued psychoanalysis in chapter 2 of *The Second Sex*, "The Psychoanalytic Point of View" (Beauvoir, 1989, 38–52) objecting to 1940s psychoanalysis that bequeathed to women a "destiny" of masochism and oppression. De Beauvoir's criticism positively empowered a generation of women. At the same time, her existentialist convictions that supported women's freedom and agency left the psychoanalytic notion of a divided subject, split by unconscious overdetermination by the wayside. Sexual difference and its discontents result from the interplay of fantasy and drive; to become more politically adept, we need to be in touch with the fact that we are "strangers to ourselves," as Julia Kristeva (1991) observed.

De Beauvoir's analysis was rapidly integrated into American feminism due to its concern for agency, choice, and identity. French feminist writers such as Irigaray and Cixous looked to de Beauvoir's critique in the service of creativity and embraced the dynamism of a non-biological but rather linguistically influenced unconscious for its writerly, wayward, and undisciplined possibilities. They celebrated the ambiguity and indeterminacy of feminine sexuality, imagination, and creativity.

In recent years, the relation between feminism and psychoanalysis has generated new interest, reinvigorated by British object relations as well as its American iteration, relational psychoanalysis. This revival of psychoanalysis is also visible in the burgeoning field of Lacanian and Kristevan-inspired criticism. Among the earlier works in the Lacanian current, we find one of our contributors, Juliet Flower MacCannell (*The Regime of the Brother: After Patriarchy*, 1991, and *The Hysteric's Guide to the Future Female Subject*, 2000). Influenced by Kristeva, another of the contributors to this collection, Kelly Oliver (*Family Values: Subjects Between Nature and Culture*, 1997, and *Subjectivity Without Subjects: From Abject Fathers to Desiring Mothers*, 1998), inflects philosophical reflection and political critique with psychoanalytic and feminist concepts.

After psychoanalytically influenced feminism, which exposed female sexuality and gender roles as constructed, motherhood was no longer seen as a natural psychic progression of femininity. By way of a reappraisal of the mother–child bond as well the mother–daughter relation and identification, the politics of the psyche (abjection, fantasy, desire, and embodiment) were taken into account. Tackling the ideological underpinning of representation, including cinema and literature, the intersections between gender, race, and power, and symptoms of these imbrications, such as pornography, racism, violence, and oppression, were critically interrogated.

From Feminism to Trans*

Feminism not only broke the ideological tie to biological essentialism, freeing women socially and politically, but also broke a natural relation to the female body as determinative of a fixed gendered meaning. Freud paved the way for this fracture between nature and culture when he permanently altered the Cartesian dichotomy between spirit and flesh as the mystery of the speaking body took center stage.

In terms of the tension between gender as identity and sexuality, as concerns the unconscious and the drives, Jennifer Finney Boylan (2015) astutely stated that sexual orientation is who you go to bed with, but gender identity is who you go to bed as. Boylan's remark opens up to a more radical understanding of sex and gender. Psychoanalysis reveals the paradoxical reality of sexuality— namely that while one may be thinking that one is going to bed as someone, in fact, due to the partial organization of the sexual drives, when we go to bed with someone, we go to bed as *something* (an object). The problem is that we are not sure what this *something* is, either for ourselves or for our sexual partner. In talking about gender and sexuality, psychoanalysis is not concerned with *who*. In any case, as Freud observed, there is more than one *who* engaged as part-object in any sexual interaction, as Tim Dean's contribution to this volume shows. In our book's opening chapter "Freud's *ménage à quatre*," Dean thinks through the difficulty of sex, and specifically the challenge of dispelling certain assumptions about it, such as its dyadic relationality, ineluctable heterosexuality, vulnerability to pathologization, as well as its status either as a symptom or as a cure. The term sex is ambiguous, referring to both sexual difference and sexual behavior. Most psychoanalytic research over the past few decades has focused on the former (often under the rubric of gender) to the neglect of the latter. Likewise, the academic field of queer theory has drifted away from thinking about sex in favor of other objects of inquiry. What may be symptomatic, in the end, is our assumption that we can say what sex is. Indeed, for Dean, what is most proper to psychoanalysis is not heterosexuality, but a sexuality that undoes stable binary categories. He refers to Freud's famous quip that there are at least four people present in any coupling of two, showing how psychoanalytic insight makes simple arithmetic not so simple at all. What may be symptomatic, in the end, are our assumptions that we can say with certitude what sex is. Our confident descriptions and prescriptions are perhaps symptomatic of the relentless pressure induced by the enigmas at the heart of sex.

Sex is more often than not marked by awkwardness and longing. Whether excessive or lacking, sex destabilizes. Quite often in fact, great sex is the exception rather than the rule. The *liebesschmerz* [love-pain] of sex is frequently treated pedagogically by focusing on its physical mechanism. From the *Kamasutra* to today's sex-help books, the assumption is that if only we could do it right, it would not be a problem. It is well known that psychoanalysis was born from Freud's listening to the suffering of women whose bodily ailments defied anatomical explanations; their symptoms resisted traditional medicine and challenged scientific understanding. Behind their pain, Freud found repressed and often traumatic sexual scenes expressed in fantasies they were not aware of but which were nevertheless spoken via their suffering. The talking-cure lifted the symptoms by bringing their unconscious motivations to light. Words revealed a mysterious link between psyche and body. The hysterical body in pain revealed more fidelity to language than to anatomy; the body that could be cured by speech.

Elaborating on the link between body and language, in Chapter 2 of this collection, "Glôssa and Logos: The Perverse Tongue of Psychoanalysis," Elissa Marder embarks on a close "counter-reading" of Freud's pre-psychoanalytic texts to reveal a non-binary conception of gender and sexuality that traverses his entire oeuvre. In the late 1880s, Freud became fascinated with the case of a woman who interrupted her own speech by making strange bird-like noises with her tongue. Marder returns to this originary "scene of fixation" of the tongue to detect a powerful counter-current to some of what have been considered to be Freud's most heteronormative views about gender and sexuality. The work of language as staged in the hysterical body influenced some of Freud's most obscure formulations regarding how a woman came into being, female sexuality, perversion, and fixation in his later writings.

Feminism questioned and reinvented the notion of what a woman is—or rather, asked as Freud did earlier, how it is that a woman comes to be, bringing this process to critical discussion. The controversial debate brought about by de Beauvoir's claim that a woman is not born but made had already elicited a debate among the early psychoanalysts whose radical ideas still reverberate today, although we are often unaware of these historical precedents. This theoretically foundational exchange is examined by Leader in Chapter 3, "The Gender Question from Freud to Lacan." Closely reading Freud's contributions of the 1920s and 1930s and bringing an often overlooked debate to life, Leader recontextualizes the castration complex—accepted by all in Freud's circle—by showing how it led to a controversy, one development of which was the notion of *Penisneid* (penis envy), a concept that was not accepted by all of Freud's circle. An outcome of this debate was the transformation of the penis (an organ) into the phallus (a symbol).

This theoretical move, usually exclusively credited to Lacan, was in fact developed by earlier female analysts, including Karen Horney and Melanie Klein. The questions that preoccupied the early analysts, such as whether Oedipal currents determined gender and heterosexuality, are shown to be consequential for subsequent queer and gender theory debates. Leader links these questions to Lacan's contributions on gender and sexuality, which echo the shifts in Freud's theoretical developments. Although Lacan distanced himself from Freud with his sexuation formulae, critics argued that Lacan perpetuated a normative paradigm of sexual difference by reinforcing a binary. Leader contributes an informed perspective on these formulae and their reception, pointing to both their limitations and possibilities in contemporary discussions of gender, sexuality, and psychoanalysis.

Further theorizing difference historically by looking back at foundational psychoanalytic texts, in Chapter 4, "Two Analysts Ask, 'What is Genitality?' Ferenczi's Thalassa and Lacan's Lamella." Jamieson Webster and Marcus Coelen recontextualize controversies from the first half of the twentieth century. They revisit Sandor Ferenczi's notion of Thalassa, an originary concept of libido, in conjunction with Lacan's myth of the lamella, an originary "undead" libidinous "inorganic" organ of differentiation, in order to unpack the pre-Oedipal origins of difference. This juxtaposition leads them to reassess the controversial concept of the phallus, contested not only by contemporary psychoanalytic theory, but by feminist and queer theory as well.

One might assume that, in today's materialistic, object-oriented, gender-fluid universe, the concept of the phallus is an outdated misogynistic relic. Coelen and Webster show its relevance in clinical work today, noting that the phallus appears when the questions of sexual difference, family romance, and the impasse of the sexual relationship emerge in the analytic transference. By approaching Ferenczi and Lacan together, they deconstruct not only the notion of the phallus but of genitality itself. The authors suggest that fundamentally, the controverted phallus functions as a hinge that opens onto what Lacan called the agalma—a precious object concealed beneath an unappealing or unremarkable exterior. This object plays an important role in the transferential bond between analyst and analysand. Webster and Coelen persuasively argue that the phallus as agalma operates as an agent of desire, something forever lost that can be ascribed to the analyst.

This loss has a subjectifying function. For psychoanalysis, identity, whether sexual or otherwise, is aleatory. Constructed around an inaugural loss, it can be traced to a mythical, ungendered moment when we fell from undifferentiated completeness into a fractured reality, infected by what William Burroughs (1962) called the virus of the word. This is played out at the precise early moment of our lives when someone sanctioned our being with the appellation "boy" or "girl," interpellating us. Butler has famously developed the role of Louis Althusser's (2010) notion of interpellation, the "material ritual practice of ideological recognition in everyday life" (1355) in the social construction of gender identities. Althusser's idea underlines both the embodied (material) and symbolic (ritual) components of interpellation that Butler develops as relating to gender. We are hailed, summoned, and come into being by way of an experience that positions us as gendered subjects. How may I claim my name and how am I claimed by it? How am I claimed by notions of identity? How am I perceived and received in the world, affecting my sense of self when declaring myself a man, woman, or anything else? For Butler, the notion of interpellation emphasizes gender as an ideologically loaded performative materialization of the socio-political environment. Genevieve Morel's Chapter 5, "Undoing the Interpellation of Gender and the Ideologies of Sex," returns to Althusser's theory of interpellation by adding the valence of the unconscious to Butler's analysis, in light of the fact that the subject of ideology is at the same time the psychoanalytic subject of the unconscious. Morel shows how gendering interpellations, which can be injurious when they are non-normative, are interpreted through each individual's unconscious fantasy, providing a frame to broker a gendered relation to the world. Making use of her experience as a clinician, Morel is able to explain how subjective transformation can undo the deleterious effect of slurs that work as interpellations, granting new possibilities for the subject beyond identification. She analyzes Guillaume Gallienne's 2013 film *Me, Myself and Mum* (*Les Garçons et Guillaume, à table!*), an autobiographical coming of age comedy that tells the story of Guillaume, raised in a French upper-class family who saw him as effeminate. He was considered gay, especially by his adored mother, an eccentric aristocrat with liberal ideas. The plot resolves with Guillaume's heterosexual coming out when he announces to his shocked mother that he is in love with a woman whom he plans to marry. The movie presents a series of metonymical gender interpellations, punctuated by two sentences which cut this thread at the beginning and at the end, operating like two metaphors of his sexed position: "not a boy," and then "not a girl." In this chapter, Morel advances an alternative theory of gender assumption, taking into account the unconscious dimension of desire and enjoyment in the formation of identity via the projection of fantasy.

The psychoanalytic concept of fantasy differs from the popular understanding of the term. Early on, Freud became aware that the memory of seduction was not always the result of actual abuse. This moment was foundational for the birth of psychoanalysis, which understood that subjectivity is involved in the construction of psychic reality. In this understanding, fantasy is not opposed to reality but sustains it; it is a frame through which the world is created. Fantasy constructs a scenario that grants access to pleasure, or more precisely, that explosive mixture of pain and pleasure called jouissance. As Freud shows in "A Child Is Being Beaten," fantasy can be reduced to a single sentence, or as Lacan does, to an axiom or mathematical formula, a primer that gives meaning to history and time as well as the subject's place in it. For Lacan, fantasy functions as a veil over a "nothing" that is at the origin of signification. A body exists, constructed via fantasy, creating difference and inscribing racialized, gendered bodies into histories of belonging and ostracism. For psychoanalysis, gendered embodiment involves desire, jouissance, and symptoms, and all of these terms concern fantasy, a fantasy with a void at its center.

As developed in Part II, Queering Psychoanalysis: Fantasy, Anthropology, and Libidinal Economy, fantasy accompanies the subject and creates a window, "framing" the world; it concerns the individual as well as shared social ideals. With this in mind, looking at queer narratives of desire, Eve Watson explores another possible destiny for fantasy beyond systems of domination. The function of fantasy has been elided in contemporary queer and critical theories of desire, save for some exceptions (Berlant, 2012; Dean, 2000, 2001). In Chapter 6, "The Role of Phantasy in Representations and Practices of Homosexuality: Colm Tóibín's *The Blackwater Lightship* and Edmund White's *Our Young Man*," Watson shows how the "nothing" of fantasy can function as a prerequisite for desire in order to stay on the side of life. In melancholia, this "nothing" metastasizes into hatred, killing desire, and often, with it, even makes a casualty of the subject, as is the case with Hamlet.

A quick detour via Hamlet will be illustrative. When the melancholy Dane responds to Rosencrantz and Guildenstern's query regarding Polonius' body, Hamlet cryptically quips, "The body is with the king but the king is not with the body," adding his oft cited, "the King is a thing of nothing." While the phrase demonstrates Ernst Kantorowicz's (1957) thesis that the symbolic "body" of the king outlasts and exceeds his real body, more significantly, it reveals Hamlet's melancholic knowledge. As a result of his father's traumatic death, having lost faith in the system, Hamlet is able to encounter the truth at the center of "the King," Claudius, his own dead father, and at the center of language itself, i.e., "nothing." Hamlet is at the crossroads of a symbolic and personal tragedy that also confronts him with the "nothing" at the heart of the fantasy sustaining his reality. As Sheldon George (2016) notes in his study of African American racial identity, it is around this kernel of nothing that the racial other is constructed. At the same time, the recognition of this "nothing" at the core of racism, sexism, homophobia, transphobia, and hatred in general is the key to its transcendence.

The "nothing" does not have to be met with paranoiac rage or melancholic lassitude; the empty hole that fuels fantasy can also propel us toward the world and to other subjects. In fact, without fantasy, there is no selfhood or freedom. Individual unconscious fantasy supports the subject by organizing subjective desire, but fantasy also plays a role in culture, providing a desiring template supported by shared ego ideals and group demands that do not need to be oppressive. Going from the individual to society, Watson notes the irony in privileging heterosexual monogamous loving object relations to buttress political, ideological, and economic ends, as it is in contradiction with Freud's (1955) observation that the unconscious does not operate by social-sexual mandates; as far as the unconscious is concerned, heterosexuality does not exist. Watson argues that in Western contemporary culture, homosexuality has been a placeholder for "excess," "otherness," "dis-ease," and loss.

Further analyzing the fantasmatic relevance of the figure of the homosexual man as a nexus of cultural excess, Ray O'Neill, in Chapter 7, explores Oscar Wilde's "comedy in art and tragedy in life" in light of the unconscious transmission of trauma. Freud, born two years after Wilde, analogously made good use of humor, revealing the power of sexuality, the legacy of parents and family *até* (malediction, fate) and of the compulsion to repeat. Interweaving the personal and political in both Wilde's dramatic success and tragic demise, O'Neill shows the primacy of unconscious repetition, unearthing the transgenerational unconscious transmission of fantasies, desires, and anxieties. Exploring the relation between repetition and transgression for Wilde, O'Neill's reading is a psychoanalytic study of how historically overdetermined sexuality and filiation can be.

The psychoanalytic understanding of filiation is predicated upon the concept of the Oedipal structure, which means that several generations are always implied. This consideration has been developed by anthropologists like Claude Lévi-Strauss in his study of the structures of kinship. In Chapter 8, "Does the Anthropology of Kinship Talk about Sex?" Monique David-Ménard asks whether the foregrounding of sexuality in psychoanalysis has an equivalent in the anthropological analysis of the kinship structure. Moving away from corporeal to symbolic coordinates, David-Ménard examines the use of categories of sex and sexual difference in the field of anthropology. David-Ménard wonders whether anthropological inquiry provides other modalities of separation from the incestuous bond with an all-powerful maternal figure in addition to the "symbolic castration" prescribed by psychoanalysis.

On occasion, it looks like the anthropological explorations of menstruation, menopause, and infertility overlap with psychoanalytic constructions about sexual difference. Looking at the work of noted French anthropologists Françoise

Héritier, Daniel Delanoë, and Maurice Godelier to critically explore issues of kinship, filiation, femininity, coupling, the body, and reproduction, David-Ménard examines how these are understood anthropologically and whether they are reduced to structural formalism. In short, David-Ménard questions how non-Western cultures, as studied by anthropologists, broach the question of sexuality and gender.

Anthropology provides us with an informed perspective on social organization and symbolic formation, making us aware of the enormous diversity found in myriad cultures that challenge normativity and essentialism. Broadening our understanding of the human family, anthropology shows models outside of what Gayle Rubin (1975) calls "the sex/gender system," that is, the patriarchal nuclear family structure, giving us access to gender roles that exceed the binary. For instance, research on non-binary gender identities such as the Native American two-spirit (an umbrella term for a combination of male and female energies) and the Indian *hijra* (a third gender that is neither entirely male nor female and challenges conventional boundaries of sex, gender, and hierarchy) have allowed us to question what Western culture sees as "natural" or "normal." In addition, the anthropology of religion has shown the importance of non-binary gender in both the mystical tradition and art historical considerations of the iconographic tradition. In the same manner that Western feminists find in anthropology a corresponding ethos wherein social organization was shown to be constructed and contingent, psychoanalysis offers a theory of fantasy and subjectivity with emancipatory potential to challenge gender oppression.

The gender revolution, brewing now for several decades, has come to a boiling point that psychoanalytic theory has to account for. In our era of destructive shatterings, as Kelly Oliver points out in Chapter 9, "From Fundamentalism to Forgiveness: Sex/Gender Beyond Determinism or Volunteerism?" voicing and inciting violent reactions have become the norm. Led by blind faith, Trump's famous "base" was devoted solely to the fact that he systematically expressed himself in anger and outrage. Civility became suspicious precisely because it was political, as if politics itself were suddenly revealed as fraudulent, instead of valued as the basis of civil society. The irony was that intolerance was shared by both Trump's supporters and opponents. Oliver draws on Julia Kristeva's notion of abjection to make sense of our contemporary preoccupation with victimhood and outrage. She examines the "fundamentalism of authenticity" to diagnose and offer a way out of our current impasse, a moment in which the critical discussion and historical contextualization of identities and desires appear impossible. Culture wars have become contests of suffering, and victimhood its unassailable fortress. Oliver warns us about a form of fundamentalism where safety has come to mean protection from difference. These polarized socio-political rifts echo in gender and sexual debates regarding identity. Following Kristeva, Oliver proposes that psychoanalytic transference opens up a space with multiple possibilities, summed up in a broader understanding of the concept of forgiveness, wherein we are able to sublimate our murderous or suicidal tendencies. Oliver invites us to interrogate "our own unconscious investments in violence and exclusion, and our own self-righteous urges towards dogmatisms or fundamentalisms as manifestations of the disavowal of abjection with its inherent ambiguity and ambivalence."

In Chapter 10, Juliet Flower MacCannell examines another iteration of our current disavowal of difference. She reminds us of Lacan's observation that "getting rid of sex" marked the inaugural moment of capitalism. Via Lacan's recourse to group psychology, MacCannell notes Freud's observation that equality "works" by erasing difference: "everyone must have the same and be the same." While paradoxically "universal," equality is based on one foundational exception: "The One who enjoys fully with no concern for his own absolute inequality in this regard with respect to everyone else." Capitalism enthrones a male logic that strives to eradicate all traces of the feminine (Other) logic. While it may sound as if it is an advance for women that the logic of capitalism insists there be no distinctions among those under its regime, the reality is just the opposite. What MacCannell calls "sexual indifference," or Lacan's "getting rid of sex," has effectively become a hidden ethical imperative to refuse recognition to a sex other than the male. This makes us wonder whether liberal "inclusiveness" is precisely the ideological fiction that Nancy Fraser (2016) has called progressive neoliberalism, the lingua franca of the West, one that focuses only on mechanisms of inclusion and exclusion at the expense of an appreciation of the basic antagonistic structure of society.

What is the role of gender and sexuality in this divisive context? As feminism has shown, insofar as this juncture between body and flesh is political, psychoanalysis continues to be instrumental to political and social movements, affecting myriad modalities of embodiment. Culture and society encounter the flesh by way of language. As the language expression reveals, one "is" not a body but rather "has" a body. "Having" a body is not a given fact. A body is made: as seen with the infant's evolution, the body becomes sexualized by language. For Lacan, the body is morphed by an unconscious that is linguistic and therefore intimately concerned with and made up of the culture one inhabits. When traversing the traditional boundaries of gender, as happens when someone changes genders, the material determination of the body as constructed by culture becomes more apparent; this intersection between language and flesh is political, individual and social at the same time.

This interrelatedness has been recently theorized by Chiara Bottici (2021) as "an ontology of the transindividual" under the rubric of anarchafeminism. Bottici opposes a singular principle (or arché) that would explain gender oppression, emphasizing the intersections of class, race, empire, sexuality, hetero-cis-normativity, and feminism. Anarchafeminism proposes that "another woman is possible" (Bottici, 2018, 2021). This new paradigm includes all types of women: those assigned the female sex at birth, those assigned the male sex at birth, as well as feminine, masculine, lesbian, trans, and queer women; this is a feminism beyond biological dimorphism, a feminism as critique, a transnational feminism (Chandra Talpade Mohanty, 2003), a feminism that pluralizes bodies and modalities of resistance to oppression in an attempt to supersede traditional divisions.

The imbrication of feminism, trans* experiences, and trans* feminism appears as a wonderful critical tool to examine cultural ideology in terms of gender determination. In this new millennium, the trans* body is changing historical notions of sex, gender, and sexuality. In the same way that psychoanalysis prioritizes the singularity of each subjective experience, even when structurally overdetermined, Heaney (2017) reminds us that trans* feminism reinstalls women and the feminine as vital categories for political activity that undo the universalist claims of the categories of sex, race, and class, of cisness and trans*-ness, reinvigorating contemporary feminist thinking. Like Bottici and Heaney, we encourage thought that engages difference and promotes invention and new possibilities. We appreciated the gesture of Preciado (2021) who, when addressing a large group of Lacanian psychoanalysts, brilliantly and movingly called for psychoanalysis to look at grand social issues from colonialism to feminism.[4] His calculated provocation, a timely wake-up call, helps us imagine a different life and potential for psychoanalysis. As Preciado contended, if there is a future for psychoanalysis, it has to be de-patriarchal, de-heterosexual, and de-colonial (97). If such a change, as predicted by Preciado, can happen, it entails engaging critically with Black, queer, feminist, and trans discourses.

Expanding on the asterisks in trans* in the opening chapter of Part III in this collection, Being and Becoming TRANS*, Sheila L. Cavanagh's "Tiresias and the Other Sexual Difference: Jacques Lacan and Bracha L. Ettinger" invites us to revisit Lacan's instructive choice of a trans* figure from classical myth, i.e., Tiresias, the blind seer who lived as a man and as a woman, and who Lacan elects as psychoanalyst's patron saint (Gherovici, 2017; Lacan, 2014). This choice highlights an ethics of sexual difference that transcends the gender binary pointing to a sexual enjoyment beyond pleasure, which corresponds to what Lacan calls jouissance. Cavanagh elaborates on the theoretical implications of Lacan's adoption of this mythic trans* figure as a way of linking feminine sexuality, the Other or feminine jouissance and psychoanalytic theory itself. Cavanagh provides a critical supplement to theoretical discussions of sexual difference by drawing on the pioneering work of Bracha L. Ettinger (2006), a post-Lacanian feminist scholar. She expands on Ettinger's idea of the "matrixial," which takes the uterus not as an organ but metaphorically as a space of relationality and difference, a site alternative to the phallus. This hybridization that trans*cends gender, sexual orientation, and sex morphology has immense potential for both feminist and trans* studies.

Trans* discourses and practices radically question and redefine what it means to embody gender. They confirm the psychoanalytic findings regarding the imbrication of body image, language, and psyche. In this collection, we return to both the power and radicality of the foundations of psychoanalysis, as well as to recent theorizations in the field as a means of rethinking what it means to have a sexed body. Feminism has made use of psychoanalysis precisely because the body in question is always the body politic, affecting not only women's bodies but other bodies as well, as we have seen. Many feminists have nonetheless attacked trans* people, especially trans* women, whose femininity they questioned, leading in some cases to a transphobic stance. This is the conflicted situation addressed by Oren Gozlan's Chapter 12, "In-Difference: Feminism and Transgender in the Field of Fantasy." Gozlan claims that the trans* body is a new feminist body participating in a new body politic, and calls for cooperation rather than division between feminist and trans* discourses. For some feminists, the trans* person's appeal for inclusion is taken as potentially obliterating women's rights to safety and stability. Underscoring the fragility of gender in order to traverse political and personal fantasies, Gozlan returns to the feminist founding credo of "the personal is political," to show how for the trans* person, the political is also personal. He argues for a space of "in-difference" that allows for the toleration of ambivalence, permitting us to hear the other's desire as enigmatic. He calls this a position of "ethical in-difference."

Observing that psychoanalytic thinking has since its very inception been in dialogue with, and partially constituted by, feminist thinking, Ranjana Khanna argues that thinking itself is a form of trans-lation. In Chapter 13, "Translation, *Geschlecht*, and Thinking Across: On the Theory of Trans-" she follows Jacques Derrida's consideration of the term *Geschlecht* or gender, as he reads Martin Heidegger, to ask what it means to think trans-, or to think across. Khanna makes use of deconstruction, the rhetorical method of criticism that reveals the implicit assumptions, relational quality of meaning, and textual tension constitutive of any narrative, loosening the constraints of what have become psychoanalytic ready-mades such as "anatomy is destiny" or "'the' woman does not exist." Deconstruction reveals that binaries unravel into undecidability, giving rise to aporias and impasses that are relevant to our psychoanalytic re-reading of gender.

Engaging feminist-informed psychoanalysis through the lens of coloniality, Khanna adds a needed corrective joining the theoretical contributions of feminism and psychoanalysis with the socio-political critique of post-coloniality to undo the trappings of universalist meanings. For Khanna, the promise of trans* is addressed in terms of the tension between the particularities of the translatable and the untranslatable. Her analysis of *Geschlecht* allows her to broach sexual difference, the "*ur*-difference for psychoanalysis," in terms of rhetoric, analogy, and metaphor. *Geschlecht*, as translation, is not only relevant for psychoanalysis—which from its very inception at the turn of the twentieth century conceived of itself as an international force—but also reveals the production of gender in its dynamic interrelatedness with sex, race, lineage, and nation.

The sex-race-lineage-nation knot overdetermines generational and cultural trauma, as examined in Dina Al-Kassim's contribution, Chapter 14, "Scenes of Self-Conduct in Contemporary Iran: Transnational Subjectivities Knitted On Site." Al-Kassim examines emergent subjectivities between same-sex players and transsexuals under modern Iranian biopolitics, revealing unforeseen networks of affiliation and fantasy. Following Laplanche's theory of sublimation, she reads the fantasy of fatality as evidence of transsexual inspiration in Afsaneh Najmabadi's *Professing Selves: Transsexuality and Same-Sex Desire in Contemporary Iran* (2014). While transsexuality in Iran is legally tolerated but not fully embraced as a category of being, it nevertheless produces spaces for non-normative living. Al-Kassim records a genealogy of revolutionary subjectivity inspired by Michel Foucault's late work, locating transsexual experience as a contemporary reworking of spirituality that offers a socially sanctioned category of identification, an acceptable category of existence in Iran. Thus, Al-Kassim shows that transphobia and notions of sexual deviance are not limited to Western culture but pervade socially conservative and religious ideologies globally. Segregation and abjection confront not only non-binary expressions of gender and sexuality but concern day-to-day public bathroom politics across the globe.

Critiquing gender segregation and its concomitant threat of a breakdown in meaning, in Chapter 15, "Lacanistas in the Stalls: Urinary Segregation, Transgendered Abjection, and the Queerly Ambulant Dead," Calvin Thomas uncovers the psychic roots of the potentially murderous transphobic logic that permeates socially conservative ideology. When we need to satisfy the most basic and urgent need, and use a public restroom, we also use language, or Lacan's symbolic order, forcing us to make a choice of meaning either as a "woman" or as a "man." The so-called laws of urinary segregation impose a distinction on otherwise identical bathroom doors, as famously illustrated in Lacan's *Écrits*. Anyone going through the "wrong" door will be seen as a transgressor, becoming neither "subject" nor "object" but what Kristeva describes as the "abject," in this case, one who dares "to be" and "to mean" as both "a man" and "a woman." In the transphobic imaginary, the "abject" would abolish the symbolic difference created by language between two otherwise identical doors, shattering the fictional but constitutively human difference, threatening the imaginary dimension of signification itself. Thomas argues that the cross-identified subject threatens vaunted heteronormative notions of privacy by erasing hygienic lines between properly socialized/sexuated bodies and the ungendered bodily excretions that are deposited on the other side of any bathroom door. Critically reading the film *V for Vendetta*, the 2005 film written and produced by the Wachowski trans* sisters, Thomas analyzes the transcultural imaginary as a queer, counter-normative, or even "terrorist" celebration that takes distance from transphobic readings imagining a less abject future.

To project ourselves onto the future, we need to understand the complex forces constructing our present, as well as the politics of narrating our past. Dany Nobus' Chapter 16, "Becoming Being: Chance, Choice and the Troubles of Trans*cursivity," pursues an original perspective by examining the socially conservative ideology that we have seen taken to task by the trans* experience. Nobus situates the popularization of a certain trans* experience as a symptom of contemporary neoliberal economic biopolitics. He assesses the dangers of non-normative, non-binary sexual identities being co-opted and recuperated by neoliberal identity politics. Critiquing the concomitant idea of "choice" presumed as the highest duty of citizenship and liberty, he sees in the "choice" of the remodeled body the prevailing ideology that individual enterprise equals freedom. In this regard, Nobus argues that the body is the ultimate site of choice and is politically and ideologically constructed as a topos of sexual expressiveness and civil liberty. In contradistinction, Nobus shows the revolutionary potential of what he calls "trans*cursivity" (a term he borrows from Félix Guattari's *The Anti-Oedipus Papers*) as a strategy that refuses the binary and counters the so-called social "smooth functioning." "Trans*cursivity" positions itself in tension with user-friendly identity politics. Similarly, psychoanalysis advocates against an unfractured narrative construction of the self; Freudian free-association is essentially and transformatively a discursive act of subjective destitution. "Trans*cursivity" promotes a radical "de-territorialization" of established structures comparable to the psychoanalytic process, a journey of freeing dis-integration. Psychoanalysis, in Nobus' view, may be inherently trans* oriented. While he challenges the idea of a trans*friendly analyst as contraindicated by the aims of analytic neutrality, which presupposes the analysts' reticence regarding preconceptions and prejudices, letting the analysands express themselves freely, thus allowing the unconscious to speak, Nobus observes that psychoanalysis offers a transitional or translational space between and beyond identification. In that space resides its emancipatory potential.

Like Nobus, questioning the unmediated trust in authenticity that appears in some trans* narratives, such as when transition is described as "becoming what one has always been," in Chapter 17, "Just Kidding: Valerie Solanas's *SCUM* and Andrea Long Chu's *Females*," Elena Comay del Junco explores the implications of Andrea Long Chu's *reductio ad absurdum* "everyone is female, and everyone hates it" (Chu, 2019, 11). Comay del Junco takes Chu's comedic lead in stride and goes after the truth behind the joke. As Lacan recommended, instead of wasting time wandering around the detours of the Oedipal narrative, she takes a short-cut—comedy. On this faster lane, Comay del Junco cuts to the chase of Chu's account of trans*, or more precisely, what it means to have a gender at all. Comay del Junco critiques Chu's appropriation of Valerie Solanas' claim that men live in terror of "the discovery that males are females." As Chu puts it, things can get worse: "we are all, men and women, cis and trans, female." Comay del Junco astutely discerns both the success and fragility of Chu's argumentation as well as the perils and pitfalls of her "philosophical" joke, pointing out that Chu's recurring use of the joke makes it fall flat. No longer funny, the joke bungled; there is nevertheless a leftover, Chu's desire, as an assertion of radical individual freedom.

Psychoanalysis takes desire seriously; it is its theoretical, clinical, and ethical compass. Lacan's famous exhortation, to not give way on one's desire, while touted by many, has nevertheless often been misinterpreted as a moral injunction, to not give way on one's jouissance, as though Lacan were handing out free-passes to a Sadean Disneyland, sanctioning practices or acts that people would later abjure after they had encountered suffering there. Several years after a patient terminated an analysis, he wrote to his analyst saying that after reading Lacan, he realized that his entire analysis could be summed up as learning to replace painful jouissance with desire. For Lacan, the divided subject is "condemned" to desire: even when fulfilled, it fails to deliver on its promise. This failure is desire itself, a principle of negativity, protecting us from the ravages of jouissance and keeping us on the side of life.

Desire is not linked to happiness or to the pursuit of the good. In the seminar *The Ethics of Psychoanalysis*, Lacan (1992) underlines this point: "There is no good other than that which may serve to pay the price for access to desire" (321). This is the lesson we take from Chu's *n + 1* essay, "On Liking Women," where she considers transition not in terms of identity but of desire. She writes, "How can you want to be something you already are? Desire implies deficiency; want implies want. … [W]hat makes women like me transsexual is not identity but desire..." Avoiding the discourse of authenticity, Chu conceives of desire, in its non-arrival, as a prime mover: "...trans women want things too. The deposits of our desire run as deep and fine as any." The feisty title of Chu's *New York Times* op ed—"My New Vagina Won't Make Me Happy. And It Shouldn't Have To"—takes explicit distance from a eudemonistic ideal that prescribes transitioning with the ultimate goal of achieving "happiness." Chu writes, "Transition doesn't have to make me happy for me to want it. Left to their own devices, people will rarely pursue what makes them feel good in the long term. Desire and happiness are independent agents." Indeed, "happiness" is often invoked to deploy biopolitical mechanisms of discipline "to neutralize dangers, to fix useless or disturbed populations," allegedly increasing the utility of individuals (Foucault, 1979, 210).

Within psychoanalytic theories, certain "disciplining," longstanding assumptions for gender formation and psychosexual development still prevail, such as the duality of sex, the foundational role of sexual difference, and a parental (usually heterosexual) couple as key contexts and references. As transgender experiences and embodiments become more variegated, they challenge the fixity of the binary of sex and the narratives of an "authentic" gender that must be discovered, established, and kept in place. The tenets of the duality of sex, the nuclear family structured by the (heterosexual) couple, and the primacy of sexual difference are also intricately bound up with now disavowed histories of coloniality and structural whiteness. Thiem's Chapter 18, "Transgender Quarrels and the Unspeakable Cisgender Whiteness of Psychoanalysis," rejects a conception of gender perceived as self-identification and proposes to address gender and race in parallel as two elaborations of embodied patterns of behavior. Transition raises the issue of raced embodiment and necessarily interpellates the neglected intersection of gender and race, an intersection overdetermined by implicit normative whiteness. As concerns for racial justice have loomed larger in the last years, we feel that such an investigation is only beginning a larger set of inroads that we reserve for a second volume. Theorizing the opposition between the inclusion granted by privilege and the exclusion determined by race, Thiem tackles the unsettled matter of gender, sex, and sexual difference by further elaborating upon the intersections of our book's title: psychoanalysis, gender, and sexuality.

We have questioned the idea of a natural order of sexuality but cannot help noting that nature has a sense of humor, for, as Hegel quipped, sex is a joke of nature, at least for cis males; indeed, sex "combines the organ of its highest fulfillment, the organ of generation, with the organ of urination" (Hegel, 1977, 210). This remark prepares the stage for a comedy of the sexes, and it is in that space that Anne-Emmanuelle Berger (2013) locates "the theater of gender." Both Freud's "bedrock of castration" and Oedipal tragedy, in Lacan's elaboration at least, tend to become a hotbed of screwball comedy, the phallus returning, as in the ancient theater, as a ridiculous gigantic prop to the laughter of all. Freudian *Penisneid* is no longer in a starring role. Whether you play it straight or not, the Lacanian sexuation comedy uses the mask of desire to perform a multiplicity of roles.

For too long, tragedy has been paradigmatic of psychoanalytic practice and critique. Lacan proposes comedy as a more productive model (Gherovici and Steinkoler, 2016). Comedy is on the side of life. Unlike in tragedy, where everyone dies at the end, in comedy, the hero jumps into the soup to become laughing stock, only to jump out again, making do with life in all its happenstance and finitude, in all its unbearable absurdity. Taking distance from a utilitarian notion of means and ends, thinking about sex beyond anatomy, gender beyond culture, sexuation beyond jouissance, and moving even beyond the theories of infantile sexuality shared by some psychoanalysts, Lacanian psychoanalysis differs from most discourses about gender and sexuality. Psychoanalysis brings to the fore the fact that the trappings of identity conceal subjective truth, while the mask of desire allows us to perform. We leave you with the mask and the particular truth that is unique for each subject, inviting you to discover your role in the ongoing comedy, now that our introduction has reached its "happy ending," wishing it had something of the fairy tale, comedy, or massage parlor.

Notes

1 Freud's *Trieb* means "drive" and not *Instinkt*, "instinct," despite many English mistranslations of the term.

2 The term "intersectionality" created by Kimberlé Williams Crenshaw in 1989 attempts to account for multiple social constructions that may include gender, caste, sex, race, class, sexuality, religion, disability, physical appearance, and height as intersecting and overlapping identitary categories that may be both empowering and oppressing.

3 By feminist psychoanalysis, we mean an effort to avoid clichés about gender as well as question notions such as "penis envy" and other concepts that invoke the patriarchal heritage.

4 On November 17, 2019, Paul Preciado spoke in Paris to an audience of 3,500 Lacanian psychoanalysts. He wittily alluded to Kafka's 1917 short story "Report

to an Academy." In the story, an ape named Red Peter has learned to behave like a human. Preciado exhibited himself as a transsexual specimen like Kafka's ape, who ironically claimed that he was as "human" as anyone in the audience. See Paul Preciado's (2021) *Can the Monster Speak?: Report to an Academy of Psychoanalysts.*

Bibliography

Althusser, L. (2010). "From *Ideology and Ideological State Apparatuses (Notes towards an Investigation),*" in *The Norton Anthology of Theory and Criticism* (pp.1335–1361, 2nd edn), eds. V.B. Leitch, W.E. Cain, New York: W. W. Norton & Co.

Badiou, A. (with N. Truong) (2012). *In Praise of Love,* trans. P. Bush, New York: The New Press.

Beauvoir, S. de (1989). *The Second Sex,* trans. H. M. Parshley, New York: Vintage Books.

Benjamin, J. (1988). *The Bonds of Love,* New York: Pantheon Books.

Benjamin, J. (1998). *Like Subjects, Love Objects,* New Haven: Yale University Press.

Berger, A.-E. (2013). *The Queer Turn in Feminism: Identities, Sexualities, and the Theater of Gender,* New York: Fordham University Press.

Berlant, L. (2012). *Desire/Love,* New York: Punctum Books.

Berlant, L. and L. Edelman (2014). *Sex, or the Unbearable,* Durham: Duke University Press.

Bersani, L. (1987). "Is the Rectum a Grave?" *AIDS: Cultural Analysis/Cultural Activism,* 43 (Winter), 197–222.

Bettcher, T. M. (2007). "Evil Deceivers and Make-Believers: On Transphobic Violence and the Politics of Illusion." *Hypatia,* 22(3), 43–65.

Bettcher, T. M. (2013). "Trans Women and Interpretive Intimacy: Some Initial Reflections," in *The Essential Handbook of Women's Sexuality* (pp.51–69), ed. D. Castenada, Westport: Praeger.

Bettcher, T. M. (2014). "Feminist Perspectives on Trans Issues." *The Stanford Encyclopedia of Philosophy* (Spring).

Bottici, C. (2018). "Anarcha-féminisme et l'ontologie du transindividuel." *La Deleuziana,* No 8, December 2018, 99–104.

Bottici, C. (2021). *Anarchafeminism,* New York and London: Bloomsbury.

Boylan, J. F. (2015). "Loving Freely." *The New York Times,* last modified October 23, 2015, http://www.nytimes.com/2015/10/24/opinion/loving-freely.html

Brennan, T. (1992). *The Interpretation of the Flesh: Freud and Femininity,* New York: Routledge.

Brennan, T. (1993). *History after Lacan,* New York: Routledge.

Burroughs, W. (1962). *The Ticket That Exploded,* New York: Grove Press.

Butler, J. (1990). *Gender Trouble: Feminism and the Subversion of Identity,* New York: Routledge.

Butler, J. (1993). *Bodies That Matter: On the Discursive Limits of Sex,* New York: Routledge.

Butler, J. (2002). "What Is Critique? An Essay on Foucault's Virtue". In *The Political* (pp. 212–228), ed. David Ingram, London: Blackwell.

Carlson, S. T. (2010). "Transgender Subjectivity and the Logic of Sexual Difference." *differences,* 21(2), 46–72.

Carlson, S. T. (2014). "Psychoanalytic." *TSQ,* 1(1–2), 169–171.

Carlson, S. T. (2017). "'Taking the Risk of a True Speech': Transgender and the Lacanian Clinic." *TSQ,* 4(3–4), 627–631.

Caserio, R., Edelman, L., Halberstam, J., Munoz, J. E. and Dean, T. (2006). "The Antisocial Thesis in Queer Theory." *PMLA*, 121(3) (May), 819–828.

Cavanagh, S. (2017). "Transpsychoanalytics." *TSQ: The Transgender Studies Quarterly,* 4(3–4) (November), 326–357.

Chodorow, N. (1978). *The Reproduction of Mothering: Psychoanalysis and the Sociology of Gender,* Berkeley: University of California Press.

Chu, A. L. (2018). "My New Vagina Won't Make Me Happy, and It Shouldn't Have To." *The New York Times,* 24 November, https://www.nytimes.com/2018/11/24/opinion/sunday/vaginoplasty-transgender-medicine.html

Chu, A. L. (2018). "On Liking Women: The Society for Cutting Up Men Is a Rather Fabulous Name for a Transsexual Book Club." *n + 1,* 30 (Winter, "Motherland" issue), https://nplusonemag.com/issue-30/essays/on-liking-women/

Chu, A. L. (2019). *Females,* London and New York: Verso.

Cixous, H. and C. Clement (1986). *The Newly Born Woman,* trans. B. Wing, Minneapolis: University of Minnesota Press.

Coffman, C. (2010). "Queering Zizek." *Postmodern Culture,* 23(1), 56–73.

Coffman, C. (2017). "Zizek's Antagonism and the Futures of Trans-Affirmative Lacanian Psychoanalysis." *TSQ,* 4(3–4), 472–496.

Coffman, C. (2022). *Queer Traversals Psychoanalytic Queer and Trans Theories,* London and New York: Bloomsbury Academics.

Corbett, K. (2016). *A Murder Over a Girl: Justice, Gender, Junior High,* New York: Henry Holt and Co.

Dean, T. (2000). *Beyond Sexuality,* Chicago: University of Chicago Press.

Dean, T. (2004). "Lacan and Queer Theory" in *Cambridge Companion to Lacan,* J. M. Rabaté (pp. 238–252), Cambridge: Cambridge University Press.

Dean, T. and C. Lane (eds) (2001). *Homosexuality and Psychoanalysis,* Chicago: University of Chicago Press.

Dimen, M. and Goldner, V. (2007). *Gender in Psychoanalytic Space,* New York: Other Press.

Dinnerstein, D. (1976). *The Mermaid and the Minotaur: Sexual Arrangements and Human Malaise,* New York: Harper & Row.

Domurat Dreger, A. (1998). *Hermaphrodites and the Medical Invention of Sex,* Cambridge: Harvard University Press.

Drescher, J. (2010). "Queer Diagnoses: Parallels and Contrasts in the History of Homosexuality, Gender Variance, and the *Diagnostic and Statistical Manual (DSM)."* *Archives of Sexual Behavior,* 39, 427–460.

Drescher, J., P. T. Cohen-Kettenis and S. Winter (2012). "Minding the Body: Situating Gender Diagnoses in the ICD-11." *International Review of Psychiatry,* 24(6), 568–577.

Drescher, J., P. T. Cohen-Kettenis and G. M. Reed (2016). "Gender Incongruence of Childhood in the ICD-11: Controversies, Proposal, and Rationale." *Lancet Psychiatry,* 3, 297–304.

Edelman, L. (2004). *No Future: Queer Theory and the Death Drive,* Durham: Duke University Press.

Elliot, P. (2001). "A Psychoanalytic Reading of Transsexual Embodiment." *Studies in Gender and Sexuality,* 2(4) (October), 295–325.

Elliot, P. (2010). *Debates in Transgender, Queer and Feminist Theory: Contested Sites,* New York: Routledge.

Elliot, P. (2014). "Psychoanalysis." *TSQ*, 1(1–2) (May), 165–168.

Elliot, P. and Lyons, L. (2017). "Transphobia as Symptom" *TSQ*, 4(3–4), 358–383.

Elliot, P. and Roen, K. (1998). "Transgenderism and the Question of Embodiment: Promising Queer Politics?" *GLQ*, 4(2), 231–261.

Eng, D. (2001). *Racial Castration: Managing Masculinity in Asian America*, Durham: Duke University Press.

Ettinger, B. (2006). *The Matrixial Borderspace*, Minneapolis: University of Minnesota Press.

Fausto-Sterling, A. (1999). *Sexing the Body: Gender Politics and the Construction of Sexuality*, New York: Basic Books.

Foucault, M. (1979). *Discipline and Punish*, trans. A. Sheridan, New York: Random House.

Foucault, M. (1990). *The History of Sexuality. Volume I: An Introduction*, trans. R. Hurley, New York: Vintage Books.

Fraisse, G. (2014). "Sex, Gender, Difference of the Sexes, Sexual Difference," in *Dictionary of Untraslatables: A Philosophical Lexicon* (pp.969–974), ed. B. Cassin, translation in English ed. E. Apter, J. Lezra and M. Wood, Princeton: Princeton University Press.

Fraser, N. (2016). "Progressive Neoliberalism versus Reactionary Populism: A Choice that Feminists Should Refuse." *Nordic Journal of Feminist and Gender Research (NORA)*, 24(4), 281–284.

Freud, S. (1953a). "Fragment of an Analysis of a Case of Hysteria," in *The Standard Edition of the Complete Psychological Works of Sigmund Freud, Vol. 7* (pp.114–115), ed. and trans. J. Strachey, London: Hogarth Press.

Freud, S. (1953b). "Three Essays on the Theory of Sexuality," in *The Standard Edition of the Complete Psychological Works of Sigmund Freud, Vol. 7* (pp.123–146), trans. and ed. J. Strachey, London: Hogarth Press.

Freud, S. (1955). "Group Psychology and the Analysis of the Ego," in *The Standard Edition of the Complete Psychological Works of Sigmund Freud, Vol. 18 (1920–1922): Beyond the Pleasure Principle, Group Psychology and Other Works* (pp.65–144), trans. and ed. J. Strachey, London: Hogarth Press.

Freud, S. (1961a). "The Infantile Genital Organization (an Interpolation into the Theory of Sexuality)," in *The Standard Edition of the Complete Psychological Works of Sigmund Freud, Vol. 19* (pp.139–146), trans. and ed. J. Strachey, London: Hogarth Press.

Freud, S. (1961b). "The Dissolution of the Oedipus Complex," in *The Standard Edition of the Complete Psychological Works of Sigmund Freud, Vol. 19* (pp.171–180), trans. and ed. J. Strachey, London: Hogarth Press.

Freud, S. (1961c). "Some Psychical Consequences of the Anatomical Distinction between the Sexes," in *The Standard Edition of the Complete Psychological Works of Sigmund Freud, Vol. 19* (pp.243–258), trans. and ed. J. Strachey, London: Hogarth Press.

Friedan, B. (1963). *The Feminine Mystique*, New York: W. W. Norton.

Gallop, J. (1982). *The Daughter's Seduction*, Ithaca: Cornell University Press.

Gallop, J. (1985). *Reading Lacan*, Ithaca: Cornell University Press.

George, S. (2016). *Trauma and Race: A Lacanian Study of African American Racial Identity*, Waco: Baylor University Press.

Gherovici, P. (2010). *Please Select Your Gender: From the Invention of Hysteria to the Democratizing of Transgenderism*, New York: Routledge.

Gherovici, P. (2011). "Psychoanalysis Needs a Sex Change." *Gay & Lesbian Issues and Psychology Review*, 7(1), 3–18.

Gherovici, P. (2017). *Transgender Psychoanalysis: A Lacanian Perspective on Sexual Difference*, New York: Routledge.

Gherovici, P. and Steinkoler M. (2016). *Lacan, Psychoanalysis, and Comedy*, New York: Cambridge University Press.

Gozlan, O. (2008). "The Accident of Gender" *Psychoanalytic Review*, 95(4), 541–570.

Gozlan, O. (2010). "The 'Real' Time of Gender." *European Journal of Psychoanalysis*, 30, 61–84.

Gozlan, O. (2014). *Transsexuality and the Art of Transitioning: A Lacanian Approach*, London: Routledge.

Gozlan, O. (2016). "The Transsexual's Turn: Uncanniness at Wellesley College." *Studies in Gender and Sexuality*, 17(4), 297–305.

Gozlan, O. (ed.) (2018). *Current Critical Debates in the Field of Transsexual Studies: In Transition*, Routledge: New York, 2018

Grosz, E. (1990). *Jacques Lacan: A Feminist Introduction*, New York: Routledge.

Hansbury, G. (2011). "King Kong & Goldilocks: Imagining Trans Masculinities through the Trans-Trans Dyad." *Psychoanalytic Dialogues*, 21(2), 210–220.

Hansbury, G. (2018). "The Masculine Vaginal: Working with Queer Men's Embodiment at the Transgender Edge." *Journal of the American Psychoanalytic Association*, 65(6), 1009–1031.

Harris, A. E. (2011). "Gender as a Strange Attractor: Discussion of the Transgender Symposium." *Psychoanalytic Dialogues*, 21, 230–238.

Heaney, E. (2017). *The New Woman: Literary Modernism, Queer Theory, and the Trans Feminine Allegory*, Evanston: Northwestern University Press.

Hegel, G. W. F. (1977). *Phenomenology of Spirit*, trans. A. V. Miller, Oxford: Oxford University Press.

hooks, bell. (1981). *Ain't I A Woman: Black Women and Feminism*, Boston: South End Press.

Ireland, M. (1993). *Reconceiving Women: Separating Motherhood from Female Identity*, New York: The Guilford Press.

Irigaray, L. (1985a). *Speculum of the Other Woman*, trans. G. C. Gill, Ithaca: Cornell University Press.

Irigaray, L. (1985b). *This Sex Which Is Not One*, trans. C. Porter, Ithaca: Cornell University Press.

Irigaray, L. (1993). *An Ethics of Sexual Difference*, trans. C. Burke and G. C. Gill, Ithaca: Cornell University Press.

Kantorowicz, E. (1957). *The King's Two Bodies: A Study in Medieval Political Theology*, Princeton: Princeton University Press.

Klein, M. (1984a). *Love, Guilt and Reparation and Other Works 1921–1945*, New York: Free Press.

Klein, M. (1984b). *Envy and Gratitude and Other Works 1946–1963*, New York: Free Press.

Kristeva, J. (1982). *Powers of Horror: An Essay on Abjection*, trans. L. S. Roudiez, New York: Columbia University Press.

Kristeva, J. (1986). "Women's Time," in *The Kristeva Reader* (pp.187–213), ed. T. Moi, New York: Columbia University Press.

Kristeva, J. (1991). *Strangers to Ourselves*, trans. L. S. Roudiez, New York: Columbia University Press.

Lacan, J. (1981). *The Seminar of Jacques Lacan, Book XI: The Four Fundamental Concepts of Psychoanalysis*, trans. A. Sheridan, New York: Norton.

Lacan, J. (1982). *Feminine Sexuality*, ed. J. Mitchell and Jacqueline Rose, trans. J. Mitchell, New York: Norton.

Lacan, J. (1992). *The Seminar of Jacques Lacan, Book VII: The Ethics of Psychoanalysis*, trans. D. Porter, New York: Norton.

Lacan, J. (1998). *The Seminar of Jacques Lacan, Book XX: On Feminine Sexuality: The Limits of Love and Knowledge*, trans. B. Fink, New York: Norton.

Lacan, J. (2006). *Écrits: The First Complete Edition in English*, trans. B. Fink, New York: Norton, 2006.

Lacan, J. (2014). *The Seminar of Jacques Lacan. Book X: Anxiety*, ed. J.-A. Miller, trans. A. R. Prince, Cambridge: Polity.

Laplanche, J. (1992). "The Drive and the Object-Source: Its Fate in the Transference," in *Jean Laplanche: Seduction, Translation, and the Drives* (pp.179–196), trans. M. Stanton, ed. J. Fletcher and M. Stanton, London: ICA.

Laplanche, J. and S. Fairfield (2007). "Gender, Sex, and the Sexual." *Studies in Gender and Sexuality*, 8(2), 201–219.

MacCannell, J. F. (1991). *The Regime of the Brother: After Patriarchy*, New York: Routledge.

MacCannell, J. F. (2000). *The Hysteric's Guide to the Future Female Subject*, Minneapolis: University of Minnesota Press.

MacKinnon, C. (1989). *Toward a Feminist Theory of the State*, Cambridge: Harvard University Press.

Masotta, O. (1991). *Lecciones de Introducción al Psicoanálisis*, Mexico: Gedisa Editorial.

Masters, W. and V. Johnson (1997). *Human Sexuality*, 5th edn, Boston: Allyn & Bacon.

Masters, W. and V. Johnson (2010a). *Human Sexual Inadequacy*, New York and Tokyo: Ishi Press.

Masters, W. and V. Johnson (2010b). *Human Sexual* Response, New York and Tokyo: Ishi Press.

Merleau-Ponty, M. (2002). *Phenomenology of Perception*, trans. C. Smith, New York: Routledge.

Millet, K. (1971). *Sexual Politics*, London: Rupert Hart-Davis.

Mitchell, J. (1973). *Psychoanalysis and Feminism*, New York: Vintage Books.

Mitchell, J. and J. Rose (eds) (1985). *Feminine Sexuality: Jacques Lacan and the École Freudienne*, London: Macmillan.

Mitchell, J. and A. Oakley (1997). *Who's Afraid of Feminism? Seeing through the Backlash*, New York: New Press.

Mitchell, S. (2002) *Can Love Last? The Fate of Romance Over Time*, New York and London: W.W. Norton & Co.

Moi, T. (1986). *Sexual Textual Politics*, New York: Routledge.

Money, J. (1955). "Hermaphroditism, Gender and Precocity in Hyperadrenocorticism: Psychologic Findings." *Bulletin of the Johns Hopkins Hospital*, 96, 253–254.

Najmabadi, A. (2014). *Professing Selves: Transsexuality and Same-Sex Desire in Contemporary Iran*, Durham: Duke University Press.

Oliver, K. (1993a). *Reading Kristeva: Unraveling the Double-bind*, Bloomington: Indiana University Press.

Oliver, K. (ed.) (1993b). *Ethics, Politics, and Difference in Julia Kristeva's Writing*, New York: Routledge.

Oliver, K. (1997). *Family Values: Subjects between Nature and Culture*, New York: Routledge.

Oliver, K. (1998). *Subjectivity without Subjects*, Lanham: Rowman & Littlefield.

Oliver, K. (2004). *The Colonization of Psychic Space: A Psychoanalytic Social Theory of Oppression*, Minneapolis: University of Minnesota Press.

Perel, E. (2014). *Mating in Captivity: Unlocking Erotic Intelligence*, New York: Harper Collins.

Posadas, M. (2017). "Psychoanalysis and Psychoanalytic Theory as a Tool to Increase Trans* Visibility." *TSQ*, 4(3–4), 647–653.

Preciado, P. B. (2013). *Testo Junkie: Sex, Drugs, and Biopolitics in the Pharmacopornographic Era*, trans. B. Benderson, New York: The Feminist Press.

Preciado, P. B. (2020). *An Apartment on Uranus*, London: Fitzcarraldo Editions; Los Angeles: Semiotext(e).

Preciado, P. B. (2021). *Can the Monster Speak?: Report to an Academy of Psychoanalysts* Los Angeles; Semiotext(e)/Intervention Series.

Prosser, J. (1998). *Second Skins: The Body Narratives of* Transsexuality, New York: Columbia University Press.

Pula, J. (2015). "Understanding Gender through the Lens of Transgender Experience." *Psychoanalytic Inquiry*, 35(8), 809–822.

Rose, J. (1986). *Sexuality in the Field of Vision*, New York: Verso.

Rubin, G. (1975). "The Traffic in Women: Notes on the 'Political Economy' of Sex," in *Toward an Anthropology of Women* (pp.157–210), edited by Rayna R. Reiter, New York: Monthly Review Press.

Ryley Snorton, C. (2017). *Black on Both Sides: A Racial History of Trans Identity*, Minneapolis: University of Minnesota Press.

Saketopoulou, A. (2014). "Mourning the Body as Bedrock." *Journal of the American Psychoanalytic* Association, 62(5) (October), 773–806.

Saketopoulou, A. (2015). "This Compromise Formation That Is Gender: Countertransferential Difficulties in Cis Analysts Working with Trans Analysands." Paper presented at the Congress of the International Psychoanalytical Association, Boston, July 24.

Saketopoulou, A. (2017). "Between Freud's Second and Third Essays on Sexuality: Commentary on Hansbury." *Journal of the American Psychoanalytic Association*, 65, 1033–1048.

Salamon, G. (2004). "The Bodily Ego and the Contested Domain of the Material." *differences*, 15(3), 95–122.

Salamon, G. (2010). *Assuming a Body: Transgender and Rhetorics of Materiality*, New York: Columbia University Press.

Scott, J. (1988). "Gender: A Useful Category of Historical Analysis," in *Gender and Politics of History* (pp.28–50), ed. C. G. Hellbrun and N. K. Miller, New York: Columbia University Press.

Scott, J. (1996). *Only Paradoxes to Offer: French Feminists and the Rights of Man*, Cambridge: Harvard University Press.

Shepherdson, C. (2000). *Vital Signs: Nature, Culture, Psychoanalysis*, New York: Routledge.

Silverman, K. (1988). *The Acoustic Mirror: The Female Voice in Psychoanalysis and Cinema*, Bloomington: Indiana University Press.

Solanas, V. (2004). *SCUM Manifesto*, ed. A Ronell, London and New York: Verso.

Stoller, R. (1968). *Sex and Gender: On the Development of Masculinity and Femininity*, New York: Science House.

Stoller, R. (1975). *The Transsexual Experiment, Volume Two of Sex and Gender*, London: Hogarth Press.

Stoller, R. (1985). *Presentations of Gender*, New Haven: Yale University Press.

Stryker, S. (2004). "Transgender Studies: Queer Theory's Evil Twin." *GLQ: A Journal of Lesbian and Gay Studies*, 10(2), 212–215.

Talpade Mohanty, C. (2003). *Feminism Without Borders: Decolonizing Theory, Practicing Solidarity* (Durham: Duke University Press, 2003).

Valentine, D. (2007). *Imagining Transgender: An Ethnography of the Category*, Durham: Duke University Press.

Van Haute, P. and H. Westerink (2017). *Desconstructing Normativity? Re-reading Freud's 1905* Three Essays, New York: Routledge.

Walton, J. (2001). *Fair Sex, Savage Dreams: Race, Psychoanalysis, Sexual Difference*, Durham: Duke University Press.

Wiggins, T. (2020a). "A Perverse Solution to Misplaced Distress: Trans Subjects and Clinical Disavowal." *TSQ*, 7(1), 56–76.

Wiggins, T. (2020b). "The Pervert on Your Couch: Psychoanalysis and Trans/Sexual Health," in *Sex, Sexuality and Trans Identities: Clinical Guidance for Psychotherapists and Counselors* (pp.155–181), ed. J. Niemira, G. Jacobson and K. Violet, London: Jessica Kingsley Publishers.

Wittig, M. (1992). "The Category of Sex," in *The Straight Mind and Other Essays*, Boston: Beacon Press.

Wright, E. (1992). *Feminism and Psychoanalysis: A Critical Dictionary*, Oxford: Blackwell.

Young-Bruehl, E. (ed.) (1990). *Freud on Women: A Reader*, New York: W. W. Norton.

Zupančič, A. (2017). *What Is Sex?* Cambridge: MIT Press.

The Genealogy of Sex and Gender

Part I

The Genealogy of Sex and
Gender

Chapter 1

Freud's *ménage à quatre*

Tim Dean

I One Plus One Equals

Let us begin with a sentence from Freud: "I am accustoming myself to the idea of regarding every sexual act as a process in which four persons are involved" (Freud, 1975, 289). It is striking how little commentators have had to say about this extraordinary remark, made in a letter to Wilhelm Fliess in 1899. The idea that every sexual act involves four persons seems to me quintessentially psychoanalytic in its defamiliarizing of the sexual. We might say that Freud's epistolary comment converts the most routine coupling into group sex. His budding psychoanalytic perspective—he writes at a threshold moment, as the field of psychoanalysis is coming into existence—enables Freud to see past the heterosexual couple to something less mundane, in which sex involves multiple bodies, perhaps an assemblage, or at the very least more than two parties or parts. I would suggest that Freud is at his most psychoanalytic when he produces apparently unintelligible observations about sex such as this one. The key to appreciating the originality of psychoanalysis lies in not rationalizing or normalizing such remarks too quickly.

This chapter meditates on Freud's comment to Fliess as a means of gauging the potential—and, indeed, testing the limits—of psychoanalytic theories of sexuality. I begin by acknowledging that the opening sentence cannot justifiably be reduced to a single, unambiguous meaning because that is not how meaning works in psychoanalysis: the unconscious stands ever ready to supply additional meanings, including contradictory ones. The point is not to resolve this sentence's ambiguities but to explore its enigmatic resonances. Doubtless Freud's multiplying the number of persons involved in "every sexual act" is connected to the way in which his theory of the unconscious multiples meaning and intention in every individual. As a multiplier, the unconscious is also a negator—of unity, synthesis, coherence, and control. A psychoanalytic exploration of our opening sentence thus entails relinquishing the satisfaction of coherence in favor of other potential pleasures.

However, nothing is easier than to curtail the significance of Freud's remark. Given the epistolary context of bisexuality, it would be perfectly plausible to

DOI: 10.4324/9781003284888-3

read the sentence as referring to a doubling of persons—a couple becoming four—attributable to the bifurcation within each into masculine and feminine dispositions. Fliess's theory of bisexuality, which hypothesized a "duality of sex" in every individual, would support that reading.[1] By doubling each person, this bisexuality of the psyche makes two into four. The late nineteenth century witnessed an efflorescence of psychological research on what was referred to variously as "dual personality," "double consciousness," "multiple personality," and even "multiplex personality"; Fliess's notion of bisexuality emerges from that constellation of ideas.[2] Intellectual history, compensating for the absence of Fliess's side of the correspondence, would render intelligible the otherwise mysterious passage with which Freud ends his letter:

> Now for bisexuality! I am sure you are right about it. And I am accustoming myself to the idea of regarding every sexual act as a process in which four persons are involved. We shall have a lot to discuss about that.[3]

Although the sentence in question is Freud's, it remains far from clear that the idea originates with him; instead, as with most intriguing psychoanalytic thoughts, the idea emerges in dialogue. As if recursively, the duality of dialogue generates a notion of sexual duality.

A normalizing interpretation would perceive in Freud's remark a man in whom the masculine predominates interacting with a woman who has assumed her feminine position in a paradigmatically heterosexual encounter; the shadow of the man's feminine disposition would be countered by an echo of his masculinity in the woman; and the incongruous doublings would fade into the background. But to reach such an interpretation, in which heterosexuality and gender normativity remain largely unchallenged, four persons must be scaled back to two, with the stranger possibilities forgotten. There is all the difference in the world between reducing four to two, on the one hand, and seeing four in two, on the other. Further, the reduction explains sexual acts in terms primarily of sexual difference. Both interpretive gestures—the reduction of four to two, and the reduction of "sex" to questions of difference—domesticate what is so distinctive about Freud's remark. Hermeneutic normalizations neutralize the sentence via the expediency of sense, repressing its puzzling qualities. Another way of putting it would be to say that reading this sentence in the historical context of Fliess's theory of bisexuality eclipses what is most psychoanalytic about it. Here, the historical is the agent of normalization.

If an eccentric reading of the Freudian sentence pulls against its normalizing recuperation, then that tension duplicates at a hermeneutic level the conflict between the normal and the strange in human sexuality itself. In order to reach a normative conclusion, the weirdness of sex must be repressed (the *ménage à quatre* must be reduced to coupledom). I want to suggest that this double movement—erotic strangeness registered but then repressed via normalization—replicates the rhythm through which human sexuality makes itself known. At another level of recursivity, I will contend that the normalization of sense-making also characterizes our theories of sexuality when they aspire to totalization or systematicity—when, that is, our conceptual accounts of sex elide the disruptions of the unconscious. Previous commentators have noticed how the double movement of registering strangeness and then repressing it determines the trajectory of Freud's *Three Essays on the Theory of Sexuality*.[4] I argue that double movement—a kind of erotically provoked epistemological rhythm that entails opening followed by closing—determines other theories of sexuality too. Our theories of sex are marked by the impact of their object on consciousness.

In order to sustain, rather than resolve, conflicts between the normal and the strange in human sexuality, I want to give free rein to Freud's weirdness, even what might be called his kinkiness. Here, I resist speaking in terms of the potential *queerness* of psychoanalysis because the category of queerness has, in recent years, been normalized via the thoroughgoing de-sexualization necessary for its successful institutionalization within the North American university. Having lost interest in sex, Queer Studies has forgotten virtually everything it learned from psychoanalysis (Davis and Dean, 2022). But this problem repeats the forgetting of sex that often occurs in psychoanalysis too. Reducing sex to questions of sexual difference is one way in which that happens—a reduction made easier by the fact that the word *sex* refers to both status (as a controverted synonym for gender) and action (sex as behavior, practice, and fantasy). Too often when critics discuss sex in conceptual terms, they are, in fact, focused primarily on the former, sex-as-difference, with merely the illusion that they're discussing the latter (see, e.g., Butler, 1993; Copjec, 1994; Scott, 2018; Zupančič, 2017). One of the goals of the present chapter is to de-prioritize sexual difference in psychoanalytic accounts of sexuality. Sexual difference functions as the great alibi of heterosexuality, fueling heteronormativity by its maintenance of a binary framework for sex. When one constructs an account of sexuality that begins with sexual difference, results are constrained in advance. From my perspective, sexual difference works to normalize the strangeness of sex.[5]

It is worth recalling that in the sentence with which we began, Freud writes not of sexual difference but of sexual acts. The context of bisexuality may prompt speculation about sexual difference, but Freud actually refers to persons, acts, and a process (by which I take him to mean a mental process that necessarily involves fantasy).[6] If the hinge that connects "sex" to sexual difference is genital sexuality—that is, already normalized *adult* sexuality—then what distinguishes sexuality for Freud is its *infantile*, polymorphously perverse dimension. Here "sexual" is not a synonym for "genital" but is defined in contradistinction to it. As Laplanche (2011, 161) encapsulates the distinction in his exposition of the psychoanalytically enlarged concept of sexuality, "for Freud, the *'sexual'* is exterior to, even prior to, the difference of the sexes, even the difference of the genders: it is oral, anal or para-genital."[7] Freudian sexuality involves a human body fully receptive to pleasure, yet without that body's necessarily being sexed.

When he refers to sexual acts "as a process in which four persons are involved," I would suggest that we are being asked to imagine adult erotic activity in which the infantile holds sway. The "four persons" of Freud's *ménage à quatre* might be read not as, say, two women and two men but as two adults and two children.

In place of the explanatory logic of sexual difference, then, I would substitute that of generational difference—or, more precisely, the difference between adult and child. The foundational difference that animates human sexuality is neither self-other nor man-woman but adult-child. Recurring social panic around pedophilia is only one element that prevents us from grasping this. What I'm trying to describe remains irreducible to either pedophilia or the Oedipus complex, though it may illuminate both. Freudian sexuality entails the disruptive persistence of the infantile within the adult, on the one hand, and the adult's sexual disruption of the world of childhood, on the other. In this account, it is not only that the lingering presence of the polymorphously perverse in adult sexuality threatens to derail reproductive genitality, but also that the emergence of the sexual well in advance of puberty risks making human sexuality entirely about pleasure, with reproduction as an incidental byproduct. Since the relation between adult and child is neither linear nor developmental but chiasmic, we have not merely the familiar situation of an adult with an "inner child" but, more strangely, a child with what might be called an "inner adult"—not an embryonic grown-up but an alien figure within the child.[8] And it is this chiasmic structure that helps to explain how the adult-child relation can be "sexual" without necessarily being genital or abusive.

Laplanche conceptualizes what I'm calling the child's "inner adult" via his theory of generalized seduction. Freud's abandoned seduction hypothesis—in which the cause of neurosis was posited as adult interference with childhood sexual innocence—is revived by Laplanche through the notion of the enigmatic signifier. It is an enigmatic message, transmitted inadvertently from the adult's unconscious to the child's in the course of routine bodily handling, that interferes with innocence. This message implants sexuality in a child in the form of an irreducible mystery, one that is no more soluble by the adult than by the uncomprehending child in whom it persists as a question, or a constellation of questions, concerning "sex." It is already a domestication of the enigma to suggest that the child's question boils down to the conundrum of where babies come from. The questions that Freud claims all children confront—including that of the difference between the sexes—are contingent interpretations *by Freud* of something that is more enigmatic because it remains unconscious. The question of where babies come from has an ultimately intelligible answer, whereas the unconscious enigma transmitted intergenerationally does not.

One significant implication of Laplanche's account is that, owing to the role of the enigmatic, human sexuality remains *under*determined by nature, family, language, society, and culture. The combination of these influencing factors, no matter how powerful, cannot predetermine a sexual outcome, since any translation of the unconscious enigma is necessarily contingent upon a singular subjectivity. As soon as one includes the dimension of the unconscious in a theory of sexuality, she has admitted an "x" factor whose incalculability undermines all determinisms. The unconscious changes everything. Hence the appeal of this psychoanalytic account for anti-essentialist and counter-heteronormative visions of sexuality. Conversely, however, the downside to creating a space within determinism is that the category of the unconscious introduces irreducible epistemological problems for any theory of sex that takes it seriously. Admitting an unknowable element renders the theory untotalizable and resistant to systematization. The moment you centralize the unconscious in your theory of sexuality (as psychoanalysts should), the theory necessarily becomes piecemeal. This problem is less often acknowledged than ignored.

II Two Ways About It

Our culture has embraced a version of Freud's polymorphously perverse (thanks perhaps to its compatibility with capitalism) on the condition that it be divorced from the infantile. Paradoxically, polymorphous pleasures have become for adults only, as the myth of childhood sexual innocence has been aggressively reasserted. Cultural panics around pedophilia are a symptom of this regression (Lancaster, 2011; Rubin, 2011). In a development that has elicited insufficient critical attention, the United States now has something approaching 1 million registered sex offenders, roughly a quarter of whom are minors, 11–17 years old (Levine, 2017, 153).[9] The massive denial of infantile sexuality has, in the name of protecting children, helped to create a judicial system in which young people are imprisoned and, indeed, branded for life as sex offenders, often for little more than youthful sexual experimentation. We have returned to a pre-Freudian era, apprehending the efflorescence of sexuality in childhood exclusively in terms of pathology, trauma, and abuse. The significance of the role of fantasy has been forgotten and become virtually unanalyzable. In this context, we might say that sex offenders need psychoanalysis not to treat or cure them but to exonerate them. The complexity of this terrain—in which the ostensibly competing realities of both abuse and fantasy need to be held in mind simultaneously—has been drastically over-simplified by a pathogenic cultural commitment to myths of innocence. Today we want our children without "inner adults."

Freud's observations about children's sexual research are especially pertinent here. Added to his *Three Essays* in 1915, the section titled "The Sexual Researches of Childhood" describes the emergence of a "will to know" directed principally to sex: "The instinct for knowledge in children is attracted unexpectedly early and intensively to sexual problems and is in fact possibly first aroused by them" (Freud, 1953). If children are the original sexual theorists, actively engaged from a tender age in speculation on issues they consider urgent, then we might wonder whether adult theories of sexuality retain any childlike elements. Also germane is the question of why all children appear as sex researchers but so few adults do. (The answer cannot be that adults have solved the mysteries of sex that perplex only childish minds.) It is significant that Freud, writing out of a culture that invented the research university, deliberately uses the term *research* (the noun *Forschung* in the phrase *die infantile Sexualforschung*) to describe this childhood activity (Freud, 1942). What the children are up to is neither idle speculation nor delinquent behavior but serious business; sexual research, far from compromising children's education, is a vital part of it—with the proviso that when it comes to sex, everyone is more or less an autodidact.

By describing children's will to know as an "instinct for knowledge," Freud universalizes it. We might redescribe this will to know—building on Laplanche—as a drive to translate. What appears as universal is less the particular riddles Freud claims children are trying to solve (*Where do babies come from? What is the difference between the sexes?*) than the imperative to make sense of the enigmatic message. It is the enigmas lodged within them that provoke children's research, though the forms and terms of their investigations remain entirely contingent. The motive for research counts more than whatever its results may happen to be. Freud concludes:

> We can say in general of the sexual theories of children that they are reflections of their own sexual constitution, and that in spite of their grotesque errors the theories show more understanding of sexual processes than one would have given their creators credit for.
>
> (Freud, 1953, 196)

In their pastiche quality, their combination of "grotesque errors" with surprising insights, children's sexual theories offer a glimpse of what may be at stake in all theorizing about sex.

Any theory of sex that does not disavow the unconscious must be a montage spliced together, with seams showing. Lacan described the drive as a montage (based on Freud's claim that "the sexual instinct and the sexual object are merely soldered together"), but I'm suggesting that the theory of this montaged phenomenon is itself a montage (Freud, 1953, 148).[10] There can be no coherent, systematic theory of sex because the object of the theory remains indelibly fractured by the unconscious and, hence, untotalizable. Only in the imaginary can theories be systematic and complete: conceptual coherence is a fallacy of the imaginary order. My reservations about certain Lacanian approaches have to do with their tendency to synthesize Lacan's fragmentary thinking into a conceptual whole, one that sometimes appears as a belief system or doctrine. When psychoanalytic theories become systematic, they become analyzable in the way that psychic defenses are analyzable.

The impossibility of a psychoanalytic theory of sexuality stems from the qualities of the object being conceptualized. Certainly, the unconscious dimension of sexuality can be theorized; but the effects on cognition of the object in question undermine the legitimacy of conceptual closure. In view of this limitation, the piecemeal aspect of *Three Essays*—what the late Steven Marcus once described as the text's "mosaic" construction—should not perturb us (Marcus, 1984, 23). The piecemeal aspect of Freud's theory of sexuality, far from incidental, mimics the piecemeal quality of the sexual drive itself. His theory is a composite because he's trying to explain the patched-together character of the component instincts or partial drives. As Marcus put it, "The disaggregation and decomposition that Freud had chosen as the analytic and expository form in which to treat the sexual aberrations is now revealed to be an essential attribute in the formation and structure of those aberrations themselves" (Marcus, 1984, 31). It is owing to the necessarily fragmented quality of what it aims to conceptualize that a psychoanalytic theory of sex cannot, in good conscience, be complete.

Freud's disaggregation of the drive offers a conceptual context for his multiplication of persons in the letter to Fliess with which we began. The psychoanalytic detotalization of the erotic body dramatically increases the number of parties or parts involved in sex; converting a couple into a *ménage à quatre* is but the beginning. One way of reading Freud's line to Fliess would involve seeing how the subjective division introduced by the unconscious automatically multiplies two persons into four. Dividing me against myself, the unconscious doubles me (this may explain why the joke about having sex with oneself retains some pungency). Of course, the unconscious is not another person but an impersonal other, a zone of alterity irreducible to personhood. Yet what would it mean to consider the psychoanalytic paradigm for sex as the group rather than the couple? And how might this idea challenge what we take group sex to represent? A *ménage à trois* tends to be regarded as the breaking of a dyad by a "third"; the third, by triangulating desire, reveals desire as necessarily mediated. But the *ménage à quatre* complicates that triangulation—potentially doubling it, yet also potentially restoring the dyad by recentering two couples. Psychoanalysts know what to do with a couple and they know how to handle a "third"; Freud's *ménage à quatre* raises questions that trouble the psychoanalytic authorities on sex.

Historically, group sex has been a feature of gay communities and subcultures, with various institutions—bathhouses, saunas, sex clubs, porn theaters, and darkrooms in bars—established in most urban centers throughout Europe and North America to facilitate sex beyond the pair. These institutions accommodate sex one-on-one, but they encourage sex among groups of men. Freud's line about "regarding every sexual act as a process in which four persons are involved" makes him sound, to a certain degree, like an urbane gay man. Either a gay man or a swinger from the pages of Catherine Millet's (2002) remarkable book about her regular and ritualized group sex life in 1970s Paris. Not the least of Millet's merits lies in her ample demonstration that group sex, far from exclusively a masculine pleasure, is for women too. If the psychoanalytic paradigm for sex is not the couple but the group, then we can see how Freud might be recognized as having laid the groundwork for the sexual revolutions of the 1960s and 1970s. Of course, the intellectual history and the sexual politics involved are considerably more complex than I'm suggesting here. My point is that, at the end of the nineteenth century, Freud intuited how human sexuality might better be conceptualized on the model of the group, with multiple partners or parts, than on the binary model of the pair. Group sex need not be established as the societal norm for it to function paradigmatically in psychoanalytic thinking.

Another way of putting this would be to say that when contemporary psychoanalysts talk about sex, they might try being a little more imaginative about it. Why does the psychoanalytic community speak frequently of group psychology but almost never of group sex? The heterosexual couple may represent a statistical norm for how adult sex is practiced, but it is far from how sex appears at the level of the unconscious. It might be desirable to exploit, rather than repress, this disjunction. Too often, the institutional respectability of psychoanalysis prevents it from being sufficiently psychoanalytic when it comes to sex. What kinds of thinking or research are needed for contemporary psychoanalysts to conceptualize sex beyond the couple?

III Is Three a Crowd?

When Freud writes that every sexual act is "a process in which four persons are involved," he may be saying that the physical interaction between two human bodies conjures additional persons. There is something about sex that brings other people into the room, even when they are not literally present. We might say that sex reproduces persons by multiplying their number in cases where pregnancy isn't an option. Is the multiplication of persons a consequence of my becoming someone else—or perhaps several others—during sex? Certainly, erotic intimacy offers an occasion for trying out different personae (as well as different positions); the psyche gets stretched and potentially reconfigured in such moments. But it may also be worth thinking about how sex enables a range of contact with others who are not actually present. Even with only two bodies in bed, there may yet be a group.

Catherine Millet (2002), the preeminent contemporary French philosopher of group sex, offers a helpful distinction for considering this possibility:

> There are two ways of envisaging a multitude, either as a crowd in which individual identities become confused, or as a chain where, conversely, what distinguishes them from one another is what binds them, as one ally compensates for another's weaknesses, as a son resembles his father even while he rebels. The very first men I knew immediately made me an emissary of a network in which I couldn't hope to know all the members, the unwitting link in a family of biblical scale and diversity. (35)[11]

Millet's distinction between dual conceptions of the multitude differentiates an essentially Deleuzean from a loosely Lacanian style of picturing group relations.

By virtue of her erotic activity with various overlapping groups of men, she identifies herself as the link in a chain whose members extend far beyond her capacity to know or identify them. Her having sex with some of these men connects her to all of them. It may be worth acknowledging that this kind of group sex—similarly to the unconscious—is at once utterly impersonal and deeply meaningful. It gives rise to what Leo Bersani and Adam Phillips (2008) call impersonal intimacy.

When, several years ago, I wrote about a newly emergent set of erotic practices in gay subculture, I invoked the term "unlimited intimacy" to encapsulate how some gay men were thinking about barebacking—that is, deliberately unprotected sex in the era of HIV (Dean, 2009). Millet's conviction that group sex confers access to a much larger set of partners than she could ever actually touch is another version of this "unlimited intimacy." What especially interested me about bareback subculture was its use of a virus to create kinship networks: the fantasy that sharing an indelible pathogen could be considered a version of the consanguinity that traditionally defines kin (rather than blood serving as what anthropologists call the "shared substance" of kinship, these men used a blood-borne virus). Some gay men employed this fantasy in group sex situations to think about their ancestors, understanding themselves as links in a network that stretched back in time to people they'd never met, much less had sex with. As with Millet, a particular conception of the multitude facilitates the idea that having sex with some of these men connects one with all of them. Involving an invisible pathogen in their erotic lives by having sex with a virus, these men were also having sex with ghosts. There were always more men in the scene than were in the room.

The impulse to conceive of gay sex as a kind of erotic contact with the dead via the living precedes AIDS. In the literary pornography of Sam Steward, written in the 1960s and 1970s under the nom du plume Phil Andros, sex is frequently imagined as a mechanism for summoning ghosts or gaining contact with the past. For example, in one story a sex partner tells the promiscuous narrator, "If you've had a lot of men ... I can 'look through you,' so to say, and see and wonder about all the ones you've had behind you" (Andros, 1992, 81). The partner who is present becomes an erotic medium who grants access, by means of his own body, to someone or something not present. In Steward's work, one witnesses the emergence of group sex as a paradigm not only for erotic contact but also for contact with the past, as if physical intimacy with other men were the route to previous generations or, more broadly, to history.[12] Here the historical would be the agent not of normalization but of alterity or strangeness. Steward casts in a new light the familiar dictum that every time you have sex with someone, you're having sex with all the people he had sex with. While contemporary sex education usually cites that dictum as a deterrent, Steward (and, subsequently, barebackers) treats it as an inducement.

Practices of impersonal group intimacy may be attempts to explore how sex is haunted by the presence of others. According to this perspective, group sex would represent neither a flight from intimacy nor a "fear of commitment" but rather a means of exploration—possibly a form of thinking—as well as a source of pleasure. I'm suggesting that group sex may furnish an occasion for working on the intergenerational enigmas that haunt erotic bodies. Freud's *ménage à quatre* stands as a prescient attempt to think the ways in which human sexuality always exceeds the primary couple that instantiates it—how sex multiplies not only persons but also otherness. There is group sex of a kind happening even in the monogamous couple; it's not an issue for only swingers or queers. Drawing on Laplanche, psychoanalyst Avgi Saketopoulou (2014, 254–268) has argued that perverse sexuality may be psychically generative, not merely symptomatic, because it aspires to shatter the ego and thus freshly to expose the subject to the enigmas of alterity. In this light, the impersonal intimacy of group sex would suggest psychical goals for erotic practice that differ from mutual recognition and intersubjective complementarity, on the one hand, or narcissistic gratification and simply getting off, on the other. Not the least of its pleasures stems from how, through the embrace of multiplicity, group sex facilitates psychic transformation.

IV Not Adding Up

Having elaborated some potential meanings of the sentence from Freud with which we began, I want in closing to resist the impulse to resolve their differences and incompatibilities. Since there is no conceptual coherence without repression, I have tried to sustain the tension between the normal and the strange in psychoanalytic thinking. The centrality of sexuality to psychoanalysis, together with the immortality of the infantile within sexuality, torques psychoanalysis in the direction of strangeness, although institutionally psychoanalysis tends to gravitate toward normativity. In view of this tension, there is something to be said for the weirdness of infantile sexual theories over their more respectable grown-up counterparts. Because adult theorizing yearns toward synthesis, coherence, and systematicity, it may in the end be oddly unsuited for capturing the disjunctive, composite dimension of sexuality. A specifically psychoanalytic theory of sexuality would need to relinquish much of what makes conceptualization recognizable as such. Drawing on Wittgenstein, the British psychoanalyst Adam Phillips (2001, xvi, 111) insists that psychoanalysis doesn't need new or improved theories: it just needs new sentences. Freud's enigmatic line about every sexual act involving four persons may be one of them.

Notes

1 Freud uses the phrase "duality of sex" to characterize Fliess's notion of bisexuality in a palimpsestic footnote that bears traces of his ambivalence toward his former friend and correspondent. See Freud (1953, 143).

2 The term *multiplex personality* comes from psychologist F.W.H. Myers's fascinating book, originally published in 1903, *Human Personality and Its Survival of Bodily Death* (1961). The best account of the emergence of "double consciousness" in the nineteenth century and its development into "multiple personality" and then "dissociative identity disorder" in the twentieth century is given in Ian Hacking, *Rewriting the Soul: Multiple Personality and the Sciences of Memory* (1995). Hacking claims that multiple personality came into being "late in the afternoon of the 27th of July, 1885" (171). By 1924, psychologist Morton Prince (1975, 207) was arguing that everyone has a multiple personality, because the normal human "mind is a composite of a lot of little minds, each concerned, however with its own business and its own interest and aim."

3 The newer English translation of this letter contains a significant difference: "I am accustoming myself to regarding every sexual act as a process in which four *individuals* are involved" (Freud, 1985, 364; emphasis added). Masson's translation appears closer to Freud's original: "*Ich gewöhne mich auch, jeden sexuellen Akt als einen Vorgang zwischen vier Individuen aufzufassen*" (Freud, 1986, 400). Yet, I prefer Strachey's translation over Masson's because "persons" resonates more significantly with the psychological and philosophical contexts in which Freud was writing.

4 See, for example, Bersani (1986), especially Chapter 2. More recently, Philippe Van Haute and Herman Westerink (2017) have sought to show how the original edition of Freud's *Three Essays* exhibits a strangeness and radical potential that subsequent editions dilute or conceal (see Freud, 2017).

5 In *Beyond Sexuality* (2000), I argued that Lacanian psychoanalysis could provide ammunition to the queer critique of heteronormativity via its development of the concept of *l'objet petit a* as "cause of desire," since the object *a* is prior to, and independent of, gender or sexual difference. Here, I'm advancing a cognate thesis in different terms, aiming to displace the primacy of sexual difference by generational difference.

6 While Foucault endeavored to bracket fantasy in his histories of sexuality, I insist that fantasy is inseparable from sexual practices as Foucault conceived them. Fantasy is itself a form of sexual behavior and, indeed, a specific sexual act undertaken by the libidinized mind. See Michel Foucault (1997, 125–126).

7 Laplanche develops "sexual" as a French neologism distinct from "sexuel" to indicate the specificity of Freud's contribution; since the French "sexuel" already translates to "sexual," Laplanche's distinction is indicated in English by italicizing *sexual*.

8 Since the "adult" within the child was also once a child with an inner alien "adult" of his/her own, the situation here is multigenerational; what I unconsciously inherit with the enigmatic message is thus at once intimate to, and notably remote from, me.

9 It is noteworthy that Halperin and Hoppe's (2017) *The War on Sex*, a 500-page book devoted to the unwarranted criminalization of sexuality, contains not a single mention of Freud.

10 See also Lacan (1979, 176): "The drive is precisely that *montage* by which sexuality participates in the psychical life, in a way that must conform to the gap-like structure that is the structure of the unconscious."

11 It is crucial to Millet's account that the erotic groups she participated in and meticulously describes "overlap with aesthetic groupings" (48).

12 For an elaboration of this account, see Dean (2017, 25–43).

Bibliography

Andros, P. (1992). *Roman Conquests*, Boston: Perineum Press.

Bersani, L. (1986). *The Freudian Body: Psychoanalysis and Art*, New York: Columbia University Press.

Bersani, L. and A. Phillips (2008). *Intimacies*, Chicago: University of Chicago Press.

Butler, J. (1993). *Bodies That Matter: On the Discursive Limits of "Sex"*, New York: Routledge.

Copjec, J. (1994). "Sex and the Euthanasia of Reason," in *Read My Desire: Lacan Against the Historicists* (pp.201–236), Cambridge: MIT Press.

Davis, O. and T. Dean (2022). *Hatred of Sex*, Lincoln: University of Nebraska Press.

Dean, T. (2000). *Beyond Sexuality*, Chicago: University of Chicago Press.

Dean, T. (2009). *Unlimited Intimacy: Reflections on the Subculture of Barebacking*, Chicago: University of Chicago Press.

Dean, T. (2017). "Sam Steward's Pornography: Archive, Index, Trace," in *Samuel Steward and the Pursuit of the Erotic: Sexuality, Literature, Archives* (pp.25–43), ed. D. A. Moddelmog and M. J. Ponce, Columbus: Ohio State University Press.

Foucault, M. (1997). "An Interview with Stephen Riggins," in *The Essential Works of Michel Foucault, 1954–1984*, vol. 1, *Ethics: Subjectivity and Truth* (pp.121–133), ed. P. Rabinow, trans. R. Hurley, New York: New Press.

Freud, S. (1942). *Drei Abhandlungen zur Sexualtheorie*, in *Gesammelte Werke, Vol. V, 1904–1905*, Frankfurt: S. Fischer Verlag.

Freud, S. (1953). "Three Essays on the Theory of Sexuality," in *The Standard Edition of the Complete Psychological Works of Sigmund Freud, Vol. 7* (pp.123–243), trans. and ed. J. Strachey, London: Hogarth Press.

Freud, S. (1975). *The Origins of Psychoanalysis: Letters, Drafts and Notes to Wilhelm Fliess, 1887–1902*, ed. M. Bonaparte, A. Freud, and E. Kris, trans. E. Mosbacher and J. Strachey, New York: Doubleday.

Freud, S. (1985). *The Complete Letters of Sigmund Freud to Wilhelm Fliess, 1887–1904*, ed. and trans. J. M. Masson, Cambridge: Harvard University Press

Freud, S. (1986). *Briefe an Wilhelm Fliess, 1887–1904: Ungekürzte Ausgabe*, Frankfurt: S. Fischer Verlag.

Freud, S. (2017). *Three Essays on the Theory of Sexuality: The 1905 Edition*, trans. U. Kistner, London: Verso

Hacking, I. (1995). *Rewriting the Soul: Multiple Personality and the Sciences of Memory*, Princeton: Princeton University Press.

Halperin, D. M. and T. Hoppe (eds). (2017). *The War on Sex*, Durham: Duke University Press.

Lacan, J. (1979). *The Four Fundamental Concepts of Psycho-analysis*, ed. J.-A. Miller, trans. A. Sheridan, Harmondsworth: Penguin.

Lancaster, R. N. (2011). *Sex Panic and the Punitive State*, Berkeley: University of California Press.

Laplanche, J. (2011). "Gender, Sex and the *Sexual*," in *Freud and the* Sexual*: Essays 2000–2006* (pp.159–180), ed. J. Fletcher, trans. J. Fletcher, J. House and N. Ray, New York: International Psychoanalytic Books.

Levine, J. (2017). "Sympathy for the Devil: Why Progressives Haven't Helped the Sex Offender, Why They Should, and How They Can," in *The War on Sex* (pp.126–173), ed. D. M. Halperin and T. Hoppe, Durham: Duke University Press.

Marcus, S. (1984). *Freud and the Culture of Psychoanalysis: Studies in the Transition from Victorian Humanism to Modernity*, New York: Norton.

Millet, C. (2002). *The Sexual Life of Catherine M.*, trans. A. Hunter, New York: Grove Press.

Myers, F. W. H. (1961). *Human Personality and Its Survival of Bodily Death*, ed. S. Smith, New Hyde Park: University Books

Phillips, A. (2001). *Promises, Promises: Essays on Literature and Psychoanalysis*, New York: Basic Books.

Prince, M. (1975). "The Problem of Personality: How Many Selves Have We?" in *Psychotherapy and Multiple Personality: Selected Essays* (pp.188–213), ed. N. G. Hale, Jr., Cambridge: Harvard University Press.

Rubin, G. S. (2011). "Thinking Sex: Notes for a Radical Theory of the Politics of Sexuality," in *Deviations: A Gayle Rubin Reader* (pp.137–181), Durham: Duke University Press.

Saketopoulou, A. (2014). "To Suffer Pleasure: The Shattering of the Ego as the Psychic Labor of Perverse Sexuality." *Studies in Gender and Sexuality*, 15(4), 254–268.

Scott, J. W. (2018). *Sex and Secularism*, Princeton: Princeton University Press.

Van Haute, P. and H. Westerink (2017). *Deconstructing Normativity? Re-reading Freud's 1905 Three Essays*, London: Routledge.

Zupančič, A. (2017). *What Is Sex?* Cambridge: MIT Press.

Chapter 2

Glôssa and "Counter-Will"

The Perverse Tongue of Psychoanalysis

Elissa Marder

In the late 1880s, Sigmund Freud became fascinated with the case of a woman who has a tendency to interrupt her own speech by making strange noises with her tongue. As soon as she thinks to herself that she must remain silent, her uncontrollable tongue erupts into clacking noises that contradict and counteract her conscious intentions. Seemingly captivated both by the specific quality of the sounds she makes and by the fact that she is apparently compelled to make them against her will, Freud describes her peculiar tongue-noises in several of his early works: "A Case of Successful Treatment by Hypnotism: With Some Remarks on the Origin of Hysterical Symptoms Through Counter-Will" (1953) and "On the Psychical Mechanism of Hysterical Phenomena: A Lecture" (1962). He also treats it in a paper, co-written with Joseph Breuer, with the very similar name "On the Psychical Mechanism of Hysterical Phenomena: Preliminary Communication" (1955).[1] In the 1893 essay, Freud devotes an entire page to her and glosses his description of the noises she makes with the suggestive addition that the sounds resemble the "cry of a capercaillie" (31). As we learn from an editorial footnote in the *Standard Edition* that refers us to a 1955 book called *Bird Recognition III* by ornithologist J. Fisher, the capercaillie's cry is described as "a ticking ending with a pop and hiss" (Freud, 1893, 31). In his original German text, Freud (1893) describes her bizarre vocalizations as *"eigenartiges Schnalzen mit der Zunge mitten in der Rede, ähnlich dem Balzen des Auerhahns"* ["her speech was interrupted by a peculiar 'clacking' with her tongue, which resembled the cry of a capercaillie"]. The word *"Schnalzen"* that Freud uses for the odd clacking or clicking sounds of the woman's tongue rhymes with the word *"Balzen"*—a word designating the mating cry of the male mountain woodcock. The evocative rhyme, *"Schnalzen"* with *"Balzen,"* establishes a sensuous phonetic link that echoes and enhances the descriptive analogy that Freud establishes between the clacking noises made by the woman's tongue and the mating call of the male bird.

Although Freud makes no further overt mention of the strikingly erotic and non-human dimension to the noises the woman makes with her tongue aside from these dramatic rhetorical flourishes, in every text in which he describes this particular symptom, he implicitly draws attention to the ways in which her human and (presumably) feminine speech is punctuated by something radically

DOI: 10.4324/9781003284888-4

other. Her involuntary clacking noises run counter to the cultural language she otherwise inhabits; her cacophonic interjections are heard by Freud as a sonorous amalgam that is marked as an erotic address, performed by a male bird. And, in response to that address, Freud formulates his first genuinely psychoanalytic account of the unconscious.

References to the woman (and her symptom) run through his early writings. As mentioned above, Freud's first discussion of the clacking tongue appears in one of his very first clinical publications: "A Case of Successful Treatment by Hypnotism: With Some Remarks on the Origin of Hysterical Symptoms Through 'Counter-Will'" (Freud, 1953, 115–132). This paper has received relatively little attention in psychoanalytic theory because it was traditionally classified as one of Freud's "pre-psychoanalytic" writings due to its apparent focus on clinical treatment by hypnosis. And yet, confronted with the paradoxical phenomenon of a woman whose speech is subjected to the mysterious force of what he calls her "counter-will," Freud begins to lay down the basic building blocks out of which he will go on to construct the architecture of psychic organization in his mature psychoanalytic writings. As Freud begins to wonder why the woman is apparently compelled to interrupt her own speech by making animal noises with her tongue, he begins to articulate, for the first time, the idea that bodily symptoms are the expressions of utterances that have been forcefully removed from consciousness. In describing the noises the woman makes with her tongue, Freud uses the term "fixated" for the first time in a (proto) psychoanalytic sense. Before examining how this use of the concept of "fixation" in the case of the clacking tongue becomes significant for Freud's later writings about female sexuality, I would like to begin by suggesting more generally that fixation both grounds and contests the place of female sexuality within psychoanalysis.

Fixation and Female Sexuality[2]

The word "fixation" designates the threshold—and perhaps the limit—of psychoanalysis. Although the term enters Freud's early (and still largely psychiatric) writings as part of the technical clinical vocabulary of hypnosis, fixation also comes to mark the very moment when psychoanalysis veers off from psychiatry. Over time, this disarmingly familiar term has not only acquired many varied meanings and functions within psychoanalysis but also has become effortlessly absorbed into everyday speech. "Fixation" is vital to Freud's first elaborations of hysterical symptom formation, the mechanisms involved in repression, and the importance of infantile sexuality. And, although Freud invokes fixation in conjunction with the so-called normal psychic operations such as mourning and love, the term is invariably associated with virtually all of the most contested zones within Freud's theory of gender and sexuality: homosexuality, perversion, pre-Oedipal attachments to the mother, regression, femininity, and the clitoris. Within the language of psychoanalysis, fixation functions as a kind of placeholder that marks many of the places where Freud himself gets stuck. Those sticking points inscribe possible counter-readings to Freud's texts that enable us to challenge some of his most hetero-normative claims from within the terms of his own writing and thinking. These counter-readings become most legible whenever Freud writes about the intimate connections between fixation and female sexuality, and they point to the fundamentally paradoxical place of female sexuality within psychoanalysis.

Simply put, the paradox is this: female sexuality both establishes the universal foundations of the Freudian metapsychology and is excluded from it. As is well known, Freud invents the language of psychoanalysis and elaborates his first metapsychological account of how human subjectivity is organized on the basis of his early clinical work with female hysterics. Likewise, although Freud discovered hysteria *in* women, he famously—and controversially—never understood it as being specific *to* women. His elaboration of hysteria enabled him to establish the essential link between sexuality and the unconscious that provides the ground for psychoanalysis's most far-reaching insights. For Freud, hysteria is the hallmark of female sexuality, the matrix of all of the other neuroses, and the bedrock of psychic organization. In later years, as Freud becomes increasingly invested in the paradigm of the Oedipal complex, he shifts his clinical gaze away from women patients and begins to develop a putatively universal (albeit exclusively male) model of human subjectivity based on his clinical work on men and boys. While in the early years, the hysterical symptoms he discovered in women instigated and substantiated psychoanalytic knowledge, in his later texts, he concedes that there is something intractably "enigmatic" and unknowable about female sexuality that eludes psychoanalytic grasp. And so it happens that female sexuality, which initially provided Freud with the original material on which psychoanalytic theory, method, and technique were founded, becomes increasingly excluded from the very metapsychology for which it was once the ground.

Faced with his inability to integrate a plausible narrative of sexual development for a girl child into his Oedipal model organized around castration anxiety, in his notorious late texts "Female Sexuality" (1961) and the lecture "Femininity" (1964), Freud suddenly proposes (in contradiction to all his own previous theories) that "femininity" is not merely a psychic position adopted by either men or women throughout sexual life, but rather a final stage of sexual development, unique to women, an end-point to which women are biologically pre-destined. But in every text that is ostensibly devoted to "femininity," Freud spends more time enumerating the various paths that lead inexorably *away* from femininity than he does showing how anyone ever succeeded in attaining it. His descriptions of the many potential stumbling blocks and obstacles to femininity are much more vivid and convincing than the speculation (never sustained with any clinical evidence) that any actual woman ever successfully managed to reach (and/or remain in) that illusory theoretical stage. On the contrary, virtually all of the clinical material he presents consists of detailed accounts of how and why the path to femininity became unavailable or (as is the case of his daughter, and all of his women analyst colleagues) was emphatically the road not taken. Paradoxically, therefore, as a universal category, femininity is a general rule for which there are only exceptions.

As Freud himself concedes in the lecture called "Femininity," the fate that awaits the rare woman who reaches femininity is tantamount to a living death because "her libido has taken up final positions and seems incapable of exchanging them for others. There are no paths open to further development... as though, indeed, the difficult development to femininity had exhausted the possibilities of the person concerned" (Freud, 1964, 135). According to Freud, when "femininity" fails, it is because archaic pre-Oedipal fixations from the past prevent a woman from moving forward in time, but when femininity succeeds, it freezes the future out of existence. Fixations impede a woman's path toward femininity, but femininity, once achieved, is nothing other than a state of pure fixation. We arrive at the paradoxically perverse conclusion that fixation is both opposed to femininity and is the purest expression of the psychic petrification that befalls the woman who might be unfortunate enough to succeed in reaching it. Happily, however, the risks for little girls and adult women are slim, as "femininity" is virtually impossible to attain.

I have re-told this familiar story because I would like to turn it inside out and upside down. I would like to claim that within and alongside Freud's hyperbolically hetero-normative attempt to use "femininity" to rescue the universality of the (male) Oedipus complex, one can discern the traces of a very queer counter-narrative about sexuality that is inscribed within his ambivalent, contradictory, and over-determined uses of the term "fixation."

Two of Freud's most marginal—but particularly evocative—case studies feature scenarios of "fixation" in which a part of a woman's body becomes animated, aroused, and strangely endowed with non-human sounds that oddly punctuate the theoretical claims surrounding it. In the first case, from the late 1880s, which I have already mentioned and to which I will return in a moment, Freud uses the term "fixation," to explain why a woman's tongue suddenly interrupts her speech and erupts into strange bird-like clacking noises. In the second case, from 1915 (which I have written about elsewhere [Marder, 2017]), Freud (1955) describes a woman who hears strange clicking noises while she and her paramour are together. Convinced that the sounds she hears come from a camera and that her would-be lover has hired someone to take compromising photographs of her while they are making love, she consults a lawyer, who sends her to Freud. He declares that the clicking noises she thinks she hears ("*Ticken/Pochen/Klopfen*") are in fact auditory hallucinations that emanate from her clitoris. According to him, the queer clicking sounds are vestigial traces of a powerful fixation on her mother that takes the form of sound-images from a primordial past that have been transmitted via her clitoris. The early case of the clacking tongue from the 1880s communicates with the later case of the clicking clitoris through the odd, non-human form of speech common to both.

The two cases speak to each other in the strange language of eroticized bodily organs that have been endowed with speech by fixation. Together, these two texts begin to reveal the traces of a kind of sound-image track—within Freud's writing—that opens onto a language of sexuality that threatens the logical coherence of his normative descriptions of sexual difference.

Both the tongue and the clitoris have an ambiguous status in terms of sexual difference and gender identification. Despite Freud's many attempts to claim that the clitoris is nothing other than an inadequate, insufficient, and stunted penis, and therefore a failed phallic organ, his own texts tell a slightly different tale. Freud insists that the clitoris is especially susceptible to fixation because, unlike the penis, it is not subject to the laws of castration. However, after arguing for decades that the existence of the phallic clitoris renders the little girl nothing other than a little boy and that with puberty and womanhood the attachment to the clitoris normally fades away in favor of the pleasures of the properly feminine vagina, in the late text "Female Sexuality," he concedes that the clitoris "continues to function in later female sexual life in a manner which is very variable and which is certainly not satisfactorily understood" (Freud, 1961, 228). Freud seems compelled to admit (even if only implicitly) that the clitoris is not merely an inferior ersatz penis, but also, and perhaps even more disturbingly for him, the corollary that the "variability" of the clitoris also consequently affects both the possibility of pre-determining the temporal organization and sexual life of the subject. The unpredictable "variable" influence of the clitoris in time and over time is arguably as threatening to him as is its indeterminate sexual identity. The clitoris thus occupies the paradoxical status of being both the quintessential figure of fixation and the element that cannot be fixed within his system. According to the logic of this counter-reading, it also follows that Freud's persistent fixation on linking the clitoris to fixation is itself an indication of the fact that the clitoris speaks in a tongue that he cannot fully assimilate into the language of psychoanalysis.

Before returning to the case in which Freud first uses the word "fixation" to describe how a woman's tongue becomes mysteriously affected by an idea that cannot be brought into consciousness, I would like to take a short detour to ask about the status of the figure of the tongue itself.

Glôssa

What is a tongue? A quick trip to the dictionary tells us that like "*langue*" in French, "*lingua*" in Latin, and "*Glossa*" in Greek, the word "tongue" in English can either designate a bodily organ in the mouth or the articulated language that is made possible in part by the muscular action of that bodily organ. But is it really possible to keep these two meanings and these two functions apart from one another? The tongue negotiates the border between the self and not-self, inside and outside. Present and active from the time of birth, the tongue is a bodily organ that makes articulated speech possible and, via the sense of taste, makes judgments about what can or cannot or what should or should not be taken in and assimilated by the mouth. Within sexual life, the tongue occupies an undetermined but undeniably powerful role. Its place within psychoanalysis is curiously nebulous: it both is and is not considered to be a sexual organ. Involved in erotic activities such as sucking and kissing, the tongue is morphologically analogous to both the penis and the clitoris but reducible to neither. Although—unlike the genitals—the tongue does not develop over time or change in form, it is nonetheless sensitive to the effects of aging and the demands of culture. In this sense, the tongue provides a model for a non-developmental, non-teleological genital-like body part: both plastic and fixed, the tongue challenges distinctions between infantile and adult sexuality and resists being simply identified with either masculine or feminine sexuality.

In literary texts from ancient days up till the present, the tongue is often a figure for a non-human element within human language. Animated tongues speak languages that undermine the will of the speaker or that bear witness to that which cannot be said. Ovid vividly describes how Philomela's severed tongue continues to writhe after being cut off from her body (Ovid, 1977). Several of Edgar Allan Poe's most famous stories feature tongues that speak against the speaker's will or—as in the case of M. Valdemar—after the speaker's death.[3] Within Christianity, forked tongues of fire communicate God's message to the apostles. When writing about translation in "What is a Relevant Translation," Jacques Derrida (2004, 424) famously invokes the figure of a "tongue of flame" to describe how the body of a text both calls for and resists translation.

According to the entry for "Language" in the *Dictionary of Untranslatables,* unlike the word *logos* (the general Greek word for language), the Greek word for tongue, *glôssa,* is not restricted to the human realm:

> Glôssa in the sense of "tongue" is distinct from the universality of the logos defining the humanity of humankind, in that it is linked to the differences between languages, and to human diversity. We tend therefore to reserve "language" (langage) for logos, and "tongue" (langue) for glôssa.
>
> (Cassin, 2014, 545)

And, as we glean from the *Dictionary of Untranslatables*'s entry "To Translate," the word *glôssa* often indicates the introduction of a foreign element and a foreign body into a given language:

> In the rhetorical and grammatical corpus, "barbarism" refers to an effect of unintelligibility: for instance, in poetry, when one diverges from the proper meaning or common use (to idiôtikon [τὸ ἰδιωτικόν], to kurion [τὸ κύριον]) and uses "foreign" expressions instead (xenika [ξενικά]). Too many metaphors result in ainigma [αἴνιγμα], a confusion of the signifier, and too many borrowings (glossâi [γλῶσσαι]) lead to barbarismos

[βαρβαρισμός], gibberish, and the confusion of the signified (Aristotle, Poetics, 22.1458a18–31; see LANGUAGE, II.A).

(Cassin and Lezra, 2014, 1141)

Glôssa, the tongue, is related to barbarism because the language of the other is perceived as empty bodily utterances that remain unintelligible. When the body of a given tongue is heard as unintelligible sound, something within the material body of language that resists being transposed into meaning also becomes audible. In this sense, the bodily word *for* language, tongue or *glôssa*, is inextricably linked to the question of the body *of* language. It is because language is *glôssa* and not merely *logos* that translation is both necessary and impossible. Necessary because, as we have said, the notion of language invoked by *glôssa* presupposes linguistic differences, but impossible because *glôssa* also recalls and retains something of the non-human bodily residue of the tongue that cannot be brought into articulated human language.

The Perverse Tongue of Psychoanalysis

In Freud's earliest psychoanalytic papers, the woman with the clacking tongue makes repeated cameo appearances as an anonymous character identified uniquely on the basis of her noisy symptom. In 1895, several years after his first written description of her odd verbal eruptions, Freud devotes his first single-authored case history in the co-authored *Studies on Hysteria* (with Joseph Breuer) to her and gives her the name "Emmy von N." While it is indisputable that the subject of the case of Emmy von N. refers to the same biographical person as the unidentified woman with the clacking tongue, Freud's theoretical interest in the figure of the clacking tongue both precedes and outlasts its place within the case history and indicates that there may be something more—or perhaps different—to be heard in way that its strange sounds resonate—and produce effects—within his later writings and his thinking more generally.

The case of Emmy von N. has generated an interesting afterlife of its own, in part because of the striking role that animals (though curiously not the capercaillie) play in the case.[4] Many of these recent reassessments draw upon material assembled in a paper written about Emmy von N. by Swiss psychoanalyst Henri Ellenberger in 1977. In this provocative and influential article, Ellenberger reveals the true identity of the patient (Fanny Moser) and, working with new documents concerning her position in society and her terrible relationship with her two daughters, he argues provocatively that Fanny Moser suffered from a form of *sociogenic hysteria*. Ellenberger rather startlingly asserts that the vicissitudes of wealth combined with the restrictions of the social roles available to her as a woman produced trans-generational toxic effects. According to him, Fanny Moser's many psychic symptoms (which included pathological fear of animals and ghosts) and her unpleasant behavior (which involved abusive treatment of her children and her domestic staff) were exacerbated, if not actually produced, by the forms of social violence associated with her privileged position in society. Although Fanny Moser was the daughter of an old aristocratic Swiss family and the young widow of an extremely wealthy industrial businessman, after her (much older) husband's sudden death, she was accused of having poisoned him by his children from a former marriage, shunned by society and forced to defend herself and her fortune in court. In the years following these events, she used her immense wealth to create a new social world for herself. She bought an enormous castle, hired an extensive staff, and invited distinguished visitors of all kinds (including Freud) to pay her court. Although in his 1895 case history, Freud is consistently sympathetic to Emmy von N. and fails to observe or report any abusive social behavior on her part, for Ellenberger, who re-opens the case in 1977 in light of new material regarding the pernicious effects that Fanny Moser had upon her daughters, there is a direct connection between her symptoms (fear of animals and the occult) and the deleterious effects perpetuated by patriarchy and capitalism run amok. In an interpretative gesture reminiscent of Emile Zola, Ellenberger claims that Fanny Moser unwittingly and unconsciously transmitted the content of her sociogenic symptoms to her two daughters, both of whom (perhaps unconsciously) devoted their lives to counteracting their negative force. The older daughter became a zoologist who was an expert on jellyfish and then subsequently developed a scholarly interest in paranormal phenomena; the younger daughter immigrated to the USSR where she founded an orphanage and wrote a children's book about learning to love animals. Ellenberger ends his paper about Fanny Moser with the suggestion that if Moser's daughters succeeded in repairing the damages of their mother's sociogenic illness, they were able to do only by transforming the unconscious conflicts manifested by her symptoms into the motivating force behind their social activism and intellectual labor. It is striking—and somewhat peculiar—that given Ellenberger's strong interest in Fanny Moser's fear and dislike of animals, he makes no mention either of her most distinctive symptom (her clacking tongue) or of the fact that Freud explicitly compares the clacking tongue to sounds made by an animal. As a counterpoint to Ellenberger's reading, I would like to point out that although Fanny Moser's phobic hallucinations of small animals (primarily mice and worms) can be readily integrated into his sociological interpretative framework, Emmy's bird-like sputterings are queer augurs that demand a different path into Freud's discovery of the language of the unconscious.

As I have already indicated, Freud first mentions the woman with the clacking tongue in one of his very first clinical publications: "A Case of Successful Treatment by Hypnotism: With Some Remarks on the Origin of Hysterical Symptoms Through 'Counter-Will.'" As the somewhat unwieldy double-barreled title of the case indicates, the case has a striking two-part structure. It is divided into two distinct sections, which feature two very different clinical examples that are ostensibly related to one another through Freud's successful use of hypnotism in both treatments. A closer reading of the case, however, reveals that the real theoretical action of the case is located in the strange new concept of "counter-will" that is announced by the case's subtitle and that serves as the hinge between the two parts. Here, as in many of his most innovative later papers (such as "Mourning and Melancholia"), Freud sets up a juxtaposition between a relatively familiar form of a psychic disturbance and presents it in relation to its more pathological—and usually more conceptually suggestive—psychic counterpart. The first half of "A Case of Successful Hypnotism..." makes for very pleasurable reading because Freud presents his clinical material in the form of a lightly humorous human-interest story. The case is about a woman who suffers from an inability to breastfeed her three children because of a sudden—and apparently hysterical—onset of uncontrollable vomiting. After having been completely unable to breastfeed her first child, she (and her family) consults Freud when she becomes ill following the birth of the next two babies. On both occasions, using hypnotism, Freud succeeds in helping to settle her stomach and increase her appetite so that she manages to breastfeed the babies. At the end of his engaging narrative account, Freud ruefully describes (in mock-heroic terms) how, despite his successful treatment, the patient and her family failed to express any appreciation for his efforts because his cure proved that the young woman was unable to conquer her symptom by the power of her own will.

Using his patient's frustration about the failure of her will as a springboard, Freud then launches into a curiously quasi-philosophical pre-psychoanalytic speculation about the specific psychic mechanism that could account for why she fell ill instead of carrying out her conscious intention to breastfeed her child. He postulates that all subjective expressions of will (intentions) are invariably accompanied by affective ideas associated with everything that might thwart or interfere with an intention's capacity to fulfill itself by merging with its corresponding expectation. However, precisely because intentions, by definition, are inherently virtual—that is, they can only be realized in the future—logically speaking they always conjure up—and are accompanied by—the specter of their potential failure. Every intention is haunted by the set of all of the negative thoughts that express the idea of its potential negation. Freud calls these negative thoughts "distressing antithetical ideas." He goes on to assert that every future-oriented thought (be it intention or expectation) invariably generates such distressing "antithetical ideas" that must be overcome and/or neutralized before the intention can be carried out.

Despite the apparent similarity between the two clinical examples in the paper (in both instances, Freud uses hypnosis in the treatment of a woman patient who suffers from a hysterical symptom that overrides her conscious intention to care for her children), there is nonetheless a subtle but critical discontinuity regarding Freud's conceptualization of hysteria in the two cases. While the first clinical example both conforms to and confirms accepted contemporary models for understanding hysteria, in the second clinical case, something slightly different happens. Although Freud frames the discussion of hysteria as a mysterious failure of "will-power" and uses hypnosis in the treatment in both cases, in the second clinical example, unlike the first, Freud does not use hypnosis in order to *treat* the symptom, but rather as a way of gaining knowledge about the very logic underlying its formation. The focus of the clinical intervention is not to remove the symptom, but rather to understand why, when, and how it comes into being in the first place. Moreover, Freud's attempts to explain how the symptom is formed motivate him to invent a new language—and a new technical vocabulary—to describe the structure of the psyche from which it arises. The brief clinical account about the woman with the clacking tongue is, in miniature, a first vignette in which Freud begins to speak of and with a new tongue: the language of the unconscious:

> Some years ago I treated a hysterical lady who showed great strength of will in those of her dealings which were unaffected by her illness; but in those which were so affected she showed no less clearly the weight of the burden imposed on her by her numerous and oppressive hysterical impediments and incapacities. One of her striking characteristics was a peculiar noise which intruded, like a tic, into her conversation. I can best describe it as a singular clacking of the tongue with a sudden interruption of the convulsive closure of her lips. After observing it for some weeks, I once asked her when and how it had first originated. "I don't know when it was," she replied, "oh! a long time ago."
>
> (Freud, 1953, 124)

> [*Vor Jahren behandelte ich eine hysterische Dame, die ebenso willensstark in all den Stücken war, in welche sich ihre Krankheit nicht eingemengt hatte, wie anderseits schwer belastet mit mannigfaltigen und drückenden hysterischen Verhinderungen und Unfähigkeiten. Unter anderem fiel sie durch ein eigentümliches Geräusch auf, welches sie ticartig in ihre Konversation einschob, und das ich als ein besonderes Zungenschnalzen mit plötzlichem Durchbruch des krampfhaften Lippenverschlusses beschreiben möchte. Nachdem ich es wochenlang mitangehört hatte, erkundigte ich mich einmal, wann und bei welcher Gelegenheit es entstanden sei. Die Antwort war: "Ich weiß nicht wann, o schon seit langer Zeit."*]
>
> (Freud, 1893, 12)

Although Freud notices the woman's speech impediment during his first encounters with her, he initially does not pay any particular attention to it because he assumes that it is a permanent *tic convulsif* of the sort that Charcot's student Tourette from the Salpêtrière had already identified and that was familiar to him. But once the woman informs him that she cannot remember exactly when the symptom started, but that it did begin at some point during her adult life, Freud realizes that there is an important correlation between the *failure* of her memory and the *origin* of her symptom. In other words, he understands that if the symptom was produced in response to a particular event, that (forgotten) event must reveal something about the necessary conditions that led to its formation. Under hypnosis, she produces memories of two related scenes during which her firm intention not to make any noise seemingly compels her to produce the very noisy sounds she is attempting to ward off: in the first scene, she recalls that while tending to her sleeping sick child, the very thought that she should refrain from making any noise so that the child could go on sleeping apparently caused her to start making noises against her will. Although this first manifestation of the symptom disappeared shortly after its first occurrence, several years later, when she once again found herself in a situation in which she wanted to remain silent, she discovered, once again, that she could not do so. In this second scene, the woman remembers riding in a horse-drawn carriage during a thunderstorm and, after seeing a tree being struck by lightning, the very thought that she shouldn't frighten the horses provokes her to do the very thing she wanted not to do. During the second event, her symptom returned and persisted thereafter.

On the basis of the link between these two recovered memories and the intractable symptom of the clacking tongue, Freud articulates, for the very first time, how hysterical symptoms are the trace of a counter-utterance that becomes removed from consciousness and becomes "fixated" in the body.

> This, however, was the first occasion on which I was able to observe the origin of hysterical symptoms through the putting into effect of a distressing antithetic idea—that is, through counter-will. The mother, worn out by anxieties and her duties as a nurse, made a decision not to let a sound pass her lips for fear of disturbing her child's sleep, which had been so long in coming. But in her exhausted state the attendant antithetic idea that she nevertheless would do it proved to be stronger; it made its way to the *innervation of the tongue*, which her decision to remain silent may perhaps have forgotten to inhibit, broke through the closure of her lips and produced a noise which thenceforward remained *fixated* for many years, especially after the same course of events had been repeated.
>
> (Freud, 1953, 125)

Freud uses the evocative term "counter-will" to describe the unsettling psychic consequences that ensue when the distressing antithetical idea that has disappeared from consciousness becomes rerouted as a bodily "innervation" that runs counter to the conscious intention of the person involved. The "counter-will" succeeds in carrying out its distressing aim of counteracting the original volitional intention precisely because it has the capacity to bypass the subject's conscious knowledge and because of its ability to express itself bodily.

> The antithetic idea establishes itself, so to speak, as a "counter-will," while the patient is aware with astonishment of having a will which is resolute and powerless.
>
> (Freud, 1953, 122)

Although this primitive notion of a counter-will is a direct precursor to the psychoanalytic notion of repression, in this early text, Freud depicts the power of the counter-will in terms that are closer to the occult phenomena of fantastic fiction and demonological possession than they are to the quasi-scientific descriptions of repression found in the later metapsychological writings. Like Edgar Allan Poe's famous "imp of the perverse" to which it bears an uncanny resemblance, Freud describes counter-will as a "perversion of will" that affects the tongue. Counter-will, he writes, "exercises greater control over the body than does conscious simulation [...] here, in contrast to the *weakness* of will shown in neurasthenia, we have a *perversion* of will" (Freud, 1953, 123).

The queer compound term "*Willensperversion*" ("perversion of will") does not appear to exist in the German tongue before Freud uses it here. Moreover, the component word, "perversion," is of Latin origin and it is not a normal German word. As a foreign word imported into German from Latin, Italian, French, and English, "perversion" would have been more or less familiar to educated German speakers. Its precise meaning, however, was not at all fixed in German. From its Latin root, the word "perversion" means turning around or turning away and, although from ancient times the word has carried moral and theological meanings (turning Good into Evil, truth into falsity), it also has more technical meanings relating to reversals in chemistry, medicine, and optical geometry as well. During the nineteenth century, in part due to the work by Richard von Krafft-Ebing, the word "perversion" became more common in German and was associated with sexuality in general and homosexuality in particular. Curiously, however, it is not primarily in this sexual sense that Freud uses it in this context. As is made clearer later in the essay, Freud uses the term "*Willenspeversion*" here to convey how the experience of the counter-will exposes the affected subject to an experience of radical negativity and radical alienation from her own conscious intentions. "Counter-will" is characterized as perverse because it introduces a radical negativity and negation into the very constitution of psychic organization.

In the following extraordinary passage, Freud establishes a direct link between "counter-will" and the driving negativity and the demonic quality of something he calls "perversity of character" manifested in hysteria:

> This emergence of a counter-will is chiefly responsible for the daemonic characteristic which hysteria so often exhibits—the characteristic, that is, of the patients' not being able to do something precisely when and where they want to most passionately, of doing the exact opposite of what they have been asked to do, and of being obliged to cover everything they most value with abuse and suspicion. The perversity of character shown by hysterical patients, their itch to do the wrong thing, to appear to be ill just when they most want to be well—compulsions such as these (as anyone will know who has had to do with these patients) may often affect the most irreproachable characters when for a time they become the helpless victims of their antithetic ideas.
>
> (Freud, 1953, 126–127)

Something happens to Freud's language as he attempts to respond to the call of the clacking tongue with a precise description of the mechanism of "counter-will." His account relies on two literary-inflected invocations of the term "perversion": *"Willensperversion"* and *"Charakterperversion."* Both terms deviate from common usage in the German tongue and from the accepted future meaning of "perversion" within the vocabulary of psychoanalysis. In this context, *"perversion"* must be understood as a fundamental constitutive estrangement that happens to a tongue and in a tongue. The affected tongue cannot be thought as simply belonging to a human body: it is the perverse organ of speech of a language that speaks its counter-utterances through a body that is charged with counter-meanings.

This originary scene, in which a perverse tongue becomes the bearer of the language of the unconscious, renders certain foundational presuppositions of psychoanalysis unfamiliar and lays down the tracks of a non-androcentric, non-binary conception of a sexualized subject of indeterminate gender that traverses Freud's entire corpus. Fixation introduces a figure of a sexualized form of body-writing that privileges neither the male genitals as the primary signifiers of sexuality nor the temporal structure of the Oedipal narrative constructed on the basis of those genitals.

As a primal figure for language that confuses the distinction between body and language, the clacking tongue confounds the ability to decide where the body ends and language begins. Likewise, the unruly temporality and uncanny technological properties of the clicking clitoris destabilize the status of the penis as the privileged signifier for sexuality and sexual difference. The peculiar sounds made by the clacking tongue reverberate in the clicking clitoris. Together, they inflect the conceptual language of psychoanalysis with a queer form of speech, born from fixation.

Notes

1 It bears mentioning that these two apparently similar texts are, in fact, subtly different. The reference to the "clacking woman" is significantly reduced in the version co-authored with Breuer.
2 This discussion of fixation and female sexuality is part of a larger on-going project, tentatively titled *On Fixation: Freud's Queer Counter-Concept*. For a related discussion of many of the issues raised in this chapter, see my essay "Freud's Fictions: Fixation, Femininity, Photography" (2017).
3 See, in particular, Edgar Allan Poe (1975), "The Facts in the Case of M. Valdemar" and "The Imp of the Perverse."
4 In addition to the groundbreaking work by Henri Ellenberger (1977), "The Story of 'Emmy von N': A Critical Study with New Documents," I am indebted to a number of notable recent readings of the Case of Emmy von N: Maud Ellmann's (2014) "Psychoanalytic Animal" and Jennifer L. Fleissner's (2009) "Symptomatology and the Novel." For an excellent critical summary of the history of hysteria within psychoanalysis, see Patricia Gherovici's "Genealogy of Hysteria" (2010).

Bibliography

Cassin, B., E. Apter and J. Lezra (eds) (2014). *Dictionary of Untranslatables: A Philosophical Lexicon*, Princeton: Princeton University Press.

Derrida, J. (2004). "What Is a Relevant Translation?" in *The Translation Studies Reader* (pp.423–446), ed. L. Venuti, trans. L. Venuti, First published in 2000, Second Edition, London and New York: Routledge.

Ellenberger, H. F. and M. S. Micale (1993). *Beyond the Unconscious: Essays of Henri F. Ellenberger in the History of Psychiatry*, Princeton: Princeton University Press.

Ellmann, M. (2014). "Psychoanalytic Animal," in *A Concise Companion to Psychoanalysis, Literature, and Culture* (pp.328–350), ed. L. Marcus and A. Mukherjee, Chichester: Wiley Blackwell.

Fleissner, Jennifer L. (2009). "Symptomatology and the Novel." *Novel: A Forum on Fiction*, 42(3), 387–392.

Freud, S. (1893). "[Vortrag:] Über den psychischen Mechanismus hysterischer Phänomene (1893)," in *Gesammelte Werke I: Texte aus den Jahren 1885 bis 1938* (pp.187–188), London: Imago Pub. Co., 1940.

Freud, S. (1947). *Gesammelte Werke, 18 vols.* Frankfurt am Main: Fischer.

Freud, S. (1953). "A Case of Successful Treatment by Hypnotism: With Some Remarks on the Origin of Hysterical Symptoms Through Counter-Will," in *The Standard Edition of the Complete Psychological Works of Sigmund Freud, Vol. 1* (pp.115–132), trans. and ed. J. Strachey, London: Hogarth Press.

Freud, S. (1955). "A Case of Paranoia Running Counter to the Disease," in *The Standard Edition of the Complete Psychological Works of Sigmund Freud, Vol. 14* (pp.261–272), trans. and ed. J. Strachey, London: Hogarth Press.

Freud, S. (1961). "Female Sexuality," in *The Standard Edition of the Complete Psychological Works of Sigmund Freud, Vol. 21* (pp.221–244), trans. and ed. J. Strachey, London: Hogarth Press.

Freud, S. (1962). "On the Psychical Mechanism of Hysterical Phenomena: A Lecture," in *The Standard Edition of the Complete Psychological Works of Sigmund Freud, Vol. 3* (pp.27–39), trans. and ed. J. Strachey, London: Hogarth.

Freud, S. (1964). "Femininity," in *The Standard Edition of the Complete Psychological Works of Sigmund Freud, Vol. 22* (pp.112–135), trans. and ed. J. Strachey, London: Hogarth.

Freud. S. and J. Breuer (1955). "On the Psychical Mechanism of Hysterical Phenomena: Preliminary Communication," in *The Standard Edition of the Complete Psychological Works of Sigmund Freud, Vol. 2* (pp.1–17), trans. and ed. J. Strachey, London: Hogarth.

Gherovici, P. (2010). *Please Select Your Gender: From the Invention of Hysteria to the Democratizing of Transgenderism*, New York: Routledge.

Marder, E. (2017). "Freud's Fictions: Fixation, Femininity, Photography." *Paragraph: A Journal of Modern Critical Theory*, 40(3), 349–367.

Ovid, P. N. (1977). *Metamorphoses*, trans. F. J. Miller, Cambridge: Harvard University Press.

Poe, E. A. (1975). *The Complete Tales of Edgar Allan Poe*, New York: Vintage Books.

Chapter 3

The Gender Question from Freud to Lacan[1]

Darian Leader

When Lacan published his two reformulations of the psychoanalytic debate on female sexuality, "The Signification of the Phallus" and the "Guiding Remarks for a Congress on Female Sexuality," he referred to the *"querelle du phallus,"* an expression that not only situated what he took to be the key issue of the debate but also evoked with some humor the Renaissance question of the *"querelle des femmes"* (Lacan, 1966, 685–695, 725–736).[2] The polemics of the 1920s and 1930s about the construction of sexuality are probably the area of psychoanalytic history that has received the most attention from scholars, and they have often been explored in relation to debates in feminist theory and critiques of psychoanalysis.

Many of these readings reduce the complexity of historical debate to a set of quite caricatured dogmas, and although there may be good reasons for disagreeing with the early Freudians, it seems an important preliminary to try to situate the nature of the research questions that bound their contributions together. These are not as obvious as they have seemed to many commentators, and as we examine the context of the debate, we will see how different theories may be seen in a new light as responses to questions that have themselves often remained implicit.

Freud's changing perspectives on male and female sexualities, filtered through the theories of the Oedipus and castration complexes, have been expounded time and time again, and the debates of the 1920s and 1930s seen as affirmations, rejections and developments of the Freudian positions. The key texts are taken to be "The Infantile Genital Organization" (1923; Freud, 1961a), "The Dissolution of the Oedipus Complex" (1924; Freud, 1961b), "Some Psychical Consequences of the Anatomical Difference between the Sexes" (1925; Freud, 1961c), "Female Sexuality" (1931) (Freud, 1961d) and the New Introductory Lecture on "Femininity" (1933; Freud, 1964). Although there has always been disagreement about why exactly Freud changed and modified his views in this period, the question of why he apparently avoided publishing anything on female sexuality between the mid-1920s and early 1930s has been somewhat neglected. The immediate response might be simply to appeal to Freud's "time for understanding": he needed to think things through and that's just how long

DOI: 10.4324/9781003284888-5

it took. But this is not the only way to explain the supposed lacuna: rather than positing a diversion of Freud's attention, one could argue that he did indeed make a major contribution during this period, a contribution that tends to be overlooked and bracketed out of the female sexuality debate. This is an argument that, as we will see, is constructed out of a footnote, a very important footnote penned in 1925.

In 1924, Freud published "The Dissolution of the Oedipus Complex" in the "*Zeitschrift*" (Freud, 1924a). The German term rendered as "dissolution" – *Untergang* – had a variety of translations before Strachey's, as "abolition," "demolition" or "destruction," although the article was first translated in the *International Journal of Psychoanalysis* as "The Passing of the Oedipus Complex," a term that, like "dissolution," is far weaker than the original *Untergang* (1924b). Writing to Andreas-Salomé in March of 1924 (Pfeiffer, 1972, 133), Freud says that he is working on the *Untergang* paper "which sounds, I hope, as tragic as the title of Spengler's book," a reference to Oswald Spengler's *Der Untergang des Abendlandes*, the second volume of which had appeared in 1922, and which was done into English as *The Decline of the West*.[3] Spengler's bestseller put forward a theory of the decline of modern civilization as a consequence less of external and contingent factors than of an internal principle. Like life forms, death and demise were built into the program as an entropy. Cultures have youth, manhood and old age. The idea of an *Untergang* written into history from the start parallels in certain ways Freud's views on the Oedipus complex as being "pre-programmed" to end in failure, and gives to Freud's title a resonance that must indeed have evoked tragedy at a time when Spengler's ideas were well known and much discussed.[4]

The force of Freud's title was certainly effective. Jones could refer to the "surprising title" of this paper, a surprise that would become considerably dampened in the Strachey translation with the choice of "Dissolution" for "*Untergang*," a term that features perhaps most famously in the phrase "dissolution of the monasteries" (Jones, 1957, 114). Indeed, it is curious how formulations of the fate of the Oedipus complex seem to take their cue from history books: when Hans Loewald took up the *Untergang* question again in the late 1970s, he gave his paper the title "The Waning of the Oedipus Complex." Where Freud took Spengler's "*Untergang*," Loewald's title evokes Huizinga's *The Waning of the Middle Ages*, just as Strachey's "dissolution" evokes David Knowles' contemporary accent on English history as being the history of the dissolution of the monasteries (Cantor, 1991; Knowles, 1940; Loewald, 1979, 751–175). Although Strachey is careful enough to add a note to the text on the term "*Untergang*," he does not seem to be aware of the reference to Spengler, and the particularity of Freud's term seems neglected.

Jones's "surprise" at the title of Freud's paper became "astonishment" when he read it (Jones, 1975, 280). Freud argues in this paper that the Oedipus complex for the boy is destroyed, not merely repressed, by the threat of castration: the narcissistic value of the penis is offset against the incestuous demand to the parent, and preserving one's sex is chosen instead of the incest (wish). Better to keep the penis than to risk losing it as punishment for erotic claims on the mother. Hence, the boy can turn away from her.

For the girl, there is a reversal: the Oedipus complex is not destroyed by the castration complex but in fact introduced by it. The girl thinks that she once possessed a penis and lost it by castration. The demand for compensation involves turning to the father, and the wish for a penis is replaced by the wish for a baby through the process of symbolic equation. The Oedipus complex is given up because the wish for a baby from the father is unfulfilled, but this slackening is hardly comparable with the brutal destruction that befalls the boy's complex. The real *Untergang* of the Oedipus complex seems to concern not the girl but the boy. By 1925, Freud could say that although the Oedipus complex may be slowly abandoned by the girl or dealt with by repression, it may also persist in "normal mental life" (Freud, 1961c, 257).

In the same paper, Freud argues that the girl's Oedipal link to the father is not entirely symmetrical with the boy's tie to the mother. In fact, it is a "secondary construction" (*sekundäre Bildung*), which has a long and by no means simple prehistory. The mother is held responsible for the girl's lack of a penis, but the Oedipal link to the father is introduced not so much as a direct consequence of this, but rather as a result of the symbolic equation: penis = child. The wish for a child that this generates will initiate the turn to the father as love object, and the girl will become "a little woman." Note that in this model, the turn to the father is explained less in terms of hatred and hostility to the mother than in terms of a desire that is itself based on a mechanism of equivalence (penis = child). The disappointment experienced now in relation to this desire will mean that the father is abandoned and an identification established in the place of the libidinal tie.

Some of these hypotheses were taken up immediately by Freud's students, but before examining their responses it is important to see how Freud himself did not abdicate from the debate after the first series of articles. Although it is usual to assume that after the *Untergang* paper and that on the psychical consequences of anatomical difference, Freud returned to the problem around 1930, he would in fact take up exactly the same questions that had been the agenda of the 1924 article in 1926. Although the short paper of 1924 seemed to many merely to recapitulate earlier Freudian ideas, Jones's "surprise" and "astonishment" need to be taken seriously. How, after all, can a complex so fundamental as the Oedipus actually be destroyed rather than repressed? And if the castration complex is so bound up with the Oedipus, what kind of fate does it have itself? If the girl's Oedipus complex is not abolished, what exactly happens to it? If destruction of the Oedipus complex allows the child to avoid neurosis, would its non-destruction for the girl imply that femininity and a form of neurosis are inseparable? The more one considers the *Untergang* paper, the more radical its consequences seem to become.

Freud (1959) would indeed take up such questions in his monograph *Inhibition, Symptom and Anxiety*, a book that was to have a strange fate in the history of psychoanalytic literature. At the time of publication, Freud could say that it "shakes up much that is established and puts things which seemed fixed in a state of flux again," a fact that many readers seem to have understood solely in terms of a change in Freud's theory of anxiety (Meng and Freud, 1963, 102). Edward Glover (1938, 109), reviewing the English translation of the work, described it as "without doubt the most disjointed presentation ever published by one who has proved himself a master of orderly exposition" (Glover, 1938). Melanie Klein would see the work as a real turning point for Freud:

> Freud himself having reached his climax in *Inhibition, Symptom, Anxiety* not only did not go further, but rather regressed. In his later contributions to theory some of his great findings are weakened or left aside, and he certainly did not draw the full conclusions from his own work.
>
> (Klein Archive)

And likewise for the larger part of its readership. When Freud commented about the work that "Analysts who above all want peace and certainty will be discontented at having to revise their ideas," he perhaps misjudged the attraction that peace and certainty had for many of them over the discomforts of revision (Meng and Freud, 1963, 102). As Glover noted in his review article, "Most of the hints and suggestions thrown out in this book have fallen on stony ground."

The title itself raises a number of questions. Translated at one point as "The Problem of Anxiety," the book was seen as contesting the field of research associated with Rank's work on the birth trauma, which had often been discussed under exactly this rubric, "The Problem of Anxiety." Although the link with Rank is not to be disputed, how could one explain the apparently unheralded introduction of the motif of inhibition? Despite his having formulated a theory of inhibition in his early work of the 1890s, it did not remain a major Freudian concept, and now it suddenly appears as one of the three central themes of a whole monograph.[5]

The standard argument here is to explain the oddity of *Inhibition, Symptom and Anxiety* in terms of Freud's emotional response to Rank's 1924 book *The Trauma of Birth*. Rank had been a close follower of Freud, whose loyalties were called in question progressively in the early 1920s as his stance on psychoanalytic technique and theory became more and more distant from that of Freud. As he elaborated his theory of the birth trauma, with its very concrete consequences for psychoanalytic practice, everything seemed to be reduced to the anxiety of birth, which became for Rank the pivot of analytic experience. Hence, it was logical to assume that Freud's 1926 book was an answer to Rank, with its central theme of anxiety: as Strachey concluded in the introduction to his English translation, it was Freud's "rejection of Rank's views (that)...

stimulated him to a reconsideration of his own, and *Inhibitions, Symptoms and Anxiety* is the result" (Strachey, 1959).

But what evidence is there for this? Rank certainly did little to modify the preconception: reviewing the book in the *American Journal of Mental Hygiene*, he could write: "In this book, perhaps for the first time, Freud does not speak from his own analytic experiences, but uses my experiences deductively and critically" (Rank, 1927). There are indeed several sections in *Inhibition, Symptom and Anxiety* that engage directly with Rank, and Freud's correspondence at the time does show that he was concerned with responding to his protege, but is this the whole story? If we choose to read it as not simply a missive to Rank, what are the questions that emerge as central to Freud's inquiry?

We should note first of all that *Inhibition, Symptom and Anxiety* was written in the summer of 1925, a time with a special significance for the history of the psychoanalytic movement. This was the summer of Melanie Klein's six lectures to the British Psycho-Analytical Society on "Early Analysis," as Jones (1925) had noted in a circular letter in June. Jones also brings up the sore point of Melanie Klein's ideas in letters to Freud at this time and given the fact that Klein's theories centered on a very precise formulation of the relation of inhibition to anxiety, Freud's choice of topic seems less surprising. It is often taken for granted that Klein's early innovations concerned the structure and genesis of the superego, the dating of the Oedipus complex and the theory of internal objects, but it is clear that up until 1926 the theory of inhibition is a cornerstone of her thinking (Petot, 1990).

This aspect of her work is linked to the program being established by Karl Abraham in the early 1920s: he had included several sections on inhibition in his study of the development of the libido in 1924 and had noted that a "further inquiry is needed into the origin of the inhibitions of the libido," an invitation that had already been taken up by Klein (Abraham, 1927b). By the end of 1925, Klein had published four articles that dealt quite directly with this theme: the 1922 paper on "Inhibitions and Difficulties at Puberty," the 1923 paper on "The Role of the School in the Libidinal Development of the Child," the 1923 paper on "Early Analysis" and the 1925 "Contribution to the Psychogenesis of Tics" (Klein, 1975).

Klein is concerned with the question of why someone may develop an inhibition rather than a symptom, and the question of the relation of inhibition, symptom and anxiety is absolutely central to her formulations in these papers. Indeed, reading "Early Analysis," one might be surprised that this dazzling paper was published before Freud's 1926 book rather than after. She explores the role of anxiety as a signal, the relation of anxiety, castration and inhibition, and the link between castration anxiety and birth anxiety. Similarly, it is well known that both Klein's and Abraham's research in this period was closely bound up with the question of melancholia and depressive states, and in *Inhibition, Symptom and Anxiety*, Freud separates inhibition from generalized inhibition, linking the latter to exactly these research problems (Freud, 1959). As

Klein pursued the program of investigating the early structures of the libido, she would emphasize mechanisms distinct from the classic repression-symptom model, and hence the importance of the inhibition problem, although her views on this would change dramatically in her work after 1926. In the papers of 1922 and 1923, inhibition is linked to castration anxiety and genital fantasies, whereas in her later work other more archaic anxieties will take center stage.

The superego is also a significant variable here. The problem of the early superego was crucial in the debate around Kleinian concepts in the 1930s and 1940s, and it is interesting that already in Freud's 1926 book, there is an allusion to this question. Referring to the issue of the establishment of the superego, Freud nuances his earlier position, according to which the superego is the heir to the Oedipus complex and cannot strictly speaking emerge prior to it, as Klein would argue. Freud (1959, 114) now refers to the "creation or consolidation (*Schöpfung oder Konsolidierung*) of the superego," the key word being the "or," as it allows for the possibilities of earlier stages of superego formation.[6]

Details like this, together with the more general concern with the question of inhibition, suggest that Freud's book can be read not simply as a response to Rank but also to the research questions being elaborated by Klein in the first half of the 1920s. Where Klein's early work addressed the question of the fate of Oedipal currents in either inhibitions or symptoms (or both), Freud's monograph sets out a theory of inhibition in relation to symptoms and anxiety and, as we shall see, knocks up against this question of the fate of Oedipal currents. This is a question about sexuality and gender, since if all of Freud's formulations of femininity and masculinity are based on a theory of a passage through the Oedipus and castration complexes, the issue of their respective destinies is the same issue as that of gender and sexuality. Or, to put it another way, any theory of the vicissitudes of the "*Untergang*" of the Oedipus complex is also by definition a theory of gender.

***

Just as the dissolution of the monasteries did not take place overnight, Freud is concerned with how the Oedipus complex does not simply vanish without trace. This question, implicit in 1924, becomes a motif of *Inhibition, Symptom and Anxiety*. Freud did not call the 1924 paper "The Repression of the Oedipus Complex": something more is at stake, and in the 1926 text, he takes up this problem by questioning the efficacy of repression itself.[7] In the 1924 paper, Freud distinguishes between a "mere repression" and the "real removal" of an old "wish impulse." The German expression here is "*der wirklichen Aufhebung einer alten Wunschregung*," a curious phrase since the term *Aufhebung* seems less powerful than *Untergang*. The complex is not being destroyed but *aufgehoben*, yet elsewhere in the paper Freud's vocabulary is generally very strong, referring to a demolition or a destruction. Jones, we remember, had been astonished by the idea that Oedipal wishes are not merely repressed but "actually destroyed or annulled" (Jones, 1957, 280). How strange this argument must have seemed to a generation formed in the belief that the Oedipus complex was repressed, and that hence one of the goals of an analysis was to undo the repression.

The 1926 book now offers, tentatively, the theory that repression is a mechanism linked first and foremost to the genital level of development, so that previous phases will have their own defensive mechanisms "of choice." "We shall bear in mind," he writes,

> for future consideration the possibility that repression is a process which has a special relation to genital organization of the libido and that the ego resorts to other methods of defense when it has to secure itself against the libido on other levels of organization.
>
> (Freud, 1959, 125)

Melanie Klein was fond of this quotation, one of its implications being that just as the superego could be the "heir" to the genital level of organization, each of the preceding stages could have its own "antecedent" of the superego, a problem debated with so much passion in the 1930s. Likewise, Freud's discussion of clinical material in the 1926 book leads him to suggest that other operations can be more effective than repression, particularly that of regression, with which he is so concerned throughout his text. Where the 1924 paper had placed "destruction" (*Untergang*) rather than repression in the local context of the exit from the Oedipus complex, by 1926, Freud is examining the question of alternatives to repression in the much larger context of early psychic life.

These issues are closely linked with the gender question. If femininity and masculinity are constructed through the vicissitudes of the Oedipus and castration complexes, it opens up the questions that Freud would treat explicitly from 1930 under the banner of the "pre-Oedipal" relation to the mother, and, crucially, it introduces the theme of the importance of operations other than repression. Although he discusses alternatives to repression, Freud by no means slights the impact of this mechanism, and the question is posed, in a seminal footnote, of the fate of whatever becomes repressed (Freud, 1959, 142). He now claims that it is not self-evident that repressed material remains "unaltered": "In other words," he asks, "do the old wishes, about whose existence analysis tells us, still exist?" The footnote appears in the section in which Freud examines the question of whether each stage of life may have its own specific determinant of anxiety, and it is the footnote that so astonished Lou Andreas-Salomé as she was reading through Freud's book: "I almost got a shock at one point (long footnote 90), because it seemed to me that by loosening a few stitches, one might make the whole fabric run into holes" (Pfeiffer, 1972, letter of 3/5/1926).

***

If what is repressed changes, what does it mean clinically to access the repressed? And if repression is not the only thing that can happen to the Oedipus complex, what are the theoretical and technical consequences for analysis? The obvious answer to the question Freud poses about the continued existence of repressed wishes is that they do continue to exist, since the derivatives of the repressed material are present in symptoms, but this does not exhaust the possibilities. There are alternatives here: the old wish may now operate only through its derivatives (*Schicksal*), having shifted its cathectic energy to them, or, "it is itself still in existence too." And third, if it has exhausted itself through the cathexis of derivatives, "in the course of a neurosis it may become re-animated (*wiederbelebt*) by regression." Freud adds at the end of this paragraph: "These are no idle speculations," and evokes the difference he had set out in the 1924 paper between the "mere repression" and the "real removal" of the impulse (Freud, 1961b).

This startling footnote invites a return to the 1924 text in the following sense: if Freud had argued there that the Oedipus complex is destroyed, rather than repressed, does this mean that all the above possibilities are ruled out? And if the complex has been repressed but not destroyed, what are the consequences for the Oedipal themes? In terms of the theory of sexual development, it is the problem of charting the possibilities of the passage from the Oedipus complex to the castration complex: if a current is not abolished, what, exactly, happens to it? That this is a central concern of *Inhibition, Symptom and Anxiety* is clear from the many sections dealing with regression as an alternative to repression. The reformulating of material from the cases of Little Hans and the Wolfman is supposed to illustrate how a regression can be "more effective" than a repression, a change "in the drive itself" being contrasted with a change in its "representative" (Freud, 1959, 103–105).

Thus, when Freud argues that women have a castration complex but not a castration anxiety, he can ask the question of whether fear of castration is the sole motive force of repression. Rather than seeing these quite complex ideas as an excursion into an abstract "metapsychology" or as a response to Rank, the focus on the vicissitudes of and alternatives to repression indicate a development of the 1924 argument about male and female sexualities, a way of exploring how it is that the Oedipus complex is not entirely dissolved, abolished or removed. And, as we shall see, the Freudian notion of a "re-animation" would prove of great significance in the gender debates.

The relation of the castration complex to castration anxiety discussed in 1926 is central to the arguments of Freud's students, although its form is usually obscured. What was the real question behind the involved polemics of the debate? Ernest Jones, Karen Horney, Melanie Klein and Helene Deutsch did not agree with all of Freud's formulations of sexual development, but what they did not dispute was the existence of an early phase of *Penisneid*. It is interesting to note that Deutsch, Klein and Horney had all been in analysis with Abraham, and that it was Abraham's 1920 article on the female castration complex that proved so significant in getting the debate going (Abraham, 1927a, 338–369). Abraham's students did not dispute the existence of a castration complex in women. The central problem was not to determine whether either penis "envy" or a castration complex was really there, but rather to understand *the nature of the relation between them*. The debates of the 1920s and 1930s share this one underlying question: *is there or is there not a causal connection between penis envy and the castration complex?*

Women might have a concern with loss of love and with ideas of adding and subtracting something from the body, and girls might spend some time comparing their own genitals with those of the boy, but what was the relation between these two sets of interests? What Jones, Horney and Klein could not accept was that the one was the cause of the other. Something, they thought, had to happen in between, and they formulated this something in their own, individual ways. If the castration complex in women was sometimes identified with the term *Penisneid*, what this meant was that there had to be more than one *Penisneid*.

The first, apparently anatomically based comparison of genitals might generate a little envy, but something had to happen to this envy to give it the powerful form of the castration complex as such. Karen Horney had the idea that after the first initial penis envy, which focused on voyeuristic and exhibitionistic tendencies, the girl had to deal with the tragedy of her failed, disappointed romance with the father. This frustration would search for a symbol, and so the first penis envy would become re-cathected and function now as the representative of the loss of love (Horney, 1926b, 54–70, 71–83). Jones agreed more or less with this formulation, except that he followed Klein in making the tragedy not the failed romance with the father but the impossibility of sharing the father's penis with the mother in coitus: "The disappointment at never being allowed to share the penis in coitus with the father, or to thereby obtain a baby, reactivates the girl's early wish to possess a penis of her own" (Jones, 1948, 444; Leader, 2000, 134–135).

In a neglected contribution to the debate, Carl Müller-Braunschweig (1936) would also argue that the penis functions symbolically here, although rather than elaborating the more Kleinian model he thinks that the relevant tragedy is the child's realization of its inability to satisfy the mother. Hence, the original perception of the image of the penis (*Das Bild des Penis*) is radically transformed into a "representative representation" (*Vorstellungsrepräsentanz*).[8] Thus, for Horney, Jones and Muller-Braunschweig, the anatomical penis of the initial penis envy *would become re-animated as the symbol of another and quite distinct loss*. An organ would thus pass to the level of a symbol:

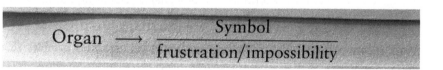

$$\text{Organ} \longrightarrow \frac{\text{Symbol}}{\text{frustration/impossibility}}$$

This would seem to explain, for Horney and Jones, how the transitory and apparently contingent episodes of anatomical comparison could generate the more global and structural complex of castration. The next question they had to tackle was the problem of the phallus itself, and how it could be possible that some women seemed to show a special sensitivity to the idea of losing something. This ought to have been the problem for the man, not for the woman: what sense could it make to speak of a female castration complex when a woman, in Alix Strachey's words, has "nowt to castrate"? (Meisel and Kendrick, 1985, 152).

***

Freud had argued in 1924 that the Oedipus complex is ushered in for the girl by the castration complex. Her search for the penis is frustrated by the mother and so she turns instead to the father. But this point was disputed, particularly in Berlin, and as Lisa Appignanesi and John Forrester (1992, 430) have pointed out, the challenge to Freud's theories came from the students of Abraham: Klein and Horney. Although it is generally assumed that Klein's contribution to the debate came significantly later than Horney's, exemplified in her 1928 paper on "The Early Stages of the Oedipus Complex," a footnote to the 1926 "Psychological Principles of Early Analysis" on the theme of the girl's turn to the father shows that she was already working carefully on this question.

The footnote is, in fact, a condensation of some of the conclusions she had arrived at in a collaboration with Horney herself, as an unpublished paper by Klein, proves. Klein's typed manuscript, in the Klein Archive at the Wellcome Institute in London, is described by her as a contribution to a joint seminar with Horney on October 31, 1925, and a note in the *International Journal of Psychoanalysis* tells us that this was the same date on which Horney (2000) gave a paper entitled "Reflections on the Masculinity Complex in Women" to the Berlin Psychoanalytical Society. This is probably the paper published as *"Flücht aus der Weiblichkeit"* (Horney, 1926a) and rendered into English as "The Flight from Womanhood: The Masculinity-Complex in Women as Viewed by Men and by Women" (Horney, 1926b, 1967).

The joint presentation by Klein and Horney came at a particularly significant moment. Freud had completed his paper "Some Psychical Consequences of the Anatomical Distinction Between the Sexes" in August of 1925, and it was read by Anna Freud in September 3, 1925 at the Homburg Congress in September. Klein and Horney's seminar took place the following month, at the end of October, and it seems likely that their papers involve responses to Freud's recent intervention, as well as constitute elaborations of the work they had been pursuing prior to this, probably since 1922. In this joint presentation, Klein develops a real revision of Freudian theory. One of the big questions in the gender debate was the turn from mother to father for the girl. Was this because she hated the mother, and then turned to the father, or was the attraction to the father independently motivated?

Freud held, in 1925, that the transformation of the wish for a penis into a wish for a child was what operated the shift, but for Klein, this first wish has complex antecedents. The castration complex will be structured, she argues, by the pain of oral frustrations and toilet training ("the training in cleanliness") administered by the mother. The girl will turn to the father not because of any idea of the inferiority of her own genitals but rather because she is searching for another object of oral satisfaction following the oral refusals associated with the mother: the father thus figures first of all not as a person but as a part object, the penis. And the initial priority is not given to a love affair with the father, but rather to the search for the satisfaction of a drive (the oral one).

In the subsequent period of female genital primacy, Klein continues, the vagina and clitoris are properly feminine, and the already existing wish for a child becomes linked to the father. When the romantic appeal to the father is disappointed, the girl assumes that she has failed in her competition with the mother, and that her genitals have been damaged. These factors generate a revival of a primary penis envy, and the girl moves into an identification with the father and the ensuing castration complex. The wish for a child has now reverted to a wish for the penis, and the disappointment of this phallic aspiration pushes her to return to the feminine position, even if only in a partial way.

Klein and Horney thus agree on a number of issues: the separation of primary and secondary penis envy, a primary femininity, a flight into identification with the father and a defensive function for the phallic phase. The idea of a primary femininity that they develop had already been brought up by Abraham in a 1924 letter to Freud. "I have recently wondered," he writes, "whether in early infancy there may be an early vaginal awakening of the female libido, which is destined to be repressed and which is subsequently followed by clitoral primacy as the expression of the phallic phase" (Abraham and Freud, 1965, 377). Freud replied with an encouragement to Abraham to explore this question, while remarking that the female side of libidinal development remained "extraordinarily obscure" to him. This theme would be developed in detail by Klein and Horney, with a special attention to the problem of how a complex of representations could become the form of expression of a different, and later, problem.

What we see emerging from both Klein and Horney's work here is a theory of re-animation: if penis envy is not the cause of the castration complex, the penis of penis envy is not the same thing as the object of the castration complex (and hence the interest of distinguishing, as Lacan did, the penis from the phallus). Freud's footnote to *Inhibition, Symptom and Anxiety* is especially interesting here as it invites a theory of re-animation that is not entirely to be equated with regression: Klein and Horney are not claiming that there is simply a regression to the initial penis envy but that the form of this first experience of pain is used to articulate other issues. Indeed, Horney is careful to refer here to the *Äusserungsform*, the "manifestation," of the female castration complex, a term that echoes the title of Abraham's initial paper on *"Äusserungsformen des weiblichen Kastrations-komplexes,"* although its specificity is lost in the translation, where *Äusserungsform* becomes "form" for Horney and "manifestation" for Abraham (Horney, 1923). And as Jones noted, it was Freud's notion of *reactivation* developed in the 1926 monograph that seemed to support the theory of such manifestations.

Klein and Horney's arguments develop the suggestions made by Abraham to Freud, and form a part of the Berlin opposition to Freud's views on sexual development. Only a month after the joint presentation of Horney and Klein, Josine Müller (1932) would lecture on the "genital phase" in girls, and emphasize the early awareness of the vagina, in opposition to Freud and Deutsch. For Klein, the turn toward the father was due to the oral libido's search for new objects and to the hatred of the mother generated by oral and anal frustrations. Later, it would be conceptualized in terms of reparation and guilt. This turn toward the father was a central question in the gender debate, and it is worthwhile pausing here to consider one of the many neglected contributions to it, a brilliant paper by Lillian Rotter, published in 1934, which radically shifted the terms of the debate and invited a new consideration of female sexuality in terms of being rather than simply in terms of having.[9]

She starts by pointing out something that is generally absent from earlier theories of sexual development: the role of the desires of the parents in relation to their children, and in particular, the hostility and disappointment a mother may express regarding the sex of a daughter. When the latter becomes aware of the phenomenon of male erection, she supposes that she has brought about this physical change herself, and that the penis belongs to her as a consequence of her causal powers. Other phenomena also support this assumption: the interest of the father or other men in her presence, for example, will signify to her the effects she can have on the male sex. She thus takes on the position of the cause of the other's desire, and Rotter thinks that this is a decisive factor in the Oedipal turn from mother to father.

One of the interests of this argument is that it gives a formative place to the encounter of the girl with the desire of the parent, and also that it widens the scope of the "penis" in *Penisneid*. It has become linked to the question of desire, of indicating the presence of a desire, and situated in some sense outside herself. As Rotter puts it, "My penis is on my father or brother, but in spite of that belongs to me." This would imply, she thinks, that the loss of the father or the man's love would constitute a castration: in other words, she no longer functions as cause of desire. The Oedipal turn to the father is thus no longer formulated simply in terms of the search for a penis or child, but as assuming this new position of being the cause of desire. The vicissitudes of Oedipal development will depend on whether and in what form this dialectic of desires has taken place.

The neglect of the role of parental desires in the constitution of sexuality is a striking feature of the debate here. The idea of a preformed sexuality, and even a preformed Oedipus complex waiting to hatch, exerted a more powerful attraction for Klein and Horney, certainly in their early work, and this belief perhaps owes something to Abraham. Abraham had trained in embryology, and his taste for neat stages and divisions, together with tabular schemes, is reflected in his pre-analytic work on the development of the urinary system and the development of the chick. Indeed, the title of his classic study of libidinal phases (*Versuch einer Entwicklungsgeschichte der Libido*) echoes the title of his doctoral thesis on the development of the budgerigar (*Entwicklungs-geschichte des Wellensittichs*) (Lewin, 1951).[10] Development is seen in terms of an unfolding of possibilities that are already contained within the organism, and, if we move along the implicit biological continuum, it will come as no surprise to find sexuality itself explained in terms of such internal principles.

Horney, Klein and Jones shared this belief, in their early work, that the Oed-ipus complex was there from the start, that the girl is naturally oriented toward the father and the boy toward the mother. This strange dogma had important consequences for their conceptualizations of female sexuality. Since Oedipal desires carry with them a lot of anxiety, Horney thought that there would be good reason to reject them. The little girl, plagued by guilt, gives up her pre-cocious femininity and changes into a little man. Thus, where Freud had at one time seen the girl as being similar to the boy in early development, with a focus on phallic-clitoral sexuality, Horney agrees, yet adds that she was really a girl first. She changes because femininity brings anxiety. In entering the order of the male masquerade, she has rejected her own "femininity." Now, rather than ridiculing this view, as is so often the case, why not ask the question of what clinical phenomena could have given her the idea?

To find this problem, we do not have to look very far. A central explanation Horney gives for the young girl's anxiety is the mismatch between her own vagina and the size of her father's penis. She thinks, according to Horney, that if her incestuous wishes were to be realized, the result would be irreparable damage to her own sexual organs. Hence the fear of vaginal mutilation that Horney finds so often in her practice. This, of course, is the old clinical problem that vexed the early Freudians from Jones to Horney to Rado: if women did not have to worry about the threat of castration in the same way as men, why would they have anxieties about damage to their genitals? Did it simply mean that they had the idea that once they possessed a penis, which was taken away, leaving a wound? (Lampl de-Groot, 1935; Rado, 1933).[11]

Horney's first answer to this question differs slightly, however, from her later formulation. In her 1922 paper on the genesis of the castration complex, she argues that the idea of genital damage functions for the girl as a proof of love. Each girl, she thinks, has the fantasy that the father has possessed her. Genital damage would thus prove the reality of rape on the part of the father, a proof of the love relation that implies the fantasy of having thus suffered castration. The male genital was lost through the sexual relation with the father, to gen-erate one of the roots of the castration complex (Horney, 1922). The interesting feature of this perspective – with its stress on being the object of the father's enjoyment – is not really developed in the later papers, although the link with incestuous fantasy remains constant.

Horney and Klein hold different positions here: where Klein saw anxieties about genital damage as a consequence of attacks made on the mother's body, Horney insists on the role of the father. It would explain, she argued, one aspect of the female dread of castration: first, in terms of the original problem of mismatch of size for the girl, and second, in terms of the consequence of her flight into masculine identification. Now, it would seem, the problems of men would become her own.

***

Horney's work is particularly important here in that she was one of the first of the early analysts to take seriously, and develop, Freud's notion of an identification being established as a response to disappointment. These ideas had been elaborated by Freud in the 1919 paper "A Child is being Beaten," in the 1920 "Psycho-genesis of a Case of Female Homosexuality," and in *Group Psychology and Analysis of the Ego* published in 1921. When a significant disappointment takes place, for example, due to the father's refusal of love, the response of the child may be an identification with him. This mechanism – disappointment/identification – would become of great importance in the psychoanalytic thinking of the later 1920s and 1930s, and Horney's thesis of the flight into identification with the father clearly supposes this development in Freudian theory. Her revision of Freud thus follows a very Freudian route, at least on this point.

These ideas take on a new sense if we introduce one further question into the context of the gender debate, a question that is not always manifest yet which is central to the whole framework of problems: when does the Oedipus complex start? Although this is usually seen as a characteristic of later debate around Klein's work, it needs to be pushed back further in the 1920s. If one thinks that the Oedipus complex is there right from the start, then one has to explain the castration complex as developing out of it, as Jones, Klein and Horney attempted. Thus, rather than claiming in a Freudian way that the move away from the mother is activated by the latter's failure to give her daughter a penis, Jones thinks it is a result of an initial rivalry over the father's penis. Klein and Jones agree with Horney that there is an original and mysterious "attraction between the sexes," which means, in turn, that there is a knowledge of the difference between the sexes from the start, and not a belief in the universality of the phallic standard.[12]

Where Freud had argued that girls and boys see the phallus everywhere until they learn the grim truth, his students would disagree by claiming that this belief is a secondary and entirely artificial construct. Thus, for Jones, the girl is perfectly aware of sexual difference, but since she has an Oedipus wish, she will fear a terrible retribution from the mother, probably in the form of a mutilation (Jones, 1932). If she is herself penetrable and her unconscious desire is for coitus, what could be more logical than to deny her own penetrable qualities?

Likewise, it is the boy's fear of the boomerang of his hostile impulses toward the father's penis contained in the mother that makes him decide that it is the mother who is impenetrable: if there's no hole, his incestuous wishes amount to nothing and he can sustain the illusion of a universal phallus. For Jones, it is not the mother's lack of a penis that is so disturbing, but rather the existence in her of a vagina with its associated idea of penetration. When the child gives up the idea of this anatomical hole, it is thereby getting rid, in a sense, of a desire, an incestuous, Oedipal one.

Thus, it is Oedipal wishes that actually produce the first part of the phallic phase, the belief in the maternal phallus and the denial of female castration. Once again, although one may dispute the details of such conceptions, they respond to the empirical fact that children may be attentive to the difference between male and female sexual organs, and then, sometimes quite suddenly, make claims about the mother's widdler. In an analogous way, children may use past verb forms ("went," "came") quite correctly and then, to the surprise and perplexity of those around them, universalize them in a series of errors ("goed," "comed"), a fact that is often evoked to refute the once popular view that the mistakes come first in the chronology of language learning. For Jones, Klein and Horney, there is an agreement that the "mistakes" come not first but second: hence the defensive function of the phallic phase.

The phallus as a symbol of loss and frustration will now take on a privileged value: if it fails, the boy and the girl will have to deal with the most terrible anxieties of mutilation and castration. In Jones's terms, this first part of the phallic phase in which castration is avoided is a defensive construction, an artificial rampart that is structurally similar to a phobia. Later, he would describe it instead, as Sachs did, as a perversion, defined as the compromise between libidinal impulses and the wish to avoid mutilation. There seems to be a tension in Jones's articles between the notion of a mutilation-castration as the motor of the unlearning of sexual difference and the idea of aphanisis, the extinguishing of the possibilities of pleasure.[13]

Where Freud had put the castration complex in both men and women, Jones thinks there is a more primal fear shared by both sexes, the fear of aphanisis. Jones's idea of a primal danger here is anticipated in *Inhibition, Symptom and Anxiety*, where Freud describes the "danger" situation of the child's non-satisfaction, "a growing tension due to need against which it is helpless," a dimension of infantile life that was perhaps most emphasized in those years by Klein and Jones. The clinical question here is the one we have already mentioned: why should a woman dread castration if she has already suffered it?

Jones's answer is that castration should no longer be identified with loss of the penis: rather, it evokes the more general threat against "enjoyment as a whole." This menace of the extinction of enjoyment is what Jones means by aphanisis, the fear of the drying up of the possibilities of having desire satisfied. Thus, to avoid this, the desire itself is given up, to generate the feeling of guilt. Jones's idea here reminds one of the Lacanian concepts of guilt in the seminar *The Ethics of Psychoanalysis*, defined as an effect of the ceding or giving up on one's desire (Lacan, 1986). The motifs of mutilation-castration can now be understood as the forms in which the specter of aphanisis appears, as they are direct results of the desires in question. One of the many problems with the Jonesian theory here is that when he speaks of "damping down" on a desire to avoid aphanisis, he does not spell out the relation of this damping down to repression. It would seem as if the problems discussed by Freud in *Inhibition, Symptom and Anxiety* concerned exactly this question of the forms that repression and its alternatives could take.

How does this fear of aphanisis allow Jones to differentiate the male and female versions of sexuality? For the boy, he gives the formula:

> I wish to obtain gratification by committing a particular act, but I dare not do so because I fear that it would be followed by the punishment of aphanisis, by castration that would mean for me the permanent extinction of sexual pleasure.

For the girl:

> I wish to obtain gratification through a particular experience, but I dare not take any steps towards bringing it about, such as asking for it and thus confessing my guilty wish, because I fear that to do so would be followed by aphanisis.

This is an extraordinary formulation: the only thing that separates the boy from the girl here is a relation to speech. The two versions are different precisely in their reference to language. While the boy simply doesn't dare, the girl doesn't dare say or confess. The boy refrains from perpetrating an act, but the girl refrains from talking about it, a formulation that reminds us of Lacan's famous comment about women keeping quiet about their special relation to enjoyment and Freud's controversial remarks about women and secrecy (Freud, 1957).

Lacan's remark can also be linked to the early debate in another way. What did Horney, Josine Müller and Sylvia Payne all dispute with Freud? What they couldn't accept was his supposition that girls had no precocious vaginal sensations, and they tried to find empirical disproofs of what they saw as an entirely unfounded dogma. According to Marie Bonaparte, Freud interpreted such sensations as anal masturbation retrospectively attributed to the vagina (Brierley, 1932; Eissler, 1939; Hann-Kende, 1933; Horney, 1933; Klein, 1928; Payne, 1936b). But if we read these authors carefully, the problem seems to be slightly different: what was in question was not the existence of vaginal sensations but the knowledge of them. In other words, the agenda of this debate was not about the mechanics of the body but about the subjective assumption of these dynamics in a knowledge, in a system of representations.

***

This problem of the relation of an enjoyment to a knowledge was reformulated by Lacan in his seminar *Encore*, when he argued that a particular form of enjoyment is not linked to knowledge (Lacan, 1975).[14] Although this might seem an unnecessarily abstract formulation, the relation of enjoyment to meaning is a very real concern: one could evoke the question of the meaning of sex. When someone says, "It didn't mean anything, it was just sex," such problems are brought into focus. While it is often said that sex and meaning are bound up for women much more than for men, it might be argued that the notorious separation made by men between sex and meaning is a desperate defensive measure brought into play precisely because sex really does mean an awful lot. Otherwise, how could one explain men's sudden "loss of desire" in certain sexual situations?

Similarly, one might question the amalgam of sex and meaning for a woman. I have been curious for many years about why so many female friends and acquaintances gravitate toward the London department store Liberty, which for a man might just seem to embody a haphazardly organized, bizarrely uneven collection of stands and franchises. Yet, it is undeniable that many women love Liberty, and, as an analysand explained to me one day, this is simply the best shop in the world "because not everything there has a meaning." In the field of sexuality, it can be this very absence of meaning that allows a bodily pleasure where, previously, it had been disallowed.

Now, to return to Jones, what is it that happens to the dread of aphanisis as the Oedipus complex moves on? The girl must choose, according to Jones, between her sex or her incest. Either she renounces her incestuous link to the father and assumes her femininity, or she keeps the incestuous link and is thereby deprived of the assumption of her sex. The libidinal attachment to the father is retained, but is now converted into an identification, which will give a "penis-complex." This is an idea that has had a checkered history in psychoanalysis. Should each identification be seen as the form of a libidinal link, in this case, an incestuous desire, or should it be separated? In his commentary on the Dora case, Lacan tried to distinguish between the object of love and the object of identification, criticizing Freud for having confused the two (Lacan, 1951). Clinically, this is often a controversial point: does the prevalent father identification in a hysteria suggest a romance or quite the opposite? Does the dependency on his image mean a libidinal tie, a way of organizing a desire or both? And in what way would a hysteria be separated here from "femininity" as such?

Jones's conception of this problem led logically to his view on female homosexuality: if sex is given up in favor of incest and a father identification established, the next step is to desire a woman. Female homosexuals are then grouped into two categories: those who retain an interest in men and want to be accepted by men as a man themselves and those with no interest in men, who employ other women to exhibit femininity for them. The latter idea is not without interest. It situates femininity as the site of the real focus in female homosexuality, which the subject investigates "at the hand of an unseen man," the one established by the paternal identification. Thus, a form of the homosexual relation is not that of two women, but two women and a man. And, Jones's hypothesis implies that femininity has to be searched for outside since the subject has not assumed it herself. The whole theory of the phallic phase and aphanisis gives an argument for why the girl has given up her implicit femininity, and she now appeals to this lacking image outside herself. Lacan would later elaborate an alternative view: the lacking image is searched for not because an implicit femininity has been given up, but because an implicit femininity cannot be symbolized in the first place.

If we take both Jones and Horney seriously, there is this implication that femininity will be a central point of interest for a woman in the world around her, an idea that it is usually assumed only Lacanian theory can account for. We should note, however, that Jones adds at the conclusion of his research that paternal identification is not the key that he had once thought it to be. Rather, the really determinant factor lies in the intensification of the oral sadistic phase, suggesting a relation to a partial object (the oral object) and not to the father as such. We thus see how a sensitivity to the phallic problematic cannot account entirely for the phenomena: there is something in addition, something more than the phallus, which Jones describes as a relation to a partial object and which Klein and Lacan would theorize in their own separate ways: the more they push their research into the phallus, the more they realize that something else matters as well.

Freud's students thus shared a set of common concerns. If the Oedipus came first, how did the castration complex affect it? How did it come about that the phallus became attributed to the mother after an initial "awareness" of sexual difference? In a sense, this question of "awareness" is central to all of the different contributions: Freud's set of alternatives to and vicissitudes of repression from consciousness, Horney's idea of a flight from the awareness of femininity, Jones's concept of aphanisis and the various contributions to the vaginal awareness debate. Framing these questions was the less obvious one of the relation between penis envy and the castration complex. If we read *Inhibition, Symptom and Anxiety* as a contribution to the gender debate, one consequence is that a theory of sexual "development" ought to contain a theory of anxiety. Horney, Klein and Jones all took this perspective seriously, and their theories of the relation between penis envy and castration are built up around it.

No less important is Freud's distinction in the 1926 monograph between the existence of a complex, the operation of a complex through its derivatives and the re-animation of a complex through the mechanism of regression. The various formulations of the revival of primary penis envy by secondary penis envy rely on a theory of re-animation, whereby the image of an organ starts to function as the symbol of a series of losses and frustrations. It is not just a question of "regressing" from one psychic "layer" to another, but of elements from one system of memory traces functioning as symbols of issues from another: in other words, the unconscious is working like a language.

It is significant that when he turned to the questions of the gender debate, Lacan would argue that the point the early Freudians had missed was the idea of the phallus as a signifier, as opposed to a real or a phantasy object. This perspective might appear with hindsight to be a logical consequence of the early debates: if the phallus is used to signify certain things, a relevant theory of symbolism and of linguistic functioning cannot be shied away from. The gender debate thus calls for an attention to the effects of language and systems of signs in the construction of sexuality. Today, probably few people would disagree with this thesis; but how exactly the early Freudians engaged with it is a fascinating and still unexhausted chapter in the history of psychoanalysis.

***

When we turn now to Lacan's contribution, it must be said that the volume of commentaries and expositions is staggering. Phallic and non-phallic logics are endlessly contrasted and opposed, and it is a real question why the same formulae are repeated again and again with so little critical perspective. The notations for sexuation from the seminar *Encore* have generated hundreds of expositions, ranging from scholarly articles to clinical case reports and even entire books. Yet, the reasons why a suggestive, illuminating yet clearly inconclusive set of pseudo-mathematical formulae should prove so popular remain unexplored.

To have a reality check on this, one need only think of the encounter with someone who enthusiastically tells us that they are in possession of logical formulae for male and female sexualities. And, indeed, to consider the question of whether any new idea about sexuality has actually been put forward in the last 50 years in Lacanian psychoanalysis. The formulae certainly have their interest, but they are hardly the philosopher's stone of sexuality, and they have had the unfortunate effect of totally blocking any further work on an area which contains many open questions. When Lacan held up a knotted piece of string to his lover and said "This is you," one might see a dazzling revelation of true structure or, on the contrary, an unfortunate reductionism which has perhaps had its effects in our field (Millot, 2016).

It is curious here that whatever the problems of Freud's theorizations – and prejudices – about women, he always tends to map out different feminine trajectories, whereas Lacan prefers to generalize about women as such. Although lip service is paid to the Lacanian shibboleth "one by one," he hardly ever contrasts different female pathways through the Oedipal and castration complexes. So where Freud offers a theory of different forms of femininity, Lacan just has one, with the caveat that this one contains what is sometimes described as infinite difference. Yet, theoretical and clinical uses of this apparent emancipation tend to be lazy and judgmental.

It is also breathtaking here that Lacan's references to a "true woman" are so often cited uncritically, as if they were immune to the effects of fantasy. Women are implicitly evaluated against this glorified standard, usually coming off badly and only occasionally managing to attain its status. Comparable – and generally negative – distinctions between a woman and a mother are also ubiquitous, as if everyone has forgotten that this splitting is precisely a hallmark of repression and fantasy. Motherhood is described as exclusively phallic, and so a woman only reaches the apex of femininity in some act whereby she renounces her children. Beyond this is of course the old equation of femininity with sacrifice, which one might have hoped that psychoanalysts would question.

What we lose out on here is a return to the questions of gender and sexuality that Freud and his students had begun to approach. Freud, Deutsch, Klein and others had a lot to say about the archaic relation to the mother's body, yet for Lacan, this question is shut down: Lacanians evoke the "ravage" of the daughter's relation to her mother, as if this term explains everything. The particularities of the daughter's relation to the mother's body invite further study, yet have we heard anything more about this since the 1970s apart from the repetition of the old formulas?

Similarly, when we move from here to Oedipal relations and the registration of kinship, it is clear that the notion of substitution (*Ersatz*) is inadequate, as Freud guessed. The idea that the Oedipus complex for the girl involves substituting the father for the mother is obviously incorrect, and it would be interesting to elaborate Freud's concept of "delegation" in this context, which he introduces in "A Child is Being Beaten" (1958). When Taylor Swift sings "I got a blank space baby…and I write your name," the key is that she says "and" and not "where," and it is perhaps in this detail that we can situate one of the central issues of female sexuality. A contiguity matters here rather than a replacement, and at the risk of reductionism, we could contrast the formula of male sexuality – "I got a blank space baby…where I write your name" with the "and" of a sexuality that is not centered on substitution.

The question of the psychical assumption, differentiation and investment of bodily zones is also important here. Taking up suggestions of Lou-Andreas Salomé and Marie Bonaparte, Lacan (2004) drew attention to the early continuity of vagina and cloaca; yet sadly, his comments have not been taken up by his students. Echoing this, Lacanians tend to repeat blindly their master's aphorism that psychoanalysis has made no contribution to sexology; yet, aside from this being false, analysts may learn something from sexologists if they bother to read the right works. I remember an evening when, as a young student just arrived in Paris, one of Lacan's inebriated followers explained to me which sexual techniques were appropriate to which clinical categories, an enlightenment that was not entirely fantastical.

The networks of innervation in the body are well worth studying here, and especially if one tries to avoid reducing them to the vaginal/clitoral binary or to the tripartite division of "jouissances" between phallic, Other and surplus. Just as Tracy Emin can declare "My Cunt is Wet with Fear," one might contrast the secretions of the Bartholin's gland with those of the vaginal wall, which are arguably precisely those of terror. The early physiology of arousal is perhaps closely enmeshed with that of anxiety, and this is a rich field of research for psychoanalysis. There is a great deal of early twentieth-century work on arousal which has not yet been linked to a rigorous psychoanalytic theory, and this study remains to be carried out.

Finally, one last observation about the sexuation table. While male sexuality is more or less contracted to the line of the fantasy, joining subject and object, female sexuality is divided between the phallus and the signifier of the lack in the Other. At a purely formal level, prior to any exploration of what each of these vectors can signify, we can note that Lacan has linked femininity not to an essence but to a relation, or, to put it another way, to an oscillation. The implication of a link not only to a man – sometimes – and to the points at which the symbolic fails to reply help us to situate many clinical and cultural phenomena, as well as Lacan's reference here to mystics. Rather than designating someone whose body is soaked in divine jouissance, the mystic here is simply someone who is unable to ever be fully alone.

Notes

1 Parts of this chapter appeared in *Freud's Footnotes* (2000) (pp. 120–152), London: Faber, and I am grateful for their permission to include them in this current work.
2 Note that Marie Bonaparte (1953, 33) refers to this debate as "the battle around the vagina."
3 On Spengler, see, with caution, Fischer (1989) and Collingwood (1927).
4 Ferenczi picked up this reference in his letter to Freud of 24/3/1924, and the use of the term "Untergang" was known to be linked to Spengler: see, for example, Alexander (1925, 456).
5 Indeed, Freud seems to have considered as an earlier title simply *Inhibition and Symptom*; see Grubrich-Simitis (1996, 167).
6 Reich's work on the superego is significant here; see *Der triebhafte Charakter*, Vienna, 1925.
7 It seems that Abraham gave a talk with exactly this title "The repression of the Oedipus complex" in Berlin in 1925, but I've been unable to find further traces of it.
8 The idea of the child's inability to satisfy the mother had been emphasized by Jeanne Lampl-de Groot (1933).
9 Other forgotten contributions include Müller-Braunschweig (1936), Bibring-Lehner (1933), Sterba (1933), Harnik (1943) and Odier (1932).
10 For more on the history of Abraham's tabular presentation of stages, see Leader (2000, 141–142).
11 See also the discussion in Payne (1936a). Payne compares the mother here to a crocodile, with the child turning to the father's penis "as a protection" against this, an image that Lacan would later use without citing its source.
12 This was seen by Elizabeth Zetzel (1970) as indeed one of the cornerstones of the Kleinian system.
13 The analysts who panicked in the 1920s when Rank proposed something to usurp the Oedipus complex (the birth trauma theory) would themselves all go on to

propose what they took to be more fundamental alternatives: for Jones, aphanisis, for Klein, the depressive position.

14 The Other jouissance is linked to the lack in the Other, which implies that it is not linked to a knowledge.

Bibliography

Abraham, H. and E. Freud (eds) (1965). *A Psychoanalytic Dialogue, the Letters of Sigmund Freud and Karl Abraham 1907–1926*, London: Hogarth.

Abraham, K. (1927a). "Manifestations of the Female Castration Complex," in *Selected Papers on Psychoanalysis* (pp.338–369), London: Hogarth.

Abraham, K. (1927b). *Selected Papers on Psychoanalysis*, London: Hogarth.

Alexander, F. (1925). "Einige unkritische Gedanken zu Ferenczis Genitaltheorie." *Zeitschrift*, 11, 456.

Appignanesi, L. and J. Forrester (1992). *Freud's Women*, London: Weidenfeld.

Bibring-Lehner, G. (1933). "Über die phallische Phase und ihre Störungen bei Mädchen." *Zeitschrift fur psychoanalytische Pedagogik*, 7, 145–152.

Bonaparte, M. (1953). *Female Sexuality*, New York: IUP.

Brierley, M. (1932). "Some Problems of Integration in Women." *International Journal of Psychoanalysis*, 13, 433–438.

Cantor, N. (1991). *Inventing the Middle Ages*, Cambridge: Lutterworth.

Collingwood, R. G. (1927). "Oswald Spengler and the Theory of Historical Cycles." *Antiquity*, 1, 311–325.

Eissler, K. (1939). "On Certain Problems of Female Sexual Development." *Psychoanalytic Quarterly*, 8, 191–210.

Fischer, K. (1989). *History and Prophecy, Oswald Spengler and the Decline of the West*, New York: Peter Lang.

Freud, S. (1924a). "Zeitschrift, 10," in *Gessamelte Werke*, 13, 395–402.

Freud, S. (1924b). "The Passing of the Oedipus Complex." *International Journal of Psychoanalysis*, 5, 419–424.

Freud, S. (1957). "The Taboo of Virginity," in *The Standard Edition of the Complete Psychological Works of Sigmund Freud, Vol. 11* (pp.191–208), ed. and trans. J. Strachey, London: Hogarth Press.

Freud, S. (1958). "A Child Is Being Beaten," in *The Standard Edition of the Complete Psychological Works of Sigmund Freud, Vol. 7* (pp.179–204), ed. and trans. J. Strachey, London: Hogarth Press.

Freud, S. (1959). "Inhibition, Symptom and Anxiety," in The *Standard Edition of the Complete Psychological Works of Sigmund Freud, Vol. 20* (pp.77–175), trans. and ed. J. Strachey, London: Hogarth.

Freud, S. (1961a). "The Infantile Genital Organisation," in *The Standard Edition of the Complete Psychological Works of Sigmund Freud, Vol. 19* (pp.139–145), trans. and ed. J. Strachey, London: Hogarth Press.

Freud, S. (1961b). "'The Dissolution of the Oedipus Complex," in *The Standard Edition of the Complete Psychological Works of Sigmund Freud, Vol. 19* (pp.171–179), trans. and ed. J. Strachey, London: Hogarth Press.

Freud, S. (1961c). "Some Psychical Consequences of the Anatomical Difference between the Sexes," in *The Standard Edition of the Complete Psychological Works of Sigmund Freud, Vol. 19* (pp.241–258), trans. and ed. J. Strachey, London: Hogarth Press.

Freud, S. (1961d). "Female Sexuality," in *The Standard Edition of the Complete Psychological Works of Sigmund Freud, Vol. 21* (pp.221–243), trans. and ed. J. Strachey, London: Hogarth Press.

Freud, S. (1964). "New Introductory Lecture on Femininity," in *The Standard Edition of the Complete Psychological Works of Sigmund Freud, Vol. 22* (pp.112–135), trans. and ed. J. Strachey, London: Hogarth.

Glover, E. (1938). "Review of *Inhibition, Symptom and* Anxiety." *International Journal of Psychoanalysis*, 9, 109.

Grubrich-Simitis, I. (1996). *Back to Freud's Texts, Making Silent Documents Speak*, Princeton: Yale University Press.

Hann-Kende, F. (1933). "Über Klitorisonanie und Penisneid." *Zeitschrift*, 19, 416–427.

Harnik, J. (1943). "Zur Streitfrage der infantilen weiblichen Genitalorganisation." *Zeitschrift fur psychoanalytische Pedagogik*, 20, 102–105.

Horney, K. (1922). "On the Genesis of the Castration Complex in Women," in Karen Horney, *Feminine Psychology* (1993, pp.37–53), New York: W. W. Norton.

Horney, K. (1923). "Zur Genese des weiblichen Kastrations Komplexes." *Zeitschrift*, 9, 12–26.

Horney, K. (1926a). *"Flücht aus der Weiblichkeit." Zeitschrift*, 12, 360–374.

Horney, K. (1926b). "The Flight from Womanhood: The Masculinity-Complex in Women as Viewed by Men and by Women." *International Journal of Psychoanalysis*, 7, 323–339.

Horney, K. (1930). *Zehn jahre Berliner psychoanalytisches Institut*, Vienna: Deutsche Psychoanalytische Gesellschaft.

Horney, K. (1933). "The Denial of the Vagina," in Horney, *Feminine Psychology* (pp.147–161).

Horney, K. (2000). "Reflections on the Masculinity Complex in Women," trans Lindsay watson, unpublished. in D. Leader, *Freud's Footnotes* (pp.237–244), London: Faber

Jones, E. (1925). *Rundbrief*, 19/6, unpublished

Jones, E. (1932). "The Phallic Phase," in Ernest Jones, *Papers on Psychoanalysis* (pp.452–484), London: Hogarth.

Jones, E. (1948). "Early Development of Female Sexuality," in Ernest Jones, *Papers on Psychoanalysis* (5th edn), London, Hogarth.

Jones, E. (1957). *Sigmund Freud, Life and Work, Vol 3*, London: Hogarth.

Klein Archive, Wellcome Institute, PP/KLE/D16.

Klein, M. (1928). "Early Stages of the Oedipus Complex," in Melanie Klein, *Love, Guilt and Reparation* (1975, pp.186–198), London: Hogarth.

Klein, M. (1975). *Love, Guilt and Reparation*, London: Hogarth.

Knowles, D. (1940). *The Monastic Order in England*, Cambridge: Cambridge University Press.

Lacan, J. (1951). "Intervention sur le transfert," in *Ecrits* (1966, pp.215–226), Paris, Seuil.

Lacan, J. (1966). *Ecrits*, Paris: Seuil.

Lacan, J. (1975). *Le Seminaire XX, Encore*, ed. J.-A. Miller, Paris: Seuil.

Lacan, J. (1986). *Le Seminaire VII, L'Ethique de la Psychanalyse*, ed. J.-A. Miller, Paris: Seuil.

Lacan, J. (2004). *Le Seminaire Livre X, L'Angoisse*, ed. J.-A. Miller, Paris, Seuil.

Lampl-de Groot, J. (1933). "Problems of Femininity." *Psychoanalytic Quarterly*, 2, 489–518.

Lampl de-Groot, J. (1935). "Review of Rado, 'Fear of Castration in Women.'" *Zeitschrift*, 21, 598–605.

Leader, D. (2000). *Freud's Footnotes*, London: Faber.

Lewin, B. (1951). *The Psychoanalysis of Elation*, London: Hogarth.

Loewald, H. W. (1979). "The Waning of the Oedipus Complex." *Journal of the American Psychoanalytic Association*, 27, 751–775.

Meisel, P. and W. Kendrick (eds) (1985). *Bloomsbury/Freud" the Letters of James and Alix Strachey*, New York: Basic Books.

Meng, H. and E. Freud (eds) (1963). *Psychoanalysis and Faith, he Letters of Sigmund Freud and Oscare Pfister*, London: Hogarth.

Millot, C. (2016). *La Vie avec Lacan*, Paris, Gallimard.

Müller, J. (1932). "A Contribution to the Problem of the Libidinal Development of the Genital Phase in Girls." *International Journal of Psychoanalysis*, 13, 361–369.

Müller-Braunschweig, C. (1936). "Die erste Objektbesetzung des Mädchens in ihrer Bedeutung für Penisneid und Weiblichkeit." *Zeitschrift*, 22, 137–176.

Odier, I. C. (1932). "Mutterbindung des Weibes: Beitrag zum Studium des weiblichen Über-Ichs." *Zeitschrift*, 18, 442–449.

Payne, S. (1936a). "A Conception of Femininity." *British Journal of Medical Psychology*, 15–16, 18–33.

Payne, S. (1936b). "Zur Auffassung der Weiblichkeit." *Zeitschrift*, 22, 19–39.

Petot, J.-M. (1990). *Melanie Klein, First Discoveries and First System 1919–1932*, Vol. 1, New York: International Universities Press.

Pfeiffer, E. (ed.) (1972). *Sigmund Freud and Lou Andreas-Salome, Letters*, London: Hogarth.

Rado, S. (1933). "Fear of Castration in Women." *Psychoanalytic Quarterly*, 2, 425–475.

Rank, O. (1924). *Das Trauma der Geburt und seine Bedeutung für die Psychoanalyse*, Zürich: Internationaler Psychoanalytischer Verlag.

Rank, O. (1927). "Review of *Inhibitions, Symptoms and Anxiety*." *American Journal of Mental Hygiene*, 11, 181–188.

Rotter, L. (1934). "Zue Genese des weiblichen Sexualität." *Zeitscrift*, 20, 367–374.

Spengler, O. (1922). *Der Untergang des Abendlandes*, Munich: Oskar Beck.

Sterba, R. (1933). "Über den Ödipuskomplex bei Mädchen." *Zeitschrift fur psychoanalytische Pedagogik*, 7, 334–348.

Strachey, J. (1959). "Introduction to *Inhibition, Symptom and Anxiety*," in *The Standard Edition of the Complete Psychological Works of Sigmund Freud, Vol. 20* (pp.77–175), trans. and ed. J. Strachey, London: Hogarth.

Zetzel, E. (1970). "The Depressive Position," in Elizabeth Zetzel, *The Capacity for Emotional Growth* (pp.63–81), London: Hogarth.

Chapter 4

Two Analysts Ask, "What Is Genitality?" Ferenczi's Thalassa and Lacan's Lamella

Jamieson Webster and Marcus Coelen

In Freud's (1953) *Three Essays on the Theory of Sexuality* (1905), the anarchic, staccato rhythms of psycho-sexual development are described in a way that places them beyond gender, object choice, and even genital anatomy. Infantile sexuality, polymorphously perverse, refuses to consolidate into either genital aims or the aim of reproduction, entering into a temporality that allows it to constantly return and disrupt adult sexuality, having been cut off from any linearity with it by latency. Sexuality is split in half. Freud leaves the question of genitality remarkably open, or perhaps simply unresolved. But what is genitality? Sándor Ferenczi translated Freud's *Three Essays* into Hungarian in 1914 and from his work on the text, imagined writing about the dark continent of genitality, which eventually became the infamous book, *Thalassa: A Theory of Genitality.*

What might be considered the most out of date in Ferenczi's rarely discussed first text—namely its emphasis on Freud's onto- and phylogenetic heritage of man recapitulated in psycho-sexual development—is what we want to argue precisely what is worth preserving, showing its necessity for thinking about sex and sexual difference. This "theoretical" speculation, and its rigor, makes Ferenczi a surprising predecessor to Jacques Lacan who wrote in a letter to Balint about his admiration for Ferenczi (though never expounded upon it) in 1953, as well as commented several times on the importance of Ferenczi for understanding the child in the adult, citing Ferenczi as the most tormented clinician by the analytic canon. Lacan is linked to Ferenczi around the question of the genital in his own elaborations on sexual love that rely on biology, and even embryology, though he does not cite Ferenczi at this point.

Freud, with Ferenczi and Jacques Lacan, is united in an act of the most audacious, wild, speculative, and material psychoanalytic theorizing, without which we do not think we can conceive of the drives, certainly not the death drive, nor sexuality and the consequences of trauma. We are speaking about their phylogenetic bio-psychological speculative fictions or myths: elements and fragments of a dimension for which Ferenczi forged the term "bio-analysis." Freud, Ferenczi, and Lacan are, as far as we know, the three theorists who really engage this mode of work as key to conceiving the clinical situation, as well as

DOI: 10.4324/9781003284888-6

the transmission of psychoanalysis. And they do so via the impossible figure of genitality as psychoanalytically conceived.

The texts we are lining up here are Freud's (1955) *Beyond the Pleasure Principle* (1920) (which helped Ferenczi to bring his text out of a latency of nine years), Ferenczi's *Thalassa*, and what Lacan called his "myth of the lamella" developed in his 1960 paper "The Position of the Unconscious" and then again in his 1963–1964 seminar *The Four Fundamental Concepts of Psychoanalysis*. What these three texts also have in common is a kind of ruthless pessimism concerning human progress as resulting from sexuality: a sense of the catastrophe of being human, the struggle with sexuality, the impossibility of transcending the body, drive, life, death, and illusion, all caught in a vast mechanism of eternal recurrence. These wild speculative writings seem to want to sober psychoanalysis, steady it, or even act as a corrective. Nothing could be further from what characterizes mainstream psychoanalytic work today.

***

Of interest is the fact that these works are born out of the soil of great conflict. Freud's *Beyond the Pleasure Principle* could be seen as a text (often considered the most controversial, the most rejected of Freud's texts) that divided the field in half: those who believed in the death drive and those who wanted to reduce the death drive to innate aggression or who just simply rejected the notion altogether. Freud takes the concept of the drive and centralizes it beyond any content, beyond any psychopathology, beyond sex itself (which was only one component of the drive), and therefore beyond even the unconscious, previously seen as the storehouse of our memories, traumatic and otherwise. Of course, the text can also be read as a response to the horrors of World War I.

Likewise, *Thalassa* takes shape in 1914, while Ferenczi worked in a military hospital, which he called his "exile" in a garrison town where he was a medical officer to a squadron of Hussars, translating Freud's *Three Essays on the Theory of Sexuality* during his leisure time. It seems that the text is in conversation, or even competition, with Freud's *Beyond the Pleasure Principle*, the two men writing these in concert in the years preceding 1919. Freud shared the development of his work with Ferenczi, who had been struggling to write, which seems to have given him the encouragement to complete it.

Furthermore, Ferenczi also sees himself as corroborating Rank's theory of birth trauma (more about this later) and finds himself in heated disagreement with Freud as to its value. Freud plays the two men off one another and distinguishes the value or lack thereof of their theories. In a series of letters in 1924, Freud writes to Ferenczi:

> The truth is that I liked the thing much better in the beginning than I do now and that, according to your own quotation, I am on the way from 66% to 33% [Ferenczi had quoted Freud saying, "I don't know if 33% or 66% is

true, but it is a significant piece of work"] [...] If the trauma of birth works not onto- but phylogenetically, only then does he have a connection to your theory of genitality, which otherwise eludes him [...] I must return to the thoroughly inept and deficient presentation in Rank's case [...] While I hold fast to the theoretical estimation of the at least 33%, from a practical perspective, all valuation fails me.

(Freud and Ferenczi, 1996, 135)

Freud then goes on impugn Rank's personality and appeals to the mutual work and amity between himself and Ferenczi, all of which is followed by long machinations about the International Psychoanalytic Association and Abraham's role as the president. Rank does fare well. Meanwhile, Ferenczi is thoroughly shaken by the exchange, appeals and pleads with Freud, and eventually falls in line, though he can be seen continually trying to vouch for Rank.

Incidentally, reflecting on his theory of genitality a decade later in the clinical diaries, Ferenczi radically differentiates himself from Freud. He writes:

The ease with which Freud sacrifices the interests of women in favor of male patients is striking. This is consistent with the unilaterally androphile orientation of his theory of sexuality. In this he was followed by almost all of his pupils, myself not excluded. My theory of genitality may have many good points, yet in its mode of presentation and its historical reconstruction it clings too closely to the words of the master; a new edition would mean complete rewriting.

(Ferenczi, 1995, 187)

Ferenczi would then go on to wonder if a more feminine element of the death drive was overlooked by Freud; that, starting from a "heterosexual direction of the drive" and an early "knowledge of the vagina," would include self-sacrifice, selflessness, kindness even, and fragmentation, as opposed to egoism and self-assertion. This finds its way into Ferenczi's work on trauma and traumatic fragmentation around the same time, when Freud writes him a letter lauding the work as "ingenious" and on par with his great work *Thalassa*. Ferenczi coolly replies that the theory is a practical addendum to the *Thalassa* work, and while he was pleased to be called "ingenious," he would have preferred to have been called correct.

The story of Lacan's myth of the lamella is even stranger. This myth not only develops Freud's contention that "the drives are, so to speak, our mythology" and articulates a new mythical figure for the libido; it also—as we will see later—thinks libido itself as mythical and, for that reason, extracts it from embryology. The lamella is the libido as developed from embryological development.

The lamella surfaces most prominently in Lacan's seminar on the *Four Fundamental Concepts of Psychoanalysis*, one of his most expository and pedagogical seminars. It was given under critical circumstances: Lacan had planned to teach on the "names-of-the-father" during the academic year of 1963/1964 only to discover in October 1963 that his status as an IPA training analyst was revoked. He then reinvented his teaching, and in the course of a couple of weeks, delivered a concentrated version of his thought. The following January, he opened the seminar with a lecture on his—and Spinoza's—"Excommunication." Lacan continued with an entirely new program envisioning the founding his own school, as he would do on June 21, 1964. The seminar becomes polemical as the doctrinal groundwork for his school and his teaching is set up.

The contentious atmosphere of the seminar is not limited to issues of psychoanalytic transmission and training. In 1960, in his "Guiding Remarks for a Convention on Female Sexuality," Lacan had lashed out at what he called some "irresponsible mental retardation" (Lacan, 2006, 615/731) regarding the common ideas of many analysts with respect to sexual difference and femininity. In a section on "Misrecognitions and Biases" (Lacan 2006, 614/730), he denounces a certain number of misconceptions in psychoanalysis concerning female sexuality, more precisely what he calls the role of "phallic mediation" that must be recognized in order for a supposedly "proper" psychoanalytic treatment. His polemics are specifically addressed "at claims to deduce fantasies of the breaking of corporal boundaries from an organic constant whose prototype would be the rupture of the ovular membrane" (Lacan, 2006, 615/731). Lacan, however, does not indicate whose fantasies those might be. The adversary remains anonymous.

More than 25 years before the appearance of the myth of the lamella, which is, in fact, centered on the idea of a broken egg, in 1938, Lacan spoke at a meeting of the Société Psychanalytique de Paris during the discussion of an oral presentation by Marie Bonaparte. Her talk can be assumed to be a spoken version of her paper, "Some Palaeobiological and Biopsychical Reflections" (Bonaparte, 1938). In that paper, Bonaparte speculates that "the act of fission [scil. cell division] involves a disintegration [rather: 'lost by crumbling {Abbröckeln}'] of the substance which if continued would result in its annihilation" (1938, 215). Bonaparte further assumes a "narcissistic aversion to fission" that "can serve as the foundation of the castration complex," inasmuch as the "fear of penetration of the protoplasm is reflected in the dread of penetration felt by so many virgins and is no doubt at the root of many cases of frigidity in women." In his response, Lacan underlines that "it is quite certain that nothing allows us to assume that the cells have a representation of anything" (Lacan, 2006, 551) and he offers, as a solution for the missing representation of what Bonaparte calls the "absolute narcissism of the earliest cells," his own "mirror stage" whose "threat of dismemberment" he "had tried to present at the International Congress" in Marienbad in 1936, that is, two years earlier. In Marienbad, Lacan introduced his mirror stage theory and was interrupted and prevented from finishing his paper by a stern Ernest Jones in an initial public rejection, a moment that seemed to haunt Lacan who would not write or theorize for many years afterward.

Bonaparte's rather straightforward affirmation of the link between the cellular and the psychical levels is nevertheless central for the inception of Lacan's
myth of the lamella. What Lacan denounced as a fantasy of "unadmitted
speculation" regarding cellular fission and narcissism travels almost unaltered
from Marie Bonaparte—who was crucial to his excommunication—to Jacques
Lacan. The myth of the lamella is born from the encounter and violent separation between Lacan and members of the IPA.

These enigmatic texts—on the death drive, on bio-analytic regression, on the
lamella myth of libido—are born out of a general situation of conflict and hostility: World Wars I and II, as well as from the wars within psychoanalysis. At least
two of their authors—Freud with regard to the drives and Lacan with regard to
the lamella—refer to their "objects" as mythic. Later on, at least two of them—
Lacan and Ferenczi—extract their myths or speculative entities from what Freud
had called the "unknown continent" of femininity. Are these mythical constructions about war at the same time myths about the feminine? If so, why?

We should remember that "myth"—a word now equivalent to the elements
of bio-psycho-analytical speculations—can be understood as having at least four
meanings or functions: first, myth not only tells a version of history, but also
itself has a history, that it is obscured by its own telling; a myth covers up the
story of its invention. Second, the invention is, as *muthos*, meaning a spoken word
or story, a creation of discourse. But while a myth is mostly considered to be story
or oral legend articulated a long time ago, passed on, and collected much later, in
the Platonic use of *muthos*, the term can also refer to an invention created in order
to provide an element of discourse that cannot be provided by rational argumentation; the *muthos* fills a gap in the chain of arguments or plugs the holes of logos.
Third, a myth usually ends up being written down, either solidifying in some
axiom-like formula or being itself an instance of a system of permutations that
works like a combinatory chart into which its elements are inscribed. Fourth, a
myth is a story of origin, either sexual or political, and usually both.

We are underlining the importance of the place from which these myths are
announced, in terms of the general historical context, and that of the history
of psychoanalysis. These myths of origin are sexual and political, and they are
also a written formula of the work of psychoanalysis. Yet as such, they are nothing in themselves; they are a result of absolute "amphimixis," to use Ferenczi's
term, which would make them analogous to the "genitals" in his bio-analytic
speculation or myth formation. Does this logic go further: is it more than just
an analogy? If that is true, is there a complex homology between the mythic
and the genital?

Part I—Ferenczi

Let us turn to *Thalassa* and the question of genitality. The whole book, it seems,
is built on a ruse, the ruse of the temptation or desire to return to the womb,
to water, as a principle of the death drive. It depicts the drive to return to

inorganic origins, to death or Nirvana, as integral to the theory of genitality. *"Regressionszug"* evokes in English the trait, pull, rift, drift, and draft of regression. In this one seemingly simple term, an abyssal, contradictory, both aporetic and infinitely disjunctive logic is at work, and all the terms involved in it are slippery like the skin of fish or tadpoles. The logic of equivalences is confusing, as confusing as the logic in *Beyond the Pleasure Principle* where Freud must finally admit that the idea of a foundational division is simply a rhetorical trope, a false distinction: there is not pure Eros or Thanatos; rather, they slip, like the death drive itself. Why would a return to sea or even to the womb, to the confines of the mother, promise Nirvana?

This slippage—both "on the surface" and "in depth"—emblematic for Ferenczi of the attempt to return to a state of bliss that becomes death manifested as "catastrophe" is precisely the point. It doesn't take Ferenczi very long to land us on the shores, place us in ponds, and impose a forced evolution, a reproductive struggle, an ice-age, and a scorched earth:

> The possession of an organ of copulation, the development within the maternal womb, and the circumvention of the great danger of desiccation—these three terms thus form an indestructible biological unity which must constitute the ultimate basis of a symbolic identity of the womb with the sea and the earth on the one hand, and of the male member with the child and the fish on the other.
>
> (Ferenczi, 1989, 50)

No psychoanalyst who has read this text can forget the analogy of the introjection of the sea inside as amniotic fluid and the semen/baby like a fish attempting to return home. For Ferenczi, this condenses a whole history of phylogenetic catastrophes: the history of the earth in crisis that is present not only in every attempt at regression, but in every attempt at coitus, which he makes the hallmark of the progressive unification of the drives in genitality, though it is less a bliss than an act of anxiety-ridden violence—another hole or forced water-pit marking an ever-increasing force of separation.

Forget breathing. Forget the inflow of air, the end of bisexuality in sexed reproduction. Forget that the origin of coitus is rape, not to mention the violence of the male member that bores a hole into the other's body. Forget the creation of limbs in order to pin her down. Forget that the age of the father is hallmarked by the Ice-age.

Let's go home to the sea where we are men and women both, where we simply release our bodily products into the fluid around us, wrap ourselves in ourselves and in an environment that is nourishing, wet, one. Let's forget that this oneness is only circumscribed in the act of fertilization that essentially happens without us ever being there; neither parent is there, nor is the child.

Ferenczi dreamed up this book, maybe even hallucinated it, while working in a military hospital, filled with war-traumatized patients, but also with dismembered bodies. He writes about genital functioning:

According to the conception here presented, the procreative function thus concentrates a whole series of elements of pleasure and anxiety into a single act: the pleasure of liberation from disturbing stimuli of instinctual origin, the pleasure of return to the womb, the pleasure of happily accomplished birth; and the anxiety, on the other hand, which has been experienced in the course of birth and that which one would necessarily feel in connection with, the (fantasied) return to the womb. Since the actual return is limited to the genital and its secretion, while the rest of the body can keep itself unscathed (and takes part in the regression "hallucinatorily"), every element of anxiety is successfully eliminated in orgasm as the procreative act that terminates with a feeling of complete satisfaction.

(Ferenczi, 1989, 43)

Complete satisfaction? How could the return to the womb be at once a happy pleasure and a scathing anxiety that returns us to every trauma, personal and geological, which must then be extinguished or "conducted off" by orgasm? Ferenczi also calls this process a complete identification with the genitals; the genital products; the desired baby, even though it is also a parasite; the fish that we once were. Identification produces the unification and organization of the sexual drive, uniting the anarchy of infantile sexuality, without mature genitals. Here, the book is at its most fantastic and it undoes itself almost completely, beautifully. Yet, this is its truth: there is no unity aside from a fantastical identification; unity of identification as a libidinal process itself—and this is what has been called, for the longest time, the "phallus." This is the only theory of genitality we can have as analysts, one that Freud pointed to in his essay on the "Dissolution of the Oedipus Complex" and that makes its appearance constantly in his letters to Ferenczi about Otto Rank, about what Freud thought was mistaken about the theory of birth trauma. The problem is always a problem with the phallus; and as it concerns genitality, Freud advocates not for the repression or triumphant assumption of the phallus, but for its total destruction or dissolution ["*Der Untergang*," which means decline, destruction, end, ruin]. Maybe we could add to destruction Ferenczi's notion of genital catastrophe.

Is this question of the phallus a return to the muddy waters between Ferenczi and Freud? With this phallic fantasy, are we pointing to what Ferenczi tries to undo, time and time again, when he attempts to find a more feminine essence in his theory, with and against his love for Freud? Freud once remarked about Ferenczi that he was too feminine and needy, almost whiny, obsessed with having a child instead of working. Ferenczi was obsessed with having a child, caught in a complex drama between mother and daughter patients. One was coveted for her fertility, sexual passion, and youth, and the other, for her intellectual adventurousness, though he had an unpassionate relationship with her, and she was unable to give him a child. It struck us while reading this correspondence, that the whole situation with Ferenczi and these two women is not really about the women themselves, or about the baby, nor even the splitting of love and desire (despite its considerable presence as a theme), but about writing to Freud. Ferenczi seems to need to find his voice or his name, with and against this man that he loves, who is also his psychoanalyst.

Given that Ferenczi wants to account for the evolution of the human species, one might find it odd that the development—or rather "event"—of language is nowhere explicitly included, which for Lacan is an experience that is catastrophic, a violent separation and alienation, even if it is structuring. This is why Lacan links the phallus and language.

In the last section of *Thalassa*, entitled "Bioanalytic Conclusions," Ferenczi makes the case for the biological unconscious as a way of conceiving of a prime mover, even if, as Freud says, "the goal of all life is death." This too-and-fro of life and death would require "a third dimension," but Ferenczi speaks of dualities such as attention and thought, and sleep and sex in the development of a sense of reality. Never is language "directly" or "as such" mentioned; never does he posit a mediating third function that would allow the assumption of a sexed body.

It comes as no surprise that at the moment he is working on this book, he struggles with the question of writing. He is concerned to find a way not to write letters to Freud, or to make his work the means of conversing with him. Ferenczi writes to Freud on May 13, 1914:

> Stemming from the problem of enuresis, some ideas have occurred to me about the 'amphimixis of partial instincts' at the onset of the primacy of the genital zone. This time I set about not to dissipate the matter with epistolary and oral discourse, but to write the matter up and—without regard for possible disgrace—to send it to you as free associations on this theme.
>
> (Freud and Ferenczi, 1993, 553)

The task would take him another nine years. During this time, he wants to have a child, and doesn't want to have a child; he wants to write a book, and cannot write a book: what else is this than a missing third, a problem of identification with the phallus?

"Language" is not being addressed "directly" or "as such" but constantly put to use and to task by Ferenczi, who was a prolific writer and inventor of terms and concepts. Language for Ferenczi might just be an internal reversal or an exteriorizing contortion of sorts, addressed in the most "direct" way possible—"as such." Imagine here a "fourth narcissistic insult" that—after Galileo's, Darwin's, and Freud's—Ferenczi would have administered to mankind by pointing out that "intelligence" is not an inherent property or capacity but has to be searched for and found "in the cosmos" by leaving oneself, turning oneself outside (see Ferenczi, 1995, 44). This intelligence is language: the most proper to it, is at the same time, the most external. In fact, its very intrinsic nature is assigned to it by what is external to it. This is a feature that "amphimixis" concretizes in the genitals. They are nothing in and for themselves; even procreation is nothing in itself: they only serve the purpose of the return they never accomplish.

Furthermore, the term "amphimixis," which Ferenczi claims as a neologism or terminological coinage of his very own making, and which is set into the title of *Thalassa*'s first chapter ("The Amphimixis of Eroticisms in the Act of Ejaculation"), makes one think of the *"Sprachverwirrung"* ("Confusion of Tongues"), the title of his famous late and very controversial essay. Both amphimixis and *Sprachverwirrung* are traumatic for thought: they hint at fundamental confusions inside language and inside the construction of reality. The concepts themselves (i.e., "language" and "reality") remain deeply altered, traumatized, estranged from themselves, and maybe forever impossible to grasp. Both amphimixis and *Sprachverwirrung* render language and reality impossible calling up the "Real" in Lacan's sense. Ferenczi might have been intuiting this dimension more than thinking it. He seems at any rate to shy away from exposing or saying explicitly what comes with these two—as well as other—traumatic notions in his own discourse and thought. *Sprachverwirrung* confuses language; amphimixis confuses representation. The elementary logical as well as spatial and temporal relations are haphazard.

Ferenczi's language evokes far more than it delivers. Multiple titles allude to various dimensions and announce multiple subjects that are subsequently abandoned or only tangentially touched upon. For instance, for the very seductive and promising, "Confusion of Tongues" stated in the title leaves one wondering whether "tongues" are used in a quasi-metaphorical sense, or whether Ferenczi wanted to address, indirectly, a confusing dimension of language. Another more striking example is the title of an entry in the 1932 *Clinical Diaries*, "Endlessly repeated 'literal' repetition" which is identified by the editors as preparatory to the "Confusion of Tongues" paper. One does not find much about repetition in this note, however, nor is there anything "literal" either—except for the literal repetition of the word "repetition" in the title itself.

Part II—Lacan

Lacan's 1960 paper "The Position of the Unconscious" was given in response to a debate by the psychoanalysts Jean Laplanche and Serge Leclaire to establish whether language or the unconscious was primary. Lacan pokes fun at them, saying that they treat the unconscious like a part of a car they are examining, whereas what they need to understand is that they are already implicated, since "psychoanalysts are part and parcel of the concept of the unconscious, as they constitute that to which the unconscious is addressed" (Lacan, 2006, 704). He carries on, "I thus cannot but include my discourse on the unconscious in the very thesis it enunciates: the presence of the unconscious, being situated in the locus of the Other, can be found in every discourse, in its enunciation" (Lacan, 2006, 704). How vain is the attempt to sustain the presence of the unconscious,

Lacan declares, but why not force the psychoanalysts to bear this impossibility—what he calls a fundamental splitting. Like trying to speak about one's analysis while in analysis, there is no meta-position possible. A new consideration of how we think about what is outside and what is inside is necessary; this is why, Lacan says, we need to invent a new topology.

In this key paper, Lacan invents two myths to speak topologically about the unconscious: the cave and the lamella, both sexual myths and myths about sexuality. "I will try to contribute something newer by resorting to a genre that Freud himself never claimed to have superseded in this area: myth" (Lacan, 2006, 716). Alluding to Plato's famous allegory of the cave that by Lacan's time had become a cliché of psychoanalytic practice, the simulacra, and shadow play, the analyst draws the patient out of the depths into the light of the day. Lacan, of course, problematizes this.

The place in question is the entrance to the cave, toward the exit of which Plato guides us, while one imagines seeing the psychoanalyst entering there. But things are not that easy, as it is an entrance one can only reach just as it closes (the place will never be popular with tourists), and the only way for it to open up a bit is by calling from the inside.

This is not unsolvable—assuming the "open sesame" of the unconscious consists in having speech effects, since it is linguistic in structure—but requires that the analyst re-examines the way in which it closes (Lacan, 2006, 711).

Lacan is being cheeky and quite funny regarding this cave, while the question for him is serious—it concerns how we understand what he calls the edge structure between the conscious and the unconscious. This is more like a rim between two sides of the same strip of paper than two distinct spaces. For Lacan, the unconscious is not an "inside."

It is due to Lacan's topology (where the unconscious is neither inside nor outside) that he called his clinical technique a "cut." The analyst intervenes so as to touch or even create this edge. This is important for several reasons: (1) What is said by the analyst has to open up something new; it cannot solidify something old or shore anything up. (2) The temporality of the unconscious mirrors that cut or punctuation of a sentence which needs to be stopped in order to understand the full import of what is being said. This is the very *Nachträglichkeit* (deferred action) structure of trauma elucidated by Freud which Lacan highlighted, meaning that what happens in the present can structure the past rather than vice versa. (3) Taken together, Lacan emphasizes that psychoanalysts need to re-examine the idea of cause and give up on naive notions of aetiology. Cause is a lure. We would do better with a Freudian notion such as over-determination, understood as the necessity for a circular, nonreciprocal, articulation. This is a reversal of Ferenczi—or perhaps paradoxically his fullest expression—since in writing *Thalassa* Ferenczi takes his singular transference to Freud as far as it would go, his transference to Freud is the cause that re-writes the past.

Lacan then situates the unconscious in relation to the categories of the subject and the Other. In this way, we shall understand the question of entry (to the cave) and of its closing. While abstract, Lacan's resituating will return us to the question of genitality. The subject is the Cartesian subject presupposed by the unconscious. In claiming "I think, therefore I am," Descartes gave us the inverse subject of the unconscious as posed by Lacan as "I am where I am not thinking." The Other, Lacan says, "is the dimension required by the fact that speech affirms itself as truth" (Lacan, 2006, 712). How to reach this affirmation? Lacan sums up elegantly: "the unconscious is, between the two of them, their cut in action" (Lacan, 2006, 712). One can almost imagine the analyst's silence addressed to the patient inside the cave, listening intently with his ear to the door, hoping that was is said grants him entry, if even only for a minute. The analyst will learn to play not only with what it means to speak, but by listening, by following the rhythm of repeated intervals in which a structure of discourse can be discerned, which usually allows the cut to function.

It is possible to peer into Lacan's cave and excavate Freud. However, the Lacanian construction is so fundamentally different to the cliché ways of imagining the unconscious. It is not a space, it is not even a pre-articulated discourse (this and that series of traumatic memories and fantasies), nor is it the storehouse of the causes of our neuroses. The unconscious is the action of a cut between speech and the subject. That is why Lacan (2006, 716) can say that "transference is essentially tied to time and its handling." Keeping the image of the cave, he then asks, "what is the being that responds to us, operating in the field of speech and language, from shy of the cave's entrance?" (716). The answer is surprising and shifts the unconscious as cave to the unconscious as cave edges: "I would go so far as to embody it in the form of the very wall of the cave that would (like to) live, or rather come alive with palpitations whose living movement must be grasped now..." (716). Psychoanalysis repositions spatial representation to the edge where the temporal being of rhythm originates. The unconscious is a cave moving outside of itself. Of course, it is hard not to hear vaginal references in the palpitating walls of the cave, and one must wonder how exactly Lacan wants to link analytic listening, the unconscious, and "feminine" sexuality.

To understand all of this better, we need to turn to Lacan's second myth, that of the "lamella." Lacan writes,

> [w]henever the membranes of the egg in which the foetus emerges on its way to becoming a new-born are broken, imagine for a moment that something flies off, and that one can do it with an egg as easily as with a man, namely the hommelette, or the lamella.
>
> (Lacan, 1981, 196/221)

Not only does he invite his audience to enjoy the fantasy of breaking an egg, but he also evokes a mono-cellular being to animate the idea even further: "The lamella is something extra-flat, which moves like the amoeba. It is just a little more complicated [...]" (Lacan, 2006, 716).

Is Lacan following Freud in *Beyond the Pleasure Principle* when he evokes pro-
tozoa, vesicles, and gametes to speculate on the drives? Lacan is following Freud
here by following the myth that Freud himself uses to speak of Eros, using the
moment in Plato's *Symposium* where Aristophanes speaks of what Lacan characterized as "primitive double-backed creatures in which two halves are fused
together as firmly as those of a Magdeburg sphere; the halves, separated later
by a surgical operation arising from Zeus' jealousy" and "represent the beings
we have become in love, starving for our unfindable compliment" (Lacan, 2006,
716–717).

The human's search for sphericity, for the mirage of the whole, speaks more
to subjective division and points to this broken egg which seems to have been
repressed since Plato's time. The sphere is a broken egg. The amoeba-like
lamella or *hommelette*—a condensation of omelette and homme ("Manlet")—a
little flat egg man, is introduced both as a "practical joke" (ibid.) and as a
"myth." Now, the breaking of the ovular membrane, transposed and multiplied as the breaking of the cells' developmental division and taken as this
mythical joke, becomes the central piece of psychoanalytic concept formation
invented by Lacan. All this pokes fun at the fantasy of complementarity between the sexes, which, for Lacan, never make a whole. Here again, as with
Ferenczi, when touching on the question of unification regarding the libido,
sexuality, and genitality, we land on the problem of the phallus, and Lacan
wants to make the broken egg man his paradigm, comparable to Ferenczi
and his fish.

Lacan turns back to embryology to elaborate on the little egg man who is
brought into the world not as a whole but with bursting membranes, perfo-
rations, cut cords, and an anatomical complement that is not the mother, but
rather a parasitic organ, the placenta or after-birth, which the new-born loses.
He then asks us to imagine this phantom organ as an infinitely "primal" form
of life

> in no way willing to settle for a duplicate role in some microcosmic world
> within a world [...], omniscient as it is guided by the pure life instinct [...].
> It is certainly something that would not be good to feel dripping down
> your face, noiselessly while you sleep, in order to seal it.
>
> (Lacan, 2006, 717)

The struggle with this fearsome being would be fierce since it has no need of
the senses; it cannot be educated or trapped and guided, Lacan says, by the
"pure real," while we have to clumsily turn what is real into a "reality" to find
our way. The only hope, he says snidely, is to get it to slip into a round enclosure
(like the one Zeus halved in Aristophanes' tale) on its own, because to touch it is
to let it take up residence in you, who knows where. It would take an invention
by the gods to contain and restrain the libido in the genitals, no less in a sexual
relationship.

The lamella becomes the closed surface that is created by the myth that ["not only [...] cut[ing]s short, but [...] fills in the gaps that Freud, surprisingly, left in his enumeration of the drives"] (Lacan, 1981, 195, 218–219). The lamella, myth, and surface are invented to occlude the holes of logos, fulfilling the anti-philosophical function of an invention in a theoretical discourse that otherwise is seen to be faltering. What leads Lacan to perform this operation?

The answer is both theoretical and connected to the specific vicissitude of the myth in the dimension of writing. The lamella is introduced to resolve the contradiction emerging from Lacan's contention. On the one hand, all drives are partial (pre-Oedipal or pre-genital sexuality), and on the other, there is the idea of "*ganze Sexualstrebung*" (the representation of the totality of the sexual drive) (Lacan, 1981, 188). The partial nature of the drives doesn't mean, for Lacan, that they are part of any whole but rather that they are distinct, each corresponding to a specific erogenous zone of an orifice, mouth, anus, ear, and eye. Second, it means that the drive must be described as a movement that starts from the edge of the orifice and returns to it; it does not close this hole but circles around an object—breast, feces, voice, gaze—that, by the fact of being detached from the zone it is related to, introduces into the circuit a gap that opens it to the dimension of virtually infinite loss. Third, the drive is partial because the movement of its circuit not only circles around the object, but also traverses the field of the Other, i.e., signifiers: no drive is "natural," as if separable from desire, demand, ideals, and identifications. The drive is thus "absolutely partial"—an amphimixis of mutually exclusive dimensions.

Lacan finally concludes, "this image and this myth seem to me apt for both illustrating and situating what I call 'libido' [...] an organ [...] qua surface" that organizes a "force field" (Lacan, 2006, 718). The libido is what goes beyond the limits of the body and it is practically palpable. Lacan illustrates this when describing a hysterical patient who "plays at testing its elasticity to the hilt" (Lacan, 2006, 719)—an image of the female patient in analysis that has captured the imagination of many. Furthermore, the myth of the lamella speaks to the important place of sex in psychoanalysis that teaches us two fundamental lessons:

First, for human beings,

> shy of being altogether in speech [...] there is no access to the opposite sex as Other except via the so-called partial drives wherein the subject seeks an object to take the place of the loss of life, he has sustained due to the fact of being sexed..
>
> (Lacan, 2006, 720; translation slightly modified)

Second, from the perspective of the Other,

> the locus of speech as it encounters the exchange of signifiers, ideals they prop up via the elementary structures of kinship, the metaphor of the

father as a principle of separation, and the ever reopened division of the subject owing to its initial alienation--on this side alone and by the pathways I have just enumerated, orders and norms are instituted which tell the subject what a man and a woman must do.

(Lacan, 2006, 720)

You are on the one side or the other, when it comes to the question of sex. You are on the side of the partial drives, or you are on the side of language that attempts to construct sexual difference which otherwise does not exist in the unconscious. As analysts, all we can do is follow the circuit of the drive and see what it animates, paying special attention to what is said about sex. This is what we learn from the myth of the lamella.

What more can we say about language? Once again, we must take up the question of the phallus, or the identification that potentially or partially fills in the gap or cut between a living being and the Other. In Lacan's article, "The Signification of the Phallus" in *Écrits*, he states from the outset that the castration complex (regarding the phallus) (1) gives to analysis what is analyzable on the one hand, as well as (2) gives a position to the subject in the unconscious on the other

> without which he could not identify with an ideal type of his sex, or answer to the needs of his partner in sexual relations without grave risk, much less appropriately answer to the needs of the child who may be produced thereby.
>
> (Lacan, 2006, 575)

Why, Lacan asks, must these be given on the basis of a threat, namely, the threat of castration? And why is biology not enough on its own, why do we also need myth, the Oedipal myth, to understand this structuring?

The mark of language and the materially unstable elements that speak through us are repressed, and return via the symptom, which is mythically structured. The function of the phallus (also mythic, referring to a rite of the Ancients) is to be found here. It is not a fantasy, nor is it simply the object (which still concerns a reality), nor is it the organ it purports to symbolize (i.e., the penis or clitoris). The phallus is there to designate the effect of meaning, or meaning effects in the human subject, i.e., what is analyzable, or what ideal the subject has found to unconsciously find stability. If it is not enough to be a subject of need or an object of love, we land upon the conundrums of desire, where all the "defects" are to be found in the psychoanalytic field regarding sexual life showing that there is no "virtue" that can be located in the "genital" (see Lacan, 2006, 580).

The phallus thus forms a copula whose links to copulation Lacan marked by pointing out that the reference to the penis in the phallus hinges on what is most salient in terms of what can be grasped regarding intercourse, that is what signifies the vital flow, turgidity, and what is transmitted between the generations. Its equivocation derives from its being symbolically the figure of the copula, an "and" that can connect all signifiers. Lacan has received a lot of criticism for this claim, but if we do not simply stoop to finding Lacan ridiculous along with Ferenczi and Freud, we can see that he is at the place where identification and sex meet; the copula inhabits a mythic site of reconstruction, and somehow, of psychoanalytic veracity. One might say that the phallus echoes Ferenczi's "amphimixis" of language, a place where letter, function, history, and body are entirely confused and nonetheless foundational in this very confusion. Here is an anchorage in what can only be called a catastrophe, a catastrophe that is nevertheless the basis of human sexuality. Lacan avoids making Ferenczi's mistake, which consists in losing the feminine side of the equation, of letting it drift away even if we have learned since then that such feminine drift is the profound truth of one half of the question of the phallus, the metonymy of desire against its phallic instantiation. Lacan thus reverses Ferenczi's picture of an organ in search of a cause; he provides the clinical picture of a cause, which is unconscious sexuation that must forever search for an organ that cannot be found except in speech, writing, or symptoms.

Let us note that "The Signification of the Phallus" was a lecture given by Lacan in 1958, two years before the myth of the lamella. It is strange to see its "vital flow" transposed soon after into the foundational myth of the bursting membranes of the egg and the placental organ of the libido. But this is also what is transmitted by psychoanalysis, an organ that un-writes itself in a transferential process, the regression that allows it to be re-written, refashioning the surface of the body in analysis—what we might simply call the work of and on the drive.

We now understand why these three psychoanalytic theorists had to give themselves over to the act of writing myth to raise the stakes of psychoanalysis, even if it is under the name of bio-analysis, which might be a way of re-claiming the ground of the sexual—of leading back to genitality indeed! When Lacan says that the phallus is an organ for which a function had to be invented, adding that this invention was, and is, psychoanalysis itself, he ushered in the most general and the most concrete amphimixis. It is more precisely the amphimixis of the general—that we could call either "death" or "life," we cannot tell—and the most concrete elements, like speech, signifiers, cuts, and remainders. Genitality appears neither as a name or an image nor as a metaphor for the pull and rift; it is the dis-attraction between them: genitality appears indeed just because it is nothing in itself.

Bibliography

Bonaparte, M. (1938). "Some Palaeobiological and Biopsychical Reflections." *International Journal of Psychoanalysis*, 19.

Ferenczi, S. (1989). *Thalassa: A Theory of Genitality*, trans. H. A. Bunker, New York: Norton.

Ferenczi, S. (1995). *The Clinical Diary of Sándor Ferenczi*, trans. M. Balint, Cambridge: Harvard University Press.

Freud, S. (1953). *Three Essays on the Theory of Sexuality*, in *The Standard Edition of the Complete Psychological Works of Sigmund Freud*, Vol. 7 (pp.155–243), ed. and trans. J. Strachey, London: Hogarth Press.

Freud, S. (1955). *Beyond the Pleasure Principle*, in *The Standard Edition of the Complete Psychological Works of Sigmund Freud*, Vol. 18 (pp.7–64), trans. and ed. J. Strachey, London: Hogarth Press.

Freud, S. and S. Ferenczi (1993). *The Correspondence of Sigmund Freud and Sándor Ferenczi, Volume 1, 1908–1914*, trans. P. T. Hoffer, Cambridge: Cambridge University Press.

Freud, S. and S. Ferenczi (1996). *The Correspondence of Sigmund Freud and Sándor Ferenczi, Volume 2, 1914–1919*, trans. P. T. Hoffer, Cambridge: Cambridge University Press.

Freud, S. and S. Ferenczi (2000). *The Correspondence of Sigmund Freud and Sándor Ferenczi, Volume 3, 1919–1933*, trans. P. T. Hoffer, Cambridge: Cambridge University Press.

Lacan, J. (1981). *Seminar: Book XI: The Four Fundamental Concepts of Psychoanalysis*, trans. A. Sheridan, New York: Norton.

Lacan, J. (2006). *Écrits: The First Complete Edition in English*, trans. B. Fink, New York: Norton.

Chapter 5

Undoing the Interpellation of Gender and the Ideologies of Sex

Geneviève Morel

Many recent events demonstrate that, despite its popularity, the notion of gender is increasingly generating discontent. The word gender is relatively new and was first used in relation to grammatical classification (masculine/feminine/neuter) or taxonomic classification (gender/species). Following the contributions of Gender Studies theory in the 1970s, gender came to designate a vast field of concepts with social and political implications, generally considered progressive. It was therefore logical that when significant social reforms were being made (marriage and adoption equality), these would be met by reactionary resistance – led by defenders of traditional family values infiltrated by religious groups revitalized by the circumstances – and resistance based on a naturalist theory of sexual difference, marriage, and filiation.

Another sort of protest, this one more surprising, came from people who benefited from the recent legal reforms supporting gender reassignment. For example, the case of "Norrie" May-Welby is very instructive in this regard. Norrie, an Australian national at age 51, was at the center of a long legal battle to obtain a high court decision that recognized gender X in 2014. As a result, this "not specified" gender, neither male nor female, was inscribed in all basic legal documents.

Norrie, assigned male at birth, first identified as female, and underwent gender reassignment surgery in Scotland in 1989. However, following the surgery, Norrie did not feel represented by any gender and asked the civil authorities that "non-specific" gender, neither one nor the other, be inscribed, written as "X," on the civil registry. During the three-year legal battle that ensued, in the Appellate Court, a three-judge panel unanimously determined that "as a matter of construction... the word sex does not bear a binary meaning of 'male' or 'female'." "Maybe people will now understand there's more options than the binary, and even if a person is specifically male or female, their friends might not be - and hopefully people might be a little bit more accepting of that," said Norrie (Bibi and Harrison, 2014). Commentators noted that this decision, which marked a wish to end the binary nature of both sexual identity and gender, opened the door not only to a third gender, but beyond that, to a multiplicity of potential genders (Bibi and Harrison, 2014). We could obviously conclude

DOI: 10.4324/9781003284888-7

that in order to avoid such dilemma, one could reform the law and suppress any mention of gender or sex on national documentation.

However, this decision of the Australian Supreme Court interests us beyond the juridical perspective. Norrie's discontent implies the idea that no classification will ever be sufficiently precise to cover all possible cases in the plurality of gender, nor can it account for the singularity of one's relation to what Lacan calls sexuation. Let us note that Lacan's notion of sexuation, which may resonate with implications appearing at first biological, designates the way in which one becomes (or not) man or woman. It is a concept absolutely not anatomical. On the contrary, it is based on a sophisticated logic of sexual enjoyment, structured around the formulas of sexuation. This logic therefore goes against any attempt at classification, and even against the binary nature under which the formulas may at first appear to be organized. Isn't this not exactly why, fundamentally, in psychoanalysis sexual difference is not coterminous with gender? Of course, I am not talking here of the traditional oppositions taken up by classical psychoanalysts who, believing in nature, stubbornly hang on to anatomical difference as if it were the only possible compass. Unable to read Freud closely, they face an impasse. It is clear that Freud encountered an impossibility early on. One can of course go on quoting his famous "anatomy is destiny"; however, we then forget that he also said that "In human beings' pure masculinity or femininity is not to be found either in a psychological or biological sense" (Freud, Three Essays). The logic of sexuation reveals how the term gender is insufficient to adequately capture the singularity of enjoyment, of symptoms, and of fantasy, and of what makes people declare themselves man, woman, or whatever else altogether.

Gender may appear as an unconcise or unspecific notion, hence not useful for psychoanalysts who have at their disposal more precise tools to capture not only the most intimate relation of an individual to sex, but also to its social and bodily consequences, issues that critics in the field of Gender Studies wrongly assume are not dealt with in psychoanalysis. This assumption leads to an unsatisfying divide, noticeable in the psychoanalytic field between the "reactionaries" who refuse the political and social implications of Gender Studies theory and the "moderns" who accept the objections and give up on their concepts completely, throwing away the baby with the bathwater. Would it not be more judicious to, on the contrary, investigate why gender is so precious to our peers and to assess at which level of analytical theory one can situate it, rather than retroactively forcing an anachronistic reintroduction of the notion of gender into Freudian concepts? From such a point of view, what would be the psychoanalytic value of gender?

I will take as a starting point the hypothesis that "gender" is at play when analysands tell us of the way they were treated and mistreated in relation to their sexed being, when they repeat the names they were called (most often, insulting ones): "tomboy," "sissy," "pussy," "butch," "faggot," "dike," "fairy," "poof," "pansy," "tranny," "queen," "she with dick," "fruitcake," and so on. If not universal, this is a common enough occurrence across cultures.

Judith Butler, in their illuminating book *Excitable Speech: A Politics of the Performative* (1997), argues that individuals can overcome this injurious name-calling. One can refuse to identify with them; even though the individual may have accepted them, they can be deflected, and the insults can be turned against the speaker and the power which spoke to them. For example, slurs such as "queer" or the "C" and "N" words were indeed deflected and reappropriated, reclaimed as a means for groups to recognize themselves as members of a community. Slavoj Žižek (1999, 264) disagrees, maintaining that a radical overcoming of the insult requires a true subjective destitution, i.e., an action wherein individuals will set themselves free from the signifying chain that had previously alienated them, via an operation of separation in the Lacanian sense of the word. Raoul Moati (2014) very clearly presented the difference in approach between the two philosophers. The debate between Butler and Žižek on this issue, however, reveals that neither of these philosophers denies the importance of Louis Althusser's theory of interpellation, a major contribution to the Marxist theory of ideology. I would indeed like to revisit this theory to demonstrate that gender is reified via interpellation in the Althusserian sense and hence a consequence of ideology, which should encourage us to tread carefully when taking a position on gender.

Theory of Ideology: Althusserian Interpellation

In 1970, the French philosopher Louis Althusser published "Ideology and Ideological State Apparatus (ISA)" (1976, see also Althusser, 2001), a text preceded by numerous articles that dealt with the subject of ideology. Althusser made extensive use of Lacan's theory of intersubjectivity to think ideology in a renewed Marxist fashion, i.e., as an interpellation that concerned the Ideological State Apparatus. Let me quote the most well-known excerpt from his book, which describes a "theoretical scene":

> I shall then suggest that ideology 'acts' or 'functions' in such a way that it 'recruits' subjects among the individuals (it recruits them all), or 'transforms' the individuals into subjects (it transforms them all) by that very precise operation which I have called *interpellation* or hailing, and which can be imagined along the lines of the most commonplace every day police (or other) hailing: 'Hey, you there!'[1]
>
> Assuming that the theoretical scene I have imagined takes place in the street, the hailed individual will turn round. By this mere one-hundred-and-eighty-degree physical conversion, he becomes a *subject*. Why? Because he has recognized that the hail was 'really' addressed to him, and that 'it was *really him* who was hailed' (and not someone else). Experience shows that the practical telecommunication of hailing is such that they hardly ever miss their man: verbal call or whistle, the one hailed always recognizes that it is really him who is being hailed. And yet it is a strange

phenomenon, and one which cannot be explained solely by 'guilt feelings', despite the large numbers who 'have something on their consciences'.

(Althusser, 2010)

While Althusser did not use examples of interpellation dealing with gender or sex, the gender terms mentioned by analysands as having stigmatized them are indeed part of the ISA framework (Ideological State Apparatus). These include experiences of being interpellated at school, the army, the scouts, the family, other educational and sports clubs, etc., and can therefore be thought in Althusserian terms.

Boys, Guillaume: Dinner Is Served!

In the Comédie Française's actor Guillaume Gallienne first film, set among the French haute bourgeoisie, one laughs a lot despite the fact that the story is rather tragic. Is this a successful form of humor, whereby being perfectly identified to our superego, we allow ourselves to laugh at our own sadism toward our neighbor?

The biographical story of Guillaume Galliene, who plays himself, is a subtle plea opposing gender stereotypes. The plot is simple: a boy, raised with his two brothers in a French upper-class family with ideals of athletic prowess and virility, is seen as too effeminate by the father. Because of his effeminate awkwardness, he is considered gay, especially by his mother, an eccentric Russian aristocrat with liberal ideas. The plot twist is that Guillaume comes out of the closet, not as gay but as surprisingly heterosexual, announcing to his shocked mother his wedding to a young woman.

The equivocal title of the movie comes from the way his mother, Melitta, would summon, i.e., interpellate her sons, whenever food was served. Guillaume only really comes to understand the significance of this call during a psychoanalytic session, where the series of interpellations he had received throughout his life crystallize. This story was first performed as a theatrical play, and later transformed into a film. In the story, the moment of insight shifts to the moment Guillaume fell in love with his future wife, Amandine. A number of past comments play over in his mind: "this child is very effeminate"; "hey! Camp boy!"; "fruitcake"; "hi there, pussycat"; "hey you, you're so gay you've become a dike"; "cut the melodrama"; "get lost, we're between men here"; "boys, Guillaume: dinner is served." Later, he hears the host of a "girls only" dinner party he is invited to call out: "Girls, Guillaume: dinner is served." It is worth noting that in French, the expression used here for "dinner is served" is "*à table*," also means to spill the beans, which is exactly what Guillaume does. He spills the beans by creating a theatrical play and a film, in which he is both an author and an actor, playing himself at different ages as well as playing his mother.

He constructs a scene that, on the one hand, brings together the metonymical thread of hurtful and insulting gender interpellations, and, on the other hand, combines two sentences which index this thread by cutting it at the beginning and at the end, like two metaphors of his sexed positioning: "not a boy," and "not a girl." The first sentence, "Boys, Guillaume: dinner is served," which is the film's title, indexed him as not being a boy, and he concluded from it that he actually wanted to be a girl. In this feminizing interpellation which differentiated him from his brothers as being an exception, he also read his mother's desire, maybe even her what she really wanted.

The second interpellation, coming from the female host of the dinner party, "Girls, Guillaume: dinner is served!" is symmetrically opposed to the first one, and puts Guillaume in opposition to "girls." This occurs at the moment of a love-encounter with a woman, confirming his heterosexuality; he therefore positions himself as a man. We should however note that such a conclusion is not at all straightforward and could even be a misinterpretation of what was meant. Let us recall that Lacan defined as "heterosexual" anyone who loves women, regardless of their gender, since women incarnate the Other (*heteros*) for both men and women. From such a perspective, a lesbian woman is heterosexual, whereas a misogynous man is not, and a woman who loves men with contempt for her own gender is not heterosexual either. Guillaume loves women so passionately that it leads him to mimic them; first of all, he imitated his mother whose voice he incorporated – he actually had to consult with a speech pathologist for years and took pains to find his own voice as he had literally adopted his mother's. But Guillaume is not only interested in his mother, as he has perfectly well understood that all women are different. "Pervious to womanhood," he makes every effort to carefully study them, one by one, in details, even including the way they breathe. In a way, we could say that he incarnates the position of Don Juan, "taking" each woman one by one, not in order to sleep with them, but to incorporate them via a perpetual disguise of *being* them, that he sublimates in his work as an actor. By way of this incorporation of women, one by one, he shows that he has understood the "not-all" essence of femininity – which is not incompatible with adopting a feminine position. Guillaume thinks that what precipitated his masculinity is to have fallen in love with a woman. This is perhaps the reason he declares himself reluctantly as bisexual. As he explains in an interview:

> I don't know what normality is; I was never interested in that question. I am not praising any position in particular. I am only explaining what I think: that there is no link between identity and sexuality. It so happens that by the love for a woman, my life is heterosexual. If people need reassurances, if they really want to stick a label on me, tell them I'm bisexual.

Here, he confuses heterosexuality – in the Lacanian sense, love for women – with virility.

His psychoanalytic treatment, which he swears has saved his life, allowed yet another transformation, here linked to the phallus, which provides the true rationale for Guillaume to conclude that he is a man and comes out as straight. As a child, people found him to be effeminate when in fact he aspired to be a girl. Guillaume notes that effeminate and feminine are not the same thing; nobody tells a girl she is effeminate. He is nonetheless not sure if he is a girl, mainly as a result of the opinionated resistance stemming from his father. Hence, the question gnawing at him formulated on a hysterical modality: "Am I really a girl?" He detested being called effeminate, and the humiliations he endured returned in his memory as a series of insulting and stigmatizing interpellations. Later, as he mourns the disappointment of an adolescent unrequited love for a boy, his mother normalizes the experience by divulging that he is homosexual. He experiences this statement as a revolting remark for the young Guillaume since he thought of himself as a girl, and his mother's comment disowns him. After this, following the advice of his aunt, he will "give it a go" with men but is not convinced that this is his path.

Guillaume understands his metamorphosis into a heterosexual man as the possibility, thanks to his analysis, of overcoming his fear of the phallus. Indeed, this fear inhibited all of his sexuality and prevented him from either loving a man or assuming himself to be a heterosexual man when confronted with a woman. By resolving his infantile horse phobia, that was in fact phobia of horses as identified with the male sex, he was able to assume himself as being *the bearer of the phallus* vis-à-vis men and women. At the moment homosexuality became possible, he became aware that this was not what he actually wanted. Cross-dressing, adopting a feminine costume, he sublimated the wish to be a girl, and this became his work, an artistic gift. From a Lacanian perspective, we could call it a sinthome. As his breathtaking performance as an actor demonstrates, another form of relation, a sexed and sexual one, is now possible with a woman, a relation made distinct through love.

Respond with Laughter?

This is how I reach my conclusion. In Guillaume's story, the problematic of gender is characterized by the series of hurtful interpellations which crystallize around a central interpellation that positions Guillaume as not being a male, by way of the summoning "Boys, Guillaume: dinner is served." Let us note that if the subject aspires to be a girl, he nevertheless considers it insulting to be seen as effeminate, since a girl would not be called effeminate. Not being a boy therefore does not imply being a girl. This opens up a question structured around his mother's desire that is broached in a hysterical manner: "Am I really a girl?"

His relation to art is a sublimatory solution on the feminine side: theater, as the art of disguise, allows Guillaume to make a name for himself on a prestigious stage. Overcoming gender interpellations implies much more than a subjective response and a readjustment of identifications, as argued by Judith Butler. The re-appropriation of the performative interpellations as humorous is transformative. They make it possible for Guillaume to laugh at the homophobia that earlier in his life had led him to a depression. As he recounts: "I was subjected to homophobia from the age of 10. I would hear pussy, fruitcake, fagot, homo. And I would turn around, knowing that they were calling me," says Guillaume, just before laughing out loud. To the journalist interviewing him, surprised at Guillaume's spirited response to the matter, he explains that he fell into a depression at the age of 12, before going into psychoanalytic treatment for years. "It saved my life, without it I wouldn't be alive today, that's for sure" (Rocher, 2013). In addition, his humorous response staging his history makes us all laugh. This successful re-appropriation was only possible as a result of a radical subjective change linked to an irreversible act: Guillaume's decision to say "no" to his mother. While the "effeminate" past remains, it now flows into art, transformed and sublimated into a socially acceptable form. Art is absolutely essential for Guillaume in order to live, and also allows him to brilliantly show us what has changed. These transformations go well beyond identifications; they bring together the drive, fantasy, and the symptoms in their singularity.

Note

1 Note from Althusser in the quote above: "Hailing as an everyday practice subject to a precise ritual takes a quite 'special' form in the policeman's practice of 'hailing' which concerns the hailing of 'suspects'" (Translator's note).

Bibliography

Althusser, L. (2001). "Ideology and Ideological State Apparatuses (Notes towards an Investigation)," in *Lenin and Philosophy and Other Essays* (pp. 142–147), Introd. Fredric Jameson, trans. Ben Brewster, New York and London: Monthly Review Press.
Althusser, L. (1976). *Positions (1964–1975)*, Paris: Les Éditions sociales.
Althusser, L. (2010). "*From Ideology and Ideological State Apparatuses (Notes towards an Investigation)*," in *The Norton Anthology of Theory and Criticism* (2nd edn, pp. 1335–1361), trans. Ben Brewster, ed. Vincent B. Leitch, New York: W. W. Norton.
Bibby, P. and D. Harrison (2014). "Neither Man nor Woman: Norrie Wins Gender Appeal." *The Sydney Morning Herald*, April 2, 2014. http://www.smh.com.au/nsw/neither-man-nor-woman-norrie-wins-gender-appeal-20140402-35xgt.html
Butler, J. (1997). *Excitable Speech: A Politics of the Performative*, New York: Psychology Press.
Moati, R. (2014). "Structure et liberté," in *Penser avec Lacan: Nouvelles lectures*, ed. G.-F. Duportail, Paris: Hermann.
Rocher, B. (2013). "Mais pour qui se prend Guillaume Gallienne?" *Grazia*, 20 November. https://www.grazia.fr/people/mais-pour-qui-se-prend-guillaume-gallienne-577238
Žižek, S. (1999). *The Ticklish Subject*, London and New York: Verso.

Queering Psychoanalysis

Fantasy, Anthropology, and
Libidinal Economy

Chapter 6

The Role of Phantasy in Representations and Practices of Homosexuality

Colm Tóibín's *The Blackwater Lightship* and Edmund White's *Our Young Man*

Eve Watson

Introduction

The concept of phantasy is what separates a cultural or psychological notion of the unconscious from a psychoanalytic one, which is premised on a void at its heart. This chapter explores a variety of fantasmatic elaborations in four illustrative texts: Tim Dean's *Unlimited Intimacy* (2009) is a provocative and insightful exploration of barebacking, the subculture of gay men who deliberately abandon practices of safe sex and embrace erotic risk, exposure to disease and infection, including HIV in search of creating a kinship; Lee Edelman's *No Future* (2004) proposes the notion "sinthomosexuality" which calls to homosexuals to embrace the death drive and its excess *jouissance*. This paradoxical satisfaction, derived from suffering, enlarges the realm of the "inhuman" to include what is radically other. This excessive dimension of *jouissance* linked with the death drive is relocated by Dean to where it rightfully belongs, democratically with everyone. Colm Tóibín's *The Blackwater Lightship* (1999) and Edmund White's *Our Young Man* (2016) are two love story novels written 17 years apart focusing on the impact of AIDS on young gay men in the late eighties and early nineties. I will explore the role and relevance of the psychoanalytic notion of phantasy in both novels relative to AIDS, death, love, kinship, and relationality.

The Importance of Excess in Queer Theory and Psychoanalysis

Human sexuality tends toward reductive over-simplification or gross complexification. This too-little or too-much hides its more elementary aspect, a sense of straining at language's limits whenever it comes to discursively capturing sexuality's vicissitudes. For both psychoanalysis and queer theory, this challenge is linked to a question of "excess" in the representability of sexuality, in its

DOI: 10.4324/9781003284888-9

symbolization and actualization. Nevertheless, as we shall see, each discipline approaches this excess differently.

> It is not that queer theory must not be owned, so much as that it should not be allowed to own us – those who invest it with meaning, practice it, live it – must not become another identity category for us to "come out" into, castigate ourselves with, dis-identify from or fiercely protect from encroachments by hostile forces.
>
> (Giffney, 2007, 8)

Queer theory is a collection of methods (epistemological, ontological, methodological, and pedagogical) which seeks to expose norms and deconstruct the categorizations of desiring subjects, particularly in relation to identity. It explores the ideological, political, cultural, and social implications of heterosexuality and its deployment as "compulsory"[1] which configures homosexuality as excessive, other, dissident, and transgressive. It does so by leaning on its reclamation of the term "queer" and using its performative power to stare back at societal norms, and challenge, destabilize, and ultimately subvert all assumptions relating to identity (Giffney, 2007, 3). This is premised in queer's refusal to define itself following Judith Butler's (1993, 229) insistence that the term queer remains forever open to interpretation. As what is excessive to identity categorization, queer is rooted in a critique of the categorization of homosexuality conceived solely as oppositional and a transgression against heterosexuality. Heterosexuality is, it can be argued, based on identity approaches fated to reconfirm its authoritarian and centralizing position, and this is what has to be resisted. Queer thus is excessive both to sexual categorization and to its homosexual lineage. The queer psychoanalytic theorist Tim Dean (2000, 268) expresses it concisely and provocatively, "In its most fundamental formulations, psychoanalysis is a queer theory." Dean (2000, 150) shows that the psychoanalytic conception of phantasy allows for sexuality to be understood beyond merely anatomical and imaginary terms. He calls for queer theory to embrace the psychoanalytic notion of phantasy because it is not normative, insofar as it refers to a relation not between two subjects but between a subject and a non-gendered object (262). Dean notes the tendency in cultural studies to focus only on the imaginary aspects of fantasy, whereas phantasy involves all three Lacanian registers of the Imaginary, the Real, and the Symbolic together (263). Similarly, the cultural queer theorist Lauren Berlant (2012, 71) asserts that "to comprehend phantasy/fantasy we need to move between unconscious structures of desire and the conventions meant to sanitize them into an intention" (71). It is not about active imagining or conscious phantasy-production nor is it a place where the identity of the subject is to be found.

But let us backtrack. For psychoanalysis, the notion of the drive instantiates excess at the heart of the subject. This is a pulsating *jouissance* that cannot be represented. This idea of excess and irrepresentability was originally posed by Freud when he famously asserted the polymorphous perverse sexual drive's recalcitrance to adaptation and normalization (1905, 171–172). Lacan, taking this further, proposes that the object we want is neither pre-ordained nor an actual object but is an empty object and is what causes desire. This is the object *a* and while it covers the gap between the Real of the drives and the unknowability of desire (Lacan, 2006),[2] it does not provide an identity. Rather, it colonizes the gap at the heart of being with aspects of the Other which we have internalized. Psychoanalysis thus shares with queer theory an appreciation of identity categorizations as modes of adaptation and normalization. While we do not choose to come into being, we gain a sense of self from the Other. In early life, our being is not discernible as gendered or sexually differentiated, and speaks a truth that cannot be encapsulated in later identifications. This subjective truth remains unconscious because the unconscious does not recognize gender; thus, our truth is an alterity that is outside or beyond identification. Thus, one can say that it is Otherness that creates *jouissance* because it is marked by the painful enjoyment of the Real of undifferentiation, or what we give up when we enter the field of speech and language. Because *jouissance* is forbidden for the speaking-being, it can often be subsequently conceived as dangerous, horrifying, and engulfing. This helps explain the psychic origins of homophobia as linked with the threat to identity contained in *jouissance*. Hence, homophobia arises as a problem of sexual identity failing to capture the essence of sexuality; the *jouissance* that is sacrificed is deemed to have been taken or stolen by "others" (i.e. gay people) who are assumed to have access to it.

Phantasy covers over an absence, the void mentioned earlier. Phantasy hinges on the absence of a signifier, a once-and-for-all designation of sexual difference. Lacan's famous dictum sums it up (1999b); "there is no such thing as a sexual relation" (12). Phantasy is made structurally necessary for subjectivity due to the fact that there is no fundamental rapport between the sexes (Žižek, 1999, 191). The inherent failure of sex to establish a rapport or a final meaning doesn't stop it from being represented as a total success in culture, social relations, and the arts, while its failure at a socio-cultural level is fantasmatically projected into an "outside" or "other." One of the aims of psychoanalysis is to first discern and then question what to do with the excess that resists symbolization; this hated, irreducible, expurgated, and incommensurate Otherness is both intimate and exterior to us at once. What do we do with our own intolerable excess? Do we "domesticate" it, do we assign it to others, and do we "liberate" it? How do we reckon with its awful truth and confront it? Do we allow love to salve and provide succor? Contemporary social, political, and institutional groups, including psychoanalytic ones, rise and fall, are sustained and dissolved, depending on how accommodating they are to this question of difference inside, not outside, the group.

Here, the psychoanalytic concept of phantasy comes in handy; it is written with a "ph" to indicate its unconscious basis, managing Otherness by staging it as a return from elsewhere, which has the effect of locating desire on the side of the subject and projecting *jouissance* on to the side of the Other. Phantasy provides a crucial and necessary veil over the nothing; it shrouds the non-rapport at the heart of human subjectivity. It does so via a representation of the nothing on the side of the Other, which does not provide an answer to what the Other desires or enjoys but only a provisional hypothesis. This nothing is designated as Real; it can neither be made into an object nor into language and the encounter with this is experienced as traumatic. This void can be summed up in Heideggerian terms as the "negation of the totality of beings" and the "nothing" that directs us to others that is at the heart of a deep antagonism (2008, 97). The "nothing" directs us via repetition because phantasies iterate and reiterate a scene, a singular *mise-en-scène* of the radical alterity of the inexpressible experience of psychical reality, alongside the desire to be recognized and to be desired by the Other. Phantasies create a scene connecting the subject to the Other, framing the Real, as Pluth (2007) puts it, under "controlled conditions" that "allow access to a colonized, tamed Real" (88), and giving a place to the subject to desire in relation to the Other as well as giving a place to the Other's desire. Lacan writes:

> The desire of the Other doesn't acknowledge me as Hegel believes it does, and which makes the question altogether easy, because if the Other acknowledges me, as it will never acknowledge me sufficiently, I just need to use violence. In truth, the Other neither recognizes me nor misrecognizes me.
>
> (Lacan, 2014, 153)

Because phantasy locates desire on the side of the subject, it enables it, and sets up a position for enjoyment in signifiers and language, giving it a "signifying structure" (Lacan, 1966–1967, 250), as well as a place and solution for *jouissance*. Thus, phantasy provides representational coherence for the subject as object for the Other (Pluth, 2007, 84). Phantasy, for example, allows the subject, in the absence of gaining the Other's recognition, to take the place of the Other who would recognize them, as, for example, in pornographic scenes where the viewer is placed as the Other who watches. However, the Other's *jouissance*, which is unrepresentable, seemingly without limit and therefore horrifying, is also given a place in phantasy. There are two sides to phantasy: on the one hand, it "stabilizes" by giving desire a dream-like, out-of-reach quality, while on the other hand, it "destabilizes" by encapsulating envy and all the irritating qualities ascribed to the Other's enjoyment (Žižek, 1999, 192). It also allows for a subject to find a position staged in phantasy that grants them a place in the Other's desire. Let us now explore these aspects of phantasy in Tim Dean's *Unlimited Intimacy* and Lee Edelman's *No Future*.

Phantasmagorias in Barebacking and Sinthomosexuality

In the 1966–1967 seminar Lacan devoted to fantasy, he elaborates:

> If there is something that is present in the sexual relation, it is *the ideal of the jouissance of the other*, and moreover, what constitutes its subjective originality. For it is a fact that if we limit ourselves to organic functions, nothing is more precarious than this intersection of *jouissances*.
>
> (Lacan, 1966–1967, 142; emphasis original)

Can *jouissance* be social? In *Unlimited Intimacy*, Dean proposes that the phantasies that underlie the practice of barebacking include the element of risk-free enjoyment for the viewer of barebacking pornography, which stages a "deep fantasy of contact without bodily limits" and "a fantasy of intimacy that involves complete exposure to the other," the overcoming of all barriers (169). As Žižek (1999, 190) puts it, phantasy works not only to veil the Real but also creates what it appears to conceal. While it may be a fact that people participate in activities together such as cruising and barebacking, the individual phantasies at work for each participant and the particularity of the singular *jouissance* engendered are necessarily not located in the communal field and shared activity. Cruising and barebacking, in effect, localize *jouissance* as the sexual *jouissance* of everyone involved as well as the limitless *jouissance* ascribed to the Other. This dynamic is promoted to the level of a group activity that can be shared via the sexual act among the group and not limited even by the intervention of viral contamination.

The intersection of these two *jouissances* provides an illusion of limitlessness which fits in with the capitalist injunction to enjoy. Contemporary society emphasizes, or rather commands, atavistic and individualistic enjoyment (McGowan, 2004, 17). Global capitalism engenders societies that are not premised on a shared social bond through which subjects identify with each other via shared prohibitions and the sacrifice of *jouissance*. In a society based on prohibition and deprivation, there is a bond that stems from a structural lack arising from the sacrifice of *jouissance,* linking people and facilitating a shared sense of dissatisfaction; nobody can do as they please. Sacrifice provides a safe outlet for gaining satisfaction through the efforts of the ego, body image, and the sense of imaginarily regaining a lost *jouissance* in a society in which no one can enjoy extravagantly (McGowan, 2004, 22). The decline of symbolic forms of authority promotes pathological narcissisms supported by media (screen and image), offering unceasing forms of enjoyment and promising plenitude. These forms of enjoyment create docile subjects, lost in a kind of imbecilic satisfaction in a society that unceasingly supplies objects and images. The subject becomes tethered to these objects, typically consumable, that provide little or no space for meaning, reflection, agitation, and political action.

In seeking to go beyond the incitement to enjoy and its inevitable apathy, docility and even cynicism, it makes sense to celebrate sexuality and pleasure, especially queer and alternative sexuality as a force that opposes the inexorable imperative to enjoy which is suffocating, frustrating, and encourages either ennui or frenetic activity. Alenka Zupančič (2006, 171) has put it well: the framework of enjoyment collapses in on itself because every enjoyment appears to be possible, as it would have been in a mythical lost original state of harmony. Ultimately, a sexual relation has two radically heterogenous *jouissances*; in the sexual act, all we can really have is the body or body-part of the partner. There is no pretense otherwise in cruising and barebacking. Moreover, the reduction of the other to body-part or genitalia fits within the psychoanalytic conception of the structure of masculine desire, which is the reduction of the other to a phantasy-object. In this respect, "there is nothing other than fantasy" (Lacan, 1999b, 80).

In our increasingly competitive world of enjoyment, homosexuality is given its special structural status vis-a-vis the drive and its social renunciation, and figures as a particular and sustaining trope of enjoyment resentfully rescinded. It was Freud (2001c) who first asserted a special status to homosexuality in groups and social relations. In "Group Psychology and the Analysis of the Ego" (1921), he proposed that an individual's identification with a group is a deflection into the social realm of individual libido with its desirous attitudes, hostile rivalries, and personal envies, which is positively cathected via a group identification (142–143). Homosexuality, because it would represent a refusal of the drive sacrifice characteristic of the social field, is phantasized as what will dissolve a social contract dependent on drive sacrifice.

Christopher Lane (2001, 149) notes the importance of Freud's "Group Psychology" essay in explaining society's ambivalence about homosexuality. Society's love and disdain for homosexuality are indicated in its reverence for highly sublimated and aesthetic forms, while castigating its highly sexual expression. Society would thus be structurally disposed to being homophobic. This was exemplified in the successful 2015 Irish referendum which sought gay marriage by popular vote. The "no" side argued that the advent of gay marriage would be detrimental to normative families and especially to children. The irrationality inherent in this position is premised on a figuration of homosexuality as the catastrophic unleashing of the drive. Catastrophic to what? To essentialized notions of kinship and sexual difference that are pitted against "hypersexualized" homosexuals, and to the fiction that the sexual relationship *does* exist. The rancor displayed by supporters of this position has had quite an effect. In Ireland, for example, the single most frequently used slight in elementary schools is "gay" and "queer," and studies of the mental health of LGBT adolescents indicate that it lags behind compared to their heterosexual counterparts.[3]

Psychoanalytically, homophobia is understood as the pathological envy of the other who is held to enjoy a "superabundant vitality" that cannot be grasped. It leads to hatred and the will to destroy what cannot be apprehended by the subject (Lacan, 1999a, 237). Homophobia and other forms of social hatred such as racism, religious, nationalistic, and ethnic hatred, all arise from the Otherness or strangeness which emanates not from others but from our relationship to our own unconscious, our own Otherness.[4] Homosexuality plays a special function in this respect. Not only is it a site in which our Otherness supposedly resides, but homosexuality is imagined as *the* place where heterosexuality fails to establish a rapport, as opposed to homosexuality's startling revelation of the (hetero)sexual non-rapport. This phantasmatic operation is supported by the internalization of socio-cultural ideals that provide a desiring template organized by group demands carefully demarcating sexual limits, and with cultural ego ideals, telling us how to "do" sexuality. This "doing" can be described as Butler's (1999) idea of gender as "a performance that is repeated" (178), "a norm that can never be fully internalized" and that is introjected into the subject as "phantasmatic and impossible to embody" (179). This is how homophobia and hatred come to be essential to the social body's demand, as Lane (2001) puts it, for a boy "to be like his father, but not to like him too much" (161). In today's societies of enjoyment, homophobia finds strong expression as a mode of locating the *jouissance* that is always "out there."

In *No Future*, Edelman (2004) takes on the phantasmatic elaboration of homosexuality as the site of unrelinquished or stolen *jouissance* and proposes the strategy that homosexuality should be put to work in a process of re-signification which has the potential to overthrow the "vivifying fantasy" of reproductive futurism (46). Reproductive futurity is the ideological emphasis on having children, in brief *the* narrative of humanity's pacification and immortality. The "marriage and children" narrative functions as pacifying precisely insofar as it dissociates itself from the *jouissance* that insists as a remainder, a sexuality that is not "over." Homosexuality, for Edelman, is a "hypostatization" of various phantasies that aim to locate and localize the anti-social in a "child-aversive, future-negating force, answering so well to the inspiriting needs of moribund familialism" (113) set against the so-called "excess" that is homosexuality.

Edelman (2004) embraces the supposedly subversive potential of the death drive in his development of the notion of "sinthomosexual," an amalgamation of "homosexual" and "*sinthome*" (38). The *sinthome*, a form of the symptom that needs not to be cured, has been proposed by Lacan late in his work; it is presented as a creative nexus that grants enjoyment, that is, an access to *jouissance* in a less lethal way. The end of analysis means identifying with one's *sinthome* and accepting one's particular modality of *jouissance* and its senseless stupid enjoyment. "Sinthomosexual" represents the radical negativity of the death drive because for Edelman the word neologistically refers to the "sin" that continues to haunt homosexuality (38–39). For Edelman as for Dean, this suggests a phantasy granting the subject a *jouissistic* position embracing the death drive and ushering in a new relational field. The optimism in this proposal is misplaced, given the destructive nature of the death drive. It may also be leaning on a Heideggerian idea about the non-relational possibility of being and the non-relational character of death, which is what individualizes *Dasein* to itself. Yet as Heidegger pointed out, the factical and ontical persuasion of *Dasein*, of the being in the world, is to avoid death (1962, 299). There is a non-relational character of death which makes it an individual *Dasein* (308). Here is what makes it similar to the Lacanian subject conceived in terms of the singularity of its own unconscious.

Death provides the subject with a fundamental limit that is constitutive, but which cannot be symbolized or relationalized. In societies of enjoyment when everything is available and distance evaporates, death as a necessity disappears and is posed as avoidable (McGowan, 2004, 85). Death and aging can be played roulette with, for they could even be something we might escape altogether. The posing of the death drive as a relational strategy bespeaks a will-to-life that is entombed in a lonely zone of one-by-one. The kinship of barebacking, based on a form of "breeding" through viral mixing in which "barebackers transform other men into fraternal relatives in order to keep having sex with them, and they do so by means of a virus" (93), can be considered a variation on the sexual theories of children. Their theories of birth and marriage, which sometimes include an anal mode of giving birth, serve to address one of the earliest psychical conflicts and, according to Freud (2001e, 214), have a determining influence on later fixations, beliefs, and attitudes in adults. For Bersani (2011, 102), barebacking's displacement of community to the interiority of bodies is the adult elaboration of childhood phantasies, "the freakish elaboration into adult categories of thought of infantile fantasies about the life within us, about what goes on inside (as well as what goes into and what comes out of) the body's holes."

Edelman (2004), for his part, posits that queerness is ultimately an embodiment of the remainder of the Real, an excess to the symbolic order, and therefore it defies representation in normative relational modes (25). His account is a strategic reading of the sacrificial *jouissance* at stake in a positionality of sinthomosexuality aiming at "negating" and "allegorizing" the negativity of the death drive. Sinthomosexuality does this by bringing out the hauntingly destructive excess and overdetermination that is reproductive futurity, destroying its fictional affirmations of life, and subversively embodying the abject and "monstrous" figuration of the death drive hidden in the social (Edelman, 2004, 153). Barebacking is also a masochistic identification tinged with sacrificial *jouissance*. Leo Bersani depicts this as a "rageful perversion" of the reproductive process. This would be akin to Edelman's notion of transmitting death instead of life (Bersani and Phillips, 2008, 45). The death drive, as Freud (2001b, 121) defines it, is sadistic, destructive, and narcissistically self-appeasing. It promotes hatred and hostility and the reduction of the other to a subhuman status. Here, the problem may lie in confusing Freud's notion of the id with that of the unconscious. The id, as Freud put it, has characteristics exceeding those of the unconscious (2001a, 75) and is therefore closer to the Lacanian notion of *jouissance*. The unconscious comprises repressed ideas; it is grammatical and therefore "language."

Is there a sacrifice, a martyrdom, in sinthomosexuality and barebacking? The positionalities are too self-consciously deliberate and appeal to a transformative potentiality. True martyrdom is unplanned. There must be something in martyrdom that provides a satisfaction in having done the right thing and in which responsibility is accepted for the consequences of actions which are not only taken for their own sake (Eagleton, 2018, 93). "The martyr," Eagleton writes, "seeks to live his death in the here and now, seeing it as incarnate in the perishable stuff of the body rather than simply as a future event" (87). Martyrdom is to be distinguished from suicide in so far as the martyr gives up what she or he considers precious, while the suicide relinquishes a life that is worthless (88). As a *jouissance* position, martyrdom offers freedom, symbolic disorder, and a refuge of the unconscious, which doesn't mean that it offers anything beyond its own enjoyment. Such a potentiality is not necessarily useful either to the subject or to society at large.

In general, the experience of *jouissance* entails suffering, profound dislocation, and often severe anxiety. Anxiety is an affective signal of the Real and of the signifying division of the subject in which the subject realizes him or herself in a move from *jouissance* to desire. Little in the way of anxiety is discernible in the celebratory style of the proposition that barebacking and sinthomosexuality proffer recuperative and transformative potential. The idea that they re-signify sexual shame by making the abject erotic and celebrating it may have more to do with the effects of melancholic identification and incomplete mourning. How does one mourn the catastrophic losses of an earlier generation to AIDS, the hundreds and thousands of men who died before their time? There is sometimes melancholic identification in homosexuality, as Dean (2000, 118–119) put it in an earlier essay. To mourn is to process the grief of loss and this involves creating a frame for absence. In Dean's analysis of barebacking, the space of absence is difficult to discern for it is dominated by the presence of the invisible virus and by sexual *jouissance*. If we do not mourn what we lose in every object-based knowledge and relation, we will be indifferent to the possibilities of creative endeavor. These creative possibilities are to be found in the emptiness of the image or the inadequacy of the partner (whoever or whatever that is) or in the sonorous vacuum that the voice elicits; these moments call us to acts and enunciations in the true and real sense of them.

Instead, transformative potential for both Dean and Edelman is leveled at normative relational modes and institutions and their dissatisfaction with "homonormativity." For them, the inclusion of gays and lesbians in marriage, conventional kinship networks, and the establishment of legal protections has done little to change those institutions, nor has it much reduced the secondary status of LGBT. Instead, the inclusion has "normativized" gays and lesbians and made them satisfied with the gains that primarily benefit white middle-class queers. For Dean (2000), the virus challenges "homonormativity" and the ideal imaging of homosexual men and women as normal. "Socially unsanctioned sex or promiscuous mixing," he writes, "jeopardizes ideal images because it muddles identification, contaminating one with the other" (20). There is, as Bersani (2011) would have it, the politically correct way of dealing with barebacking, which is to call it self-destructive, and even suicidal and murderous behavior that is linked to a catastrophic self-hatred (93). Alternatively, a psychoanalytic approach would consider, as Bersani (2011) puts it,

> every individual's responsibility for the violent impulses that are consti-
> tutive of our psychic structure. We are now in psychoanalytic territory
> (anathema to many queer theorists), by which I mean territory ontically
> prior to social inscriptions, and "beyond" such intersubjective categories as
> shame and pride.
>
> (94)

There remains, I suggest, an intersubjective dimension and therefore relational aspect to the efforts at de-prioritizing the heterosexual couple and the affirmation of the communal models of impersonal intimacies of Dean and Edelman. Barebacking and cruising break down the distinction between phantasy and reality, between the potential of the unconscious and the apotheosis of reality (Bersani, 2011, 107). *Jouissance* is regulated by desire, but in a society of *jouissance*, desire is denounced and denigrated. Two novels, *The Blackwater Lightship* (1999) and *Our Young Man* (2016), are implicit considerations of desire, *jouissance*, and the relevance of love between men. Both novels are meditations on the impact of AIDS and do not flinch from inviting the reader into the trauma and devastation visited on families and communities. The writings indicate an openness to death and aging and relating to the other at their most needy and desolate. Lacan's aphoristic assertion that "only love allows jouissance to condescend to desire" (2014, 179) will provide a guide in exploring the two novels.

Love, Beauty, and Death in *The Blackwater Lightship* and *Our Young Man*

To turn again to Eagleton, he proposes, showing a Heideggerian affinity, that death is one of the "few residues of the absolute in a secular age" and it is therefore opposed to prevailing orthodoxies in functioning as a limit, a boundary to human existence within which it is motivated by its very limit (2018, 75). Today's secularism, in so far as it is underpinned by globalizing and consumerist forms of capitalism, is a discourse and social link that refuses the notion of limit. It manages "excess" (*jouissance*) by offering consumable objects to mitigate a demand for them that it cunningly foments. Death throws a spanner in the works of the seamless operation of consumerism by removing the subject-consumer. It is interesting that Tóibín's novel, *The Blackwater Lightship*, written in 1999 at a time when the Irish "Celtic Tiger" was approaching its apex and the economy was booming, is set in 1993 prior to this propitious and ultimately calamitous level of capitalistic enterprise, and just before the arrival of the anti-retroviral drugs that would remove the death sentence of the HIV-AIDS virus. The novel is a reclamation of a limit point, a subjective reclamation of life and existence through a confrontation with death.

The Blackwater Lightship is an unflinching account of the main character's last months, which serves as the catalyst for three generations of his family to be reunited after a long and difficult hiatus. Its unsentimental matter-of-fact portrayal of Declan's physical decline shows us what a practical, complicated matter dying is, how much logistics and paraphernalia it requires. Its gritty style is a kind of respect paid to this. Few pieces of fiction remind us so unpreachingly that in the midst of death we are, as Eagleton (1999) put it, in life. Declan's impending death also forces Declan's family to come into contact with his private queer life. As a conduit for the rapprochement of three generations of women, Declan's impending death and bodily decline offer a touchstone that breathes life into stultified familial relationships. The setting is on a crumbling coastline where the Blackwater Lightship is a metaphor for what has been lost: there were once two lighthouses, looking at each other. For Virginia Woolf too, going to the lighthouse was about a confrontation with loss and death, and in her case, the death of her mother.

The novel depicts alternative, non-normative forms of kinship and relationality. Declan's gay friends, Paul and Larry, are portrayed as better caregivers than his family, due to the fact that they were present in his life from the beginning of his illness. Paul and Larry know more about Declan's life than his own mother, Lily, and sister, Helen. At one point, Paul and Lily have a heated argument that manifests when Paul interferes in Lily's attempts to comfort her son, and this prompts Lily to kick Paul out of her home (223). Declan, Paul, and Larry function thus as a family unit and they understand each other, and unlike Declan's family, stick together and do not abandon each other when things get rough. Blood is not thicker than water, even if it carries a deadly virus. The novel also leads to a queering of normative institutions such as marriage and religion. When Paul tells Helen how a Catholic priest performed a secret marriage ceremony for him and his partner, François, he poses a distinct and unambiguous alternative to heteronormative marriage and to the Catholic Church. His membership of a Catholic group called "Cruising for Christ" and the depiction of the marriage ceremony sets this out:

> [The priest] changed into his vestments and said Mass and gave us Communion and then he married us. He used the word "spouse" instead of husband and wife. He had it all prepared. He was very solemn and serious. And we felt the light of the Holy Spirit on us…
>
> (172–173)

White's *Our Young Man* (2016), set in the eighties and nineties in New York City, is an exquisite and hilarious novel about a beautiful seemingly ageless self-obsessed French fashion model named Guy who begins to lose those around him to what will eventually become known as AIDS. The hedonism of Guy's sexual life is set alongside rich representations of a range of both personal and impersonal intimacies. From the poignant yet laugh-out-loud rendering of ideas, like his insistence that cocaine is not addictive (238) or that only men with STD's could catch the HIV virus, the text nonetheless confronts the ravages of aging, sickness, and death. Guy, whose livelihood and relationships require him to lie about his age and fight constantly against the passage of time, nonetheless is interested in, albeit suspicious of romantic coupling, love, and security. His partner, Fred's, illness, decline, and death are painstaking and horrifyingly captured.

While filled with sexual adventures, the novel also explores romantic coupling, love, and desperately sought security. Throughout the novel, Guy has three lovers: Fred, the film producer who bequeaths Guy estates in Fire Island and Manhattan's West Village after he dies of AIDS; Andrés, a Colombian art-history grad student who forges artwork to keep up with Guy's high-fashion lifestyle; and Kevin, a young college-aged youngster who steps in while Andrés is in prison. Yet, the novel and the protagonist remain deeply suspicious about coupling as a middle-class heterosexual romantic fantasy. For all that, Guy falls in love, begins to age, and in the end settles down to a life with Andrés.

The novel nods in its own way to the contemporary equal marriage movement but in an ambiguous way. Fred's death from AIDS offers an occasion for Guy to explain to Kevin that "we don't have any rights" (197). But the "rights" in question aren't typical legal protections but rather concern Guy's pending inheritance of an estate left to him by Fred on Fire Island. Undoubtedly, this is a privileged white gay experience. For all that, Guy is both a consumable image and an image of consumption, and he reflects the rigid fantasies of mass culture. "In a world of shiny consumer goods," he thought, "he was the shiniest one of all" (166). In opposition to such a world dedicated to filling lack with never-ending replaceable consumables, a discourse like psychoanalysis would remind us of the gap at the core of human subjectivity, not only in terms of desire but also in terms of the subject's interaction and engagement with the public and community domains.

Let us evaluate how both novels do not shirk from presenting love and what can be made of this. There is, psychoanalytically speaking, the possibility of a love that does not only exist in the field of reciprocity, which is narcissistic. There is also love that has real effects, love in this sense being what allows *jouissance* "to condescend to desire." This is a type of love based on lack, based on not having. For both Guy and Declan, the castrating effects of lack involve encountering death and loss and for Declan there is no reprieve. No matter what, for both, love exists and all the more as their worlds start to crumble and fall away. Aesthetics also play a role, and in particular the aesthetic of beauty, so important for gay men. It is a mode of responding to the dilemma of what to do with Otherness, which principally emanates from within ourselves. From Heidegger, to Lacan, Tóibín, and White, beauty is an aesthetic overlay of the mortal being; it is a death mask in so far as it veils decay but is also proximate and intimate with death (Lacan, 1999a, 295). It is the tragedy of aging, sickness, and death to take away beauty. The efforts of both novels to include these (im)purities of existence, the pure movement of life, the danger of carnal attraction, the inconsolability of loss and trauma, the fractured space of desire, and the deeply significant phantasmagoria of yearning which stand against the embodied joylessness and temporal pleasure of sexual *jouissance*. The violence and savagery of our real reflexes are tempered by love, by beauty, and by phantasy, which, in its orientation to a lost object, circumscribes a relationality to difference that is particular for each subject. In its particularity, determined by unconscious desire, phantasy is non-normative and is irreducible to sexual acts, gender relations, sexual orientation (Watson, 2017, 464). Phantasy veils the intractable essence of the Real.

Notes

1 The idea of "compulsory heterosexuality" was formulated by Adrienne Rich (1993) as the key mechanism that shapes and defines the sexual order. The logic of compulsory heterosexuality inevitably produces identity categories such as homosexuality that conform to norms of cultural intelligibility as well as discursive categories that can appear as developmental failures or logical impossibilities within that domain.

2 Phantasy comes in as support to sexual difference, which occurs as follows. The impact of speech and language produces logic in addition to a jouissance-laden product, the *object a*, which is, quoting Lacan from his seminar on phantasy, "a piece of refuse from the inaugural repetition" (Lacan, 1966–1967, 188).

3 An important study was published in 2016 documenting poor mental health and high risk of Irish LGBT youth between the ages of 14 and 25, especially those between the ages of 14 and 18.
See http://www.glen.ie/attachments/The_LGBTIreland_Report_-_Key_Findings. pdf.

4 Our relationship to our own unconscious is a problematic of the Otherness of desire which we must assume as our own, but which emanates in the first instance from outside of us. From the beginning, we are made by the Other. The Other is understood less as "who" and more as a "what," it is the familial discursive context as well as the broader socio-cultural discourse which includes language, history, sexual, and social mores. This is "Che vuoi," or in translation, "what does the Other want" or "what does the Other want of me?" (Lacan, 2006, 690).

Bibliography

Berlant, L. (2012). *Desire/Love*, New York: Punctum Books.
Bersani, L. (2011). "Shame on You," in *After Sex? On Writing Since Queer Theory*, ed. J. Halley and A. Parker, Durham: Duke University Press.

Bersani, L. and A. Phillips (2008). *Intimacies*, Chicago and London: University of Chicago Press.

Butler, J. (1993). *Bodies that Matter: On the Discursive Limits of Sex*, London: Routledge.

Butler, J. (1999). *Gender Trouble*, New York: Routledge.

Dean, T. (2000). *Beyond Sexuality*, Chicago and London: University of Chicago Press.

Dean, T. (2001). "Homosexuality and the Problem of Otherness," in *Homosexuality and Psychoanalysis* (pp.120–143), ed. T. Dean and C. Lane, Chicago and London: University of Chicago Press.

Eagleton, T. (1999). "Mothering." *London Review of Books*, 21(20) (14 October). https://www.lrb.co.uk/v21/n20/terry-eagleton/mothering.

Eagleton, T. (2018). *Radical Sacrifice*. New Haven and London: Yale University Press.

Edelman, L. (2004). *No Future: Queer Theory and the Death Drive*, Durham and London: Duke University Press.

Freud, S. (2001a). "The Dissection of the Psychical Personality," in *The Standard Edition of the Complete Psychological Works of Sigmund Freud, Vol. 22* (pp.57–80), trans. and ed. J. Strachey, London: Vintage.

Freud, S. (2001b). "Civilization and Its Discontents," in *The Standard Edition of the Complete Psychological Works of Sigmund Freud, Vol. 21* (pp.69–143), trans. and ed. J. Strachey, London: Vintage.

Freud, S. (2001c). "Group Psychology and the Analysis of the Ego," in *The Standard Edition of the Complete Psychological Works of Sigmund Freud, Vol. 18* (pp.64–145), trans. and ed. J. Strachey, London: Vintage.

Freud, S. (2001d). "Civilized Sexual Morality and Modern Nervous Illness," in *The Standard Edition of the Complete Psychological Works of Sigmund Freud, Vol. 9* (pp.181–204), trans. and ed. J. Strachey, London: Vintage.

Freud, S. (2001e). "The Sexual Theories of Children," in *The Standard Edition of the Complete Psychological Works of Sigmund Freud, Vol. 9* (pp.209–226), trans. and ed. J. Strachey, London: Vintage.

Giffney, N. (2007). "Quare Theory," in *Irish Postmodernism and Popular Culture*, ed. M. Sullivan, A. Mulhall and W. Balzano, Basingstoke: Palgrave Macmillan.

Heidegger, M. (1962). *Being and Time*, trans. J. Macquarrie & E. Robinson, Oxford: Blackwell.

Heidegger, M. (2008). "What is Metaphysics?" in *Basic Writings*, ed. D. F. Krell, London: Harper Perennial.

Jagose, A. (1996). *Queer Theory: An Introduction*, New York: New York University Press.

Lacan, J. (1966–1967). *Book XIV: The Logic of Phantasy*, trans. C. Gallagher, http://www.lacaninireland.com/web/wp-content/uploads/2010/06/14-Logic-of-Phantasy-Complete.pdf

Lacan, J. (1999a). *Book VII: The Ethics of Psychoanalysis*, ed. J.-A. Miller, trans. D. Porter, London: Routledge.

Lacan, J. (1999b). *Book XX: Encore, On Feminine Sexuality, the Limits of Love and Knowledge*, ed. J.-A. Miller, trans. B. Fink, London and New York: W.W. Norton and Co.

Lacan, J. (2006). "The Subversion of the Subject and the Dialectic of Desire in the Freudian Unconscious," in *Ecrits: The First Complete Edition in English* (pp.671–702), trans. B. Fink, London: W.W. Norton and Co.

Lacan, J. (2014). *Book X: Anxiety, The Seminar of Jacques Lacan*, ed. J.-A. Miller, trans. A Price, Cambridge: Polity Press.

Lane, C. (2001). "Freud on Group Psychology: Shattering the Dream of a Common Culture," in *Homosexuality and Psychoanalysis* (pp.147–167), ed. T. Dean and C. Lane, Chicago and London: University of Chicago Press.

McGowan, T. (2004). *The End of Dissatisfaction: Jacques Lacan and the Emerging Society of Enjoyment*, New York: State University of New York Press.

Pluth, E. (2007). *Signifiers and Acts: Freedom in Lacan's Theory of the Subject*, Albany: State University of New York Press.

Rich, A. (1993). "Compulsory Heterosexuality and Lesbian Existence," in *The Gay and Lesbian Studies Reader* (pp.227–254), ed. H. Abelove, M. A. Barale and D. Halperin, London: Routledge.

Rubin, G. (1993). "Thinking Sex: Notes for a Radical Theory of the Politics of Sexuality," in *The Lesbian and Gay Studies Reader*, ed. H. Abelove, M. A. Barale and D. Halperin, London: Routledge.

Tóibín, C. (1999). *The Blackwater Lightship*, New York. Scribner Paperback.

Watson, E. (2017). "Afterword," in *Clinical Encounters in Sexuality: Psychoanalytic Practice and Queer Theory*, eds. N. Giffney and E. Watson, New York: Punctum Books.

White, E. (2016). *Our Young Man*, London: Bloomsbury Press.

Žižek, S. (1999). "The Seven Veils of Fantasy," in *Key Concepts of Lacanian Psychoanalysis* (pp.190–218), ed. D. Nobus, New York: Other Press.

Zupančič, A. (2006). "When Surplus Enjoyment Meets Surplus Value," in *Reflections on Seminar XVII: Jacques Lacan and the Other Side of Psychoanalysis* (pp.155–178), ed. J. Clemens and R. Grigg, Durham and London: Duke University Press.

Chapter 7

Oscar Wilde
Father and *Som*

Ray O'Neill

All happy families are alike; each unhappy family is unhappy in its own way.
Anna Karenina (Tolstoy, 1998, Chapter 1)

Children begin by loving their parents. After a time, they judge them. Rarely, if ever, do they forgive them.

(Wilde, 1997, Second Act)

A libel trial brought upon oneself over alleged extra-marital sexual relations with a younger person led to the Wilde's family forfeiture of reputation as well as social exile; one can only imagine how these family trials of 1864 were reported and transmitted to the then ten-year-old Oscar, who undoubtedly connected this "terrible blow" (Hanberry, 2011, 147) to his disgraced father's consequent self-imposed exile to the West of Ireland, the successive deaths of his three sisters, and his father's own premature death 12 years after.

Thirty years later, Oscar Wilde would enter the courts to accuse his lover's father of libel, having been named neologistically as a "somdomite," only for this Wilde to again lose case, reputation, and career. The English authorities had hoped that Oscar would abscond to France to avoid his subsequent trial for "gross indecency," but the writer refused to flee, indubitably influenced or directed by his mother, who having pushed her own husband, Oscar's father, toward his own tragic downfall, told her son, Oscar, "if you stay, even if you go to prison, you will always be my son. It will make no difference to my affection. But if you go, I will never speak to you again" (Ellman, 1988, 468). The Wildean drive to repetition which created perfect comedy in art, but forged such tragedy in life, is that the son repeats the mistakes, patterns, and indeed the crimes of the father, spurred to its wretched conclusions by his mother.

Born less than two years after him, Freud, analogously to Wilde, made solid use within psychoanalytic discourse, not only of the potency within humor, but also the hidden power of sexuality, the formative legacy of parents and family *até* (malediction, fate), and our unconscious compulsion to repeat. An inherent piece of contemporary psychoanalytic work is to appreciate and seek to unearth

DOI: 10.4324/9781003284888-10

the transgenerational unconscious transmission of desires, anxieties, repetitions, and traumas, in order to hold a gap in the family patterns of repetition.

The Wildean legacy evidences a sexual, parental compulsion to repeat, to redress, to lose, as a reiteration of the sins of the father that fall on the son. Some damn hideous "it" is named, seen and unseen in this "hideous" neologism of Queensbury's "somdomite" that baits Wilde, who immediately railed to his former lover and continuing friend, Robbie Ross, against this "libellous" claim: "Bosie's father has left a card at my club with hideous words on it. I don't see anything now but a criminal prosecution" (McKenna, 2004, 454). For what was it that Wilde who savored "the love that dare not speak its name" experienced in the father Queensbury's calling card, in the misspelling, parapraxis, neologism of being accused of "posing as somdomite" or of posing as a son dammit? Wilde was a victim of both sexual oppression and the unconscious compulsion to repeat. Exploring the relation between repetition and transgression, a forensic psychoanalytic study of both sexuality and filiation follows here.

Not to be hard on your father.

"Try not to be hard on your father. Remember that he is your father and he loves you. All his troubles arose from a hatred of a son for his father, and whatever he has done he has suffered bitterly for" (O'Sullivan, 2016, 432). So wrote Constance Holland-Wilde, wife of Oscar, in 1898 to her 11-year-old son Vyvyan the week before she died undergoing surgery, warning her son against a son's hatred for his father. Final words haunt us. Psychoanalysis is a discourse grounded in final words, in finalizing words, in tragedies of parents and children that result from such words.

The Oedipal myth is a tragedy of unheeded words, of the forewarned son who nonetheless unknowingly, perhaps unconsciously, kills his father and marries his mother. It is a tragedy never finalized within one generation, but one that blindly marches forth in repetitions of rivalries, murders, and buried histories passing on to Oedipus' children Eteocles, Polynices, and Antigone, a name evoking "in place of one's genitor."[1] Similarly, the Wildean tragedies are tragedies of parents and children, of fathers and sons, never limited to one generation, but always repeated in and through the next. Few recall the downfall of William Wilde, Oscar's father, whose knighthood and fame resulted from revolutionizing the treatment of middle-ear infections. They do, however, remember his son Oscar's ruin and disgrace, who died from meningitis caused by chronic middle-ear infections.[2]

The birth of psychoanalysis is indebted to Freud's relationship to both his parents. Freud himself remarked on the influence of his own Oedipus Complex, conceived within *The Interpretation of Dreams (1900)* and delivered through the death of his own father, Jacob, something Freud openly acknowledged in his preface to the second edition:

For this book has a further subjective significance for me personally — a significance which I only grasped after I had completed it. It was, I found, a portion of my own self-analysis, my reaction to my father's death that is to say, to the most important event, the most poignant loss, of a man's life.

(Freud, 2001c, xxvi)

Freud underlines that a father's death is "the most important event … of a man's life." Freud, like most men, had a complex, if not ambiguous relationship to his father Jacob, which agitates many of the thoughts, memories, and dreams inhabiting *The Interpretation of Dreams*. One such childhood memory is a story Jacob told Freud of his being publicly racially attacked and insulted, yet passively accepting this humiliation. Such humiliation became transgenerationally transferred onto Freud who was not only ashamed of his father's humiliation, but even more embarrassed by his father's naïve telling of this story to the ten-year-old Sigmund, a story transmitted without any conscious awareness of just how humiliating it was for them both. In Freud's mind, this was the "unheroic conduct on the part of the big, strong man who was holding the little boy by the hand" (Freud, 2001c, 197).

Humiliation through/from/with the father is something that drives Freud's unconscious desire for success, manifested in his becoming "the father of psychoanalysis." Freud's deliberate childhood urination in his parents' bedroom might not only be a marking of territory, "in revenge, of course," but also a reply to his father's words, "The boy will come to nothing" (Freud, 2001c, 216). Paradoxically, such a mantic prophecy of destiny to the young child spurs the adult Freud to triumph. He recognizes the father's words as

a frightful blow to my ambition, for references to this scene are still constantly recurring in my dreams and are constantly linked with an enumeration of my achievements and successes, as though I wanted to say: 'You see, I *have* come to something'.

(Freud, 2001c, 216)

Jacob Freud was 40 years of age when he married 20-year-old Amalia, Freud's mother; it would be his third marriage. Freud, like Wilde, was adored by his mother, who called him "my golden Sigi" and her devotion and unconditional love marked her son.

I have found that people who know that they are preferred or favored by their mother give evidence in their lives of a peculiar self-reliance and an unshakable optimism which often seem like heroic attributes and bring actual success to their possessors.

(Freud, 2001c, 398)

Such idealization only further enclosed both son and mother, separating them from the significantly older Jacob. This was compounded due to the father's financial failures and their resulting move from rural idyllic Moravia to urban

Vienna. "I never felt really comfortable in the city. I now think that I never got over the longing for the beautiful woods of my home, in which scarcely able to walk, I used to run off from my father" (quoted in Gay, 1988, 9). Freud writes:

> My father was made into a man of straw in order to screen someone else; and the dream was allowed to handle in this undisguised way a figure who was as a rule treated as sacred, because at the same time I knew with certainty that it was not he who was really meant ... I became involved in the same emotional conflict which when a misunderstanding arises between a father and son, is inevitably produced owing to the position occupied by the father.
>
> (Freud, 2001c, 436–437)

Coincidentally, *The Interpretation of Dreams* was conceived in July 1895, just two months after Oscar Wilde was sentenced to hard labor in the wake of three high-profile, well-publicized, and ultimately scandalous trials. Freud and Wilde, born 19 months apart, were both incredibly clever, excellent, and excelling scholars, who appreciated, indeed utilized wit, the power of language, to advance their socio-psychological theories against a contemporaneous cultural collision between Victorian sensibilities and modern sexuality. In their different yet parallel discourses, both men prized, challenged, and exposed the truth that "one's real life is so often the life that one does not lead" (Wilde, 1882, 23).

Both men recognized the importance of being earnest. Wilde argued that though "'Know thyself' was written over the portal of the antique world; over the portal of the new world, Be thyself' shall be written" (Wilde, 1994, 1179), thereby effectively moving the philosophical message from self-awareness, to self-actualization. "Be yourself; everyone else is already taken," Wilde advised. Freud's psychoanalytic discourse similarly holds that only self-awareness can facilitate self-actualization: "Being totally honest with oneself is a good exercise" (Freud quoted in Masson, 1985, 272).

During fin de siècle Vienna, Wilde, his theater, his dandyism, and his personality were everywhere. Lothar, chief Viennese theater critic, remarked, "Nowadays, Oscar Wilde has become a theatrical trump card in Vienna" (Mayer, 2010, 208). In 1905, in the *Neue Freie Presse*, Bernard Shaw wrote of Wilde's reception in Vienna:

> Vienna will more easily get used to the style of Oscar Wilde, for Wilde embodied the artistic culture of the 18th century. Seeing that Vienna, apart from Paris, is the most regressive city in Europe it ought to appreciate Oscar Wilde far more greatly than he will ever be appreciated anywhere in Germany or England.
>
> (203)

Fifty years earlier, William Wilde had stayed and studied in Vienna, publishing in 1843 from these experiences a noteworthy text which would foreshadow

Freud's own later interests in combining literary, cultural, and scientific appreciations of Vienna in *Austria, Its Literary, Scientific and Medical Institutions* (de Vere White, 1967, 68).

Although Freud treasured theater, and shared "the greatest thrill" (Jones, 1961, 177) of Wilde's theatrical crush on Sarah Bernhardt, "After the first words of her vibrant lovely voice I felt I had known her for years" (177), Freud never mentions either Wilde or any of his plays, despite their proliferation of both, particularly with the scandal of Wilde's trials in fin de siècle Vienna. And again, although Freud edited Rank's 1914 essay, "The Double" with its explicit Wildean demonstrations of narcissism, interestingly, and perhaps significantly, only twice does Freud in all his collected works and correspondence refer to Wilde. First in *The Psychopathology of Everyday Life* with a reference to a case of Ferenczi's involving the forgetting of Jung's name (Freud, 2001a, 26–27) and the second, occurring perhaps more uncannily (Freud, 2001e, 252) in his essay *"Das Unheimliche {The Uncanny}*," an essay dealing with the familiar unfamiliar involved in unconscious repetition compulsion: "The uncanny proceeds from (a repetition of) something familiar which has been repressed" (247).

"All women become like their mothers. That is their tragedy. No man does, and that is his" (Wilde, 1994, 371). Both Freud and Wilde uncannily shared similar places in their own Oedipal dramas, adored sons of much beloved mothers, while consciously or unconsciously in the shadow of their disappointing, disappointed fathers. Both carry the premature death in childhood of the next sibling born after them. Their legacies from their parents spurring them both forward, for better and for worse, bolstered by maternally formed self-belief, haunted by death, infant survivor's guilt, loss, and paternally informed fear of failure.

> Now I have no idea of where I stand... The expectation of eternal fame was so beautiful... certain wealth, complete independence, travels, and lifting the children above the severe worries that robbed me of my youth. Everything depended upon whether or not hysteria would come out right.
> (Masson, 1985, 265–266)

Both Wilde and Freud's intense attachments to their mothers while living in the ambiguous shadow and legacy of both bereavement and their fathers' histories demanded of both to be great, to justify and avenge their mothers while vilifying the realities of their fathers' bankruptcy, socially and financially. Fears of privation from their childhoods repeatedly resurfaced to compel and haunt them, (mis)directing their lives and careers.

> He [was] a little boy who was in his own understanding the apple of his mother's eye and his father was his rival, and he won. And that can be as difficult as losing to triumph over your father can induce a great feeling of guilt, particularly when they die. If you, for example, wanted them to.
> (Gay, 1988, 11)

Gay's words about Freud could equally refer to Wilde, whose academic and social success in his scholarship entry to Magdalen College, Oxford, was marked by a tour of Europe with his mother during summer of 1874 while his father William Wilde was dying in the West of Ireland. William's final months were marked with financial and emotive arguments regarding Oscar's flirtatious conversion to Catholicism (Ellman, 1988, 54) though Oscar's final embrace of Catholicism would only take place on his own deathbed in 1900. There is an impossible affect a father's death has on a son, regardless of the nature of the relationship or intimacy, a being "uprooted." Freud tells us of his own difficulty, that we may only imagine was shared by Wilde:

> I find it so difficult to write just now... The old man's death has affected me deeply... With his peculiar mixture of deep wisdom and fantastic light-heartedness, he had a significant effect on my life... I now feel quite uprooted.
>
> (Masson, 1985, 202)

Is the death of the father, a threat to the son who loses his position as a child for the father and moves a step closer to its own death? Is the death of a parent also the death of childhood? Does unresolved childhood unconscious guilt, or survival shame of the death of a loved sibling rival become re-triggered with a paternal love rival's demise? Freud recognized that creative writing, like dream-work, is a manifestation of the unconscious, "a continuation of, and a substitute for, what was once the play of childhood," a creative playing with language invested in "childhood memories in the writer's life." Freud establishes such connections between writing, childhood, and memory:

> A strong experience in the present awakens in the creative writer a memory of an earlier experience (usually belonging to his childhood) from which there now proceeds a wish which finds its fulfilment in the creative work. The work itself exhibits elements of the recent provoking occasion as well as of the old memory.
>
> (Freud, 2001b, 151)

Just as the child's game of Fort-Da, throwing an object away and finding it again, exclaiming Gone! and There! is a game that seeks to signify unconscious anxieties of loss and separation, so "the creative writer does the same as the child at play" (144). The creative writer is playing with words, with fantasies, wishes, and stories. Fantasy, as the root of creative writing, drives the writer to exorcise childhood anxieties and desires, by way of inspiration, via condensation and metaphor, "by equating his ostensibly serious occupations of today with his childhood games, he can throw off the too heavy burden imposed on him by life" (145).

Throughout Wilde's plays and creative writing, family legacies consciously trouble parents, and unconsciously haunt their children. In *The Importance of*

Being Earnest, Lady Bracknell censors Jack Worthing with the famous quip that adds a farcical overtone to the tragedy of being an orphan: "To lose one parent, Mr. Worthing may be regarded as a misfortune; to lose both looks like carelessness" (Wilde, 1994, 369). In Wildean drama, having secret parents and parents' secrets intimates disaster. In the play *Lady Windermere's Fan*, the revelation that Mrs. Erlynne is in fact Lady Windermere's mother, coupled with her recognition of her secret daughter's risk of repeating her own mistake of leaving her husband for another lover, is only avoided by way of not exposing her identity as her mother. The Windermere's marriage is restored through mutual silence and concealment of secrets by both partners, albeit with the audience's complicity. "It concludes with collusive concealment rather than collective disclosure" (Ellman, 1988, 364).

Similarly, in the play *A Woman of No Importance*, the (un)known sexual activity of parents unconsciously haunts the child. Gerald forges a relationship with Lord Illingworth, not recognizing him as the father whose refusal to marry his mother forced her to live a scandalized life as a single mother. This is a secret that his mother, Mrs. Arbuthnot, is determined to hold in order to protect her son's social position and romantic future. Pointedly, Hester, Gerard's love interest, remarks, "It is right that the sins of the parents should be visited on the children" (Wilde, 1994, 499). While Mrs. Arbuthnot herself recognizes that "Children begin by loving their parents. After a time, they judge them. Rarely, if ever, do they forgive them" (513). This line is itself a repetition, though expanded, from Wilde's famous novel, *The Portrait of Dorian Gray*: "Children begin by loving their parents; as they grow older, they judge them; sometimes they forgive them" (59). In this novel, Dorian is orphaned; yet, his tragic history, "an ugly story... hushed up" of "an extraordinarily beautiful" (38) mother and her jealous, controlling, vengeful father, that was never disclosed to Dorian, but to Lord Henry, is the motivation for both Dorian's frantic, charming, fatal beauty and his exacting emotional and social vengeance. Over and over again, parents' secrets haunt their children.

> She was an extraordinarily beautiful girl, Margaret Devereux, and made all the men frantic by running away with a penniless young fellow – a mere nobody, sir, a subaltern in a foot regiment, or something of that kind. Certainly. I remember the whole thing as if it happened yesterday. The poor chap was killed in a duel at Spa a few months after the marriage. There was an ugly story about it. They said Kelso got some rascally adventurer, some Belgian brute, to insult his son-in-law in public; paid him, sir, to do it, paid him – and that the fellow spitted his man as if he had been a pigeon. The thing was hushed up, but, egad, Kelso ate his chop alone at the club for some time afterwards. He brought his daughter back with him, I was told, and she never spoke to him again. Oh, yes; it was a bad business. The girl died, too, died within a year. So, she left a son, did she? I had forgotten that.
> (38)

Again, in *An Ideal Husband*, we see on stage the ways in which secrets from the past threaten to destroy not only one's social position, but one's relationship and marriage, in this case, the ideal husband. Mrs. Cheveley blackmails Robert Chiltern warning, "even you are not rich enough, Sir Robert, to buy back your past. No man is" (529). This is something he later laments to his wife Lady Chiltern saying, "No one should be entirely judged by their past" (532). To which his wife replies, "One's past is what one is. It is the only way by which people should be judged" (532). It is not without coincidence that the central themes of *An Ideal Husband* emphasize a need to be forgiven for past sins and highlights the futility of ruining lives of great value to society merely because of society's hypocrisy. Such social hypocrisy was precisely what was at stake in Wilde's own story of blackmail. Though, at this juncture, as both a father and a son, Wilde could equally be aware, consciously and unconsciously, as much of his father's sexual past, as of his own then current indiscretions.

If there was to be a tragic climax, a deciding, defining moment in which the tragedy of Oscar Wilde became catastrophic, it would be April 6th, 1895, when Wilde was arrested at the Cadogan Hotel in London. First, Oscar, in deciding to pursue an unnecessary failed libel trial, his first trial, against Queensbury, had placed himself as the author of his own arrest. But more significantly, there seemed to be both precipitation and delay on issuing the warrant for Wilde's arrest. High-ranking politicians had to balance their fears between both the wider names and associations that would be revealed in the event of a trial, against the public outcry in failing to prosecute Wilde.

During that fateful day, Ross tried unsuccessfully to persuade Wilde to flee the country as everyone had expected him to. His wife Constance told Ross, "Poor Oscar! I hope he is going abroad" (McKenna, 2004, 506). Even Queensbury, though demanding Wilde's prosecution, told reporters "If the country allows you to leave, all the better for the country!" (506) Ross had given him £200 from his bank account, what today would be equivalent to £25,000. At 5pm, a sympathetic reporter from the *Star* warned them that the warrant had already been issued, but there would have been enough time to flee, because it was only at ten past six, allegedly after the last train for the Dover night crossing to France had left, that two detectives arrived to arrest him. Wilde had fatally, stoically decided, "I shall stay and do my sentence whatever it is" (Ellman, 1988, 456).

They wished he would flee, but he did not. It is often said that Oscar Wilde's arrest was delayed by several hours to allow him to catch the last boat-train and escape to the continent[3]. This silent escape would have facilitated social authorities, but Wilde did not flee; the trials had to happen, and everything became public, spoken and visible.

(O'Neill, 2015, 97)

The opportunity to flee to the continent and avoid imprisonment or further humiliation again presented itself between May 7th, 1895 upon Wilde's release on bail following the hung jury of his second trial, and before his being found guilty at the third and final trial on May 25th, 1895. But again, Wilde did not try to get away. Did Wilde believe that he would not be found guilty? Given the libel trial and the level of sexually compromising evidence Queensbury had amassed, this would have been naïve, if not downright stupid. Further publicity was endangering not only Wilde's liberty, but his two great legacies, his literary bequests and his wife's and children's lives and position in society. But Wilde seemed swayed and influenced by other family attachments.

Both his brother Willie and his mother Lady Wilde "were determined that Oscar should stay and stand trial" with Willie evoking a proud Irish separatist discourse, assuring visitors, "Oscar is an Irish gentleman, and he will face the music" (Ellman, 1988, 468). As we have seen before, his mother

> declaimed to Oscar in her grand manner, 'If you stay, even if you go to prison, you will always be my son. It will make no difference to my affection. But if you go, I will never speak to you again.' Wilde promised her that he would stay.
>
> (468)

And then *jacta alea est*, the die was truly cast. Perhaps his mother's desire for Oscar's staying and standing trial was for him to be a martyr in the Irish nationalist model against English justice and law, a fulfillment of her historical fantasy of herself as Speranza, the nationalist savior of the Nation, the separatist seditious writer of 1848's *Jacta alea est*. Whatever her desire here, the price was so absolute, so apocalyptic, that one can only wonder what lack within her it pursued.

In Wilde's infamous prison letter to Bosie, *De Profundis*, amidst the many and multiple wounds and punishments his fall brought, of his enforced immediate bankruptcy Wilde underlines the loss of the "beautifully bound editions of my father's and mother's works" (Wilde, 1994, 1003), the literary legacy bestowed to, and borne by him. In his greatest tragedy, he bewails the loss of the birth right:

> She and my father had bequeathed me a name they had made noble and honoured, not merely in literature, art, archaeology, and science, but in the public history of my own country, in its evolution as a nation. I had disgraced that name eternally. I had made it a low by-word among low people. I had dragged it through the very mire. I had given it to brutes that they might make it brutal, and to fools that they might turn it into a synonym for folly.
>
> (1010)

In Oscar's lowest point, *de profundis*, he "forgets," represses the name, dishonor, and scandal that were his family's bequest. For Oscar was not the first Wilde to be doggedly surrounded by rumors of sexual scandal involving the corruption of youth which would result in an unnecessary libel trial demanded by Lady Wilde, ultimately ending in the family ruination, shame, dishonor, bankruptcy, and death. Oscar's tragedy was also a paternal confrontation and repetition of following his mother's desire into shadowing an uncanny reprise of his father's downfall, ignominy, and ultimate death. "The uncanny proceeds from (a repetition of) something familiar which has been repressed" (Freud, 2001e, 236).

The Wildean family tragedies put in relief Jacques Lacan's four fundamental concepts of psychoanalysis: the Unconscious, Repetition, Transference, and the Drive, all of which are hallmark to transgenerational traumatic legacies, where "something" gets uncannily *unconsciously transferred* in *drives* to *repeat* the past. Contemporary psychoanalytic treatment upholds Freud's theories on the power of sexuality, the legacy of parents, the unconscious compulsion to repeat, seeking to unearth and bring to consciousness the transgenerational unconscious transmission and repetition in order to facilitate conscious choice and decision. What psychoanalysis does could be explained by Wilde's Salome's own words, because psychoanalysis asks us to self-reflect, to go beyond mirages and blind spots by looking "Neither at things, nor at people [...]. Only in mirrors should one look, for mirrors do but show us masks" (Wilde, 1994, 601). And psychoanalytically, there are no better, more intimate, clearer, and opaque mirrors that mask, than those of our own families.

The Terrible Blow of Repetition

Freud's 1914 article "Remembering, Repeating and Working-Through" underscores the distinctions between remembering and repeating, core distinctions within any literature of transgenerational trauma, as Toni Morrison movingly expressed in her famous novel of transgenerational trauma *Beloved*, trauma freezes time, "But her brain was not interested in the future. Loaded with the past and hungry for more, it left her no room to imagine, let alone plan for, the next day" (Morrison, 1997, 70). As Morrison shows, the act of unconscious repeating (re)presents that which cannot be allowed into consciousness and as a result, cannot be forgotten; it is just repeated as a way to be remembered. Freud writes, "he cannot escape from this compulsion to repeat; and in the end we understand that this is his way of remembering" (Freud, 2001d, 150). These experiences that can only be repeated and never remembered "are experiences which occurred in very early childhood and were not understood at the time" (149). The psychoanalytic situation allows this potential impasse to be addressed insofar as the transference itself is a repetition. Freud writes:

> We soon perceive that the transference is itself only a piece of repetition, and that the repetition is a transference of the forgotten past not only on to the doctor but also on to all the other aspects of the current situation.
>
> (151)

Of the many discourses with "psych" on their name, only psychoanalysis recognizes, indeed, mandates the truth inherent in Santayana's oft quoted saying that "Those who cannot remember the past are condemned to repeat it" (Santayana, 1905, 284) or as another Irishman, the philosopher Edmund Burke, phrased it: "People will not look forward to posterity, who never look backward to their ancestors" (Burke, 1970, 274). In the tragedy of Oscar Wilde, one need only look at his ancestors, at his parents, to contemplate what went before, to appreciate the insistence of the damning repetition. A libel trial over extra-marital sexual relations with a young person leads to the family's bankruptcy, forfeiture of reputation, and premature death. There is no doubt that original family trials would have impacted the ten-year-old Oscar. The "terrible blow" (Hanberry, 2011, 147) was the unconsciously familiar shame Oscar knew as a child due to his father's disgrace and subsequent death. But what cannot be remembered is almost inevitably repeated.

It all began with Mary Travers, an incensed 28-year-old woman, suing Oscar's mother Jane for libel in 1864 because of an intemperate letter Jane had written on May 6th that year to Mary's father Dr Robert Travers, complaining of her behavior. Lady Wilde writes:

> Sir – You may not be aware of the disreputable conduct of your daughter at Bray, where she consorts with all the low newspaper boys in the place, employing them to disseminate offensive placards in which my name appears.... As her object in insulting me is the hope of extorting money, for which she has several times applied to Sir William Wilde, with threats of more annoyance if not given, I think it right to inform you that no threat or additional insult shall ever extort money for her from our hands. The wages of disgrace she has so loosely treated for and demanded shall never be given to her. Jane F Wilde.
>
> (139)

Mary Travers had been a medical patient and subsequent intimate of William Wilde's since 1854, when Jane Wilde was pregnant on Oscar, and Mary was 16. As Mary aged and her demands and expectations on William increased, that intimacy had turned decidedly sour, and she found herself excluded from the Wildes' home at Merrion Square. Travers then began persecuting the Wildes by publicly distributing pamphlets insulting the celebrated couple in desperate attempts to provoke both father and family into any form of meeting or confrontation, including publishing her own death announcement. When Travers discovered Jane Wilde's letter, her solicitor issued a writ against her, claiming damages of £2,000 taking particular exception to the phrase "the wages of disgrace." Rather than settling or mediating the case, Jane instructed her solicitors to enter a defense of justification, the same plea Queensbury would later use against Oscar's libel suit.

A more remarkable case has never been tried here... it was alleged that when O' Connell was on trial there was not a more general anxiety evinced to be present than has been displayed this week to hear the 'great libel case'.
The *Morning Post,* 19th December 1864 (O'Sullivan, 2016, 124)

Against the backdrop of the zenith of William Wilde's social stature and acclamation with his knighthood earlier that year, on December 12th, 1864, the case of Travers v Wilde opened in Dublin, with Wilde as a co-defendant with his wife Jane. The case, which *The Irish Times* called "extraordinary... that shook society in Dublin like a thunderclap" (132), soon mesmerized Ireland with its public accusations of sexual assault and hints of illicit affairs against a much-loved celebrity couple. Travers had a strong case to make for libel, but Mary's design was revenge and humiliation against her former intimate and his wife, to make the hidden relationship between her and William Wilde publicly "known." Under Travers' instructions, her legal counsel Isaac Butt, the nationalist MP and alleged former lover of Jane, shifted focus away from Jane's angry letter to insinuations that Wilde and Travers had been lovers of long standing with Jane's compliance, and that Jane's letter only came in the bitter aftermath of the ending of the affair and Travers' accusation of rape.

The case lasted a week, during which William Wilde's private letters would become public property, instruments of the vengeful Travers and her legal team in an unsuccessful attempt to force Wilde father into taking the stand in court, which he refused to do. This was something the parliament member Butt derided, calling it unmanly and cowardly. "Shall I call it, I must do, a cowardly plea by which he shelters behind his wife ... it was not the part of a man" (130). A claim echoed through the media and public presses. Arthur Jacob, a colleague of Wilde, publicly admonished him in the *Dublin Medical Press,* for his failure to take the stand and clear his name (132).

It was Lady Wilde who was determined to take the stand and have her day in court in which she reportedly conducted herself excellently, accustomed as she was to the glare of judicial and media publicity. Her presence in court was also a performance, that of the suffering faithful wife, although she wore widow's black while in the witness box (129). She remained unwaveringly steely throughout. *The Freeman's Journal* wrote of her "All through the trying ordeal of her examination, she displayed great self-possession" (130). She resisted Butt's attempts to force an admission that she knew her husband and Mary were lovers, instead claiming the alleged affair as a symptom of Travers' hysterical and maddened imagination.

In contrast, when Travers took the stand, on December 14th, her calamitous ability to contradict herself turned any public sympathy against her with Wilde's lawyer undermining both her case and her credibility through her letters in which she demanded financial recompense from William, as well as making allegations of Travers' laudanum addiction.

On December 19th, the jury took only 80 minutes to find in Travers' favor – but nevertheless awarded her a paltry farthing in damages for her honor. However, the burden of legal costs, which were in excess of £2,000 (about £250,000 today), fell to the Wildes. Had they settled the case, the Wildes would have saved themselves money, financial difficulties, and great personal embarrassment. William Wilde's biographer T. G. Wilson claims that William never recovered from this "terrible blow" (Hanberry, 2011, 147). Shakespeare's Hamlet warns, "When sorrows come, they come not single spies. But in battalions!" This was the case for the Wilde family. In 1867, their only daughter, Oscar's treasured sister, Isola, died of "a sudden effusion on the brain" (Ellman, 1988, 25). The 12-year-old Oscar never fully recovered from losing his sister despite his mother's declaration to "live for my sons.. they are as fine a pair of boys as one could desire" (O'Sullivan, 2016, 138). When Oscar died in utter personal and financial bankruptcy in 1900, an envelope drawn in 1867 by the then 12-year-old Oscar containing a lock of "my Isola's hair" was found among his few meager possessions (138).

William's two daughters from before his marriage, Emily 24 and Mary 22, died tragically, four years later in 1871, their dresses catching fire at a party. This series of events could only have pushed William into further decline. John B. Yeats, writing of the incident to his son, correctly observed that because of the girls' illegitimacy, "there is a tragedy all the more intense, because it has to be buried in silence. It was not allowed to give sorrow words" (O'Sullivan, 2016, 150). For it was not only the silence of death, but the silent burials of the result of past sexual misadventures, his publicly unrecognized children and his grief.

Back in 1848, against the backdrop of the Irish Famine, a group of Irish nationalists, The Young Irelanders, planned a rebellion against the British Government, which, with the suspension of *habeas corpus* by Westminster on July 22th, 1848, led to the mass arrests of its leaders and a raiding of its newspaper *The Nation*. On July 29th, the then Jane Elgee, later to be mother of Oscar Wilde, wrote the paper's editorial *Jacta Alea Est* – The Die is Cast, a call to arms "of the most warlike kind: 'Now, indeed, were the men of Ireland cowards if this moment for retribution, combat, and victory were to pass by unemployed'" (Hanberry, 2011, 147). The British Government responded immediately in appropriating any editions of the paper and suppressing it. Although in jail at the time, one of the leaders, Charles Gavan Duffy, was tried for treason and sedition with *jacta alea est est*, cited as evidence. Jane was determined to accept responsibility for her article, but Duffy refused to let her appear in the witness box. She tried to influence proceedings by going in person to see the solicitor general – "I denounced myself as author" (O'Sullivan, 2016, 54). Isaac Butt, then Duffy's defense barrister, argued *jacta alea est est*, as "penned by one of the fair sex – not, perhaps, a very formidable opponent to the whole military power of Great Britain" (55). Through the determining desire of Oscar's mother to stand trial, to take the stand, to defend her beliefs, to own her sedition and its consequences was born the legend of Jane as the nationalist poet, ready to make a stand and take the stand, an Irish martyr, living up to her pen name, Speranza (hope). It is also important to note that through this denunciation of herself as an author, she adds a hint of transgression to being a writer.

A father who refused to face his accuser, and his past, and sent his wife to stand trial in his place. A wife, who in her youth, had offered to stand trial and accept responsibility for her seditious illegality. A mother, whose son in his darkest hour, faced a post-libel trial that promised only absolute humiliation, public ruin, bankruptcy, and loss of marriage and family. This is the family story that constituted Oscar Wilde family *até*, the curse of the gods, the delusion or blindness that made him behave irrationally. Having propelled herself into the national bosom, she pushed her husband to his own tragic downfall in her desire to take the stand. Jane sealed her son's tragic fate and with her demanding phrase that functioned as an ultimatum, desired that if Oscar would stand trial and even go to prison, she would always love him, but if he would leave, she would never speak to him again (Ellman, 1988, 468). And so what *The Illustrated Police News* called "the most gruesome tragedy of the nineteenth century" (Goodman, 1988, 78) began with nothing of the family past being remembered, only for history to repeat itself. The newspapers wish that "the best thing for everybody now is to forget Wilde … let him go into silence and be heard of no more" (79). Once again, a father disappears into ignominy and again two young boys are left without a father.

One of Oscar Wilde's two sons was Vyvyan, who received his mother's final words a few days before she died in a note:

> Try not to be hard on your father. Remember that he is your father and he loves you. All his troubles arose from a hatred of a son for his father, and whatever he has done, he has suffered bitterly for.
>
> (O'Sullivan, 2016, 432)

Constance Wilde had taken her sons to Europe, and in order to avoid shame, social ostracism, and burdensome debt, changed their name to Holland. Perhaps, Oscar's wife was hoping to terminate the familial legacy of the name Wilde. Yet, Vyvyan could only make his peace with his father not by erasing his father's legacy but rather by acknowledging his name and instantiating it for himself, publishing in 1954, at the age of 67, the book *Son of Oscar Wilde*. This is a book whose public response gave Vyvyan "a new aspect of my father's final years" as well as gathering messages, letters, and testimonies from witnesses from his father's life that allowed him an appeasing of the tumultuous family history. Vyvyan spent the remainder of his life reclaiming his name, successfully emerging from Vyvyan's own bankruptcy only through restoring his father's literary estate and reinstating the name Wilde.

Cyril, Oscar's other son, was not so fortunate. Seventeen months older than Vyvyan, he bore the weight of his father's tragedy and ruination more than his brother, writing to him about it in 1915:

'I was nine years old when I saw the first placard. You were there too, but you did not see it. It was in Baker Street. I asked what it meant, and I received an evasive answer. I never rested until I found out.' His opportunity for doing so soon arose. He went to stay with cousins of my mother's in Ireland, where it was intended that I should follow him later. While he was there, he read the newspapers left lying about and realized that something was desperately wrong. He was terribly distressed, and the hackneyed expression 'he never smiled again' was for him almost true.

(Holland, 1999, 60–61)

Cyril's childhood curiosity had given him too much information, information he could neither understand nor handle, or more importantly, share with anyone. In June 1914, he wrote from India to Vyvyan explaining that since 1900:

When I returned to England in 1898, I naturally realized our position more fully. Gradually, I became obsessed with what had been lost. By 1900, [the year Oscar died] it had become my settled object in life... All these years *my great incentive has been to wipe that stain away; to retrieve, if may be, by some action of mine, a name no longer honored in the land. The more I thought of this, the more convinced I became that, first and foremost, I must be a man."*

(Holland, 1999, 140; emphasis added)

Cyril, obsessed with what had been lost, determined to wipe that stain away, "to retrieve a name" he had to be a man, a man not like his father. He allowed himself "no cry of decadent artist, of effeminate aesthete, of weak-kneed degenerate" (140). He would be like neither his father nor grandfather, but a man as only British masculine culture dictates, indeed allows, a soldier, a real man:

For that I have labored; for that I have toiled. As I roughed it month after month ... over difficult country and in dangerous times, when I was weary and ill with dysentery and alone in a strange and barbarous land.

(140)

Thus, this son of Oscar Wilde and grandson of Speranza and William would take a stand against them all and fight not against, but for King and Country, championing the very Imperialism his forebears and, especially, his grandmother, Speranza had rallied and railed against. This was Cyril's "fate," "purpose," and "despair" to be "no *wild, passionate, irresponsible hero. I live by thought, not by emotion. I ask nothing better than to end in honorable battle for my King and Country*" (140). This wished-for end of Cyril's was granted to him in being shot by a German sniper on May 9th, 1915 on World War I's western front. His grave is marked by the surname Holland, with no mention of either his father or his family name. He died un-Wilde (Figure 7.1).

Figure 7.1 Captain C. Holland's grave (photos by the author)

We often reconstruct our own past in this manner; in fact, whenever we join some phenomena of the present with analogous phenomena of the past, for the purpose of creating a conceptual or general idea ... we ipso facto reconstruct the past and revise our previous judgements in the light of later acquired knowledge.

(Cyril Holland, quoted in Holland, 1999, 143)

Vyvyan, author of *Son of Oscar Wilde*, noted that, "to this day, (1954), in the *Radley School Register*, which is a list, published periodically, of all the boys who have been educated at Radley, my brother's is the only name against which the words "son of-" are still omitted." Brother's name is the only name against which the words "son of-" are still omitted (Holland, 1999, 141). It is a curse to carry a family legacy, the *até*, and a fatal curse to deny it.

Post-Script

Merlin Holland, Vyvyan's only son, had himself only one son, Lucian, who at 21 years of age studied classics at Magdalen, Oxford, where Wilde had himself been the brilliant classics scholarship winner. When Lucian was given a room at 71 High Street, where his great-grandfather Oscar Wilde had lived for a term, Merlin thought that the similarities between his own grandfather and his son were getting out of hand. "I said to Lucian at the time, 'I don't give a damn about your sexuality, but for goodness's sake keep out of the courts.' The coincidences had gone far enough" (Guardian, 2000). But of course, psychoanalysis is always suspicious of coincidences. We attend to "coincidence" as a word often used when one cannot see, or refuses to recognize, deeper unconscious forces at work within our desires, our dreams, and our lives. The unconscious propels singular destinies for ourselves, delineated through familial shadows following the fault lines of intergenerational trauma, memorialized in repetition. Strange coincidences are never strange nor coincidental, but familiar uncanny repetitions of a lost or denied past. They may often be "hardly considered" but are pivotal for the unique considerations a psychoanalysis proffers and helps someone to say that repetition has "gone far enough." In Oscar's own words, "I need hardly tell you that in families of high position strange coincidences are not supposed to occur. They are hardly considered the thing" (Wilde, 1994, 414).

It has been repeatedly intimated that Merlin Holland will reclaim the family name Wilde for himself and his son, Lucian. "I do think about it," he said,

> but if I did it, it would have to be not just for Oscar, but for his father and mother, too, for the whole family. It was an extraordinary family before he came along, so if I put the family name back on the map for the right reasons, then it's all right. ...I am one of them. I may not have done what Oscar did or his parents, but I'm still a Wilde.
>
> (Owens, 1998)

Notes

1 Antigone is Greek: *anti* "opposite, in place of" and *gone* "womb, childbirth, generation" from *gignesthai* "to be born" related to genos "race, birth, descent" from gene "give birth, beget" with derivatives referring to procreation and familial and tribal groups. See also Rokem (2016).
2 See Markel (2020).
3 http://www.theguardian.com/books/2003/may/07/top10s.oscar.wilde

Bibliography

Burke, E. (1790). *Reflections on the Revolution in France*, London: Penguin.
De Vere White, T. (1967). *The Parents of Oscar Wilde*, London: Hodder and Stoughton.
Ellmann, R. (1988). *Oscar Wilde*, New York: Vintage Books: Random House.
Freud, S. (2001a). "The Psychopathology of Everyday Life," in *The Standard Edition of the Complete Works of Sigmund Freud, Volume 6*, trans. and ed. J. Strachey, London: Vintage.
Freud, S. (2001b). "Creative Writers and Day-Dreaming," in *The Standard Edition of the Complete Works of Sigmund Freud, Volume 9*, trans. J. Strachey, London: Vintage.
Freud, S. (2001c). "The Interpretation of Dreams," in *The Standard Edition of the Complete Works of Sigmund Freud, Vols 4 and 5 9*, trans. and trans. J. Strachey, London: Vintage.
Freud, S. (2001d). "Remembering, Repeating and Working-Through," in *The Standard Edition of the Complete Works of Sigmund Freud, Volume 12*, trans. and trans. J. Strachey, London: Vintage.
Freud, S. (2001e). "The Uncanny," in *The Standard Edition of the Complete Works of Sigmund Freud, Volume 17*, trans. and trans. J. Strachey, London: Vintage.
Gay, Peter. (1988). *Freud: A Life for Our Time*, London: J. M. Dent.
Goodman, J. (1988). *The Oscar Wilde File*, London: W. H. Allen.

Guardian (2000). "The Importance of Being Merlin." *Guardian*, 24 Nov. https://www.theguardian.com/books/2000/nov/24/classics.oscarwilde.

Hanberry, G. (2011). *More Lives Than One: The Remarkable Wilde Family through The Generations*, Dublin: The Collins Press.

Holland, M. (2003). *The Real Trial of Oscar Wilde*, New York: Harper Collins.

Holland, V. (1999). *Son of Oscar Wilde*, London: Robinson Publishing.

Jones, E. (1961). *The Life and Work of Sigmund Freud*, New York: Basic Books.

Lacan, J. (1986). *The Seminar. Book XI. The Four Fundamental Concepts of Psychoanalysis, 1964*, trans. A. Sheridan, London: Penguin.

Markel, H. (2020). *Literatim: Essays at the Intersections of Medicine and Culture*, Oxford: Oxford University Press.

Masson, Jeffrey Moussaieff. (1985). *The Complete Letters of Sigmund Freud to Wilhelm Fliess 1887–1904*, Cambridge: Harvard University Press.

Mayer, S. (2010). "When Critics Disagree, the Artist Survives: Oscar Wilde, An All-Time Favourite of the Viennese Stage in the Twentieth Century," in *The Reception of Oscar Wilde in Europe* (pp.203–216), trans. S. Evangelista, London: Continuum.

McKenna, N. (2004). *The Secret Life of Oscar Wilde*, London: Arrow Books.

Morrison, T. (1997). *Beloved*, London: Vintage, Random House.

O'Neill, R. (2015). *Nommo-Sexuality: Naming Homo-Sexual Desire, A Dis-Story*. Unpublished Doctoral thesis, DCU. http://doras.dcu.ie/20780/1/PhD_Final2015_(1).pdf

O'Sullivan, E. (2016). *The Fall of the House of Wilde: Oscar Wilde and His Family*, London: Bloomsbury.

Owens, M. (1998). "On Irving Place with/Merlin Holland; The Importance of Being Honest." *New York Times*, May 28. https://www.nytimes.com/1998/05/28/garden/on-irving-place-with-merlin-holland-the-importance-of-being-honest.html?src=pm

Rokem, F. (2016). "The Ludic Logic of Tragedy." *Performance Research*, 21(4), 26–33.

Santayana, G. (1905). *The Life of Reason: The Phases of Human Progress Volume 1*, New York: C. Scribner's Sons.

Tolstoy, L. (1998), *The Project Gutenberg eBook of Anna Karenina*, trans. Constance Garnett Project Gutenberg available at www.gutenberg.org/files/1399/1399-h/1399-h.htm (last accessed March 23, 2022)

Wilde, O. (1882). "L'Envoi (Introduction) to Rose Leaf and Apple Leaf," in *Verses by James Rennell Rodd*, J Philadelphia: M. Stoddart & Co.

Wilde, O. (1994). *The Complete Works of Oscar Wilde*, trans. M. Holland, Glasgow: Harper-Collins.

Wilde, O. (1997). *The Project Gutenberg eBook of A Woman of No Importance*, Project Gutenberg available at www.gutenberg.org/files/854/854-h/854-h.htm (last accessed 24/3/22)

Wilde, O. (2000). *The Complete Letters of Oscar Wilde*, trans. M. Holland and Rupert Hart-Davis, London: Fourth Estate.

Chapter 8

Does the Anthropology of Kinship Talk about Sex?

Monique David-Ménard
Translated by David Maruzzella
Translation edited by Manya Steinkoler and
Patricia Gherovici

For some time, I had intended to title this essay, "What Anthropology Teaches Psychoanalysis about Filiation." I had hoped that anthropologists, who have described multiple forms of filiation, would provide a way out of the psychoanalytic framework. Psychoanalysis is well known for its articulation of filiation and sexuality wherein the paternal function allows two distinct phenomena to converge: the limiting of the omnipotence of infantile desires and the generational order. The father's desire separates the infant not from the mother but from the omnipotent wish that makes the child, male or female, cling to the maternal. The father would then introduce both girls and boys to the first loss of jouissance that would allow the child, in a second moment, to desire other "objects" and tolerate the fact that what they desire in other people is marked by inadequacy. Queer and feminist critiques of this unidirectional framework have long overlapped with the clinical insight that this "symbolic castration" is not the only way for a child of either sex to abandon this quest for omnipotence.

There are other experiences of the incompleteness of sexual desire. The Oedipal is not the only experience of heterosexuality. Moreover, sexual difference need not be the exclusive form taken by the experience of sameness and otherness in the formation of sexual life.

By modifying the title of my essay, I would like to make use of the disappointment I experienced reading several anthropological texts that linked sexual practices to filiation. To put it provocatively, I would say that it is hardly ever a question of—in the texts I have in mind—what we call in psychoanalysis, "sexualities." Perhaps I expected too much from anthropology. Perhaps anthropology even neglects the very field of sexualities that it nevertheless puts into play. Let's call "sexualities" the experience [*expérience*] and the trials and tribulations [*épreuve*] (both of these French terms translate the German *Erlebnis*) of pleasures, unpleasures, and anxiety that produce human singularities. Such a definition is not, of course, without its presuppositions: it requires that we isolate, at least relatively, subjects—not in their individuality (since desires are formed in relation to other desires and in specific contexts)—but in their singularity. What makes human beings so different from one another is a result of the way these first trials and tribulations [*épreuves*], which are marked from

DOI: 10.4324/9781003284888-11

the start by inadequacy, are dealt with and experienced [*traversent*]. That this inadequacy is also called a confrontation with prohibitions is no doubt precise, but the problematic of prohibitions (of incest and murder) has been essential to the classical Oedipal schema and its "paternal solution," to use Michel Tort's (2007) expression. Therefore, in order to think about the way in which someone distances themselves from a limitless jouissance, I prefer the term inadequation, i.e. the inadequation between every object that is actually encountered and the sexual desire that aims at it. This definition of the sexual references the psychoanalytic clinic from the outset, since what is repeated in the form of symptoms can lead someone to address their hope for jouissance and the end of their suffering to a total stranger (i.e. the analyst). The latter are precisely the failures experienced in the various domains of social life, love, and in the confrontation with death.

By "framing" sexuality in this way, I do not presume to know whether it is a mythical story continuous with only one of the forms of subjectivation that have existed in human societies, or whether it is an eternal truth. On this point, anthropology moves in the same direction as the Foucauldian critique, even if it does so for different reasons. To isolate sexuality by boiling it down to the truth of the subject and its relation to sexual jouissance is perhaps only one narrative among others, but it is in no way a fully constituted science of the vicissitudes of sexuality. The practice of psychoanalysis is indissociable from the deployment of sexuality [*dispositif de sexualité*]. Be that as it may, this discursive practice has some descriptive relevance, at least for the so-called Western societies, where subjects both believe in their own free will and come to see themselves, in experiences of repetition, as constituted by relations of pleasure, unpleasure, and anxiety whose processes they fail to master either by way of knowledge or by way of actions, but which nonetheless shape their existence.

My inquiry thus consists in determining whether or not anthropology addresses the question of sexuality or whether it ignores it, and how it does so. I will take up three examples: Françoise Héritier's *Masculin/Féminin: La pensée de la différence* (1996), Daniel Delanoë's *Sexe, croyances et ménopause* (2006), and finally, Maurice Godelier's *Metamorphoses de la parenté* (2004). An attentive examination of these works will allow me to establish the following theses: (1) The anthropology of kinship almost never touches on the question of sexuality in the sense defined above (I will elucidate this "almost" later in the essay). (2) However, its choice of subject matter, such as menopause, makes the indeterminacy of the feminine appear in anthropology. As anthropologists often highlight, it is through these limits encountered in the construction of an object, in this case menopause, that the specificity of this object is known: menopause is a figure of feminine unclassifiability in a theory of gender. The fact of taking into account this feminine unclassifiability prevents the inscription of sexualities within a gender dichotomy. In this way, we can bring psychoanalysis and anthropology together. (3) Finally, sexual desires as such are invoked by anthropological research when it posits a direct link between the reproduction of social relations and the modes of jouissance of its agents. If the rules of kinship do not suffice by themselves to define the characteristics of a society, it is because these rules are tightly woven into the reproduction of politico-religious relations. In turn, an interplay with norms is established where sexuality is at stake. For example, when Maurice Godelier explains "how sex becomes gender," he hardly distinguishes between gender and sexuality; however, his analysis presupposes this distinction. On the one hand, the reproduction of social relations enlists the subject's jouissance in order to establish and perpetuate itself by means other than kinship alone. On the other hand, and at the same time, sexualities have to be defined in a singular struggle with the norms that impose in advance the sacrifice of sexuality. Sexuality must therefore exist in order to be the terrain of these struggles.

"Sexual-Life-and-Procreation": The Inseparables

In *Masculin/Féminin*, Françoise Héritier rarely uses the term "sexuality," and when she does, it is used in a less specific way than the one I have just discussed. For example, in her detailed analysis of the "sacrifices of puberty" that a young girl's father must carry out among the Samo people, Héritier (1996, 113) writes that "it is a girl's right to have her parents perform in due time the rituals that will permit her to enter into sexual life and procreation." The rituals that the girl's parents carry out require them to abstain from sexual relations during the important and dangerous moment when the girl becomes an adult. It would be dangerous for the entire society and for the cosmic order if a mother or grandmother were to give birth at the moment when the young girl enters into "sexual life and procreation." Furthermore, the young girl, who remains secluded during puberty and marriage ceremonies, is not allowed to see her father, the one whose sexual power engendered her and whose erasure will allow her to be a woman (Héritier, 1996, 116). Sexual practices are always linked with the necessity of respecting the order of generations. It is because the risk of sterility, drought, devastating rain, or ancestral retaliation must be averted during this critical period that the parents must make way for the sexual and procreative life of their daughter.

Significantly, sexual desires are not mentioned as soon as it becomes a question of entering "sexual life." They are nevertheless present if we read between the lines, since catastrophes in the universe as well as in procreation are attributed to failing to respect these rules. It must indeed be that someone transgressed. Young girls have rights but they also have obligations: a girl "must not do anything" "as long as she has not bled." In the Samo, Ashanti, Bobo, Ojibwa, and Muria, "violating this rule is either punished socially with death, expulsion, various penalties, or mystically, for having 'cut ties with the preceding generation' with this offense to ancestors" (Héritier, 1996, 112). We are also able to infer that sexual relations between women exist, since they have led to catastrophes. It is often after the fact that a violation of social rules is inferred, sometimes even against the opinion of the individuals in question. "Women's masturbation, since the beginning of time, has given birth to monsters, according to the Navajo. The Ojibwa people, as well, explain hydrocephalus in young children brought into the world by two married women, an aunt and her niece, by the supposed fact of sexual relations between the two women prior to their marriage" (Héritier, 1996, 127).

Not isolating sexual desires is, in the first instance, a methodological decision on the part of Héritier. This is the case for all anthropologists: it is a matter of not importing a Western conception of subjects of desire into the description of a given society. But in Héritier's case specifically, throughout her examination of sexual practices, what counts more than the subjects involved are the bodily substances. These must be put in relation with, or excluded from, mixtures[1]: blood, sperm, bone, and various fluids that must circulate according to rules in order to establish a viable lineage. For example, in the Nyakyusa, "the young bride brings to her mother a fowl and the millet ears that she rubbed with her hands, with which she had just cleaned the sex of her husband after having had intercourse with him... By this symbolic consumption of the body of the son-in-law, the parents become, like the bride herself, one and the same flesh as her husband. Their blood becomes mutually tolerant. She says to her mother, 'I cleaned the sex of my husband, I have grown up'" (Héritier, 1996, 123). The creation of a new mixture of substances runs the risk of giving the mother diarrhea, an outcome that would mark the refusal of it. In the same way, in what we would call adultery, what is important is that the mix of substances is rejected and is signaled by diarrhea in the husband: "a way of evacuating the harmful contact" between bloods that must not come in contact in the same womb. Héritier is careful to clarify that in this case, "the danger indeed comes from the encounter with the semen, thus with the blood, and not with the adulterer himself" (Héritier, 1996, 124). The desires of the subjects are not primary in this analysis.

The Conception of Thought in "The Thought of Difference"

Throughout her structural study of the permitted and prohibited mixtures of bodily fluids, the question for Héritier is not only to not isolate the subject's sexuality, but also to conceive of society as a system of ideas: "Each society has a particular idea of what is considered human and what is not; it constructs an order of things in the limits within which social life exists" (Héritier, 1996, 124). This system of ideas makes use of the substances active in procreation, that is, makes use of bodies for reasons that are intellectual: "since it is the first place for the observation of sense data, and because for every complex problem, the solutions always rely on explanations whose reasoning in turn leads to more and more simple facts until these explanations run up against elementary evidence" (Héritier, 1996, 234).

Here, we recognize the principle of structural anthropology: the so-called primitive thought is classificatory and structural by way of the systems it establishes between sense data whose relations of compatibility and substitution matter more than their isolated perceptible and sensorial content. This logic of qualities was formulated by Aristotle in terms of oppositions such as hot and cold, dry and wet, active and passive, heavy and light (Héritier, 1996, 202). Héritier shows that this logic is linked to the rules that structure the relations of same and other in the incest prohibition, which allows for the positive institution of sexuality and kinship. Lévi-Strauss showed that the so-called primitive thought is actually just as rational as Western reason. It is even more rational than the latter, which deludes itself by privileging history as the supposed explanation of events: there is no history without the establishment of a chronology. Furthermore, chronology is one mode of coding among others, and it does not make the way events unfold in time any more intelligible. History as a chronology of events is our myth. In this famous claim from *The Savage Mind* (1962), Lévi-Strauss unified human thought in all of its apparently diverse forms. But it was not only historical and classificatory thoughts that were unified. Every mode of thought risks being reduced to a matter of cognition as its norm and aim.[2]

What differentiates Hériter from Lévi-Strauss is that among the elementary sense data that structure kinship and society, there is only one that has political importance: if the original material of the symbolic is the body, "I will claim that the reason for this is perhaps a characteristic anchored in the female body (and which is not "its inability to produce sperm"). What is valorized in man, from the man's side, is that he can make his blood flow, risk his life, take the life of others, by way of an arbitrary free decision; woman 'sees' blood flow outside of her body (one says in French colloquially 'to see' to mean 'to have one's period') and that she gives life (and sometimes dies in doing so) without necessarily wanting to or being able to avoid it" (Héritier, 1996, 235).

By reading these well-known texts, my objective is not to determine up until what point the logic of bodily humors as materials of kinship confirms the structuralist view, nor to what extent this logic returns us to a theory of signification that would not be strictly structuralist. I am rather seeking to determine when and how anthropology encounters the question of sexuality as difference without essence in the philosophical sense: if structural anthropology overlooks sexualities in the psychoanalytic sense, this is not only, as I first maintained, because the approach to the societies being studied must not begin from a conception of the subject of desire proper to Westerners (to which researchers often belong), but it is also because the structuralist conception of thought privileges what is called cognition. To think is to organize elementary sense data and evidence by way of a structured system. That structure, made explicit in the logic of knowledge, or implicit in the practice of kinship, does not prevent what we call here "thought" from being homogeneous.[3] We are here defining all thought by the structural correlation established between the sensible and the intelligible. Now precisely, sexualities in the psychoanalytic sense require a conception of thought that leaves behind the presuppositions of intellectualism: cognition is neither the aim nor the model of all thought, explicit or symbolic. Neither drives nor fantasies are conceived of according to a cognitivist conception, that is to say an intellectualist conception of thought.[4]

Consequently, there is no self-evident sense data that thought would collect and that would be the foundation of the concept of sexual difference. The subtitle of Héritier's book is *The Thought of Difference*. But what is called difference in the anthropology of kinship is conceptually distinct from what psychoanalysis calls difference. Indeed, for the latter, the terms "feminine" and "masculine" are not separate because their role in procreation is not sufficient to define the relation that we are positing. Each pole of this relation seeks its own definition with respect to the other without finding it in a determination that would be fixed or essential. The materials that attempt to give a determination to the feminine and masculine are all borrowed: they are taken from the determinations of gender in each society, from the partition of powers and from all the other activities, uses, experiences, and sensations of desiring beings. It is surprising that in the social imaginary of psychoanalysis, we have not held onto Freud's (1955) precise formulation of 1920: psychoanalysis has no a priori notion of masculine and feminine and no privileged expertise in determining it. Psychoanalysis takes these notions such as they are presented once an analytic treatment begins and puts them to work. Furthermore, as Lacan and the Lacanians who followed him clarified, what we call sexual difference provokes a crisis in the fixed logic of difference presupposed in the relation between separate terms. It is on this point that all of the authors, philosophers, and psychoanalysts that have treated it between the years 1970 and 2000 are for once in agreement. The privilege of visible differences between men and women nourishes, among other things, the fantasmatic constructions of the difference between masculine and feminine. The visible is one of the scenes of the drive's scopic montage. It is not an elementary bit of sense data whose perception and cognition would naturally form the basis for constructing kinship. Having or not having a penis, even when transformed into a symbolic phallus, does not truly stabilize the "question" of sexual difference. We can indeed then catch sight of how anthropology rejoins psychoanalysis: it shows the extreme diversity of social content, mythical and religious rituals to which each society has recourse in order to construct "theories" about sexual life and procreation. But in the expression "sexual life and procreation," the roles in procreation seem, as they do in the works of Héritier, to establish a fixed point, a unified dimension. While if "sexual difference" is an issue that exceeds the roles of mother, father, brother, sister, or parent, which are sites among others from which we can glean materials for constructing an idea of this differentiation, then nothing forces us to make the correlation between sexuality and procreation the exclusive guiding thread in fantasy and in the experiences of pleasure, unpleasure, and anxiety by which each subject is defined sexually.

This difference without essence borrows content from the available gender distinctions, and establishes a relation between poles relative to one another. That these poles are relative from a logical point of view is the way to conceptualize the fact that in the experience of the sexual, we always address ourselves to interlocutors that are at once real and fantasmatic. Our desires do not seek to know these others, but to give them a form, a form that would guarantee our jouissance.

Menopause, an Unclassifiable "Reality"

This leads me to my second point: the more the relations described by sociology or anthropology bear the mark of an ambiguity with respect to the organization of genders as separated (which is the social rule), the more sexuality (which deploys determinations without essence but not without reality in the register of fantasy and the vicissitudes of the drives) will proliferate in studies in which sexuality is nevertheless overlooked at the level of methodology. It is, however, true that the objects that anthropology studies are correlated with methodological decisions. In his book *Sexe, croyances et ménopause*, Daniel Delanoë ups the ante by multiplying the disciplines studying menopause,[5] constructing his object at the same time as he deconstructs it. The "hard kernel" of the phenomenon is weak: women, at the moment when their ovarian cycles regulating their fertility stop, often suffer from hot flashes and, for a certain percentage of them, there is a risk of bone density loss due to hormonal changes. These modern medical facts are not enough—far from it—to make of menopause an established scientific entity as the bourgeois society of the nineteenth century supposed: "It is moreover in this society, in the 19th century, that medicine created the term menopause, subsuming under a single stigmatizing notion the end of menstruation and fertility, physical and mental illnesses and the loss of status" (Delanoë, 2006, 197).

Epistemologically, menopause is then a myth of the era of scientific medicine. Delanoë shows how the economic interests of the pharmaceutical industry contributed to forging this myth at the time of the discovery of hormonal treatments supposed to counteract the disappearance of "femininity." This modern myth is every bit as good as the myths that ensure male domination in most societies. In this sense, Delanoë's problematic is inscribed in the wake of Françoise Héritier's work. Around humors and blood,[6] societies construct a distribution of genders that designate the place of individuals, and, in particular, their place in the succession of generations and in the order of the cosmos. These myths, which leave no system of kinship and power unscathed, falter or stutter as soon as it is a question of determining whether a menopausal woman remains a woman, or becomes a third or fourth gender. The book itself confronts this paradox of method: in order to identify a phenomenon, we have to stabilize the criteria valid for both primitive and civilized societies:

By working on menopause, we quickly see that this term covers a set of heterogeneous biological and cultural phenomena. So much so that we do not always know what this notion entails...In order to escape this polysemy, I have defined five dimensions of menopause. First the cessation of menstruation and [second] fertility. Then the [third,] development of health and [fourth] aesthetic capital. The fifth element resides in the social value of the individual, the symbolic capital.

(Delanoë, 2006, 112)

Now, we must avoid this polysemy while at the same time respecting it in order to bring to light the manner in which both the so-called primitive societies and the so-called scientific societies confront the feminine when they encounter the transformations produced by the appearance and cessation of women's fertility.

How are we to isolate the social phenomena of "menopause"? On the one hand, menopause is a recent definition in particular cultures, and, on the other hand, even in these cultures linked to scientific medicine and the pharmaceutical industry, the phenomena of menopause contain mythical and economic elements that maintain these myths. The response consists precisely in bringing together the social treatment of the aging of women in all types of societies, scientific or not, and also by multiplying the perspectives. Delanoë examines the status of women in contemporary Morocco; in the same context, he discusses a tragic example in Bertrand Blier's 1974 film *Les Valseuses (Going Places)*. In classical Arabic, the cessation of fertility is called "the age of despair" (*Sinelyas*), which indeed explains why the majority of Moroccan women wish to get rid of it by using hormonal treatments (Delanoë, 2006, 70–71). In *Going Places*, a woman, released after a long stay in prison, commits suicide when she stops menstruating. The complexity of the status of elderly women in contemporary Japan is itself another example similar to the prohibitions and obligations surrounding access to and retreat from sexual activity for the Samo women of Burkina Faso. Finally, the history of medicine and the synthesis of the ethnological data are combined with a sociological survey in France compiled during the 2000s that shows the extreme diversity of social and psychological reactions to the cessation of menstruation and procreation. This diversity, however, does not take into account the distinction between the so-called developed societies and societies supposed to be "other."

The insistence on this diversity is however anything but disordered: Delanoë highlights the Thaïs, the Nuer, the Nas, court societies, career women of the French petite bourgeoisie, and women for whom this life stage affords them an authority confirmed both in the family and in society. The study shows, despite the fact that everywhere the cessation of menstruation and fertility bolsters the social belief in the danger of the feminine, that this is even subsumed into the maternal. There are, however, exceptions worth mentioning in order to leave essentialism behind. The examples of the Mojave in North America and that of the court societies of the eighteenth century studied by Norbert Elias offer examples of the realization of the role of women when the social and cultural uses of the feminine are dissociated from biological fertility. The book ends with an evolutionary hypothesis and a bit of humor: we know that sexual reproduction and the development of the brain have been biologically linked in human evolution. Furthermore, there is a certain evolutionary advantage to the temporary character of women's procreative functions. This made it possible for those women liberated from pregnancy to develop, even in the education of children and grandchildren, forms of intelligence that epigenetically modified their brains. This brain development is missing in men precisely because they can procreate until their death.

> This problematic situation fails the species while a physiological cessation of masculine fertility at a certain age would avoid the creation of widows and orphans subject to the greatest fragility. Perhaps masculine violence formerly sought to kill men well before the physiological age of death, like what happened in feudal society where the lord died in war long before his wife turned 50. Whatever the case may be, we can henceforth consider that this absence of the cessation of masculine fertility is a biological aberration that evolution passed over, and whose consequences become more striking with the recent augmentation of life expectancy.
>
> (Delanoë, 2006, 200)

The "Becoming-Infertile" of Women

I would like to consider for a moment a particular point in Delanoë's study: not only the diversity, often times favorable, of women's social status when they are no longer fertile, but the ambiguity, multiplied by menopause, of the feminine. It is because women who are no longer fertile become unclassifiable in terms of gender that social figures of the feminine post-menstruation accumulate paradoxes and rejoin—depending on the reader—the paradoxes of the sexual in psychoanalysis and the Deleuzian philosophy of "becomings." In fact, it is not only by the regular mention of pleasure and women's seductive powers as long as they are fertile that sexuality is present in *Sexe, croyances et ménopause*. It is also present in the series of feminine figures whose very ambiguity is deployed due to the fact that women and fertility are dissociated. Delanoë proceeds by accumulating these small differences, all ambiguous, in which a line of flight takes shape. We see this in the strange longings of Peruvian women during their *"nervios,"* which can either turn into madness or establish new social relations.[7] We also notice it in the "woman-who-helps," the one who "makes babies and makes corpses," whose extra-territoriality dwells within the village. The author lingers over this figure and describes its paradoxes in the ethnographic study of the Minot village in the Bourgogne region (Verdier, 1979). Invulnerable and inoffensive, Yvonne Verdier nicely summarizes these two qualities that allow menopausal women to enter into contact with dangerous, even mortal elements. She is invulnerable because her fertility has passed, and inoffensive because she no longer produces menstrual blood; yet, she is deemed dangerous and is the object of many precautions. This unassignability, Delanoë (2006, 91) clarifies, is inscribed nonetheless in the social relations around sex: "we bear witness to an infinite recognition of this despised woman." Let us follow the list of figures of this strange being post-fertility. She is the "woman with the heart of a man" for the Piegan Indians (Delanoë, 2006, 91; and also Héritier, 1996, 226–228) or the Breton matrons and other figures—young widows—of feudal nobility. She is better known in Western Christianity[8] as the old sorceress and she is found in the religious texts of the Abrahamic religions. She is the go-between that we find in fairy tales such as "Little Red Riding Hood" among others. These impressive figures are akin to those we find in the Bororo myth studied by Lévi-Strauss, where the grandmother produces illnesses and kills children.[9] By including these figures in his research, Delanoë (2006, 101) arrives at the myth of the ultimate seductress, who is not dependent on men, and even less so on women. In the Kabyle culture, according to Pierre Bourdieu, this figure deploys imaginary powers. She is "sterile, savage, untamed; she is the opposite of the feminine-masculine [dichotomy] of the fertile woman, who is domesticated, cultivated." No longer only the "woman-with-the-heart-of-a man," but the feminine par excellence! Delanoë confronts the paradox of these emblematic characters by asking if a third or fourth gender would have to be defined to distinguish the "like-a-man" from the hyper-feminine (Delanoë, 2006, 106).

Does the classificatory approach encounter its limit here? We will rather inscribe each of these figures, imaginary and yet real since they correspond to functional social relations, either in a psychoanalytic logic wherein we accentuate, case by case, the ambiguity of these emblematic characters, or in a Deleuzo-Guattarian perspective in which the feminine, in the series of examples, is constituted by drawing a line of flight from the "becoming-infertile."

Finally, we encounter some formulations of the feminine as the unclassifiable and the paradoxical: in 1914, Freud (1964) had compared narcissistic women to wild animals and decoded this imago as a masculine fantasy. He also made of this "refusal of the feminine" by the two sexes one of the conditions of sexuation. Monique Schneider (2004) keenly interpreted the cruelty of elderly, devouring female animals in fairytales. Lacan describes, in a more theoretical manner, the way in which the phallic function can be considered a display in place of the absence of any essence of the "sexual non-relation." Men, in fact, tend to believe more easily than women that the use of their genitals guards them against the confrontation with an anxiety-provoking difference, confronting them with their unmasterable and unassignable pleasure. In *Seminar XX: Encore*, Lacan tells us that the phallic function is struck by contingency as the direct result of the sexual "masquerade." In fact, "masquerade" belongs to the woman who plays at being "nothing" other than the object of desire for the other.[10] There is a second possible reading: if we are attentive to the remarkable series that Delanoë constructs and in which the social relations of sex and fantasies cannot be differentiated, menopause can be read in the Deleuzo-Guattarian perspective of becomings.[11] Would there be, owing to the cessation of menstruation and fertility, a "becoming-infertile" of women? A becoming is the process by which a particular reality or a specific idea is disqualified. Its prior identity (in this case, the feminine-maternal) exhausts what allows for the knotting of new relations, against nature:

> Starting from the forms one has, the subject one is, the organs one has, or the functions one fulfills, becomings is to extract particles between which one establishes the relations of movement and rest, speed and slowness that are closest to what one is becomings, and through which one becomes. This is the sense in which becomings is the process of desire. The principle of proximity of approximation is entirely particular and reintroduces no analogy whatsoever.
>
> (Deleuze and Guattari, 1987, 272)[12]

It is by the exhaustion of every identity that a new intensity is invented, forming connections that defy any essence. I am glad to find a Deleuzian series in *Sexe, croyances et ménopause*. While the author's aim is here neither philosophical nor psychoanalytic but anthropological, the work shows how critiques of sexual essentialism overlap in the diverse fields that it explores. Dissociation, which has a concrete effect on the life of women, is conceptual in the theories of the sexual guiding this critique.

Thinking through the menopausal figure allows us to move toward a consideration of diverse notions of sexuality. Delanoë distinguishes sexual life from procreation by turning again to the sociological and theological tendency that associates them:

> The venerable age might also signify an age on the basis of which it is no longer legitimate to have a sexual relationship, child-bearing or not. Many women also spoke to me of the scorn that struck only a few years ago when an aunt had a child when she was between 40 and 50 years old. Inversely, certain societies favor, indeed, prescribe a non-marital sexuality to the menopausal woman. In the Tin Dama in New Guinea, the menopausal woman physically initiates young men into love—a perilous moment since the young man might become mad and kill himself a few days later
>
> (Delanoë, 2006, 84)

It is a question in this work, not of refusing all linkages between the feminine and the maternal, but to open up feminine becomings [devenirs-féminin].

Godelier's Ventriloquism of Gender and Ventriloquism of Sexuality

If gender is the social use of biological sexual difference affirmed in a dichotomous way, then social relations of sex expose not only the differential valence of the sexes in kinship systems, but also the domination that is exercised in the production and reproduction of the economic, political, and religious powers that characterize each socius. Rather than making kinship the organizing center of the socius, Maurice Godelier shows in his work that it resides in a narrow connection between rites that initiate men and women to their powers, and the organization of their sexual jouissance. For many decades, Godelier opposed the Freudian myth of the murder of the father with what he called the "sacrifice of sexuality" that demands the reproduction of social relations. What makes of a kinship group a society endowed with unity draws on the secret arrangement of powers that mobilize jouissance, by instituting some jouissances and sacrificing others. Since I have elsewhere shown (David-Ménard, 2015, 2020), how the different moments of this thesis are constructed in Godelier's work, here I am going to concern myself with the examination of a particularly pertinent point in order to clarify how anthropology encounters sexuality. Many illuminating pages of *The Metamorphoses of Kinship* show how a set of political-religious relations are woven together to "make a society a whole." These concern the imaginary of procreation and the life of bodies:

> But above all, what matters most is the body, with all of its visible and invisible components, when it is placed (according to a determined symbolic code) at the service of the production and the reproduction of both kinship relations and the political-religious relations that encompass them and together with them make up the sites and forms of power that dominate a society at a given time.
>
> (Godelier, 2012, 312)

Relations of power are instituted via representations of kinship and are bound up with them. Organized homosexuality in the Baruya people in New Guinea, which has been extensively studied, does not only serve to establish the belief that sperm, the only active element in the creation of children, is also what produces milk in women's breasts.

> Sperm is thereby overvalued, not merely because it legitimizes the appropriation of children by the father's clan, but because it legitimizes the political-ritual supremacy of men over women, and their right to represent and to govern their society by themselves, alone. This is not the same thing as representing their clan and preserving its lands, functions and knowledge in order to transmit them to their descendants. In order to dominate, the bodies of the dominant must be disjointed from the dominated, their

substances and essence, altered. The Baruya practice of ritualized homosexuality brings about this disjunction and transmutation.

(Godelier, 2012, 310–311)

Such a capture of sexual relations and procreation by politics and religion characterizes each society. Things play out differently, for example, among the Polynesian Tonga people:

> it is the sperm of male commoners that is devalued, stripped of the power to give life, to the benefit of the spermatic breath of the Tu'i Tonga, the man-god who fertilizes all the women in his kingdom, whose importance is not denied in the aristocratic theory of procreation.

(Godelier, 2012, 311)

In this sense, politics and religion are made manifest in the life of procreating bodies, but kinship does not exhaust the social field that is shaped and totalized by the political-religious dimension. In the passage that concludes the chapter on the "Sexed Body," Godelier mentions that all of the singular interpretations of the child-bearing processes "insert a not-yet born child into three relationships": a place in the socio-cosmic order, a place "in a network of personal relations with a number of individuals who are close or distant, of both sexes and of different generations" that the child will learn to call brother, sister, father, cousins, etc., and finally, a third type of relation that constitutes the social relations of sexuality. Individuals will find themselves "placed in advance in relations of superiority (or even domination) or inferiority (or even subordination) with regard to those of the other sex" (Godelier, 2012, 313).

We find in this preceding dimension, but now in another place, the differential value of the sexes described by Héritier as well as the forms of domination mentioned by Delanoë. Delanoë assigns women, after their period of fertility, a place "apart" that is difficult to situate in the play of bodily substances: blood, bone, sperm, and feminine bodily fluids with regard to the transmission of biological, imaginary, and social life. As we have seen, this is why the woman-who-helps has a direct relation with the arrival of children and the departing of the dead whose bodies she looks after. This is also why these women bring to light the fantasmatic paradoxes of the feminine. Godelier is careful to first clarify that these fantasies are not specific to the individual, but that they are the ones that socially constitute gender.

Let us proceed to the second part of Godelier's analysis: these three types of relations produce a "two-fold metamorphosis." By this "two-fold metamorphosis," we must understand that each of the three dimensions represents the other and gets represented by the other: property relations are spoken in the language of kinship. For example, in the Yako of Africa, a society where the individual belongs both to the patrilineal line and to the matrilineal line, land is transmitted by the men in their patrilineal line, while religious functions go through the women in their matrilineal line. Material means of existence (land) and essential—ritual, for example—social functions are transformed into attributes of the relationship a person entertains with relatives.

(Godelier, 2012, 313)

This also goes for close relations where we see that the older sister will be the one to inherit the ritual function rather than the younger sister. Inversely, in a given society, kinship does not only speak of itself but of properties and the prerogatives of individuals according to their sex. Godelier calls this game of hide-and-seek or this mutual covering over of kinship, and the social and political-religious functions that have nothing to do with kinship, "two-fold metamorphosis." This is because each dimension is at play in the other: the transmission of property is spoken by the function of the sexes and the substances that intervene in the conception of children and vice versa. Calling members of the family "sister" or "father" grants them power in the access to sacrifices or to the inheritance that each acknowledges. Godelier calls this metamorphosis "sex becoming gender."

But there exists, as we have said, a third dimension that is called "ventriloquized sexuality." This concerns not only kinship and socio-political functions, that is to say, not only the cosmic order and the moral and social order, but the sexual order. What does this mean? In the concluding passage of the chapter on sexed bodies, Godelier employs the terms gender and sexuality without distinction. Godelier is often concerned gender, that is to say, social and economic roles that are in a relation of mutual concealment with the rules of kinship, as we have just seen. Often, on the contrary, he is concerned with sexuality, that is to say, the way in which each individual is not only socially a "ventriloquist's dummy which speaks on behalf of society"[13] that puts into motion the mutual concealment of these two distinct dimensions, but also a "desiring machine" that makes the experience of the sexed body the place where the ventriloquism becomes effective: it either confirms the expected sexual order or attempts to subvert it. Ventriloquism is first of all social:

This 'impersonal', as it were, and general subordination of sexuality is the starting point of a mechanism that stamps into each person's innermost subjectivity, into his or her body, the prevailing order (or orders) in society, which must be respected if the society is to reproduce itself. The machinery works through representations of the body and the person, and of the role ascribed to each of the sexes and other genders in the process that ends with the birth of a child, with life.

(Godelier, 2012, 315)

But this social logic invested in sexed bodies and that makes of the body "a source of evidence about the social and cosmic order" is also the site of an eventual subversion that can only be subjective. For example, when Godelier describes the experience of menstruation for Baruyan women, are we to consider this an issue of gender or sexuality?

> From being alienated, sexuality goes on to become an instrument of alienation. Ultimately, when a Baruya woman sees the blood running down her thighs, she can no longer object to her fate; she knows she is guilty, she feels her guilt and, consequently, feels responsible for whatever happens to her. *We now understand why sexuality is lived as something that can, at any time, challenge and subvert the order of society and the universe. And it is why it is hedged about with so many taboos.*
>
> (Godelier, 2012, 316; emphasis original)

When reading these lines, we might underline a fourth dimension. There is the cosmic order, the moral and social order, the gendered order, and also the sexual order in the Freudian sense of sexuality or the sexual in Laplanchian terms, which must be distinguished from the sexual that is considered in terms of kinship.

Godelier continues:

> In every society, representations of the body draw a sort of ring of social constraints around the individual, a metal ring that tightly encircles the person, a ring that is the very shape—paradoxically an impersonal and anonymous shape—of the individual's intimate inner subjectivity. It is in this anonymous social form of personal intimacy imposed on the individual at birth and which already organizes its encounters with others that the child will begin to experience desire for the other. Whereas the child has already been appropriated by others, by its relatives, their social group, and so on, it is spontaneously going to want to appropriate them in turn. That is when the child will discover that it cannot appropriate everyone, that some—father, mother, sister brothers, etc.—are off limits to his desire. Sexuality as a 'desiring machine' is confronted with itself as a 'talking machine', a ventriloquist's dummy, which speaks on behalf of society
>
> (Godelier, 2012, 316)[14]

We might say that this is a question of terminology: both sexuality understood as the ventriloquist's dummy which speaks on behalf of society and sexuality as a desiring machine can make use of the same term "sexuality." However, in Godelier's text, which is at once illuminating and difficult, isn't it worth distinguishing gender from sexuality? Gender inscribes social norms on the body in an intimate way; sexuality is the way sexual jouissance seeks to define a fantasmatic and effective identity for each singularity. Do these become locatable by the struggles that the desiring machine carries out via the ventriloquist's dummy that speaks as society? This distinction, which seems baroque, is decisive: is this struggle with norms exclusively political? Or does it also constitute a struggle and thus a division that concerns the desiring machine in its relation the ventriloquist's dummy?

Finally, the two-fold metamorphosis that Godelier announced is no longer only the mutual relation of kinship and economic and political-ritual functions; it is also the mutual relation of these two machines, socially gendered and desiring.

> This is the source of the fantasized figures, which necessarily emerge from our sexual condition. Here two opposing imaginary displacements and two symbolic productions occur. Here the social instantiates itself and hides, disguised in the imaginary representations of the body. Repressed desire, which suppressed, has not disappeared, buries itself in the body beyond conscious awareness, only to resurface elsewhere, in 'respectable' forms and activities. It betrays itself occasionally in a slip of the tongue, feeding as much on personal successes as on personal failures in society. The social is hidden in the imaginary representations of the body. In short, sexuality conceals itself as much as it hides the ambivalence that structures it.
>
> (Godelier, 2012, 316–317)

What better way to define the always transposed and yet distinct character of sexuality?

The Ventriloquist's Dummy Speaking on Behalf of Society and the Ventriloquist's Desiring Machine

Let's clarify the stakes of the reading that I am elaborating: the first side of the "metamorphosis" described in the text conceals kinship in property and power relations. At the same time, kinship speaks of something other than itself: properties and religious privileges. Certainly, there is a game of hide-and-seek between these two dimensions. But each remains identifiable: even if it is the transmission of lands that is spoken by the appellations father and son, or mother and daughter among the Trobriand, a patrilocal society that is matrilineal where women own the land, while the husbands use it. The fact remains in this example that one of the registers does not disappear in the other. Here, the ventriloquism is not complete. On the contrary, it seems to me that sexuality, as Godelier shows, is an experience that struggles with predetermined norms of pleasure, unpleasure, and anxiety where the child "will begin to experience desire for the other." The child encounters this "social form of personal intimacy imposed on the individual at birth, and which already organizes its encounters with others that the child will begin to experience desire for the other." Sexuality, deployed in the field of drives and fantasy, is even more unstable and difficult to distinguish from gender norms and the social relations of sex. We often justifiably reproach psychoanalysts for getting stuck in individualized sexuality without successfully determining in what way sexuality is, at the same time, social. This concerns gender, that is to say, the dominant norms of heterosexuality, but also this subtle relation by which sexuality "conceals" itself in something other than itself more radically than kinship. If there were not slips of the tongue, subjective revolts, and personal failure in society, perhaps sexuality would remain indiscernible from the materials of which I spoke of at the beginning of this essay. From the point of view of the subject's drives and fantasies, they are all borrowed.

We are not making light of the importance of the social-sexual relations nor ignoring the importance of gender trouble but naming a difficulty. As soon as we isolate sexuality, since it conceals itself in something that has nothing to do with it, what we can glean of it always runs the risk of poorly reconnecting to its social conditions of existence. It would be better to say that since sexuality is invested in what it is not, being formed by displacements and transpositions, it always appears, empirically, "to conceal itself." Inversely, in clinical work, social conditions of existence become the material of drives and fantasies, even if they are also the real conditions of the game with regard to gender norms and the struggle with social-sexual relations.

In *Les Constructions de l'universel* (2009), I claimed that the subject's fantasies that contribute to form what can seem a "purely" conceptual problematic of a philosophy always risk not being readable, not universally readable, in the form of a completed system precisely because these fantasies forged by subjects of desire are partially without "predetermined" essence, as Godelier would say.

Is this not a question of the same sexual ventriloquism that Godelier speaks of? The sexual is always invested in something other than itself, in social relations of sex, kinship, or beliefs, and in a logical problematic that seems independent of the thinker. Let us return to the example of the Baruyan woman: Godelier writes, "she knows she is a victim" all the while affirming that this experience might also be subversive. But this subversion is two-fold. On the one hand, there is a collective and/or public struggle against victimhood, and on the other, a displacement of this Baruyan woman whose jouissance and desires might follow other paths than those of a victimizing jouissance for which she was designated. For example, recently an extremely athletic woman, a runner, decided during a sporting event to not "protect" herself, to let the blood of "her" period flow. How would we distinguish between gender and sexuality in this example?

Whatever the knot that renders gender and sexualities indiscernible, ventriloquism is more totalizing in the example of menstrual blood, than in the example of the determination of kinship in the transmission of land. Early in his work, Godelier brought up the fact that his inquiry into the determination of kinship led him somewhere other than kinship. Working on a site with forest villagers responding to questions concerning their uncle, sister, brother, and so on, Godelier was able to glean the mythical origin and the political history of the struggles between lineages where the conquest of cultivated lands was at stake. However, in the Baruya or the Samo, as in our own societies, even if the transmission of properties is spoken by the appellations of kinship, one of these dimensions does not disappear into the other. When one of our parents dies, we find out, upon visiting a lawyer, that we are now the owner of whatever it may be. When one's wife dies, the husband might find out that he is no longer the owner of the apartment that was once his, since his children can claim ownership. In inheritance, however, the lines of kinship and the determination of property rights do not disappear into one another. The first level of ventriloquism is not absolute. The example of the Baruya woman (used by Godelier and taken up again by Héritier) shows the imbrication of social relations and sexuality. The Baruyan woman sees the flowing of her menstrual blood, and knows that she is the victim, since she is inscribed by way of her body in a cosmic and politico-religious order. But if there is in this experience a risk of subverting this order, is this not because of an impersonal "knowledge" that might be troubled by what she experiences, as well as by an initiative concerning the relations of pleasure that link this woman to certain members of her group and not to others? In fact, these experiences do not automatically follow the accepted social rules of alliance. Sexuality, Godelier tells us, does not speak; it is always something else that speaks in it. Are we so sure? Does the making of this hypothesis require that we import a deployment of sexuality that is only valid for monotheistic societies?

Conclusion

By giving this text the provocative title "Does the Anthropology of Kinship Talk about Sex?" my objective is not to discredit the anthropological research that Françoise Héritier, Daniel Delanoë, and Maurice Godelier make use of in order to distance themselves from current social prejudice. Héritier indeed knows that relations of desire exist between a daughter and her parents. She even gives the example that copulation for the Bush people, sexual violations (incest and adultery committed with the wife of a brother for a Samo man), zoophilia, and necrophilia are ranked by ascending order of abomination (Héritier, 1996, 126). She also knows that incestuous desires do not all have the same objects or the same internal organization. She clarifies, for example: "In sum, for the Nyakyusa people, a girl must have the consent of her father to enter into a sexual relation, and the consent of her mother to conceive" (Héritier, 1996, 118). Which desire must be surmounted in both cases so as to not "violate the impediments of kinship?" (Héritier, 1996, 126). We see the desire for jouissance in the relation to the father or of the father for his daughter since it must be erased, and we see the mother's supposed desire for destruction which is always capable of destroying the femininity of her daughter. What is profiled here by way of social sanctions are fears and fantasmatic desires, but they are binding desires, even if they are spoken as "violations brought against the impediments of kinship."

When Delanoë, in his study of menopause, clarifies that women do not think of themselves as seriously inhibited by hot flashes while their husbands are disturbed by them, and that the women then begin to doubt whether their husbands desire them, he deems this a question of sexuality. As in a hysterical symptom, the physiological component is worthless on its own, but makes an entrance into the stage of desire, that is to say, into a relation.

Psychoanalysis isolates these relations, revealing that they require a specific approach in order to be recognized in their paradoxically drive-ridden and fantasmatic reality. It is always a question of relations wherein the rules of kinship and the relationships of domination are mixed with experiences of desire. Is this so different from talking about the ventriloquism of sexuality? To say that these relations are devoid of any essence, to speak as Lacan does, of the "sexual non-relation" to clarify how we conceive of them by understanding how they exist at the limit of every logic (science of relations), outside any formalizable social function, is this any different than speaking of the ventriloquism of sexuality?

Notes

1 For other anthropologists, such as Anne-Christine Taylor (2004, 98–99), this methodological decision, which converges with Foucault's critique of "the deployment of sexuality" proper to Christian and psychoanalytic societies, is based upon Amazonian ethnology: for the Jivaro, the organizing framework of social existence is predation and its multiple variations. What we call sexuality is not isolable, nor is the difference between nature and culture, nor are persons susceptible to being defined by their desires. Predation is the concept of a relation that encompasses both affective and sexual relations.

2 Certain contemporary readers propose a renewed understanding of structure in Lévi-Strauss. Patrice Maniglier (2008) turns it into a system of transformations and not a fixed order. The aim of such a rereading is to show that a structure does not only belong to cognition, but also to action. This would make the positions of structuralism regarding the political question of gender something other than a wait-and-see position.

3 In order to leave behind the intellectualist presupposition that plagues structuralist anthropology, Philippe Descola (2014, 235–239) proposes, by way of a "conceptual reform," to return to the notion of "mode of identification" taken from Marcel Mauss. This would cover all of the correlations of structure without presupposing that all thought be cognitive.

4 Many of my works develop this point (e.g. 2014 and 2000).

5 Critical history of medicine, anthropology, and sociological surveys conducted in Tunisia and France literary analysis, myths, and tales.

6 Cf., in particular, the chapter "The Blood of the Warrior and the Blood of Women" in Héritier (1996). This chapter is excerpted and translated in Oliver and Walsh (2005, pp. 66–68).

7 "In Peru, nervios designates a psychical trouble specific to menopausal women. Nervios can degenerate into locura, a permanent state of madness. Nervios

frequently provoke an irresistible need to take walks, to go to the movies with friends, or to look for a particular kind of tea at the market or at a friend's house... the principle social function of nervios is to offer a certain autonomy to women whose husbands must tolerate the displacements" (Delanoë, 2006, 77).

8 "Beginning in the 16th century, the midwife became one of the privileged target of inquisitors" (Delanoë, 2006, 91).

9 "Taking maternity from femininity, the stench remains" (Delanoë, 2006, 101).

10 "...the sexual relationship doesn't stop not being written. Because of this, the apparent necessity of the phallic function turns out to be ere contingency. It is a mode of the contingent that the phallic function stops not being written. What submits the sexual relationship to being, for speaking beings, but the regime of the encounter is tantamount to contingency" (Lacan, 1999, 94).

11 The notion of becomings is defined on the basis of anomalies:

> ...a correspondence of relations does not add up to a becomings... Must we not lend credence to Jean Duvignaud's hypothesis that there are 'anomic' phenomena pervading societies that are not degradations of the mythic order but irreducible dynamisms drawing lines of flight and implying other forms of expression that those of myth, even if myth recapitulates them in its own terms in order to curb them?
>
> (Deleuze and Guattari, 1987, 237)

12 By taking the examples of "becomings," Deleuze and Guattari enter into a debate with psychoanalysts and anthropologists (Marcel Detienne):

> When the man of war disguises himself as a woman, flees disguised as a girl, hides as a girl, it is not a shameful transitory incident in his life. To hide, to camouflage oneself, is a warrior function, and the line of flight attracts the enemy, transverses something and puts what it traverses to flight; the warrior arises in the infinity of a line of flight. Although the femininity of the man of war is not accidental, it should not be thought of as structural, or regulated by a correspondence of relations... It is just as difficult to see how the general bisexuality, or even homosexuality, of military societies could explain this phenomenon, which is more initiative than it is structural, representing instead an essential anomie of the man of war.
>
> (Deleuze and Guattari, 1987, 278)

13 TN: The published translation of Godelier's book uses the expression "ventriloquist's dummy which speaks on behalf of society" to translate the French *machine ventriloque de la société*, literally "a ventriloquist machine of society." I have maintained the longer English translation chosen by Nora Scott in her award-winning translation. However, David-Ménard is explicitly referencing the machinic element when introducing the Deleuzian notion of a desiring machine alongside the ventriloquist machine. Godelier too is clearly making reference to this machinic element, which is unfortunately not captured in the existing English translation.

14 We can note that in order to describe the knot of the social and the sexual, Deleuze and Guattari are invoked here by the term "desiring machine."

Bibliography

David-Ménard, M. (2000). *Tout le plaisir est pour moi*, Paris: Hachette-Littératures.

David-Ménard, M. (2009). *Les constructions de l'universe. Psychanalyse, Philosophie*, Paris: PUF (Quadrige).

David-Ménard, M. (2014). *Corps et langage en psychanalyse*, Paris: Campagne Première.

David-Ménard, M. (2015). "En écoutant, en lisant Maurice Godelier," in *Parentalités et Filiation*, Introd. Patrick Avrane, Paris: Éditions Campagne Première.

David-Ménard, M. (2020). *La Vie sociale des choses. L'animisme et les objets*, Lormont, éditions Le BORD DE L'EAU.

Delanoë, D. (2006). *Sexe, croyances et menopause*, Paris: Hachette-Littératures.

Deleuze, G. and Felix Guattari (1987). *A Thousand Plateaus*, trans. B. Massumi, Minneapolis: Minnesota UP.

Descola, P. (2014). *La Composition des mondes. Entretiens avec Pierre Charbonnier*, Paris: Flammarion.

Freud, S. (1955). "The Psychogenesis of a Case of Homosexuality in a Woman," in *The Standard Edition of the Complete Psychological Works of Sigmund Freud, Vol. 18*, trans. and ed. J. Strachey, London: Hogarth Press.

Freud, S. (1964). "On Narcissism: An Introduction," in *The Standard Edition of the Complete Psychological Works of Sigmund Freud, Vol. 15*, trans. and ed. J. Strachey, London: Hogarth Press.

Godelier, M. (2012). *The Metamorphoses of Kinship*, trans. N. Scott, London and New York: Verso.

Héritier, F. (1996). *Masculin, Féminin: La Pensée de la difference*, Paris: Odile Jacob.

Lacan, J. (1999). *Seminar XX: Encore*, trans. B. Fink, New York: W. W. Norton.

Maniglier, P. (2008). "La Condition symbolique." *Philosophie*, 98 (June), 37–53.

Oliver, Kelly and Lisa Walsh (eds) (2005). *Contemporary French Feminism*, Oxford: Oxford University Press.

Schneider, Monique (2004). *Le Paradigme féminin*, Paris: Aubier-Flammarion.

Taylor, A.-C. (2004). "Corps, sexe et parenté. Une perspective amazonienne," in *Ce que le genre fait aux personnes*, ed. I. Théry and P. Bonnemère, Paris: CNRS/EHESS Éditions.

Tort, M. (2007). *La fin du dogme paternel*, Paris: Flammarion.

Verdier, Y. (1979). *Façons de dire, façons de faire: La laveuse, la couturière, la cuisinière*, Paris: Gallimard.

Chapter 9

From Fundamentalism to Forgiveness

Sex/Gender beyond Determinism or Volunteerism

Kelly Oliver

From Simone de Beauvoir's claim that one is not born a woman but becomes one, to Judith Butler's theory of gender as performance, feminists have celebrated the fluidity of gender and gender norms. The very notion of gender is itself an attempt to dislodge sexual identity from biological sex. The idea is that if women are not bound to femininity or even femaleness through biology, then there is hope for alternative ways of taking up womanhood beyond oppressive stereotypes and patriarchal expectations. Gender freedom as the freedom from biological determinism has, however, led to sex/gender volunteerism, which discounts the body and material existence entirely. The notion of identity as performance, when taken to its extreme, can lead to an unrealistic gender volunteerism that discounts the role not only of the materiality of the body, but also of social norms and historical context in the constitution of gender. Just as we cannot separate bodies and social norms (insofar as bodies are always interpreted through social norms), we also cannot and do not invent ourselves wholesale.

As psychoanalysis teaches us, our conscious desires and fears are linked to unconscious desires and fears that are not immediately obvious. Thus, we must look beyond what we think we want to understand about where our desires come from and why we fear what we do. Why do we love some and hate others? For psychoanalysis, our affects are not givens inaccessible to interpretation or analysis. To the contrary, our affects and intense libidinal investments are precisely the loci of our most intractable desires and fears. Indeed, those places where we feel the most confident and secure (or the most insecure and vulnerable) in our own identities, desires, and fears are precisely the places in need of the deepest analytic excavation.

Within contemporary culture, social media exacerbates the notion that affects need no interpretation or analysis. Social media fuels the flames of extremes and outrage that stand in for authenticity and truth. Social media makes it possible for people to take on virtual identities as whatever they like and for whatever purpose they like, which nourishes overly simplistic notions of identity as performance. At the same time, however, debates over the status of trans women as "real" women highlight the desire for stable and oppositional gender

DOI: 10.4324/9781003284888-12

categories, on both sides of the debate (see Bettcher, 2014). As the history of feminism shows, the category of woman is not only contested but also evolves. In addition, the history of feminism's relationship to the category "woman" makes evident the political necessity of simultaneously keeping the category as open and inclusive as possible, while also maintaining its power as a political tool to fight against gender oppression. Identity politics is both necessary and contested, and always complicated by the histories of identity categories, whether of race, ethnicity, or gender and sexuality. Thus, in seeking to address the complexities of sex/gender identity, psychoanalysis cannot appeal to transhistorical categories or structures—including the unconscious—but, rather, must also account for evolving social and historical contexts.

The psychoanalytic notions of the unconscious, abjection, and transference can be adapted to a type of social psychoanalysis that is always open to reconfiguration and evolution in relation to changing social norms. As we will see, the concepts of the unconscious, abjection, and transference can serve as antidotes to overly simplistic conceptions of identity politics that easily become defensive reaction-formations, on the one hand, and overly simplistic ideas of sex/gender volunteerism or gender as performance, on the other. Psychoanalysis can complicate both the idea that we are born with an authentic or real identity (whether anatomical or some internal essence or self) on the one hand, and the idea that we can choose whatever identity we want to be (through body modification, performance, or simple self-declaration), on the other. The problem, then, is to articulate a theory of sex/gender identity that acknowledges the ways in which identity concepts and categories change with changing social norms, while also acknowledging each individual's lived experience of their own sex/gender identities.

As feminists, we might ask how we can formulate a theory of sex/gender identity that acknowledges that the category of woman is socially constructed and evolving—perhaps to the point of exploding the man-woman binary—and therefore fluid, while at the same time acknowledging and legitimating our investments in the category "woman," even as it includes more and various types of bodies? This takes us back to the decades-old question central to 1990s feminism, which is still relevant today, namely, how can we both analyze the ways in which sex and gender are socially constructed and still leave room for individual agency? In more contemporary terms, as I suggested above, we might ask: how can we both acknowledge the ways in which identity categories are shaped by social norms and at the same time acknowledge the singularity of the ways in which each individual experiences those norms in their own experience and embodiment? We need a theory of sex/gender that accounts for the ways in which sex/gender categories are historical, and that legitimates each individual's experience of their own gender and sexual identities as unique. There may be as many gender identities and sexualities as there are people. And yet, those identities are neither entirely determined by social norms nor wholly freely chosen by individuals. To hold the former leaves us with a type of gender totalitarianism, while to hold the latter leaves us with a type of free market individualism. Neither of these options seems true to experience—particularly when we posit the existence of the unconscious—nor politically sound. This is the place where psychoanalysis meets politics.

At the one extreme, contemporary trends toward new forms of authenticity and the absolute authority of personal narratives of free choice foreclose the possibilities of both critical discussion and historical contextualization of identities and desires. In psychoanalytic terms, new forms of authenticity and absolute authority of narratives of choice disavow the ambivalence and ambiguity that constitute personal identity formation, not to mention unconscious desires and fears that drive identity "choices." Psychoanalysis interrogates those unconscious desires and fears and how they shape identity in all of its forms. From strategic essentialism and gender performance to lived experience and bodily urges, identity is a negotiation between the soma and psyche that is filtered through cultural norms and prohibitions. Furthermore, identity is not formed once and for all, but is rather an on-going process; the subject is never fully formed, but always what Julia Kristeva calls a "subject-in-process."

Freud's bisexuality thesis—that all human beings are originally bisexual— challenges any neat distinction between masculinity and femininity or heterosexuality and homosexuality. The bisexuality thesis, however, continues to maintain a binary schema for both gender identity and sexual object choice. Freud's hypothesis that infantile sexuality is polymorphous goes further than the bisexuality thesis to suggest the fluidity of human sexuality, or what today might be called gender fluidity. This strand of psychoanalysis not only challenges binary notions of gender and sexuality, but also diagnoses commitments to fixed or absolute identities as defensive reaction-formations against the ambiguity inherent in gender identity formation and the ambivalence inherent in sexual desire, and thereby navigates between volunteerism and determinism.

Our gender identities and sexual desires are neither freely chosen nor biologically and culturally determined. They are, however, governed by cultural norms, which are at once contradictory and changing. That is to say, both gender and sexuality have a history; and this history is not a neat linear history, but rather a messy one that involves changing norms in medicine, biology, psychology, and sociology, which are often inconsistent norms. Moreover, different factions of society, and different class, race, or ethnic histories, along with different cultures or nationalities, further complicate notions of gender and sexuality. Social position plays a part in identity formation.

While we cannot deny the biologistic thread in Freudian psychoanalysis, we also should not overlook Freud's repeated descriptions of the role of cultural and social norms in shaping the unconscious. The Freudian unconscious, then, is not an ahistorical concept, but rather thoroughly social. If there are as many sexualities as there are individuals, then, within the dynamics of the psyche, neither gender nor sexuality can be limited to binary oppositions. On a psychoanalytic interpretation, oppositional binary identities of all kinds are the result of the disavowal of ambiguity and ambivalence. Following Kristeva, we might describe this process of fortifying identity against ambiguity by disavowing the process of abjection.

Identity as a Defense against Abjection

In *Powers of Horror* (1980), Kristeva develops a theory of abjection and its relation to identity that helps us understand what she later calls the "archaeology of purity" (1996). She describes abjection as that which "disturbs identity, system, order. What does not respect borders, positions, rules. The in-between, the ambiguous, the composite" (1980, 4). The abject is excluded in order to set up the clean and proper boundaries of the body, the subject, gender, and sexual identity, at the level of the individual, and at the societal level, to set up the boundaries of cultural and national identities. Identity operates by excluding the abject, which, simply put, is the ambiguity out of which identity is constituted. Above all, ambiguity is excluded or prohibited so that identity can be stabilized. Stable identity, then, is constituted by disavowing the ambiguity at the core of identity constitution. This is why we are more comfortable with clear-cut oppositions, even when they lead to war or violence, than we are with the mess of ambiguity. We are more comfortable with notions of identity that divide the world into neat categories of black or white, male or female, heterosexual or homosexual, man or woman, than we are embracing the fluidity, ambiguity, or ambivalence inherent in any of those distinctions. We are threatened by ambiguity, even more so than by what we take to be our enemies. Indeed, enemies reassure us of our own stable identity. We thrive on oppositional thinking as a defense against ambiguous identities and our own ambivalent desires.

We don't need psychoanalysis to teach us that identity is fluid; we merely need to look to history to acknowledge the shifting norms of identity. Specifically, we can trace changing ideals of female, male, masculinity, femininity, heterosexual, homosexual, pansexual, transgender, etc. In terms of gender and sexuality, we need not even look to ancient history, but merely reflect on changes within our own lifetimes. Sex/gender norms have a history and change as cultural norms change. Although tied to the materiality of the body and bodily drives, sex and gender are always governed, if not determined, by cultural context and social norms. Denying the social and historical contexts of sex/gender and insisting on biologically determined or culturally essentialist notions of binary opposition is a quest for identity purified of ambiguity and naturalized into an artificially stable category.

The quest for "pure" identity through the violent excising of all ambiguity or "impurity" is clearly seen in ethnic cleansing, racial segregation, and apartheid; and perhaps not as clearly seen, but still very much operative in, binary gender categories that trade on the distinction between real men and real women. The notion of "real women," whether policed by right-wing conservatives insisting on biological sex, or used by trans activists arguing that trans women are real women, is a defensive reaction (what in psychoanalytic terms we would call a defensive reaction-formation) against ambiguity. Investments in defending the category of woman (or man) against interlopers result in border policing that cracks down on ambiguity at the heart of all identity. Disavowing the process of abjection that excludes ambiguity is part and parcel of the process of constituting a stable, or clean and proper, identity. To complicate matters, the categories of identity have political valences and may need to be deployed in political struggles for recognition. Even so, when they are deployed categorically, they risk exlusionary violence.

Abjection is not what is seen as dirty, unclean, or unwanted per se, but rather what clouds the waters and blurs borders. Abjection is what thwarts the border police, what they cannot categorize as this or that, man or woman, black or white. Knowing what something is reassures us. Knowing our enemy makes us feel safe. The unknown, what resists categorization, is the real threat of abjection. What is stunning in Kristeva's articulation of abjection is her suggestion that although abjection prompts exclusion, this is not because of otherness or difference per se, but rather because otherness and difference are part and parcel of the process of identification, which expels ambiguity. What is threatening about otherness or difference, then, is not its opposition to sameness or identity, but the ambiguity between otherness and sameness through which opposition is constituted in the first place. In other words, oppositional binary identity is a defense against ambiguity.

When excluded ambiguity returns, which is bound to happen, it can result in one of two responses. First, it can lead to sublimation (through which our fears of ambiguity and otherness are transformed into art, literature, or philosophy, and even into revolutions in thinking about the world and our experience). Or, second, this return of ambiguity can lead to violent attempts to destroy it through various forms of dogmatism, repression, and oppression. This violent reaction is an attempt to purify or exonerate the subject or group of its own guilt over the exclusions that it perpetuates in order to set up its identity as whole or unified. Negotiating abjection can lead to the best in humanity—sublimation—or to the worst, murder. Sublimation is the antidote to fundamentalism. Fundamentalism is the danger of fixed identity. And fixed identity is the result of the disavowal or repression of ambiguity and the process of abjection that excludes it. In order to avoid dangerous fundamentalisms of all kinds—including sex/gender fundamentalism—we need to understand the drive for purity. Psychoanalysis can help us investigate the urge for purity in contemporary culture, politics, and in our own lives.

One of the ways in which this urge for purity emerges in contemporary culture is through a renewed insistence on authenticity or realness based on the presupposition that affects cannot be interrogated. The realm of affect or feelings stemming from each individual's own experience has become the basis for an absolute authenticity seemingly beyond analysis or critical questioning. The flip side, which is equally dangerous, is that individual experience is discounted and members of oppressed groups are "gaslighted" about their own experiences such that those in power control and distribute what is "real." In part, the dismissal of the experiences and feelings of oppressed peoples has led to the privileging of affects as a way to insist on the validity of this experience. The risk of privileging affect and subjective experience as beyond critical analysis, and the need to validate the experiences of those oppressed, is one of the dilemmas of contemporary identity politics. We must be able to critically analyze experiences and their concominant affects, along with sex/gender identities, in order to better understand the social and historical contexts that give rise to them; and yet, we must do so without delegitimating each individual's suffering or challenging their lived experience. For, without critical analysis, affect becomes a form of fundamentalism, and righteous hatred legitimates violence in the name of an outrage beyond critique. However, without taking into account affects as lived, analysis becomes merely an academic exercise. Furthermore, how can we arbitrate suffering and victimhood in a culture where affects are beyond critical analysis?

The Fundamentalism of Authenticity

In a culture that increasingly value pure feelings uncontaminated by analysis, the uncritical legitimation of emotions as the basis for moral authority becomes a form of political leveling. If unexamined outrage is the new authority, then we are moving dangerously close to a form of reactionary politics that closes down discussions that are too difficult; and cannot distinguish between, on the one hand, sexism and racism and, on the other, critical discussions of them. Certainly, as Pascal says, the heart has its reasons, but we need to analyze what they are in order to better understand ourselves and others.

Privileging feelings over analysis of them not only fuels anti-intellectualism, but also conceals the socio-historical context that produces those feelings. In other words, affect is never completely raw or pure, but always already cooked and contaminated. So, too, analysis is never completely devoid of emotion. Pathos and logos aren't polar opposites. Yet, to authorize outrage (whether on the left or on the right) as somehow foundational and beyond analysis is to deny the ways in which race, class, gender, politics, upbringing, culture, and history shape our emotions. When outrage becomes an end in itself, it becomes a form of fundamentalism and part of a dogma of purity that can be as potentially aggressive, hostile, and violent as other forms of fundamentalism. When political activism becomes self-righteous or dogmatic and punishing, it uses the same techniques of exclusion and oppression that it rejects, only now in the name of liberation. In fact, with social media, punishments can be quicker and harsher, and anyone with a computer, time, and righteous outrage can play the role of sheriff.

While it is crucial to acknowledge that political purity and fundamentalism can be expressions of real distress, they close down self-critical examination of that distress, and our own investments in violent reactions to it. In addition, political purity and fundamentalism produce a need for ever more and stronger outrage. If raw feelings and pure outrage always trump cooked arguments and analysis, then the unhappy consequence is that white nationalists and rapist frat boys will *seemingly* be as justified in their claims to victimhood and safe spaces as black men and women abused by police or women who've been raped. I say *seemingly* because analysis of social and historical contexts, along with investments in violence, including racist and sexist violence, makes it clear that the suffering experienced by rape victims and that experienced by their rapists is not equivalent. Far from it. Psychoanalysis teaches us to analyze our own investments in violence rather than proclaim ourselves immune from or above violent impulses. On the one hand, the postulation of the unconscious renders self-righteous claims to transcend racism or sexism suspect. And, on the other, it should lead us to investigate and interrogate not only our own investments in violence but also the unconscious fears and desires of those who perpetrate violence against us.

Leveling violence and harm, and ignoring socio-historical contexts, risks undermine the voices of victims of the worst abuse and oppression. Comparing the suffering of perpetrators of racial or sexual violence and hate speech to that of their victims is an unacceptable consequence of accepting outrage as the source of moral authority. Comparing the pain and suffering of being raped to the pain and suffering of being accused of rape not only belittles the experiences of the rape victim, but also co-opts the discourse of victimhood in ways that demand analysis. So too, comparing teachers and scholars criticizing sexism and racism to perpetrators of violence and hate speech closes down discussions necessary to address—and hopefully overcome—those very harms.

Affects may be the beginnings of personal and political transformation, but they must not be the ends. Rather, affects must not only be channeled into action, but also analyzed. While a necessary component of political action, affects are not immune from analysis. When they are taken as unassailable givens, they risk becoming a new fundamentalism based on an illusion of authenticity and purity that feed a *certain* identity politics as a politics of transhistorical purity. Again, psychoanalysis can help us analyze the—sometimes displaced— origins of these affects, and thereby help us to understand the meaning of our feelings. Why do we feel this way? Why do we suffer? What are the origins of our suffering? What actions are most appropriate given our suffering? Psychoanalysis can help us answer these questions. Psychoanalysis can also help us address our own investments in suffering and claims to victimhood. We have become a society that values suffering and victimhood, and psychoanalysis can help us figure out why.

In addition to the fundamentalism of affects and the unassailable authority of feeling, contemporary outrage culture has fostered a competitive atmosphere wherein suffering is a zero-sum gain, and victims measure their suffering against the suffering of others. In some sense, culture wars have become contests of suffering, and the position of the victim has become the privileged position in our society, what Lauren Berlant calls "citizen-victims" (Berlant, 1997, 1). Who suffers most? Who is the most oppressed? There is a competition to claim the most suffering, as if only the most extreme victimization warrants fighting. As we have seen, as suffering authorizes truth, white men claim the position of victims of racism and fraternity rapists claim the position of victims of accusations. In other words, cut off from social and historical contexts, it is difficult to adjudicate the position of victimization. Indeed, the competition for victim status among various factions of our society is symptomatic not only of widespread feelings of suffering but also of a culture that values suffering and fosters competition over victimization.

With challenges to patriarchy and to stereotypes of the strong father as a punishing father, the suffering father has become a new icon of patriarchal power. Kristeva (2018) suggests that the sadomasochistic identification with the beaten father is a defense against the father of the law and his punishment. She maintains that identification with the suffering father has become an essential part of the process of idealization that enables the revolt necessary to negotiate social norms. The suffering father's victimization allows the child to bond with a paternal agency most like itself, vulnerable and weak. That is to say, the child as a victim of the authoritarian and threatening paternal law can find an alternate ideal in the suffering father as a victim. This identification supports the revolt against paternal or parental authority by authorizing suffering. And this revolt against the authoritarian father (or parent), in a paradoxical move, authorizes the child's subjectivity and its entrance into the symbolic.

An identification with the beaten father counterbalances the punishing paternal super-ego by allowing the child sadomasochistic pleasure in punishment, which is doubled by sadistically turning the tables on the punishing father of the law and subjecting him to a beating, and then, in turn, masochistically identifying with his victimhood and what becomes "sweet" suffering (Kristeva, 2006a, 5, 6). The Christian fantasy of the passion of Christ is Kristeva's prime example of the "a father is being beaten to death" fantasy (2006, 7). This beating/beaten fantasy transforms the passive victim of parental love and punishment into an active agent, while also turning the threatening parents into passive victims. The punishing father becomes the beaten father and the castrating mother becomes the catatonic mother (see Oliver, 2013, chapter 5). The perpetrator becomes the victim—but one with whom we identify; and, with these sadomasochistic fantasies, we find both revenge and reunion through imaginary and symbolic satisfactions.

Through identification with suffering, we not only separate from our parents to become individuals, but we also cope with the pain of that separation—the loss that prefigures all others—through an imaginary revenge. The beaten father fantasy combines the experience of passive suffering with active paternal prowess and authority. And yet, importantly, this suffering ideal father is not the punishing authoritarian father of the law. Rather, Kristeva associates the suffering father with what earlier she called the imaginary father, which is a paternal agency responsible for the transference of affects into language. On her account, the imaginary father gives form to the prelinguistic semiotic elements of signification bound up with the maternal body. Leaving aside the paternal–maternal binary that this analysis presupposes, we could say that through identification with suffering, affect is bound to signification such that language serves as a compensation for the loss and separation inherent in the process of individuation. Only when affects are bound to signification can language play this crucial compensatory role. On the contrary, when affects are cut off from signification, then somatic symptoms and acting out are possible consequences, and suffering perpetuates itself.

By positing the suffering father and the imaginary father along with the father of the law, Kristeva multiplies father figures and explodes any neat binaries between paternal and maternal. So too, she complicates the maternal function, expanding the various roles of the maternal body within psychoanalytic theory. Freud arguably also postulates various paternal and maternal agencies. Elaborating the multitudes of paternal and maternal agencies in the writings of either Freud or Kristeva is beyond the scope of this chapter. Suffice it to say, even the paternal–maternal binary, seemingly foundational to psychoanalysis, is multiplied beyond oppositional categories. More important for my analysis here is a discussion of why and how negotiating ambiguity can result in either sublimation or fundamentalism. What happens in the imaginary bind between affect and language, or body and thought, that leads to either sublimation or fundamentalism (and various stages of idealization in between)?

For Kristeva, representation not only compensates for the loss of, or separation from, our first loves, but also transforms desire for them into desire for language itself. She also insists that imaginary and symbolic identification with suffering is a depassioning. Identification with suffering not only transfers erotic drives into representation, but more importantly, transforms those drives from passion to depassion, from eroticism to de-eroticism. And it is this transformation that allows us to give form to passions or affect and thereby transforms outrage into sublimation. Ultimately, with and against the death drive, representation makes the primary separation—which comes to stand for all pain, loss, trauma, and the very meaninglessness of life—into something meaningful (cf. Kristeva, 2006b, 8).

When meaning becomes fixed in any form of fundamentalism, it becomes dogmatic and risks becoming the justification for violence. It becomes what Kristeva calls "the malady of ideality." But if the process of idealization necessary for a meaningful life is held open to constant questioning and reinterpretation through new forms of representation, then there is the possibility for sublimation of the sadomasochistic drives, which might prevent such violence. Rather than latching on to the ideal and becoming fanatical about it, we open it up to new ways of seeing, new fantasies of death and rebirth. New beginnings are possible only through continued questioning that resists rigidity or dogmatism. Questioning is the antidote to what Kristeva sees as an adolescent desire for absolutes as a defense against the ambiguities of life. Questioning is also the antidote to the fundamentalism that is the consequence of desperately clinging to those absolutes in order to ward off the messiness of ambiguity. Interpretation and reinterpretation are essential to the process of sublimation with and against our need for categorization, universals, and absolutes.

Transference as Forgiveness

With its constant reinterpretations of our losses and frustrations, psychoanalysis allows us to turn the pain of separation into language. In the psychoanalytic session, through transference, the analysand projects onto the analyst his or her unconscious desires and fears in relation to the primary loss or separation from parental figures. More generally, transference allows anybody or anything to stand in for lost loves insofar as libidinal cathexis binds primary affects to transferential objects through the imagination. In other words, through the operation of transference on the imaginary plane, primary affects can be transferred to others. Transference opens up a radical fluidity of identity and identification insofar as the imagination is not limited by anatomy, biology, or social norms, even if it operates in negotiation with them.

While transferential identification opens up the possibility of radical fluidity, and the transfer of affects, psychoanalytic interpretation provides an elaborative support for those affects and the process of identification. Psychoanalytic interpretation adds elaboration and understanding to transference and sublimation. Interpretation becomes a necessary support for affect, which moves us beyond the notion that feelings are intractable or transparent, and toward a critical analysis of affects. Through analytic interpretation, affects are connected and reconnected to words in order to give them meaning and context. Without elaboration and critical analysis, unbound affects threaten the social fabric. This is not to say that they don't have an important role to play in social interaction and the constitution of identity. They do. But they are not ends in themselves, but rather means to transformation, whether individual, social, or political transformation.

Kristeva calls analytic interpretation a form of forgiveness through which the analyst suspends judgment and allows the analysand to bring affects into language: "psychoanalytic listening and analyst's speech within transference and countertransference could be considered an act of forgiveness: the donation of meaning with the effect of a scansion" (1989, 235). Applying Kristeva's insight beyond the analytic situation, we could say that meaning is fore-given in the sense that each individual, through what Kristeva calls intimate revolt, must make the clichés of their culture their own by revolting against social norms in order to authorize and reauthorize their own identity with and against those norms. In other words, we become who we are in language, a language that is always fore-given, even as we adapt to it and adapt it to our own affective experiences. The forgiveness of signification, then, is a temporary, precarious, and always on-going reconciliation between social norms and individual affects. Forgiveness marks both the transgression against the community inherent in asserting one's own identity, and the necessity of belonging to that community. Forgiveness allows us to become individuals who still belong to a community.

For Kristeva, forgiveness forges a "third way between dejection and murder" (1989, 199). Forgiveness makes it possible to become a subject without murdering the other or dejecting or abjecting oneself. Through forgiveness, we sublimate our murderous or suicidal tendencies. Sublimation is the movement of the force of the semiotic drive into signification, of affect into law, by virtue of the imagination, through which idealization "authorizes destructive violence to be spoken instead of being done. That is sublimation, and it needs for-giving [par-don]" (Kristeva, 1989, 200). Forgiveness allows us to "speak" our violent affects and still return to the community with a sense of belonging. This sense of belonging is the result of sublimation supported by forgiveness that makes it possible for the individual subject to transgress the norm in order to authorize her own discourse.

Sublimation enables one to put into signification the pain of separation from the community; and through this articulation of the pain of transgression, the individual speaks to, and through, the community as one who belongs. In other words, in order to become an individual, the subject necessarily transgresses the social and linguistic codes, driven by affective unconscious impulses, and then sublimates that transgression by resignifying it within the very same social and linguistic codes modified to incorporate the singularity of the subject, who is always a subject in process. Indeed, forgiveness is the on-going process of becoming an individual who belongs to a community.

This process of transgression, however, brings with it existential guilt, and the need for forgiveness. In a sense, we need to be forgiven for becoming individuals with and against social norms. Forgiving ourselves—or more precisely the process of forgiveness that enables and constitutes the subject—depends on not only a suspension of judgment, but also on a suspension of time, since linear time is the time of judgment. Forgiveness requires the suspension of the time of cause and effect, responsibility, and blame. The psychoanalytic secular forgiveness moves us beyond blame and shame and toward an embrace of the process through which we become who we are. By negotiating abjection and the ambiguity of the process of identification, with and against social norms that require the exclusion of abjection, we become beings who mean through an on-going intimate revolt in language. This process of bringing into language the ambiguity of identity and the ambivalence of desire necessitates forgiveness, both as the fore-giveness of meaning and as the forgiveness of transgression, so that the individual can belong to the community.

The difficulty comes in navigating the ways in which our communities themselves are the result of processes of abjection and exclusion. In order to forgive, we must avow the ambiguity and ambivalence that constitute those communities. And, the reverse, we must avow the ambiguity and ambivalence inherent in those communities to forgive. Forgiveness is lacking in today's culture of outrage based on blaming and shaming. Social media fosters outrage and discourages analysis. Outrage cannot abide forgiveness. To be clear, the psychoanalytic notion of forgiveness that I'm proposing, following Kristeva, cannot be reduced to our everyday notion of forgiveness, insofar as it does not presuppose a sovereign forgiving agent or judge. Instead, the agency of psychoanalytic forgiveness is located in language itself, or more precisely in listening. The psychoanalyst listens without judgment in order to open up the space within which the analysand forgives him or herself by reconnecting words and affects.

In an important sense, social media does the opposite. Social media encourages affect in place of thoughtful exchange. For example, emojis are an extreme form of flattening affect and closing off discussion. Social media also encourages reaction in place of response. Moreover, insofar as it reduces the possibilities of interpretation, social media also reduces the chances for forgiveness. In the psychoanalytic sense of forgiveness, social media radically limits signification and thereby radically limits the possibility of the fore-giveness of language; and through the concomitant homogenization of signification (witness emojis) restricts the possibilities of making the clichés of one's culture one's own. In our everyday sense of forgiveness, social media fosters blaming and shaming. While blaming and shaming can be community building, those communities are formed on the basis of exclusion and violence, in ever more fractious groups. And while it is increasingly difficult to avoid blaming and shaming as part of group identity, it is imperative that we continue to try to find ways of community building across differences, rather than enclosing ourselves in increasingly shrinking bubbles of people who think exactly as we do.

In our current moment, community building is especially important, and exceedingly difficult, for political liberals, progressives, and those on the left. We blame each other for the election of Donald Trump. In the face of the overt racism, sexism, and bigotry of the 2016 presidential campaign, and the hate speech and discrimination against targeted minorities and women that the Trump administration continued to endorse, instead of working together, too often, we turn against each other to point a finger. In order to move forward through—and hopefully beyond—the current reactionary moment in American politics, we must find ways to work together to rebuild communities and belonging through various forms of forgiveness.

At the same time, it is imperative that we try to understand the suffering of those others whose viewpoints we don't comprehend, especially when those worldviews threaten our own. We need to understand why there is so much hatred and fear in the United States today, not in order to legitimate it or embrace it. Far from it. Only by understanding the desires and fears—conscious and unconscious—that drive hatred and violence, can we hope to move beyond that hatred and fear by analyzing its social, political, and psycho-dynamic contexts.

Analysis, critical thinking, deliberation, the step back—all of these forms of taking time to think about the meaning of affects and examine their social contexts help move us beyond reactionary politics toward ethical response. With its postulation of the unconscious, psychoanalysis adds another dimension to other forms of critical reflection on the meaning and context of affects. Once we posit the unconscious, we are responsible to interrogate our own unconscious investments in violence and exclusion, and our own self-righteous urges toward dogmatisms or fundamentalisms as manifestations of the disavowal of abjection with its inherent ambiguity and ambivalence. Psychoanalysis can help analyze our compulsions to react and turn and return those impulses into more deliberate responses. Finally, ethical decisions and responsible actions are possible only when we critically respond rather than merely react.

Bibliography

Berlant, L. (1997). *The Queen of America Goes to Washington City*, Durham: Duke University Press.

Bettcher, Talia Mae (2014). "Feminist Perspectives on Trans Issues," *Stanford Encyclopedia of Philosophy*, January 8.

Kristeva, J. (1980). *Powers of Horror*, trans. L. Roudiez, New York: Columbia University Press.

Kristeva, J. (1989). *Black Sun*, trans. L Roudiez, New York: Columbia University Press.

Kristeva, J. (1996). *New Maladies of the Soul*, trans. R. Guberman, New York: Columbia University Press.

Kristeva, J. (2006a). "A Father Is Being Beaten to Death." Paper presented at Columbia University Press.

Kristeva, J. (2006b). *This Incredible Need to Believe*, trans. B. B. Brahic, New York: Columbia University Press.

Kristeva, J. (2018). *Passions of Our Times*, trans. C. Borde and C. Malovany-Chevallier, New York: Columbia University Press.

Oliver, K. (2013). *Technologies of Life and Death*, New York: Fordham University Press.

Chapter 10

Sexual (In)difference in Late Capitalism

"Freeing Us from Sex"

Juliet Flower MacCannell

Lacan once said that getting rid of sex was the inaugural moment of capitalism. I puzzled for quite some time over this cryptic remark, which he made in an interview published as *Télévision* in 1974 (p. 51). As I began looking more intensively into his late work and teaching it, I realized how this conclusion flowed from the impressively insightful analysis he had made of the structure of capitalism in his seventeenth seminar, *The Other Side of Psychoanalysis* (1969) (see MacCannell, 2006). There, Lacan saw capitalism's advent as highly correlated with a new calculus of pleasure, a new quantification of enjoyment and of surplus *jouissance* (which also means "profit," i.e., the engine of capitalism's advances).[1]

> Something in the master's discourse changed at a certain moment in history. We are not going to break our necks to find out whether it was because of Luther, or Calvin, or the shipping traffic around Genoa, the Mediterranean sea, or elsewhere, because the important point is that on a certain day, surplus pleasure becomes calculable, it can be counted, toted up. There, the so-called accumulation of capital begins [...]. Surplus pleasure links up with capital—no problem, they are homogeneous—and we are into the region of values. Moreover, in this blessed age we live in, we are all swimming in it.
>
> (Lacan, 1992, 207; my translation)

Capitalism's commodification of *enjoyment* generates what Lacan called a new *discourse*, a new type of social group formation: a socio-cultural order defined by an ethos of granting each member equal opportunity to obtain this *enjoyment* (or *profit*). In this discourse, if everyone is permitted free entrée to the wealth that capitalism produces, then its corollary is a demand for there to be equal access to its enjoyment. But the principle of a universal ability to enjoy fully has a hidden side; it masks an unconscious imperative to make sure no one gets any more satisfaction than you do. Everyone, as Freud once put it, must have the same and be the same (Freud, *SE* 18, 1921, 120–121). Thus, a fundamental rule that *everyone must have the same and be the same* becomes a universal prohibition

DOI: 10.4324/9781003284888-13

on *jouissance*—akin to Max Weber's famous spirit of capitalism as it merged with Protestantism's worldly asceticism.[2] People curtail their own enjoyment in order not to appear to have excess—and to block others from surplus *jouissance*, too. After all, to install a Barthesian type of myth in our social order (the myth of universal direct access to *jouissance*), it is of the essence that there be both a tacit and a symbolically mandated indifference to difference—the purest form of equality.[3]

It seems, moreover, that there is always a crucial exemption from any regime of hypothetical universal equality: there is always One—the "exception" Freud called it—who has unique access to full enjoyment, One granted license to have it all, a One thus absolutely unequal with respect to everyone else.[4] Once *jouissance* gets fully quantified, counted up and metered out under capitalism, its lopsided distribution belies the ideological ideal of equal access to it.

In *Seminar* XVII, Lacan (1969) modeled the "One" in the primordial case as the primal Father who alone possesses all the women—the imagined figure of Freud's totemic father (or Lacan's later *père jouissant*), who reserves all pleasure to himself, and who maintains power over the whole social group in order to do so. Lacan's analysis demonstrates the hollowness of late capitalism's putative equality by exemplifying "the exception" not as a primal father, but as "the *wealthy*" (or in current parlance, the "1%")[5]: the avatars of "the exception" today are billionaires and corporate CEOs who represent unlimited enjoyment/profit.

Lacan did not stop at demonstrating how the calculating and toting up of surplus *jouissance* generated the formations of the new social group, the *discourse* of capitalism, as a whole. Shortly after his work on the seventeenth *Seminar*, he began to think about how the commodification of *jouissance* affects relations (or non-relations) between the sexes. While Lacan never engaged much with the historical economic outcomes of capitalism for the subgroups in its social order, he did pave the way for an analysis of its specific and real effects for women (and men) today. In *Seminar XX: Encore (1972–3)*, Lacan (1975) extended the application of his model of capitalist enjoyment to the concept of a sexual split in the *ways of enjoying*, a differentiation that he notices capitalism was particularly bent on doing away with.

Lacan delineated two contradictory ways the logical organization of each sex permits or restricts their access to enjoyment: a *universal masculine logic* and a *universal feminine logic*. Two universals co-existing in the same social space? Could such a thing be without one ultimately dominating or displacing the other? This is a crucial question.

Lacan's exploration of a *logical* difference in *sexuation* is based on the fundamental tenet of his psychoanalytic theory: that language/speech (the signifier) shapes an originally *animal* body into a *human* body, and reorganizes it according to the logic of language rather than according to its natural organic functions.[6] The signifier or speech "castrates" the body, expelling simple animal organic satisfactions and replacing them with socially acceptable forms of enjoyment regulated by symbolic dictates. Freud argued that speech itself is the origin of repression and Lacan found that unconscious drives are the "echo of speech in the body." Repressed animal enjoyment does not simply disappear, but instead sinks into the unconscious, where in fantasy form it stamps itself on the body ("the letters of the body") and marks it erogenously. Lacan tried to establish both that this is what occurs and that it works differently for masculine and feminine bodies.

A body that results from the signifier's shaping (Lacan calls it a "carving") of the erotic body is the same as that famed body without organs ("BwO") Gilles Deleuze named, although unlike Lacan, Deleuze did not seem as curious about distinctive and dissimilar ways BwOs relate to their lost animality, their lost organic satisfaction, as was Lacan. Recall that the BwO is entirely distinct from an organically configured body, so one's biological sex organ does not determine your relation to enjoyment and its restrictions: the organically male may well have a feminine logical ordering to his BwO, while conversely those who are biologically female may well have bodies without organs configured according to a masculine logic.

In Lacan's theory of sexual division, illustrated with his "Diagram of Sexuation" in *Encore*, the masculine logic of enjoyment bars complete satisfaction for all but One; none may enjoy fully except for this One, who is exempt from the repression that rules all others in its regime. This figure of unbarred *jouissance*, a big Other unrestricted in his enjoyments, is the sole exception to the rule of universal castration by the signifier.

How does this logic work itself out in shaping the masculine body's actual experience? This seems fairly clear: sexual satisfaction for the masculine body is largely centered on the penis, symbolically doubled as a *phallus*; its loss of unlimited organ satisfaction is compensated for with symbolic social power. For Lacan, the logical endpoint of masculine sexuation is the singular pleasure the ego-phallo-centered masculine body enjoys: the "*jouissance de l'idiot*" (idiot as individual, not connected to another), self-pleasuring.

The feminine body of enjoyment is shaped differently; it is a logic wherein *not all* people, nor all of my body is strictly under the rule of the signifier, nor have my organic enjoyments been as severely cut from my body as the cuts the masculine BwO has suffered. On this side, that of the *not-all* universal, only *some* are castrated by language, while there might be others who are not so, and at any rate, the signifier has not necessarily carved *me* in that way. For the feminine BwO, *jouissance* is de-centered and dispersed throughout the body, not focused on one main erogenous zone, and there is for the feminine body no one sex organ endowed with symbolic power as the penis-as-phallus is.[7] And no part of the feminine BwO is experienced as the unique locus of or focus for her erotic pleasure.[8]

By now, it should be abundantly clear from Lacan's investigation that he saw how the logic of capitalism paralleled just one side of the sexual equation in its allotment of *jouissance*—masculine logic has obviously been favored, despite capitalism's ideological indifference to sexual difference. Might capitalism have developed otherwise? Does capitalism *need* to have been shaped almost exclusively along masculine lines? Must it therefore strive to eradicate all trace of feminine logic in its regime? If distinctions among a society's members must be denied, must these include distinctions of gender?

Effacing distinctions might very well be a goal of capitalist discourse, but one should stop to wonder about this, lest we imagine that erasing the borders around gender constitutes an advance for women. Does disregarding distinctions among those under its regime constitute an advance in equality for all people in that regime? That is indeed the existential reality Freud confronted in his work on groups centered around the ego (and late capitalism seems to be that if nothing else): no one who is *different* is permitted full membership in a group constituted by its identification with the One who has it all: wealth and power. Each ego models (or rather re-models) itself on that of the exceptional One.[9]

Sexual indifference, the final "getting rid of sex" that Lacan says is foundational for capitalism, has effectively become a hidden ethical imperative to refuse recognition to any *sex* other than masculine—and nowadays, to refuse recognition to *everyone* deemed to be unlike *us*—especially if they are immigrants, or are poor and de facto insufficiently identified with *wealth.*

What are the real results, the everyday consequences of collapsing sexual and other differences? First of all, socially and politically ignoring those who are different is a time-honored way of reserving symbolic social and economic political power to one group alone. So it seems to be just a way of trapping everyone inside masculine logic. A willed absence of *recognition of difference* among a society's members permits you to dispense with the requirement of bridging divides with verbal communication, compromise, gestures, empathy, etc.

For most of human history people have expended great efforts to devise ways of crossing such divides, of appealing across chasms and gaps between peoples (as especially between sexes) via words, poetry, metaphor and its variants in song. The alternative to metaphor is brutality and violence, with all the gratification on the one side without care or concern for the other. When you claim that there is no difference, you are claiming that there is no need to care about the other. Given what we have now learned about the one-sided definition of what constitutes *sex* for men in positions of power in our present economic order, we can see how prescient Lacan's analysis is.

For Men of Power today have clearly identified with the Exception as they have acted out a capitalist fantasy of complete sexual indifference—by overpowering women, often those who are rendered unconscious by drugs or drink. Their hallmark is a total disregard for the other sex's enjoyment. Thus, these men have engaged in acts such as wrestling a fully clothed woman to the floor in order to masturbate to ejaculation over her. Following a woman into the ladies' room just to masturbate to completion in front of her—no contact with her necessary; grabbing a woman fleeing down a hallway just to force her to watch him pleasure himself in front of her. Are these new forms of perversion—or simply the inevitable conclusion to permitting one sex to become the *only* sex? These are ferocious (and yet also pathetic) gestures of (pseudo)mastery that seek to demonstrate that the perpetrator identifies with the One who "has it all"— all the power, all the money, all the prestige—and all the pleasure.

While not all people in the United States were terminally shocked by the cavalier attitude Donald J Trump displayed toward the wealthy and powerful directly assaulting women (e.g., his infamous, "I just grab them by the pussy" confession/boast), they have not finally failed to be appalled by the detailed descriptions of what not so powerful men have engaged in toward women over whom they hold the slightest control. It is especially gruesome to discover the extent of the abuse of female bodies (or better, feminine ones, as many victims who have come forward are gay young men or transsexual males who identify as feminine) simply as the means to their "self-abuse": masturbation or *"la jouissance de l'idiot."*

When actress Catherine Deneuve among other women in France demurred from the #*balance ton porc* and #Me Too movements as potentially destroying the amorous relations between the sexes (relations delicately built on flirtation, seduction, courtly persuasion and romance), they seemed never to have been subjected to the coercive means to self-gratification that the Harvey Weinsteins, Bill O'Reillys (and other men too numerous to name) indulged in and that was denounced by #Me Too and #Time's Up women. While Deneuve et al. were likely naïve or perhaps somewhat disingenuous about their own experiences, it is indeed possible that their personal demeanor, dignity or even their sense of entitlement to a place of pride in our order may have shielded them from such predators. Yet, our late capitalist economy, which has made all workers feel that they *must* hang on at any price to whatever job they are hired for (or potentially hired for), makes it unlikely that the Deneuve model is the general experience.

The effects of the capitalist ethos of "freeing us from sex" are further being reinforced, even dramatically so, by the technologies that displace face-to-face human interaction from the physical to the electronic. In a recent article about our current generation of teenagers, psychologist Jean Twenge (*The Atlantic*) attributes entirely to the iPhone the fact that American teens today no longer date while in high school and leave their homes (or bedrooms) far less often than eighth graders did only a few years ago. Her claim is that the i-technologies have displaced actual person-to-person interaction to such a degree as to preclude young people's living a real life in touch (literally) with others. She found that a majority of teens actually sleep with their phones beside them in their beds. They also have far fewer actual sexual experiences than the high schoolers of the generation before them as well. (Interestingly, the young people call connecting with another romantically over the phone "talking.")

In "Instincts and their Vicissitudes," Freud (1955b, 124) proposed that "two groups of [...] primal drives should be distinguished: the *ego* or *self-preservative* drives and the *sexual* drives": the latter seeks to unite and form relationships, the former to reduce all to one. He hypothesized that the "conflict between the claims of sexuality and those of the ego" are at the root of psychoneurotic disorders. What distinguishes Freud's "sex drives" from "ego drives" is that the former must link to someone or something *other* to seek out its satisfaction—in all its vicissitudes, while the ego needs no link to others for the direct satisfaction of its drives. For the sex drives, Freud details that *others* are integral even in sado-masochism, scopophilia, exhibitionism and in taking oneself as another: "turning round upon the subject's own self." The sex drive is also ultimately what makes one a link in a longer reproductive chain, tying you to your forebears and progeny. But most crucially, what this also means is that, in terms of attaining organ pleasure beyond self-pleasuring, you need another, a partner, to whom you are *linked*.

Have we reached the endpoint of what Freud distinguished as the "ego drives" from the "sex drives"? *So, it seems, and consonant with the dictum that society does not exist* (Thatcher; Reagan), *that we have simply set aside the sex drive in favor of the ego drives.*

The sexual couple, Freud said in the afterword to his "Group Psychology," is a "protest" against group psychology. If there is an absolute difference between the masculine model of enjoyment and the feminine one, we must recognize it and realize that such difference may well characterize even "same sex" couplings—they, too, may be the coupling of a masculine with a feminine mode of enjoying.

Despite the many feminist denunciations of Lacan for even trying to make distinctions highlighting sexual difference, it is nonetheless the case that to acknowledge sexual difference is to signify that there is no singular way of enjoying, no one way of feeling—i.e., there is no sole, unified way to *jouir.* And if that conception gains widespread acceptance, it seems to me that the discourse of capitalism will undergo—or must undergo—a deep and abiding change in its structure.

In other words, it could change the world greatly if the deep psychology of capitalism could be brought to articulate—and thereby dissipate the power of its fundamental fantasy of being powered by and centered on a closed masculine ego, devoid of any necessary relation to others and who thus gets to win it all. We would have to re-imagine the *ego* as no longer a closed off form, but as perhaps more open than it has been conceived until now—and we might have to explore new forms of how we can experience rather than deny or fantasize about *jouissance.*

Notes

1 Lacan also defined his "plus-de-jouir" or "surplus jouissance" as parallel to Marx's concept of surplus value, as I mentioned in my 1986 book, *Figuring Lacan: Criticism and the Cultural Unconscious.* In his seventeenth seminar, Lacan saw this version of the equality=inequality of the distribution of enjoyment as "plus-de-jouir"—a parallel to Marx's concept of surplus value: as a surplus of enjoyment that is really— for all but the One—"no more" enjoyment.

2 In Freudian/Lacanian theory, this would be like the Superego that presides over the child after the waning of Oedipus (SE 24, 1924). It urges the child to just go ahead and enjoy while installing prohibition after prohibition on doing so.
3 From this perspective, any communism or socialism that demanded the same uniform relation to enjoyment would be no different from the capitalist regime, except rhetorically.
4 Freud (1955c) terms this exceptional One "the Leader" in "Group Psychology"; for Lacan, the One is "Capital" or accumulated wealth itself—only It actually enjoys.
5 Lacan (1969) asks, in Seminar XVII, "What is wealth?"

> Ever since there have been economists nobody, up till now, has—not even for an instant [...] ever made this remark that wealth is the property of the wealthy. Just like psychoanalysis which [...] is done by psychoanalysts [...] why not, concerning wealth, begin with the wealthy?
>
> (94)

Because its answer is tautological: "Wealth is an attribute of the wealthy." He continues:

> The wealthy have property. They buy, they buy everything, in short—well, they buy a lot. But I would like you to meditate on this fact, which is that they do not pay for it. One imagines that they pay, for reasons of accounting that stem from the transformation of surplus jouissance into surplus value. [...] And very much in particular, there is one thing that they never pay for, and that is knowledge.
>
> (94)

A more apt description of the business practices of one Donald J. Trump could not be found even today.

6 Logos/"speech" is from the Greek for "word, speech, discourse," and also "reason."
7 The same holds for the psychical structure of the pervert's body, which may account for the attraction of the hysteric to the pervert I described in the first chapter of my book, *The Hysteric's Guide to the Future Female Subject.*
8 And the "power" ascribed to her principal sex organ is on a mythic, not social, plane: as "the head of the Medusa," the "vagina dentata" or women as a natural force that brings chaos into exclusively male-created culture (per Camille Paglia's theses).
9 Lest we forget, Lacan put together his analysis of the discourse of capitalism using Freud's "Group Psychology" to anchor his interpretation.

Bibliography

Copjec, J. (1994). "Sex and the Euthanasia of Reason," in *Read My Desire*, Cambridge, MA and London: The MIT Press.
Freud, S. (1955a). "Thoughts for the Times on War and Death," in *The Standard Edition of the Complete Psychological Works of Sigmund Freud, Vol. 14*, London: Hogarth. [Original 1915]
Freud, S. (1955b). "Instincts and Their Vicissitudes," in *The Standard Edition of the Complete Psychological Works of Sigmund Freud, Vol. 14*, London: Hogarth. [Original 1915]
Freud, S. (1955c). "Group Psychology and the Analysis of the Ego," in *The Standard Edition of the Complete Psychological Works of Sigmund Freud, Vol. 18*, London: Hogarth. [Original 1921]

Freud, S. (1961). "The Dissolution of the Oedipus Complex," in *The Standard Edition of the Complete Psychological Works of Sigmund Freud, Vol. 19*, London: Hogarth. [Original 1924]

Lacan, J. (1969). *L'Envers de la Psychanalyse, Seminar XVII*, Paris: Seuil.

Lacan, J. (1974). *Télévision*, Paris: Seuil.

Lacan, J. (1975). *Encore: Seminar XX*, Paris: Seuil.

MacCannell, J. F. (1986). *Figuring Lacan: Criticism and the Cultural Unconscious*, London and Lincoln: Routledge and University of Nebraska Press.

MacCannell, J. F. (2000). *The Hysteric's Guide to the Future Female Subject*, Minneapolis and London: University of Minnesota Press.

MacCannell, J. F. (2006). "More Thoughts for the Time on War and Death: The Discourse of Capitalism in Seminar XVII," in *Jacques Lacan and the Other Side of Psychoanalysis: Reflections on Seminar XVII* (pp.194–215), trans. J. Clemens and R. Grigg, Durham and London: Duke University Press.

MacCannell, J. F. (2012). "Making Room: Women and the City to Come" [*Raum schaffen: Woman und die künftige Stadt*] in *Bauarten von Sexualität, Körper, Phantasmen: Architektur und Psychoanalyse* (pp.200–221) [Ways of Building Sexuality, Bodies, Phantasms: Architecture and Psychoanalysis], ed. O. Knellessen and I. Härtel, Zurich: Scheidegger & Spiess.

MacCannell, J. F. (2016). "Refashioning Jouissance for the Age of the Imaginary," *Filozofski vestnik*, 37(2) (special issue, trans. S. Jottkandt and J. S. Riha), 167–200.

Twenge, J. (2017). "Have Smartphones Destroyed a Generation?" *The Atlantic*, September.

Part III

Being and Becoming Trans*

Chapter 11

Tiresias and the Other Sexual Difference

Jacques Lacan and Bracha L. Ettinger

Sheila L. Cavanagh

Sexual difference has a mythic history in the figure of the Theban prophet Tiresias. He appears in Homer's *Odyssey* and has an important role in Sophocles' tragedies of *Antigone*, *Oedipus the King*, and in *Oedipus at Colonus* as well as in Euripides' *Phoenician Women*, among other literary and theatrical works. He reappears in high modernism in T.S. Eliot's "The Waste Land."

This chapter draws upon the mythology of Tiresias to explicate Feminine[1] sexual difference in the post-Lacanian feminist theory of Bracha L. Ettinger. Ettinger (2006) critically engages Lacan's proposition that a man can know nothing about feminine sexuality (Lacan, 2006). Contra Lacan, Ettinger wonders how it is that a man cannot know something about the Feminine dimension. The figure of Tiresias has something to teach us about what Ettinger calls the Other (Feminine) sexual difference as distinct from Lacan's sexuation. In what follows, I draw upon versions of the Tiresian myth to explicate Ettinger's formulation of the Other Sexual Difference. For Ettinger, the Other Sexual Difference is trans-subjective and without recourse to the Oedipus complex. In her elaboration, trans-subjectivity is not a synonym for trans-identity, nor does it concern sexual positioning; it refers rather to what Ettinger calls transitive matrixial subjective elements in everyone (Ettinger, 2006). Ettinger's matrixial borderspace gives form to a Feminine sexual difference that is "subsymbolic," as distinct from Lacan's Symbolic. It has more in common with artistic encounters, telepathy, and unconscious pathways between partial-subjects in matrixial terms, than with Lacan's signifier. This difference is before gender determination but elaborated upon, by Ettinger, in relation to the female child in relation to another woman/m/Other. The matrixial difference of concern to Ettinger is rooted in an enigma stemming from the "woman-beneath-the-mother" and the "woman-beneath-the girl" (Ettinger, 2006, 182–183).

Ettinger invites us to apprehend this Other of Sexual Difference that is, for her, missing in Lacan's theory of sexuation. Ettinger's Feminine dimension is about "becoming" with, and alongside, Others (as non-I's) in the matrixial borderspace (a sub-stratum of feminine difference recalling the m/Other). "The matrixial difference conceptualizes the difference of what is joint and alike yet not 'the same,' of what is uncognized yet recognizable with-in a shared

DOI: 10.4324/9781003284888-15

transubjectivity" (Ettinger, 2006, 183). Ettinger sometimes refers to the matrixial borderspace as a field of non-conscious differentiation and co-emergence.
The borderspace should not be compared to the phallic cut theorized by Lacan
in his discussion of the signifier. The matrixial borderspace is an ever-changing
space-event of cross-pollination whereby two or more partial-subjects encounter and co-affect each other in non-conscious ways. Ettinger refers to partial-
subjects, as opposed to individual (castrated) subjects.

While for Lacan, the conundrum of sexual difference is resolved by two
forms of failure – phallic and not-all phallic, for Ettinger, sexual difference is
demarcated by differing partial relations to the m/Other independent of and,
in fact, preceding masculine or feminine sexual positioning. In other words,
the sexual difference that matters to Ettinger is the difference between the
becoming-subject and the m/Other. Sexuation, as understood by Lacan, follows
matrixial sexuality. In Lacan's formulation, the two sexuated positions are demarcated by language and logic: they produce the feminine and the masculine
positioning. For Ettinger, there is an Other order of Sexual Difference that
predates phallic sexuation and continues to operate concurrently, throughout
one's life, as a transitive sexual relation. In their discussion of Ettinger's feminist thought and mythology, Vanda Zajiko and Miriam Leonard (2008) explain that the Feminine is an "inter/trans-subjectivizing structure/encounter/
space where potentially human subjects co-emerge and co-transform" (30). As
such, the Other Sexual Difference concerns the subject-as-encounter (severality)
as opposed to differentiated sexuated (castrated) subjects. To understand the
other axis of Sexual Difference, it is helpful to consider the mythical Tiresias
as a shape-shifter who becomes a woman in both matrixial and phallic terms.
Ettinger's Other Sexual Difference is predicated upon a definition of Woman
that differs from the Lacanian Woman, who, famously for Lacan, does not exist.
For Lacan, there are only women; Woman, like Tiresias, is a myth. But in Ettingerian theory, Tiresias exists as a Woman in a Feminine dimension.

Along with Ettinger's writing on the Feminine, Tiresias offers an important supplement to an otherwise limiting focus on Oedipus in the psychoanalytic literature. Ettinger's main reference to Tiresias appears in a chapter titled,
"Transgressing With-In-To the Feminine" (2000) that was based on a presentation she gave in Belgium in 1997. The transgression with-in-to the Feminine
involves an Other Sexual Difference that cannot be reduced to Lacan's analytic
of sexuation where the phallic signifier is determinative. As Griselda Pollock
(2013) explains, the Other Sexual Difference "generates a specific proto-ethical
dimension in all human subjectivity irrespective of later gender identifications
as masculine or feminine subjects under the sign of the Phallus" (167). In what
follows, I offer a brief sketch of the mythical character, Tiresias, to illustrate the
Other Sexual Difference as explicated by Ettinger. I will establish its divergence
from the Lacanian formulation of sexual difference. I use the Lacanian conception of the Real (the psychic register beyond images and words) as it pertains
to Tiresias' breasts, to address transitivity, and feminine/Feminine difference

as understood by Lacan and Ettinger, respectively, offering a new Ettingerian reading of the Oedipal myth.

Tiresias

Tiresias was the son of Everes, a shepherd, and Chariclo, a nymph. There are multiple versions of the Tiresian mythical destiny, but I will outline the two most often cited versions involving the goddesses Hera and Athena, respectively, along with another well-known version involving Hera, Zeus, and the Olympian court.

Tiresian Myth #1

In Ovid's *Metamorphoses*, Tiresias came upon two snakes copulating on Mount Kyllene in the Pelloponese. In Book III, under the heading "The judgement of Tiresias," Ovid writes, "Once, with a blow of his stick, he had disturbed two large snakes mating in the green forest, and, marvelous to tell, he was changed from a man to a woman, and lived as such for seven years." One might ask: Why did Tiresias do such a thing? Maybe Tiresias could not tolerate the primal scene; perhaps he could not bear two snakes appearing as One (and made a Lacanian cut), his staff functioning to make two from One. Might we attribute the act to an instance of masculine narcissism and Oedipal aggression? Or from a Lacanian take, we might wonder, was he striking imaginary sameness with his stick? From an Ettingerian perspective, could it be that Tiresias was afraid to see the female snake as a symbol of another non-phallic axis of sexual difference? Whatever the explanation, Tiresias becomes a woman for seven autumns and in so doing, is said to have acquired intimate knowledge of feminine sexual pleasure.

Tiresian Myth #2

As told by the Hellenic poet Callimachus in the poem "The Bathing of Pallas," a young male Tiresias is bathing alongside his mother, the nymph Chariclo, in a spring. During his bath, he accidentally lays eyes on the naked goddess, Athena. Furious about being seen in the nude, she lashes out in anger. Night befalls Tiresias and later, at high noon, he is blinded by her spell for life. It should be remembered that Athena, the goddess of wisdom, civilization, law, and warfare, is not only a virgin, but, like Tiresias, also a shape-shifter. Throughout Homer's *Odyssey*, she assumes multiple and varied forms including those of animals and trees. Not unlike Tiresias, Athena was closely linked to snakes and birds. For instance, Athena takes the shape of a sea-owl in the third book of *The Odyssey*. Odysseus tells the goddess that she is hard for a mortal to know by sight. Despite Odysseus' cleverness and reputation for strategizing and disguise, he comments that the goddess' shapes are endless. Notably, Athena also appears in men's clothing which is not uncommon in Greek mythology. Achilles, Heracles, and Dionysus, among others, cross-dress. In Book VIII, Athena approaches Odysseus looking now dressed like an elegant youth in a gallant costume. Athena's changeability ensures that the contemporary reader can never be sure about her gender, let alone her anthropomorphism.

It is productive to ask what exactly Tiresias sees when he catches a glimpse of the naked Athena. Did he see something more than breasts and female genitalia? A brief intertextual detour with respect to Eliot's "The Waste Land" and to Apollinaire's play, *Les Mamelles de Tirésias* (later an opera by Francis Poulenc, 1947), is helpful to consider how the breasts as such figure in the fictive Tiresian history. In Eliot's modernist poem, "The Waste Land" published in 1922, Tiresias has breasts as he is referred to as the Old man with wrinkled woman's bosom. Does Tiresias give body to something he saw (or did not quite see) on Athena's body? In the play by Apollinaire, Tiresias is given balloon breasts that fly away. As dramatized on stage in *Les Mamelles de Tirésias* (The Breasts of Tiresias), the character Thérèse pops her balloon breasts, leaves her husband, adopts the name Tiresias, and ventures out into the world. While the breasts of Tiresias are worthy of a psychoanalytic and literary analysis in their own rite, let me confine my commentary to a few Lacanian notes.

Breasts – Tiresian and otherwise – have an important history in psychoanalytic theory. For Melanie Klein, they are the quintessential part-object. For Donald Winnicott, they are good and bad, respectively. Lacan refers to what he calls the analyst's breasts to illustrate the role of the analyst in the treatment. Specifically, he takes the "breasts" as the prototype of the object *a* (the object-cause of desire) in the analyst. As object *a*, the breasts are not material but represent a forever-lost object propelling desire from which the subject needs to separate and that guides the analytic task. For transference to occur, the analyst must occupy this position of object to be the cause of the analysand's desire. Richard Webb et al. (1993) argue in a Kleinian manner:

The breasts the analyst has are those the analysand wants him or her to have. In effect, the analysand places breasts on the analyst. Having placed these breasts on the analyst, the analysand then desires the analyst, desires this "truth" in the analyst (Webb, Bushnell and Widseth, 1993, 599).

Imagined breasts support analytical work. Lacan writes (1988) that the analytic task is to support the "function of Tiresias," which, in other words, is to embody difference in the flesh (2006, 321). Put another way, analytic breasts are catalysts for the transference doomed to burst, pop, or simply fly away like the balloons in Poulenc's opera. They enable the analysand to work; they are something of a prop that the analyst is assumed to have. Lacan's use of breasts as an object in analytic work is instructive. Referring to weaning, he insists that it is the "breast specified in the function of weaning which prefigures castration" (Lacan, 2006, 719). The analyst must tolerate the tit-play and give the analysand what they, as analysts, do not have. This is, for Lacan, the meaning of love. In "Science and Truth," Lacan explains the function of the object *a* in analysis and proposes that knowledge of the object *a* is the science of psychoanalysis (2006, 733).

While the object *a* foregrounds shared loss, the phallus underlines power. Nicole Loraux (1995) writes that Athena was a powerful virgin patroness of Athens. Does Tiresias see something phallic, rather than something lacking in Athena? Born from Zeus's forehead, Athena is not like other deities; she is not born from a woman's body. Does this mean that she is phallic or, alternatively, does it mean that like Tiresias, she is a shape-shifter with a birth-story relevant to Ettinger's matrixiality? Let us recall that Metis, the Oceanid goddess of wisdom, is said to have been pregnant with Athena before Zeus swallowed her in an attempt to give birth to Athena himself. Athena's birth, like Tiresias's transformation into a woman, has various versions. In some of them, she was born more than once. In any case, the origin is polyvalent and overdetermined for both figures. We might agree that what Tiresias sees as he lays eyes on Athena cannot be said or represented in linguistic terms. In other words, it was something in the order of the Lacanian Real.

In Lacanian psychoanalysis, the Real is the psychic register beyond representation. We might think of the Real as a dimension of the psyche that is structurally beyond symbolic or linguistic representation. The Real cannot be integrated into the socio-Symbolic structure and has the status of an unspecifiable remainder. Since for Lacan, the relationship to the body is not natural but entails a process of becoming a body, the dimension of the Real may add a traumatic quality associated with the assumption of a body. Perhaps the Real concerns that negativity, that nothing that Tiresias glimpses in Athena on Mount Kyllene in the Pelloponese. The Real as such can be gestured to as a conspicuous absence or vacancy, but not said or seen. Associated with trauma and anxiety, the Real is that space in a puzzle that remains because the pieces slide and do not fit together seamlessly as one might expect. But this lack of fit is ultimately functional. Lacan contends that the subject is caused by a gap in signification, a structural impasse. Let us recall that Lacan discusses the Real as an overdetermination in relation to a story whereby the proverbial die of one's being has already been cast. This is the lot we are born into. Always enigmatic, Lacan writes that we can "pick it [the die] up again, and throw it anew" (1988, 219). The image of the die already having been cast refers to the way the subject has already been constituted and, also, to an impossibility covered over by the Imaginary. Interestingly, Lacan does not refer to Oedipus in this context, but to Tiresias to make his point:

> If Tiresias encounters another Tiresias, he laughs. But in fact, he can't encounter another because he is blind, and not without reason. Don't you feel there's something derisory and funny about the fact that the die has already been cast?
>
> (1988, 219–220)

Crafted by the paradoxical contingency of what returns to the same place, the Real is an invitation for Lacan to "take a detour" (1988, 219) that concerns the body and in particular Tiresias' breasts. Lacan speaks of the Other's lack in terms of an infant's fear of the maternal "breast drying up" (2014, 234). This fear is not about actually losing breast milk, as object relations theorists may conclude, but is rather an encounter with the Real of castration. Lacan notes that from the infant's perspective, the breast is an extension of the child's body, a part-object the child does not willingly separate from, ergo, the analytic work of making the breasts fly away. This internal self-separation is made possible by encountering the mother's own castration. For Lacan, the first Other that needs to be lacking is the m/Other. The desire of the Other enraptures and causes us. In this regard, for both Lacan and Ettinger, the fact that usually a mother is a woman is of consequence.

For both theorists, the question of subjectivity with regard to sexual difference is significant. For Lacan, subjects desire because they are constituted by a lack associated with object a. For Ettinger, lack only occurs to the extent that the subject negates the Feminine dimension. The mother does not lack as such. Ettinger argues that object a is a "phantasmatic *trace* of the pre-Oedipal partial-drive's engagements with the archaic part-object and with the archaic mother" (Ettinger, 2001, 111; emphasis added). Read from a matrixial perspective, the object a is a trace-like link to the m/Other that inscribes a sexual relation as opposed to a cut, as Lacan would have it. Ettinger thus contends that Lacan's feminine and masculine sexual positions only make sense in an order of sexual difference where the phallic signifier reigns. The difference between "being" the phallus (woman) and "having" the phallus (man) takes place at the level of the signifier, but it also "renders unreal the relations to be signified" (Ettinger, 2006, 582). For Lacan, questions about sexual difference are ultimately about contingency in being.

Speaking about an analysand who presents with questions about sex formulated as "What am I there?" Lacan writes, the "fact that the question of his existence envelops the subject, props him up, invades him, and even tears him apart from every angle, is revealed to the analyst by the tensions, suspense, and fantasies that he encounters." Lacan also adds that the questions, am I a man or a woman? or am I either?, are knotted in the "symbols of procreation and death" (2006, 459). In the Lacanian formulation, the act of naming engenders the subject but interferes with being. This interference operates in the Real as an excess of the signifier. Lacan thus asks, what is left of the Real after the subject is constituted by the signifier in that inaugural moment of interpellation "boy" or "girl"? A remainder Lacan tells us. This remainder is laced with trauma as we are all the product of a signifying cut that we might experience as harrowing. He later writes that in the process of becoming a body, there is a remainder, a non-specular corporeal residue that comes along, by a certain detour to make itself felt in the place laid out for lack, and in a way that, not being an image, cannot thereafter be marked out and its presence triggers anxiety (Lacan, 2014,

60). It should not escape notice that Lacan's discussion of the detour in his seminar on anxiety ends with a direct reference to Tiresias.

Ettinger's engagement with Tiresias enables us more fully, or perhaps differently, to consider questions of being and desire in the realm of the feminine/Feminine. In this context, the status of the phallic signifier is, among other things, a question for contemporary readers of Tiresian stories. One may wonder whether Tiresias "has" it, be it a penis (coded as phallus) or something else that cannot be said. For Lacan, there is something about the feminine position that decompletes the phallic signifier (the not-all). But for Ettinger, the phallic signifier is inconsequential altogether. The phallus has nothing to do with the Other axis of Sexual Difference relevant to matrixiality. Ettinger claims that phallic subjectivity involving the Lacanian notion of castrated subject is predated by the original, primordial trans-subjective (or transitive) elements of the Other (as non-I) in the matrixial borderspace. Trans-subjectivity does not adhere to sexual positionings delimited by Lacan's phallic premise. Moreover, what Lacan calls the Real involves what Ettinger calls matrixial sub-knowledge as imprint. Ettinger writes that "experiences concerning the prenatal, the intra-uterine, gestation, and pregnancy can deconstruct and dissolve the concept of the unitary separate phallic subject split by the castration mechanism, rejecting its abject, and mourning its m/Other" (2006, 183). These transitive experiences are foundational to Ettinger's Feminine-matrixial. It should be made clear that Ettinger's formulation of Feminine difference is not essentialist or predicated upon biology, pregnancy, or even gestation. I will argue that the Ettingerian Feminine is in fact best described as Tiresian because he embodies what Ettinger calls trans-subjectivity, being with and alongside Others in transformation. Tiresias knows about being/becoming a woman from both a phallic and matrixial angle.

To contextualize Ettinger's conception about the feminine/Feminine difference, let us also remember that she responds to Lacan's now famous comments on feminine sexuality. In 1960, at the University of Amsterdam, Lacan delivered a paper later published in *Écrits* (Lacan, 2006) saying that we should not be fooled by Tiresias; the mythological character cannot know anything more about feminine sexuality than we do, which amounts to nothing. For Lacan, the feminine is a mystery out of symbolic bounds.

For the Parisian psychoanalyst, it is structurally impossible to alter one's sexual positioning and Woman as a category does not exist. For Lacan, the feminine position is not universalizable and thus eludes the confines of the phallic signifier. Consequently, she is "not-all" because not all of woman is one by one and does not exist as a phallic category. She is, therefore, closer to the Real than men. As Lacan explains, there is no symbol for the woman's sex as such. There is something about the woman that is Real because, unlike the man (who is fully subject to the phallic signifier), there is something about the woman that escapes the signification of the phallus. From an Ettingerian angle, it is very possible that as a young man, Tiresias did, in fact, intercept something of this non-phallic difference in what he glimpsed in Athena. Likewise, I wonder if Tiresias may have come close to apprehending something about feminine/Feminine difference in the copulating snakes that he could not bear. For Lacan, these suppositions would be untenable. Interestingly, at this same conference in Amsterdam, he faults female psychoanalysts for co-conspiring to keep feminine sexuality a mystery. The irony is that he might have used both Athena and Hera, who were equally enraged by Tiresias as well as what he said or saw about feminine/Feminine difference, to illustrate his point.

Although Lacan seems to suggest that there is something pertaining to feminine sexuality that may not fit into his formulation of sexuation, in his later work, he nevertheless insists that there are only two sexual positions based upon a structural relation to the Other and to jouissance. This binary choice, between feminine or masculine positionings, is central to Lacan's theorization of the subject. He insists that we should not be hoodwinked by Tiresias the great prognosticator. Sexuation is a Real problem of language and logic that is irreducible to what we in English call gender identity. Gender identity and gender expression largely concern what Lacan calls the Imaginary register, including, but not limited to, identity, affect, embodiment, and body-image. The Imaginary, which takes shape during the mirror stage, involves a structure of appearances beholden to an Other. Subjects gain a semblance of unity by identifying with an image given to be seen by an Other. The problem with identity, as Lacan sees it, is that it is inherently alienating and based upon a false semblance of subjective cohesion. There is, for Lacan, a lethal gap in the mirror stage.

Did Tiresias encounter this lethal gap? I continue to wonder about what Tiresias did or did not see in Athena's body and how it relates to matrixial sexual difference. Tiresias seems to have apprehended something in Athena's nudity as well as in the scene of the copulating snakes that goes without representation in the phallic order of language. What remains unrepresented nevertheless concerns psychoanalysis; both Lacan and Ettinger agree on this point. For Lacan, Tiresias deserves to be "the patron saint of psychoanalysis" (Lacan, 2014, 183). Despite Lacan's skepticism about the Tiresian myth, he notes that there is something about the clairvoyant that is of great relevance to the psychoanalytic project. While Lacan's reference to Tiresias in Amsterdam was not the first (or last) time he refers to the prophet in his teachings, in fact the Theban seers show up often in Lacan's works, here the myth is a poignant reference used to explicate what he refers to as the impossibility of knowing anything, ultimately, about the feminine.

The Other Sexual Difference

While Ettinger does not contest Lacan's theory of sexuation, she believes that it is only part of the equation. There is, in addition to the phallic axis of sexual difference, a matrixial axis of sexual difference (which everyone, regardless of gender and later sexual positioning, can and does experience). Additionally, Ettinger takes issue with a conception of woman that reduces her to an object, to a symptom of man, and, finally, to a radical otherness or Thing. This formulation of women is specific to the phallic premise that is confined to an "axis of the One and the Infinite, with its same and oppositions, all and nothing, as its surplus, residue, Other, impossibility, contingency" (Ettinger, 2006, 113). Moreover, Feminine heterogeneity is not registered on the phallic axis in a way that would be "independent from the all to which it is related and from the experience to which it is supplementary" (Ettinger, 2000, 188). There is, in Lacanian theory, nothing (signifiable) beyond-the-phallus and this, in Ettinger's interpretation, reduces the Feminine to a masculine phantasy and experience based on the Oedipal model. What has been "taken as the neutral and universal concept of the subject is in fact a phallic model premised on an on/off logic that positions the feminine negatively, below the threshold of any kind of symbolization" (Pollock, 2006, 2).

Ettinger thus posits an Other order of (Feminine) Sexual Difference, one that predates, yet operates alongside, the Lacanian formulation of sexuation. Ettinger's Other Sexual Difference does not concern castration (severance) by the signifier, but borderlinking to Others in the Real. This borderlinking is a feminine Eros particular to matrixial borderspace. For Ettinger, there is a primary and unavoidable incestuous relation with the m/Other that makes the Other Sexual Difference a sexual coefficient. The Feminine for Ettinger is a "non-phallic, non-Oedipal, nongendering redefinition of a subjectivizing apparatus that is, nonetheless, sexuated and sexuating" (Ettinger, 2006, 14). Ettinger writes about an "incestuous in/outside rapport" foundational to gestation and ultimately to subjectivity and sociality. This non-prohibited in/outside rapport enables trans-subjectivity as unavoidable sub-knowledge about difference in the matrixial borderspace (Ettinger, 2006). The non-Oedipal incestuous relation involves a "non-prohibited incestuous in/outside rapport" (Ettinger, 1997, 376) that predates individuality, castration, and severance from the m/Other. This trans-subjectivity involves "transformational potentiality for intersubjective transactions" (Pollock, 2006, 11) relating to feminine cross-inscription; it is fundamentally transitive.

Let us recall that in all mythical Tiresian stories, there is an Other (as female deity or archetype), an unauthorized transgression (snake-hitting or gazing), and the relinquishment of forbidden knowledge concerning sexual difference. It is possible to see that Tiresias is a matrixial figure because he embodies a sexual difference that is transitive and co-emergent. In her discussion of transgressing with-in-to the feminine, 40 years after Lacan's famous Amsterdam conference, Ettinger (2000) counters Lacan's claim that we can know nothing of the feminine dimension. She suggests that Lacan can only see Tiresias through a phallic axis of difference while in her formulation, there is an Other Sexual Difference that is matrixial (and thus Feminine), a difference having nothing to do with the phallic signifier. She writes:

Under the matrixial light, the transgression in the figure of Tiresias between man and woman is not a transgression of a frontier between known
maleness and unknown femaleness. Rather, since the matrixial I carries
traces of experiences of the matrixial non-I, inasmuch as I know in the
other and my other knows in me, non-knowledge of the feminine, in the
matrixial borderspace, is impossible, by virtue of the transgression itself.
(Ettinger, 2000, 189, emphasis in original)

In other words, it is impossible, from a matrixial angle, to not know something about women and the Feminine dimension. Ettinger's conception of
Woman differs substantively and fundamentally from Lacan's. The Ettingerian Woman is a configuration of more than one partial-subject in a given
matrixial web. For Ettinger, there is no separation between the "I" and the
Other (or otherness) at the level of what she calls partial-subjectivity. Building
upon Lévinas, Ettinger explains that the Feminine is the "irreducible difference inside subjectivity" that makes us human (2006, 190). The resulting
subjectivity is thus partial, and subjects are affected by one another as partners
in non-symmetrical ways. The Woman appears as the "co-emerging partial
self and Other, or a different kind of relation to the Other" (Ettinger, 2006,
72). Within this framework, Tiresias with-in and alongside Athena is, for example, a Woman in Ettingerian terms. Ettinger's main point is that Woman
is a condition of transitivity and a co-relationality that can be symbolized in
an expanded Symbolic (which she refers to as a sub-symbolic). In the matrix,
Woman is a "border-Other, a becoming in-ter-with the Other, never a radical
alterity" (Ettinger, 2001, 129).

Ettingerian theory gives form and interpretation to an Other Sexual Difference that is transitive, involving at least two partial-subjects, but not regressive
or symbiotic. Her writing on transitivity as a modality of sexual difference is,
in part, inspired by a belief in the limitations of the Lacanian formulation of
the mirror stage. The mirror stage is a foundational stage of ego formation
for infants who identify with their image as reflected in a mirror that will become a template for emerging perceptions of selfhood. Transitivism is a process
whereby the child identifies with another to the point where they experience
the other's symptoms. "A child who beats another child says he himself was
beaten; a child who sees another child fall, cries" (Lacan, 2006, 92). This is, for
Lacan, a structural ambivalence associated with the mirror stage. Lacan stresses
that transitivism is an indicator of how the subject can identify with the other's
image and take on the other's feelings. It is also an example of how we take on
an image that is other to our own.

Although Lacan views transitivism as regressive, for Ettinger it serves as the
basis for an ethics of Feminine difference. Given the porousness of the matrixial
web as it pertains to partial-subjects, transitivity is about "subjectivity as encounter." In this sense, transitivity is a sexual difference that co-occurs before
and after birth. Sexual difference in the matrixial is not about the One (and its

binary oppositions between object and subject), but about "thinking transmissivity and co-affectivity" (Ettinger, 2006, 183) in utero and after birth. It isn't about "having" or "being" the phallus, for example, but about the unthought time-space of borderlinking in the Real. The Feminine is, for Ettinger, a matrixial co-effecting encounter-event outside phallic logic. Working creatively with the Imaginary and the Real, the Feminine-matrixial inscribes a trace beyond the visible. This trace is fundamentally about the elaboration of a traumatic and phantasmatic border shared between two or more partial-subjects. In the original borderlinking between the mother-to-be and the subject-to-be, there is a Feminine sexual relation. Contra Lacan, Ettinger contends that the sexual relation exists and can be intercepted in a matrixial sub-symbolic. In Ettinger's theorization, sexual relations are possible and not inevitably marked by what Lacan calls "the sexual impasse." In other words, from the perspective of the matrixial, there is a sexuating co-emergence between *I* and *non-I*. This is a transitive sexual relation between partial-subjects in the matrixial borderlinking.

Mythically, we could say that the question of a sexual relation is in a nonsymmetrical way, arbitrated on Mount Olympus. Tiresias is called upon to resolve an impasse between the king and queen of the gods in *The Odyssey*. Hera and Zeus argue over the question of sexual pleasure – which sex enjoys more. Zeus insists that women have more pleasure than men during love making, while his wife, Hera, argues that it is in fact men who have more pleasure. In order to resolve the dispute, the couple consult Tiresias who supposedly has first-hand knowledge of sexual pleasure from both male and female perspectives having been a man and a woman. The problem is that the formulation of the question leaves no room for Tiresias to elaborate upon a structural difference between feminine and masculine sexual pleasure (as represented by Hera and Zeus, respectively), only a measurable difference in degree between two positions erroneously arranged upon a common axis. Tiresias is, in other words, asked to provide a phallic measure of sexual pleasure, specifically who has more of it. This is a phallic question, one that negates feminine difference in Lacanian terms and matrixial difference in Ettingerian terms. The very nature of a quantitative measure is arbitrated by a phallic principle and precept. The Other (feminine) jouissance, in Lacanian terms, cannot be measured (let alone said or known). Similarly, the Ettingerian Feminine defies quantitative measure or phallic comparison.

In both Lacanian and Ettingerian terms, the question presupposes a comparison that is not possible. I believe both Lacan and Ettinger would sympathize with Tiresias. The seer understands that the truth can only be half-told (as Lacan would say), and that there is an Other truth pertaining to what Ettinger calls Feminine sub-knowledge (as Real). The Real of the situation will always complicate and confound anything that can be said by way of an answer. Tiresias responds: "for ten parts pleasure, women have nine, which is to say women receives nine times the pleasure of men" (Madden, 2008, 36).

Moved to fury, Hera renders Tiresias blind for siding with her husband. Zeus takes pity on the prophet but cannot undo the spell of blindness cast by his wife. As compensation, he gives Tiresias the gift of prophesy, a second sight and a long life. Consequently, the truth-telling diviner lives alongside seven generations of Thebans for over 300 years. During this time, he again finds himself subject to a demand in Oedipus the King. Oedipus demands that Tiresias, the gifted prophet, tell him who killed King Laius. Oedipus does not know that he is the villain he seeks. Nor does he know that the late king is his father and that he has unknowingly married his mother, Jocasta, fulfilling the very oracle he tried to avoid. Oedipus is searching for a knowable truth. But he is searching for something that is unknowable in the sense that it is unimaginable. Tiresias occupies the position of analyst or "subject supposed to know," and Oedipus, occupying the position of analysand, demands the murderer be named.

Tiresias again finds himself in a bind structured by a denial sewn into the very nature of the question. Just as Zeus and Hera insist upon a quantitative measure for a sexual pleasure that disregards a qualitative difference that cannot be determined, Oedipus demands a truth precluded by the very nature of his question, specifically that it must be someone else who killed Laius. The Other (as murderer) is, in fact, Oedipus. In the tragedy, he ignores the difference between the Other (as murderous non-I) and the subject-Oedipus (as I). Oedipus finds himself ensnared in a transitive difference that cannot be disentangled, or understood, without troubling patriarchal and monarchal subject positions. The subject (Oedipus) is party to an (incestuous) encounter that interferes with his standing as king. From an Ettingerian perspective, we might say that he is more than One as a partial-subject, but alienated to the extent that in his familial web he is unrecognized. By trying to avoid his fate, he fulfills it. Oedipus wants to know the "truth." Tiresias tries to evade his questions. In Lacanian terms, Tiresias tries to refuse the Oedipal demand for knowledge. As careful readers of the Oedipal story will recall, Tiresias pleads:

> Just send me home. You bear your burdens,
> I'll bear mine. It's better that way,
> please believe me

(Sophocles, 1912)

Tiresias knows that the truth is tragic and best approached in another way. For Lacan, the analyst must introduce the truth as absent. The truth that matters is, for Lacan, in the unconscious. It can, at best, be half-told. In "Science and Truth," Lacan is emphatic, the truth "as long as pure reason can remember, has always kept its mouth shut" (2006, 737). In other words, the analyst refuses the analysand's demand to tell his/her truth in order to let the analysand find it. "The truth comes alive in the discourse between analyst and analysand (two subjects); it is 'other' (Other) than either of them" (Webb, Bushnell and Widseth, 1993, 599).

But Oedipus cannot bear Tiresias's refusal to tell the truth. He resorts to name-calling and "acts-out." Referring to Tiresias as "unlawful" and "unfriendly," Oedipus persists in scornful cross-examination:

> What? You know and you won't tell?
> You're bent on betraying us, destroying Thebes...
> you scum of the earth, you'd enrage a heart of stone!
> You won't talk? Nothing moves you?
> Out with it once and for all!

(Sophocles, 1912)

> Tiresias is indignant:
> You criticize my temper...unaware
> of the one you live with, you revile me.

Oedipus rages on, accusing Tiresias of murdering Laius. Pushed to his limits, Tiresias reveals the devastating truth that Oedipus not only killed his father, but married his mother:

> You are the curse, the corruption of the land!
> ...I say you are the murderer you hunt
> ...you and your loved ones live together in infamy,
> you cannot see how far you've gone in guilt.

When Oedipus is confronted with the truth, he cannot assimilate it. Oedipus gouges out his eyes to punish himself for his hubris of sight. But the truth that acts like a signifier cannot be evaded by blinding. Although the Real is in excess of what can be said or seen, it is enacted by murder and incest in *Oedipus the King*. What kind of man kills his father and marries his mother? In what configuration of sexual difference does the son maintain such sexual ties with the mother? Is there another way to read the Oedipal tragedy? Is it something more than a cautionary tale about patricide and incest immortalized by Freud in his writings on the Oedipal Complex? Might the story of Oedipus, especially as it involves Tiresias, tell us something about an Other order of Sexual Difference that has gone undertheorized in psychoanalysis?

I submit that *Oedipus the King* involves the dangers of disavowing the Ettingerian Feminine dimension. This is a dimension of being where others (as non-I's) are not strangers but internal to the partial-subject in a matrixial web. In the Feminine axis of difference, the "I" is not (only) One (as individual), but intimately tied to and co-affected by others. The "I" and the "non-I" are names for the partial-subject and its Other(s). Oedipus is not a lone actor in the drama arriving from elsewhere that he believes himself to have departed from. He is bound to and co-inhabited by his predecessors as "partners in difference" in a matrixial (familial) web he has yet to avow. Others have come before him and co-exist alongside him.

In Ettingerian terms, Tiresias is asked to reveal the sub-knowledge of an Other Sexual Difference that Oedipus, as a king and patriarch, cannot understand. There is, in other words, a disavowed Feminine relation tying Oedipus to an Other unknown familial web from which he was torn in infancy. As the story of Oedipus goes, the son of Laius is banished from his family of origin because the king is warned of an evil prophesy: that his son will take his father's life. Consequently, Laius instructs a shepherd to kill the baby Oedipus. The shepherd takes pity on the infant, allowing him a chance to live and be raised by an adopted family in a distant village.

While Freud elevates the Oedipal drama to the status of a universal complex without even once acknowledging Tiresias, Lacan and Ettinger both reflect upon the position and predicament of the prophet. Ettinger's supplement to Lacan gives us another way to read the Oedipal story. It is prudent to question a supposedly natural human inclination to patricide and incest borne out in the Oedipal tale. In Ettinger's reading, the play reveals a Feminine trauma engendered by familial abandonment, exile, and war between cities. In *Oedipus at Colonus*, Oedipus dies in exile, away from his family in Thebes, while his sons wage war and ultimately take each other's lives. Let us be clear about the fact that patricide and incest do not cause Oedipal turmoil but are a response to it. Oedipus is, in the first instance, traumatized by a rupture in his familial web. He unknowingly kills his father and marries his mother. Is this a desperate unconscious attempt to repair a matrixial tear in the fabric of his lineage? Oedipus is not just heterosexual in his lust for his mother and masculine in his over-identification with his father (as indicated by his literal usurpation of his father's position as a king); he is suffering at the hands of an un-symbolized loss, a Feminine loss connected to others in his matrixial web. What does his very public transgression of the incest taboo reveal if not a yearning to avow connections to those familial (partners-in-difference) from whom he was separated at birth? Loss of the m/ Other (Jocasta) is first and foremost in the Sophocles trilogy; patricide and incest come after the fact. While Oedipus has played a significant role in the story of psychoanalysis, it is time to pay attention to what others, like Tiresias, can see and tell us about sexual difference(s). There is more than one axis of difference at stake in the history of the subject and it may take Tiresias, a blind prophet, to see and give form to something beyond the phallic premise.

Note

1 I use the lower case "f" when referring to Lacan's conceptualization of feminine sexual positioning and capitalize the "F" when I am referring to Ettinger's conceptualization of Feminine difference.

Bibliography

Eliot, T.S. (2001). *The Waste Land*, ed. M. North, New York: Norton.

Ettinger, B. L. (1997). "The Feminine/prenatal Weaving in Matrixial Subjectivity-as-Encounter." *Psychoanalytic Dialogues*, 7(3), 367–405.

Ettinger, B. L. (2000). "Transgressing with-in-to the Feminine," in *Differential Aesthetics* (pp.185–209), ed. P. Florence and N. Foster, London: Ashgate.

Ettinger, B. L. (2001). "Matrixial Gaze and Screen: Other Than Phallic and Beyond the Late Lacan," in *Bodies of Resistance: New Phenomenologies of Politics, Agency, and Culture* (pp.103–143), ed. L. Doyle, Evanston: Northwestern University Press.

Ettinger, B. L. (2006). *The Matrixial Borderspace*, Minneapolis: University of Minnesota Press.

Euripides (1994). "The Phoenician Women," trans. A. Wilson, The Classics Pages. http://www.users.globalnet.co.uk/~loxias/phoenissae.htm

Homer (1996). *The Odyssey*, trans. Robert Fagles, London: Penguin.

Lacan, J. (1975). *The Seminar of Jacques Lacan, Book XXIII: Joyce and the Sinthome (1975–1976)*, trans. C. Gallagher, Dublin: Translation for private use.

Lacan, J. (1988). *The Seminar of Jacques Lacan, Book II: The Ego in Freud's Theory and in the Technique of Psychoanalysis 1954–1955*, New York: CUP Archive.

Lacan, J. (2006). *Écrits: The First Complete Edition in English*, trans. B. Fink, New York: Norton.

Lacan, J. (2014). *The Seminar of Jacques Lacan, Book X: Anxiety*, ed. Jacques-Alain Miller, trans. A.R. Price, Cambridge: Polity Press.

Loraux, N. (1995). *The Experiences of Tiresias: The Feminine and the Greek Man*, trans. P. Wissing, Princeton: Princeton University Press.

Madden, E. (2008). *Tiresian Poetics: Modernism, Sexuality, Voice, 1888–2001*, Madison: Fairleigh Dickinson University Press.

Pollock, G. (2006). "Introduction. Femininity: Aporia or Sexual Difference?" in *The Matrixial Borderspace*, ed. B. Massumi, Minneapolis: University of Minnesota Press, 1-40.

Pollock, G. (2013). "From Horrorism to Compassion: Re-facing Medusan Otherness in Dialogue with Adriana Caverero and Bracha Ettinger," in *Visual Politics of Psychoanalysis: Art in Post-Traumatic Cultures*, ed. G. Pollock, London: I. B. Tauris, 159-189.

Sophocles. (1912). *The Three Theban Plays: Antigone, Oedipus the King, Oedipus at Colonus*, trans. F. Storr, Cambridge: Harvard University Press. https://www.gutenberg.org/files/31/31-h/31-h.htm

Webb, R. E., D. F. Bushnell and J. C. Widseth (1993). "Tiresias and the Breast: Thinking of Lacan, Interpretation, and Caring." *International Journal of Psycho-Analysis*, 74, 597–612.

Zajko, Vanda, & Miriam Leonard, eds. 2008. *Laughing with Medusa: Classical Myth and Feminist Thought*. Oxford: Oxford University Press.

Chapter 12

In-Difference

Feminism and Transgender in the Field of Fantasy

Oren Gozlan

The capacity to transform the body in the twenty-first century is greater than it has ever been. We live in an age where body parts are malleable and replaceable. An array of possibilities opened that dramatically affected transsexuality and the effects of these possibilities continue to proliferate. Transsexuality, as understood in contemporary discourse, has multiplied gender positions, raising the question whether femininity and masculinity are polar gender binaries or whether they properly describe a field of gender possibilities. In addition, the transsexual choice raises a moral dilemma wherein the desire to change one's sex becomes a potential moral conflict: Does one have the right to change? In recent years, there has been a surge in studies attempting to understand the clinical, political, cultural, emotional, and psychological situations of trans individuals, including studies of the everyday lives of trans people, as well as concerns over the rights of young people transitioning. As a result, new understandings of affects have been revealed that exceed the trans experience invoking the quest for recognition, as well as the demand for rights and self-definition. In addition, we confront the question whether identity can be taken outside of a particular position. At the same time, in the quest for self-definition, the Freudian idea of the unconscious as a site of "interminable self-questioning" (Rose, 1993, 232) makes self-definition impossible. This impossibility is often ignored or foreclosed, turning both feminist and transsexual demands into what Jacqueline Rose calls a bankrupt "rhetoric of certainty" (Rose, 1993, 232). In most political discourses, the unconscious is overlooked precisely because it is impossible to fully account for; the experience of the unconscious is traumatic as is its suppression.

The unconscious as traumatic is taken up in Rose's (2019) essay, "One Long Scream," where she reflects upon the relation of trauma and justice in South Africa. Not only is she concerned with traditional notions of trauma, i.e., putting the unspeakable into words, but also of trauma as an expression of one's current situation, for example, as in a long scream. The rhetoric of those affected by trauma has shifted from say, the demand to be strong and to grin and bear it, to one that acknowledges their human vulnerability. Rose writes her essay after attending a 2018 conference on "Recognition and Reconciliation" in Stellenbosch,

DOI: 10.4324/9781003284888-16

South Africa. She had found something different about this conference that allowed her to connect to her own vulnerability. She was able to think about the way in which she was not implicated in the conflict, and yet she could be easily mistaken for an oppressor rather than an interlocutor. "One Long Scream" approaches trauma via identity abjuring the security of a position, which is akin to the trauma of trans.

How to think of the political as concerning the unconscious or the unconscious as concerning the political? The grounds for truth and reconciliation, Rose (2019) suggests, cannot be separated from the affect of those who have been excluded, dehumanized, and oppressed. This affect is often ruthless, steeped in desire for revenge. The scream, she suggests, is both symbolic revenge against the prohibition to experience as well as a protest against altruistic surrender. Rose illustrates how trauma can transform into a political demand. Some have theorized trauma as an instance of helplessness without a witness. In such a case, the residue of this experience of neglect can be translated into "I must be quiet." The scream is a result and the individual pain is not seen as a part of political protest. The long scream is the return of what the political represses. Any political transformation, Rose suggests, must lean upon the reconciliation between ideation and the return of affect. It cannot be grounded on their dissociation.

Earlier social movements allowed for new ways of understanding social structures and power. For example, the women's movement's idea of choice opened up a different notion of control over the body. The fight for abortion and birth control made possible the wider use of hormones and surgery, paving the way for transsexual rights. In turn, transgender demands have reconstituted what is considered feminine and masculine, de-essentializing and destabilizing gender positions. Feminist demands for political rights also wed political protest to conceptual change: transgender demands present new questions for feminism, shaping primary notions of gender in the first place. The language of desire that would allow for complexity in feminist and transsexual discourses, however, is largely absent and rarely moves beyond the question of rights.

Political protest can risk collapsing politics into a rigid certitude. At the same time, such a collapse is often necessary for reasons of intelligibility and for political action. Certitude, however, risks wrecking the capacity for communication. If we hold on to certitude, we risk wrecking the capacity for communication, however sensitive it could be. If we are unintelligible, all we have is communication without recognition. On the one hand, there is certainty, on the other, a subtlety so oppressive that we become politically mute.

What ethics can result from such paradoxes presented by the potential antinomy between political action and unconscious truth? We are reminded that ethics is not a set of rules to follow, but a creation in dialogue, and in this way close to a fantasy. It is inherently affected by what it must also contain. The tension between demand and desire also plays out in the tension between social movement and personal preoccupation. How can we tell the difference between demand and desire? Here, a series of hypothetical registers are developed: failure, unpredictability, and difference. These registers can also be read as stories of origin that link the personal to the political in novel ways.

Failure

Feminist demands for control of the body began with struggle for agency and choice regarding abortion, adoption, fertility, and breastfeeding. More recent demands for medical intervention in the form of infertility treatments, surrogate mothering, and artificial insemination have also shifted the notion of nature as static and given, to issues of culture and ideology. After all, how can nature be a measurement of what is right and what is wrong when nature pays no attention to human moral codes? For instance, what kind of "natural" justice is involved when some people are able to get pregnant, while others are not? The demands for medical intervention for infertility, surrogate mothering, and artificial insemination have also shifted the notions of what counts as natural, destabilizing the notion of motherhood. Denunciations of sexual harassment, misogyny, and violence, whose victims are generally women, brought to the surface the question posed by Catherine MacKinnon (1999) whether women were human, while assessing power dynamics and privilege. Both feminist and gay and lesbian movements have created a path for transgender rights by interrogating and expanding the fundamental structures of gender: men vs. women (patriarchal laws), and the way in which these seep into every social arrangement, by posing as natural.

However, a cursory look at today's news headlines reveals that historic gains made regarding these demands, at least in North America, are once again being contested, and that a re-entrenchment of patriarchal control over women's bodies is both imminent and undeniable. Simultaneously, new destabilizations of traditional gender arrangements have brought to the fore tensions within feminism's conceptions of what is a woman, and while feminism has long theorized gender as separate from sex, essentialist claims about genetic make-up or about a shared history of female oppression have led, in some cases, to an outright dismissal of transwomen's singular experiences and their vulnerability to gender violence, rejecting transwomen as threatening. The failure of feminism to address trans misogyny, some argue, allows "one of the most pervasive forms of traditional sexism to go unchecked" (Serano, 2007, 312). In turn, many transwomen are "oblivious to the impact that traditional sexism has on their lives" (Serano, 2007, 312).

Jacqueline Rose's (1993) feminist critique of feminism insists on making possible a language of desire in feminist discourse through focusing on the particularities of the conflicts between rights and wants, i.e., the tension between concrete material demands for social transformation and the responsibility of not relinquishing subjective desire. Both rights and wants are subject to drives, and therefore potentially destructive and retaliatory. How may feminist and trans movements account for wishes to turn the tables, seek revenge, and perform "an eye for an eye?" If we were to include one's own jouissance in writing about feminism or transgender movements, one would need to include one's fantasy of one's personal omnipotence. Rose argues that "the very moment when feminism is saying that the personal is its prerogative" (Rose, 1993, 235) actually is the very moment that something personal is compromised. What is left behind is the question of desire and the conundrum of self-difference that is both a human condition and a subjective situation. If identity politics moves us toward particular experience, one of its failures is that of excluding self-difference, and consequently, subjectivity is compromised. Rose points out a dilemma: a social movement is also a personal preoccupation and, as such, is steeped in ideality, the bed-fellow of omnipotence. Can we come to an ethics issuing from this paradox that resists collapsing into a form of "us and them?"

In this context, we can ask: Has feminism claimed ownership of woman-hood? This question points to an impossibility. On the one hand, there is a demand for intelligibility that is in contradiction with the reality of systematic sexual objectification, in particular, in relation to those most privileged – white, heterosexual men. On the other hand, this demand for inclusion and humaniza-tion of women seems, for some, to be dependent on the social foreclosure of the transsexual person as human. How do we account for this blind spot? Both the trans view of feminist hostility and feminist fantasies of how trans ruins gender remain opaque to each discourses' own investment in a fantasy of certainty that accompanies demands for recognition. While feminism opened the door to the idea of self-determination over one's body, biology appears to remain positioned as a stable ground, particularly in radical feminist movements.

Rose's (2019) recent essay, "One Long Scream," and Sally Swartz's (2019) new book *Ruthless Winnicott*, propose new psychoanalytic understandings of political movements that demand radical subjective change. In discussing the role of ruthlessness in political protest, Swartz gives an example, that of the exclusion of trans students from an exhibit organized by the "Rhodes Must Fall" (RMF) movement at a university which led to a spirited protest by trans activists who challenged the legitimacy of the movement's claim to an inclusive and trans-formative ethos. The trans protest—vocal, defiant, and exhibitionist (some pro-testers showed up naked or covered in paint; some were photographed throwing feces at the statue)—forced the closure of the RMF movement. In Swartz's ac-count, this example vividly shows the urgent need to think through conflicts *between* movements and legitimate political claims *as* internal conflicts *within* each movement, that is, as struggles of self-differentiation. These struggles are ruthless, Swartz argues, because what is at stake is nothing less than the very integrity of these movements, often configured around a demand that a need be met.

Often, political protest involves rage and indignation over not being recog-nized and makes demands for recognition. The less one feels recognized, the more passionate and even violent, the demand for recognition will be. That,

Swartz (2019) argues, is what the social realm must tolerate. Swartz's theory is that if the environment can tolerate it, the demand can also be surrendered in a manner that allows it to be less hostile. It will be an understanding that not all demands will be met, and the conclusion will not be limited to a riot.

Revolt, however, at times involves destruction of meaning. In the process of a demand for action, insight is often rebuked. For instance, revolts against access of transwomen to the women's washroom or to an all-girl's school, and denial of transmisogyny in the name of women's rights are scenes emblematic of the ways in which the transgender pledge itself is seen as clashing with, and potentially undermining, the long-fought-for rights of women. In this configuration, the trans person's appeal for inclusion is seen as potentially obliterating women's rights to safety and stability (Gozlan, 2016).

If demands for change, for transition of any kind, lean upon ruthlessness, what form of social containment may simultaneously "hold" the demand while setting firm boundaries against destructive rage? Swartz (2019) finds in Winnicott's (1971) notion of a "good enough mother" (according to Winnicott, a mother who is not "perfect" but "good enough" turns out to be better for the child who learns to deal with frustration) a useful framework to think through the paradoxical position of holding, while confronting demands whose force may eclipse their own legitimacy. While it is true that change and transition require the destruction of the old, the configuration of the new cannot happen without coming to terms with one's own limitations. Transsexuality and feminism are, and need to be, ruthless in their own ways. Ruthlessness could be the beginning of ethics inaugurated by a rupture that requires repair. The demand that gives rise to potentially obliterating rage may also inaugurate a rupture into a new order.

What would it mean then for transsexual and feminist movements to really listen to the ruthlessness of their demands? Or, in Rose's words, how do we fashion "a political movement that tells it how it uniquely is, without separating one struggle for equality and human dignity from all the rest?" (Rose, 2019, 312). Perhaps this task requires us to develop the capacity to contain both legitimate rage and legitimate fear.

Unpredictability

The idea of self-determination over the body as a central tenet is shared by both trans and feminist discourses. Nevertheless, self-determination over the body raises a conundrum: If freedom is predicated upon self-determination, how is it possible for self-determination to have a limit? And how does one decide who has control over bodies if one believes that control over bodies is predicated on the notion of biological realism?

Let us explore an example of the tensions between trans and feminism. Susan Faludi's (2016) memoir, *In the Dark Room*, describes her slow process of accepting her 76-year-old father's transition from male to female. Faludi narrates the transformation in a singular manner. Hers is not a story of continuity, one of "I always was," but one of contiguity. Faludi's father is a master of disguise. He hides. He creates changes without experiencing them. Transitioning is his way of coming to life. Notably, Faludi becomes most creative when she gives up trying to understand. She follows her father, surrendering to his questions. In the process of witnessing her father's transition, Faludi discovers many things about him: the mystery of his femininity, his history, and his relationships. Faludi must come to terms with the fact that, as much as she tries to figure things out, her father remains opaque. She moves away from trying to understand and in the process, her aggression becomes something else that transforms her and her father. He too must surrender. Both Faludi and her father accept experiences that have never been anticipated. At the limits of understanding, there is a coming to terms that forces Faludi to reconceptualize everything she knows. It is not only an attempt to understand the other that is an ethical stance, but also a study of one's own resistance to giving up something in order to understand. Those strategies are defenses and failures of imagination. Faludi's own transformation as she witnesses her father's transitioning, I suggest, offers an ethical view of transitioning as discontinuous. Faludi's memoir is not just an attempt to understand but a study of one's own resistance to giving up something in order to understand. In this way, it is paradigmatic of the way in which something of the self has to be surrendered (ideality, hatred) for understanding to occur.

As the reader follows Faludi's quest for clues wondering what her father "will have been" for what he is in the process of becoming, she sees identity itself as an obstacle course where truth can never be found. The transitioning father is seen as a stranger, and the readers, as witnesses of this estrangement, also have to come to terms with a similar opacity in their own selves. The thus opened space of intersubjectivity, that of the readers reading the text, that of Faludi and her father, is incommensurable. Another way of thinking about this estrangement is through Georg Simmel's (1950) description of the stranger as someone that comes and stays. Like Simmel's stranger, the unconscious makes us all strangers to the others and to ourselves. Given the unconscious, transformation is not as a simple story of a before and an after, that is, of a strange body that is now here and then gone. Rather, the transformation affects many aspects of the human condition. Faludi's memoir also teaches us that history to be truthful must be, to paraphrase Swartz (2019), disillusioned.

The fracture between feminist and trans movements and communities can be seen as a relational problem. Non-binary identification, for instance, de facto challenges rigid identity labels such as "woman" or "trans" that exclude self-difference and forecloses the capacity for transformation. It is precisely at the moment when someone confronts the illegibility of non-binary gender that essentialism emerges as a defense against anxiety. This anxiety is reflected, for example, in some feminist views of trans as subjects who appropriate and reify gender norms in their very desire for readability. It is similarly evident in trans women practicing misogynist forms of femininity that preserve the patriarchal and heteronormative status quo.

The same attitude is true in radical strands of feminism which exclude trans subjects from "women only" events or facilities, thus insisting on the "realness" of sexual identity, where an F to M transsexual is seen as a woman who "plays" at being a man or, more threateningly, a man (with a penis) who "plays" at being a woman (Gozlan, 2016). This essentialist clinging to gender categories, I suggest, reflects a struggle with the enigmatic qualities that transsexuality brings to gender. Transsexual discourses – in their desire for stability through the insistence on the fantasized notion of righting a "wrong body" – attempt to escape from the disorienting destabilization of sexuality. As Rose argues, these defensive essentializations

> oblige the trans person, whatever the complexity of their experience, to hold fast to the rails of identity. It turns the demand to take control of one's life, which is and has to be politically non-negotiable, into a vision of the mind as subordinate to the will (the opposite of what the psychic life can ever be).
>
> (Rose, 2016, 12)

The meeting of feminism and trans discourses is itself affected by sexuality and hence by the murkiness and fragility of gender which functions both as a placeholder and as a prison house.

The irony is that neither the feminist movement nor the transgender movement can escape the confines and fragility of gender – they are both caught up in a quest for authenticity and intelligibility predicated on treacherous grounds. The category of gender promises to render something intelligible and coherent. The promise of gender as a guarantee of meaning or stability is simply a fantasy or a defense to cover over something that will always remain unintelligible. In clinging to the fantasy of "the political nature of the sexual," in which the notion of self and other are supposedly known, what is left behind, as Rose (2016) argues, is the sexual and hence fantasized elements of the political. Examining the ruthlessness of both feminist and trans political demands from the point of view of their unconscious underpinnings would reveal that all gender ideation is already contaminated and in constant tension. The insistence of feminist discourse on authenticity already reveals an internal failure: its incapacity to recognize that the movement has already accepted transgender subjectivity based on their own assertion of freedom from biological determination. However, the implications of this assertion, and the impact of its reception, remain unpredictable. With the advent of transsexuality and non-binary identity, we can no longer predict the future of gender. Historically, in terms of identity politics, essentialism has taken two directions. One is that of "I have always been this or that" as a coming out story. These stories present a belief in an essential core that is stable and in agreement with itself. A second kind of essentialism is not about a biological core but about an experience: my experience of being oppressed allows me the privileged viewpoint and the right to essentialize the other. It is a firm tactic of language of reversal into its opposite and a claim over suffering.

While one essentialism is at the level of the body, the other essentialism is existential and may express a fear of disintegration – we cannot take an unstable position because it is impossible to survive there. While there may be a political exigency to stabilize gender positions, must this demand for political intelligibility make for totalizing narratives that conflate identity with subjectivity? For both Rose (2016) and Swartz (2019), the answer lies in the feminist and trans movements' potential to explore their own properties and practices of exclusion, in their willingness to confront their "unthought known" (Bollas, 1987).

Uncertainty is often experienced as a threat to the integrity of a positioning and there is inevitable resistance to letting a coherent story unravel. The transsexual movement ruthlessly ruptures feminist ideality. However, the trans insistence on access—to all-girls' school and colleges, to medical services, to washrooms of their choice—is not unlike the feminist revolt against patriarchy. Yet, every movement rooted in fighting exclusion and demanding recognition faces a dilemma: how much aggression can the structure bear?

Difference

Feminism introduced the idea that the personal is political. Now feminism has to contend with the idea that the political is also personal. How do we protect the right to be non-intelligible when rights both presuppose and configure stable, legible subjects? This is not a new question. Feminism has evolved from a shared collective identity and consciousness that constantly demands self-differentiation. Present divisions between feminist and trans movements bring a new urgency to this challenge. How do we overcome binary states of mind, a logic of "us versus them," particularly as these divisions obscure experiential affinities and political lines of solidarity around issues such as gender violence, economic precariousness, state and police repression? Winnicott (1971) would suggest that the only cure for immaturity is time because with time, preoccupations give up their obsessive insistence. This trajectory becomes evident in the transformation of feminist agendas from an insistence on being included into the male world, to an insistence on being recognized one's singular difference.

The third and final move concerns the experience of non-binary gender and involves a new form of subjectivity, one that is no longer oriented by an appeal to the Other. Non-binary identity can become a place of protest, of a new ruthless, made of a pleasurable moment of omnipotence, a destruction of meaning, a fall of idealities, but it can also be thought of as a transitional space, as a malleable in-between space to challenge the fantasy of "normal sexuality." While it is a space of play, it can turn melancholy because it is subject to disillusionment, not only because we can never have all that we want and that when we have we no longer want it, but also because the very thing that we value about ourselves, our identity, is in fact a defense against loss, a loss that remains unconscious. The non-binary subject is a reminder that gender is a conundrum and that sexuality, as Kohon (2016, 258) suggests, cannot offer any stability and does not point to any "'thing' that men and women can conquer and/or possess." Human subjectivity concerns a relation to the void – things that we do not and cannot know. Much like dreams, our theories and ideations of gender are emblematic of the kaleidoscopic ways in which we try to make sense of ourselves at the threshold between reality and fantasy.

Simone de Beauvoir's (2010) insistence, over 70 years ago, that women are not born but become, welcomed the possibility of a new subject. We live amidst new and ever-changing reconfigurations of desire, of femininity and masculinity that appear as unstable directions and positionings. Indeed, even if we might be at the verge of freedom from the shackles of gender, difference remains a condition of human subjectivity and thus relations are structured by failure and no social arrangement will ever be fully satisfactory. The idea of difference was discussed by Winnicott (1971) as a developmental achievement that he related to the concept of maiming. As Swartz (2019) observes, maiming is a quality of protest which Rose (2016) describes as a way of "being" that is not oriented by the quest for satisfaction or the belief that one can know, possess, and control the other. Maiming accompanies the child's ruthlessness, which is a "quality of vigor arising from a self, making a demand, as well as the steady receipt of the ruthless attack without collapse into compliance or retaliation" (Gozlan, 2016, 2). Ruthlessness, Winnicott suggests, characterizes the move from relating to an object with no recognition of otherness, to object usage, where the other's difference is recognized. In Winnicott's account, the mother cannot possibly meet every single demand of the child. She must limit the child's ruthlessness, and in doing so, let desire emerge. Containment will be based on an understanding that not all demands will be met, gradually increasing the capacity to come to terms with the other's difference. Swartz (2019) and Rose (2019) imagine ruthlessness as characterizing a desperate demand that is not simply merciless but that also contains a gesture of conviction and vulnerability. The maiming that accompanies ruthlessness signifies "a dependency on an intractable exteriority of the maternal body which survives the baby's ruthless attacks" (Gozlan, 2015, 6) but maiming is also a creation of boundaries: not only a separation between the self and its outside, but the permeable boundary of the embodied self – an intermediate space between the self and itself.

Let us channel Winnicott and ask, could feminist and transsexual movements allow themselves to be "used and eaten" by the protesters while at the same time "holding hatred" in a way that both contains and makes productive use of aggression? In the text "The Uncanny," Freud (1958) poses an intermediate space of thinking. Taking inspiration from Freud's venture into aesthetics, I propose a space of in-difference, of the most strange, even unthinkable, and at the same time familiar, a space positioned as "neutrality" in opposition to loving and hating. This space of in-difference allows one to tolerate ambivalence, and to hear the other's desire as enigmatic. This in-difference is a way out of the ideality that permeates the meeting of the political and the personal; it is a recognition of a limit – my worldview, whatever it may be, cannot be imposed on anyone else. It hinges on a shift from the "eye for an eye" (and an I for an I) that is often a feature of political activism, to an ethical in-difference where people are able to disagree without destroying the other or themselves. It is a creative engagement with something that cannot be known in advance.

Bibliography

Bollas, C. (1987). *The Shadow of the Object: Psychoanalysis of the Unthought Known*, New York: Columbia University Press.

de Beauvoir, S. (2010). *The Second Sex*, trans. C. Borde and S. Malovany-Chevallier, New York: Random House.

Faludi, S. (2016). *In the Dark Room*, New York: Metropolitan Books.

Freud, S. (1958). "The Uncanny," in *The Standard Edition of the Complete Psychological Works of Sigmund Freud, Vol. 7* (pp.217–256), ed. and trans. J. Strachey, London: Hogarth Press.

Gozlan, O. (2015). *Transsexuality and the Art of Transitioning: A Lacanian Approach*, London: Routledge.

Gozlan, O. (2016). "The Transsexual's Turn: Uncanniness at Wellesley College." *Studies in Gender and Sexuality* 17(4), 297–305.

Kohon, G. (2016). "Bye-Bye, Sexuality," in *Psychic Bisexuality: A British–French Dialogue* (pp.258–276), ed. R. J. Perelberg, London: Routledge, 2016.

MacKinnon, C. (1999). "Are Women Human? Reflections on the Universal Declaration of Human Rights." Last modified May 12, 2020. http://www.ivr.uzh.ch/institutsmitglieder/kaufmann/archives/HS09/vorlesungen/Text_no_3.pdf

Rose, J. (1993). *Why War? – Psychoanalysis, Politics and the Return to Melanie Klein*, Oxford: Blackwell Publishing.

Rose, J. (2016). "Who Do You Think You Are?" *London Review of Books*, 38(9), 3–13.

Rose, J. (2019). "One Long Scream: Jacqueline Rose on Trauma and Justice in South Africa." *London Review of Books,* 41(10), pp. 10–14.

Serano, J. (2007). *Whipping Girl: A Transsexual Woman on Sexism and the Scapegoating of Femininity*, Emeryville: Seal Press.

Simmel, G. (1950). "The Stranger," in *The Sociology of Georg Simmel* (pp.402–408), trans. Kurt Wolff, New York: The Free Press. Last modified May 12, 2020. https://www.infoamerica.org/documentos_pdf/simmel01.pdf

Swartz, S. (2019). *Ruthless Winnicott: The Role of Ruthlessness in Psychoanalysis and Political Protest*, London: Routledge.

van der Heijden, B. and B. Tahzib-Lie (eds.) (1999). *Reflections on the Universal Declaration of Human Rights*, The Hague: Martinus Nijhoff Publishers.

Winnicott, D. (1971). *Playing and Reality*, London: Tavistock Publications.

Chapter 13

Translation, *Geschlecht,* and Thinking Across

On the Theory of Trans-

Ranjana Khanna

In the work of psychoanalysis understood in conjunction with the legacy of colonialism, deconstruction has come to play an important role. Sexual difference in this work has been proffered as something that is yet to come even as it is rendered as an overdetermined binary whether in a biological language of male and female or in a cultural and linguistic frame as men and women, boy and girl, with those cultural categories producing, in turn, masculine and feminine characteristics. In feminist reflections on psychoanalysis, those masculine and feminine traits have been analyzed variously through an anchoring to the biological, for example, in the criticism of Freud's infamous phrase "anatomy is destiny," which, in turn, is understood, albeit through a conflation of the anatomical and the biological, as demonstrative of a "biological essentialism" whereby biological traits determine the manner in which we are in the world and determine what we mean by the terms man and woman as ideations.[1] In that view, cultural understanding of normative feminine traits, for example, weakness or kindness, passivity, or indeed desire for men, is attributed to the biological entity. If one accepts that reading of Freud, this might be centered on the genitals and the question of the presence or absence of the penis.[2] Today, it may also be attributed to hormonal or neural distinctions in bodies. In either case, there is potentially a teleological thinking that leads from one, that is presumed to be pre-existent as matter, to the other that is cultural. Simone de Beauvoir's famous phrase (1976, 13) *"On ne naît pas femme, on le devient"* ("One is not born woman, but becomes one") took issue with that essentialism, and in returning to the question of birth, reinscribed a story of attributes being culturally assigned to a pre-existing body.

Jacques Lacan's (1975) notion of sexuation, elaborated in *Encore* in 1972–1973, prioritized a process through which a subject is inscribed into sexual difference through the signifier of castration, that is, the phallus. But while that notion created the idea that recognition of man and woman was attributable to the signifier rather than to biology, it nonetheless presented gender as a binary, and whether that binary was descriptive or prescriptive has been the object of many courses and books since. The idea of sexuation that was further elaborated by Jean Laplanche underscored the process of sex assignment through gender

DOI: 10.4324/9781003284888-17

categories, whereby the adult assigns sex to the child through the injunction to repress the *sexual*—i.e., the non-reproductive polymorphous perversity of that sexual force that precedes binarization through gender assignment (and through translation as the social process of naming, etc.), within a reproductive dualistic framework of sex. The untranslated (and individuated) remainder becomes the sexual as such.[3]

Jacques Derrida's (1983, 1987, 1993, 2018) four essays on the German term *Geschlecht*, which mostly constitute readings of Heidegger, take up this question in profound ways in a sense by bringing Freud to Heidegger on the one hand, and by elaborating on the process and the question of translation on the other. *Geschlecht*, he tells us through the lens of a consideration of translation, is indeed gender, but it is also the sign for a series of other kinds of blows, one might say cuts also, and is thus to some extent a signifier of differentiation. In the first of those essays, *"Geschlecht:* Sexual Difference, Ontological Difference," he turns specifically to a reading of the lack of an idea of *Geschlecht* in the formulation of the category of *Dasein*, of There-Being, or existence or presence, which is the existential category that expresses the distinctiveness of human beings in the world, who are aware of their existence in it while also understanding their finite contingent nature within it as an active agent in the consideration of what it means to be. Derrida poses the problem of the characterization of *Dasein* as neutral, and how one raises the question of whether sexuation, of the blow (Geschlect is related to *schlagen* or to strike or blow, or, as Derrida elaborates in *Geschlecht* II and as Peggy Kamuf reminds us, "to mint or stamp a coin") happens pre-ontologically or in the world as such, and in so doing poses the question of the distinction between and the leaning toward each other of the ontological and the ontic, that is, the consideration of being in its underlying existence on the one hand, and the understanding of the specific realities within which that being exists on the other. In understanding *Dasein* as neutral, Derrida asks, does Heidegger attribute neutrality to that (the neutral) which has actually anyway been appropriated by the masculine, to borrow a formulation from Luce Irigaray (1985, 133), or does the positing of the neutral render sexual differentiation as coming into being entirely in the realm of the ontic? In that scenario, paradoxically for Derrida, Heidegger would open up the possibility of a pre-sexed Being that is perhaps suggestive of a plurality (a polymorphous perversity? An asexuality?)—a more or less than one (and therefore more than two) sexes that exists prior to the differentiation into a binary through the blow or strike (*"Ein Geschlecht"*—a (singular) blow) of gendering.[4]

In compelling ways in that scenario, *Geschlecht* is rendered as an act of translation. Derrida writes, "...we will even come to see the thinking of *Geschlecht* and the thinking of translation are essentially the same" (Derrida, 2008, 17). Translation is understood here as an act of naming, an engagement with the proper name, whereby the proper name that confers lineage (and thus potential reproduction) is an instance of this *minting*, or a blow that engenders and thus establishes sex differentiation as the binary that leads the neuter away from either asexuality or polymorphous perversity through the process of gendering (*ein Geschlecht*). That which exceeds gendering and sexing would elsewhere be described by Derrida (in conjunction with a reading of Nicolas Abraham and Maria Torok) as the anasemic, or indeed as an anasemic poetics which allows for a manifestation of the untranslatable in and through dissemination (Derrida, 1979, 4–12). The question remains for Derrida as to whether sexual difference understood as sexual differentiation can be relegated to the sphere of the anthropological and the elements of "concretion" that go along with that (Derrida, 2008, 12).

It is this question that brings into play the problem of translation. *Geschlecht* is analyzed in the German because "gender" is actually not an adequate translation, and neither is blow or cut or minting. "*Geschlecht* will be charged with all its polysemic richness: sex, genre, family, stock, race, lineage, generation." Additionally, in *Geschlecht III: Sexe, Race, Nation, Humanité*, Derrida puts the word *Geschlecht* to work on Heidegger's investment in the question of nationalism, and a kind of spatialization that nonetheless roots *Dasein* (Derrida, 2008, 12). In addition, Derrida adds in "Heidegger's Hand" the implied but nonetheless troubling for Heidegger blow that initiates the distinction between man and animality, something he will take up in more detail in *The Animal That Therefore I Am* (Derrida, 2008). This unpacking of the blow cast by *Geschlecht* opens up something quite specific for the text of psychoanalysis, and that is whether sexual differentiation is an *ur*-difference for psychoanalysis, or whether it is one difference among many. It also begs the question of whether the inscription of gender is in the service of production of a binarized notion of biological sex for the sake of reproduction, and in Laplanche's terms, as distinct from the sexual.

The sexual, rendered prior to differentiation, would, in that scenario, be described in the zone of the metonymical and the polymorphous, that is, in the zone of sexual difference which is yet to exist as such in the field of metaphorical differentiation. Rendered thus, all sexual differentiation, realized through assignment by the social (in Laplanche's terms) or identification (in Freud and Lacan's terms) or translation (in Laplanche's, Derrida's, and Abraham and Torok's terms), would belong to the fetishization of the binary in the service of reproduction, and in the terms of "civilized" society as described by Freud, the reproduction of a masculinist economy of the same rendered through lineage (and then through Marx and Engels through the reproduction of the labor force). Whether that fetishization that reproduces a binary actually results in a child or not, and whether it is an identification and assignment that is produced by and alongside parents, doctors, or religion, normative behavior of scalpels and surgery, in principle would not make a difference. Sexual differentiation would be a symptom, and no more or less pathological if it was produced through surgery (for the transsexual) or through ideology (for the so-called cis-female or male). That zone of indistinction would be the anticipation of a sexual difference that is yet to come, yet to be conceived.

The essay began with the topic of the colonial legacy and claimed that deconstruction had been important to the bringing together of psychoanalysis and postcoloniality, which is evident in the texts of Derrida, Gayatri Chakravorty Spivak, and Homi Bhabha, among others. Spivak in her reading of Derrida's *Glas*, and *Spurs/Éperons* questioned whether Derrida's concept of woman was distinct enough from Nietzsche's in its rendering as she who must fake pleasure in her role in this masculine economy. That faking marks her as unable to be the self-same subject of masculine lineage and also as the figuration of deconstructive analysis as it both resides in and outside an economy simultaneously. Spivak tackles the problem of how one offers a critique of phallocentrism and the representation of woman that nonetheless seeps into the polymorphous zone of indistinction in its theorization by male philosophers. Derrida's analysis of Genet in *Glas* puts stress on Hegel's concept of the familial through the figure of the maternal and her relationship to fetishism, which rewrites the fetish as less a substitute for the missing penis and more as a signifier for the swinging of the pendulum between knowing and not knowing whether the mother has the phallus or not. This inscription into the masculine economy, however, is for Spivak (and possibly also for Derrida?) inadequate to the task of understanding phallocentrism and the figuration of woman.[5]

Spivak highlights the double bind explored in Derrida's text, which is to say that he reads Nietzsche's phallocentrism and attempts to understand the aphoristic (feminine) style of Nietzsche as embodying a certain performance of the problem of the staging of woman as performative of such deceit. Is the acknowledgment of the style sufficiently distant from the utterance of the idea of the deceitful woman? Immersed in the contagion of the Western philosophical text, how does one, then, she asks, affirm deceit without reinstating the belittling description of woman? To acknowledge that woman is the problem for psychoanalysis doesn't necessarily provide the way out of constantly being the/a problem, particularly if one is attempting to claim that the theory of the subject in psychoanalysis is inadequate to the task of understanding the displaced subject of woman or indeed of the non-European whose structures of the familial, the assigned, and the identificatory may be quite distinct from those of Europe.

Psychoanalytic thought has, after all and since its inception, been in dialogue with and has been partially constituted by feminist thinking. In its early years, many thought with and against Freud on the topic of female sexuality and femininity, for Helene Deutsch to Karen Horney, and from Karl Abraham to Ernest Jones. Feminist psychoanalysis contended with masculinist thinking and did much to change it. In feminist thought more generally, psychoanalysis has had a mixed status. Some have rejected it more or less wholesale, others have had more measured responses, and there have been elaborate and important interventions from feminist thinkers working within particular psychoanalytic traditions (for example, the Lacanian, the Freudian, or the Kleinian). The imbrication of psychoanalysis with feminism has been massive, and more often than not, it has shared with other strands of psychoanalytic social theory more generally a deep investment in Western Marxist analysis of culture following the work of critics such as Louis Althusser. From the 1970s onward, the discourse linking feminism, sexuality studies, and psychoanalysis has been vibrant and has been among the most compelling forms of critical analysis attempting to grasp what Jacqueline Rose, and later Judith Butler, understood as the psychic life of power (Butler, 1998; Rose, 1994).

What that body of work often failed to engage until more recently, however, was that psychoanalysis imagined itself from its inception at the turn of the twentieth century as an international force. Psychoanalytic institutes emerged all over the world in the early years of Freud's work, and his correspondence (the movement back and forth, the pendulum of fetishism) with those setting up institutes or grappling with local conditions and psyches marks psychoanalysis as a particular internationalist modernist enterprise. Coming to grips with the world, or perhaps more appropriately, the worlds of psychoanalysis, how it came into formation at a particular moment of empire and of state formation, how it spread, became distinct in its formation, how it erred from its original path but was informed by it, and how we understand those questions through a lens of sexual difference have been the priority of studies over the last 20 years or so. In this regard, we may think of the various projects of literal and practice-based translation and parochialization that documented the early internationalism of psychoanalysis. These include histories of the psychoanalytic institutes and practices in various countries, as well as readings of Freud's letters that show his international collaboration and knowledge and that between the center (constituted as Freud who perhaps had the knowledge and perhaps did not) and the periphery. One may think of Christiane Hartnack's (2001), Ashish Nandy's (1995), Salman Akhtar's (2005), and Pratyusha Tummala-Nara's (2005) works on India; Joy Damousi's (2005) on Australia; Mariano Plotkin's (2002) on Argentina; Martin Miller's (1998) on Imperial Russia and the Soviet Union; Omnia El Shakry's (2017) on Egypt; Jingyuan Zhang's (2010) on China; and Eran Rolnik's (2012) on Palestine and Israel in the more historically focused work. In turn, they addressed some of the attempts at shifting the structures of psychoanalysis in the early years as well as in more recent times by people like Grindrasekhar Bose, Sudhir Kakar, and Wulf Sachs. We might join with these figures people like Patricia Gherovici (2003), Willy Apollon (1996), and Gohar Homayounpur (2012).

Translation, then, takes on a particular vibrancy and is the vehicle through which not only do we find instances of gendered individuation, but also particularities that put pressure on those processes of individuation. In the 1990's and 2000's, there was an effort to parochialize psychoanalysis and to consider the mechanics of translation. There was a desire to read psychoanalysis's internationalism through the lens of the periphery and to ask of those letters and exchanges a questioning of the way in which psychoanalysis developed in an international frame. This project of parochialization, and indeed of provincialization of the discipline in its colonial European formation belonged largely to an anthropological attempt to understand the context and its relation to subject formation. And in terms of untranslatability, this was understood in terms of the inadequacy of the theory to the contexts in which it was also at work. The project of *worlding* in many ways was reduced to a form of necessary parochialization. However, the worldmaking potential of worlding was often neglected. To place these works and their significance back into the theoretical plane on which I began, we may need to rewind.

The late 1980s and the early 1990s marked the publication of Butler's *Gender Trouble* and Bhabha's *The Location of Culture* (and many of the essays of course predated their appearance in the book and had already made a huge impact on the manner in which postcoloniality was being imagined). The essays were in conversation sometimes explicitly, sometimes implicitly with those by Gayatri Chakravorty Spivak, Luce Irigaray, Hélène Cixous, Julia Kristeva, Stuart Hall, and Jacques Derrida. The essays subsequently published in *The Location of Culture* opened up avenues for a certain kind of new conversation about psychoanalysis and difference beyond the thematic of sexual difference. Of course, there had been precursors in Fanon and Althusser, and implicitly in those who were thinking through Althusser's psychoanalytic Marxism to understand coloniality and different kinds of identification brought into play by post-fordism. These included Stuart Hall's work on different models of identification in what was (for a short moment) referred to as "new times" theory in *Marxism Today*, and many leftist feminists who were invested in the questions posed by psychoanalysis, most significantly Jacqueline Rose, Laura Mulvey, and many of those who published in *Screen*. While British Cultural Studies did not focus on fine art or the experimental arts scene, many of the visual artists of the moment—Isaac Julien, Mona Hatoum, and Derek Jarman, for example—were also in conversation about the different forms in which one might imagine colonial histories, sexuality, and sexual difference, and were often more experimental than their theoretical and clinical counterparts in the elaboration of the pre-assigned sexual, but also the understanding of the material category of "women" in their variety produced through the conditions experienced by them as a group who underwent or were prone to undergo those conditions by virtue of the fact that their genders were associated with certain aspects (often reproductive) of their bodies. And Robert Young's *White Mythologies* from 1990 was similarly trying to understand the coloniality and postcoloniality of writing from the "west" to reveal the importance of understanding Europe as postcolonial space.

Obviously, Bhabha's work was also deeply in conversation with critics elsewhere, Henry Louis Gates, Fredric Jameson, Edward Said, Gayatri Spivak, etc. But it does seem as if a certain configuration of thinking around identification and psychoanalysis was marked by these conversations that shaped the status of sexual difference and the use of psychoanalysis in his work in a particular way.

At the time I was writing my dissertation, I admit to a certain frustration with feminist psychoanalytic thought that failed to deal with any colonial histories (the tedium of flinging around the metaphor of the dark continent even if it was apparently in the service of celebrating the unconfinable), and equally postcolonial thought that was inadequate to the task of addressing the complexities of sexual difference. But I was also trying to tackle a problem that continues to be of interest to me. In psychoanalysis, sexual difference is the *ur*-concept of difference whether one considers psychoanalytic theories that are more anatomically based or not at all, and whether that sexual difference is defined narrowly as distinctions between or among sexed and gendered people, or more broadly (as I would prefer to do) as the yet to be imagined forms of difference marked by phallogocentrism and the idea that Lacan had articulated in *Encore* that "woman does not exist." At that time and still, it intrigued me how the question of sexual difference would play out in Bhabha's work—it often appeared at that time as a supplement—so, for example, in the introduction to *the Location of Culture*, he wrote: "The great connective narratives of capitalism and class drive the engines of social reproduction, but do not, in themselves, provide a foundational frame for those modes of identification and political affect that form around issues of sexuality, race, feminism, the lifeworld of refugees or migrants, or the deathly social destiny of AIDS" (6).

Bhabha was clearly getting at something significant, and it also seemed to address what I always thought a major problem in theories of intersectionality that emerged in the legal setting through Kimberlé Crenshaw's work and failed in various ways to address the processes of identification beyond the interpellations of the legal apparatus and its various forms of understanding sex, race, and gender. The terms, fixed by their very distinct legal origins, engendered forms of identitarian thinking themselves rather than elaborations of processes of identification. Marxist and even Marxist feminist work at a certain moment created its own hierarchies of identification through the base and superstructure models, and efforts to parochialize those narratives did not always give a solution to thinking through coloniality and sexual difference side by side.

I had initially found Bhabha's use of the discourse of difference in psychoanalysis that had been so carefully excavated by feminists, frustrating because it seemed to me to replace sexual difference with colonial difference through analogy. But I was yet to grasp fully the importance of the conceptualization of analogy that was in play at that time, even though I had written the entire introduction of my dissertation on Derrida's essay "White Mythology: Metaphor in the Text of Philosophy" which is in many ways a thesis on the specificities of analogy, or the analogical part of metaphor—its transportation device or automobility (Derrida, 1974, 5–74).

Psychoanalysis is of course a form of analogical thinking played out through ideas of latent and manifest meaning, of the analogy between savage and neurotic, or the manner in which Freud would write and think through archaeological and anthropological analogies to the psyche or ontogeny recapitulating phylogeny. And yet, as the old argument staged between Derrida and Lacan went, the truths it provides in its conclusions often fail adequately to account for analogy itself. Because of the *ur*-status of sexual difference in psychoanalysis, nothing can however be exactly analogized to sexual difference without itself begging the question of analogy, its function as the transportation device of metaphor, and its specific requirement of a literary reading.

In fact, analogy provides the means through which to understand the various forms of identification that take place. If feminist psychoanalysis had developed less through identity (as is sometimes pronounced particularly in the context of the U.S.) and more through identification and materiality, analogical thinking provided the means through which one could understand ambivalence and how multiple identifications could simultaneously take hold and resist each other.

What characterized a certain moment of psychoanalytical thinking in feminist and postcolonial theories was the necessity of thinking it through deconstruction. Clearly, Derrida's work itself owes a huge amount to psychoanalysis, but psychoanalysis, in spite of itself and in spite of its reliance on analogical thinking, often fails to see its own bound nature to "truths" and ur-categories if it's thought outside of the deconstructive mode. This was one of the many lessons learned from the work of Gayatri Chakravorty Spivak. Deconstruction gave a way for Bhabha, and for those after him, to see how thinking coloniality with psychoanalysis revealed the importance of the relationship between deconstruction and psychoanalysis. Thanks to Spivak, the relationship between psychoanalysis and deconstruction had become clearly understood through the lens of coloniality. The specifics of analogy, as Derrida has shown us, create four possible meanings (or indeed identifications) out of one, bringing to the fore identifications and textuality, ways of thinking the one, the dominant, and the ambivalence produced out of the more than one (which is always more than two).

Today, we may take that task more fully to psychoanalysis itself in thinking identification and supplementarity and to more adequately address those inadequate lists that 30 years later still plague our thinking (the race, gender, sexuality, etc., etc. LGBTQ...). Freud of course famously used analogy and metaphor—female sexuality as the dark continent; rephrasing Napoleon's *geography is destiny* to produce *anatomy is destiny*, the correlation of the primitive or savage with the modern neurotic. The metaphors betray perhaps an analogy of which Freud himself was very aware as he corresponded with psychoanalysts all over the world in the early years of psychoanalysis inception and its attempt to understand the modern psyche through the technologies of thinking across the geographies of psychoanalysis, and the significance of that for feminist postcolonial thinking.

But the question of translation, and indeed of *trans-* more broadly, begs the question again of the blow or the cut that marks one through gender as sexed. Do we understand analogy as displacement in the text of psychoanalytic theory, whereby as I wrote in the previous paragraph, displacement of geography by sex is a betrayal? Surely, one would have to say both yes and no, because the history of psychoanalysis has shown us that the sexual (polymorphous, metonymical, anasemic, unassigned) has always been denied in favor of sexual differentiation (through assignment and identification). If we are to take the project of psychoanalysis and of worlding seriously as one of translation and worldmaking, then we should heed Jacques Derrida's advice in his essay "Geopsychoanalysis 'and the rest of the world.'" There, he implores psychoanalysts to respond to violence in Argentina not with liberal calls for justice alone, but for a truly psychoanalytic grappling with the instruments of violence and an understanding of the law.

Geschlecht, as a translation, allows for an understanding of every production of gender as a blow that creates the realization of sex in the world, and that sex is to be understood as the bringing into being of sex, race, lineage, and nation. If we are to follow Laplanche, the dominant notion of sex has been in the service of reproduction and thus constitutes an understanding of a binarized duality (the ur-category of sexual differentiation) even as it manifests as more complex than that in any instantiation. Psychoanalysis has often reinscribed the metaphor of woman in that normative function, rendering those other distinctions held in the category of *Geschlecht* as incidental aspects of sexed being. And yet it is through these and thus through the particular remainders, the particularities of translation and the untranslatable, that manifest as the anasemic poetics of the unassigned, that worlding or worldmaking occurs. It is that tension between the translatable and the untranslatable, then, that allows for the oscillation between knowing and not knowing to manifest in the world.

Notes

1 Jean Laplanche (2007) elaborates on this point.
2 In turn, some would counter this reading of Freud by citing his 1932/1933 essay on "Femininity" from the "New Introductory Lectures to Psychoanalysis" in which he writes, "In conformity with its peculiar nature, psycho-analysis does not try to describe what a woman is—that would be a task it could scarcely perform—but sets about inquiring how she comes into being" (Freud, 1964, 116).
3 Judith Butler (2019) considers this question of translation in relation to gender in a recent article.
4 For a discussion of the singular nature of "Ein Geschlecht," see Derrida (2008, 54–55).
5 Sarah Kofman's "Ça Cloche" (1989) is an important reading of Derrida's understanding of the fetish in *Glas* and is a useful text to read alongside Spivak's (1983) "Displacement and the Discourse of Woman."

Bibliography

Akhtar, Salman (ed.) (2005). *Freud along the Ganges: Psychoanalytic Reflections on the People and Culture of India*, New York: The Other Press.

Akhtar, S., & Tummala-Narra, P. (2005). *Psychoanalysis in India*. New York: Other Press.

Apollon, W. (1996). "Post-Colonialism and Psychoanalysis: The Example of Haiti," trans. T. McNulty. *Journal for the Psychoanalysis of Culture & Society*, 1(1) (Spring), 43–51.

Butler, J. (1998). *The Psychic Life of Power: Theories in Subjection*, Stanford: Stanford University Press.

Butler, J. (2019). "Gender in Translation: Beyond Monolingualism." *philoSOPHIA*, 9(1) (Winter), 1–25.

Damousi, J. (2005). *Freud in the Antipodes: A Cultural History of Psychoanalysis in Australia*, Sydney: University of New South Wales Press.

De Beauvoir, S. (1976). *Le Deuxième Sexe*, Paris: Gallimard.

Derrida, J. (1974). "White Mythology: Metaphor in the Text of Philosophy," trans. F. C. T. Moore *New Literary History*, 6(1) (Autumn), 5–74.

Derrida, J. (1979). "Me-Psychoanalysis: An Introduction to the Translation of 'The Shell and the Kernel' by Nicolas Abraham," trans. R. Klein, *Diacritics*, 9(1), 4–12.

Derrida, J. (1983). *"Geschlecht:* Sexual Difference, Ontological Difference" (otherwise known as *Geschlecht I*). *Research in Phenomenology* 13, no. 1, 65–83. Reprinted in Jacques Derrida, *Psyche: Inventions of the Other Volume II* (pp.7–26), ed. P. Kamuf and E. Rottenberg, Stanford: Stanford University Press, 2008.

Derrida, J. (1987). *"Geschlecht* II: Heidegger's Hand," in *Deconstruction and Philosophy: The Texts of Jacques Derrida*, trans. J. Sallis, trans. J. P. Leavey (Chicago: University of Chicago Press, 1987), 161–196. Reprinted in Jacques Derrida, *Psyche: Inventions of the Other Volume II* (pp.27–62), trans. P. Kamuf and E. Rottenberg, Stanford: Stanford University Press. 2008.

Derrida, J. (1993). "Heidegger's Ear: Philopolemology (Geschlecht IV)," in *Reading Heidegger:* Commemorations (pp.163–218), ed. J. Sallis, trans. J. P. Leavey, Studies in Continental Thought, Bloomington: Indiana University Press.

Derrida, J. (2008). "Heidegger's Hand," in *The Animal That Therefore I Am*, ed. Marie-Louis Mallet, trans. D. Wills, New York: Fordham University Press.

Derrida, J. (2018). *Geschlecht III: Sexe, Race, Nation, Humanité*, Paris: Seuil.

Derrida, J. (2020). *Geschlecht III: Sex, Race, Nation, Humanity*, ed. G. Bennington, K. Chenoweth and R. Therezo, trans. K. Chenoweth and R. Therezo, Chicago: University of Chicago Press.

El Shakry, O. (2017). *The Arabic Freud: Psychoanalysis and Islam in Modern Egypt*, Princeton: Princeton University Press.

Freud, S. (1964). "Femininity," in *The Standard Edition of the Complete Psychological Works of Sigmund Freud, Vol. 22* (pp.1–267), trans. and trans. J. Strachey, London: Hogarth.

Gherovici, P. (2003). *The Puerto Rican Syndrome*, New York: The Other Press.

Hartnack, C. (2001). *Psychoanalysis in Colonial India*, Oxford: Oxford University Press.

Hiltebeitel, A. (2018). *Freud's Mahabharata*, Oxford: Oxford University Press.

Hiltebeitel, A. (2018). *Freud's India: Sigmund Freud and India's First Psychoanalyst Girindrasekhar Bose*, Oxford: Oxford University Press.

Homayounpour, G. (2012). *Doing Psychoanalysis in Tehran*, Cambridge: MIT Press.

Irigaray, L. (1985). *Speculum of the Other/Woman*, trans. G. G. Gill, Ithaca: Cornell University Press.

Kofman, S. (1989). "Ça Cloche," in *Derrida and Deconstruction*, ed. H. J. Silverman, New York and London: Routledge.

Lacan, J. (1975). *Le Séminaire. Livre XX. Encore, 1972–73*, ed. Jacques-Alain Miller, Paris: Seuil.

Laplanche, J. (2007). "Gender, Sex, and the Sexual," trans. S. Fairfield, in *Studies in Gender and Sexuality*, 8(2), 201–219.

Miller, M. (1998). *Freud and the Bolsheviks: Psychoanalysis in Imperial Russia and the Soviet Union*, New Haven: Yale University Press.

Nandy, A. (1995). *The Savage Freud and Other Essays on Possible and Retrievable Selves*, Oxford: Oxford University Press.

Plotkin, M. (2002). *Freud in the Pampas: The Emergence and Development of a Psychoanalytic Culture in Argentina*, Stanford: Stanford University Press.

Rolnik, E. (2012). *Freud in Zion: Psychoanalysis and the Making of Modern Jewish Identity*, London: Karnac History of Psychoanalysis.

Rose, J. (1994). *States of Fantasy*, New York: Oxford University Press.

Spivak, G. (1983). "Displacement and the Discourse of the Woman," in *Displacement: Derrida and After* (169–195), trans. M. Krupnick, Bloomington: Indiana University Press.

Zhang, J. (2010). *Psychoanalysis in China: Literary Transformations, 1919–1949*, Ithaca: Cornell University Press.

Chapter 14

Scenes of Self-conduct in Contemporary Iran

Transnational Subjectivities
Knitted on Site

Dina Al-Kassim

Afsaneh Najmabadi's *Professing Selves: Transsexuality and Same-Sex Desire in Contemporary Iran* (2014) narrates a fantasy reported by several candidates for sex reassignment surgery (SRS), whose transitions happen in serial operations over an extended period for several reasons, among them the fact that the government only pays a small portion toward surgical reassignment, an expensive and arduous proposition. "Imagining death", Najmabadi writes, becomes the condition of a wish that expresses an ideal. "When my body is…washed for burial, I want the washer woman to see a completely female body./When my body is…washed for burial, I want the washer man to see a completely male body" (245). Although legally able to live as and to enjoy the rights of their reassigned gender, including marriage and adoption, many transitioners persist on the SRS path even after having earned their new certification. State recognition of gender reassignment is insufficient to appease a yearning that is again and again expressed in these terms of a finitude that paradoxically promises new life.

With the publication of this study of the history of transsexuality in law, medicine, popular culture and transactivism in Iran from the 1930s, scholars of Middle East, West Asia and North Africa are newly able to test our speculative theories of contemporary subjectivity and its entanglement with modern state power.[1] Arguing that Iran's Islamicized modernity elaborated new subjectivities through the regulation of sexual and gendered morality, habitus and identity, in medicine and civil status, *Professing Selves* locates a crucial techne of state power multiplied in the proliferation of interview, questionnaire, affidavit, testimony and case study that sediments official state discourse on trans habitus. Najmabadi's historical approach locates attitudes in popular media, psychiatry and law in the pre-revolutionary period the better to track the medicalization of transsexuality as co-eval with that of Europe and North America at that time. The medical view, one preceding the Revolutionary Islamic Republic yet surviving the transition of state, that transsexuality reflects a "gender identity dysphoria" dovetails with one traditional, religiously informed view that the trans person suffers a discrepancy between soul and body (rather than gender, for on this account there is no clear notion of gender) that can be corrected by acknowledging social reassignment. As early as 1964, Ayatollah Khomeini

DOI: 10.4324/9781003284888-18

published the view that sex change is permitted in Islam, while his 1984 formal ruling or *fatwa* affirmed the piety of sex change in response to a transwoman's request. This laid the foundation for the refinement over the next 20 years of a bureaucratic and medical apparatus resulting in the institutional approach to trans habitus today. SRS is as achievable, partially funded and regulated as highly as is immigration, education or any of a host of other government functions that shape our citizen being. This is to say that gender reassignment is not a matter of sovereign choice but a form of agency highly mediated by a social process. And yet, the juridical change of status proceeds from and requires as foundation, the personal perception of suffering and key, of a suffering soul whose social appearance and physical body fail to reflect inner being.

Despite significant disagreement among Islamic jurists, the weight of Khomeini's fatwa is indisputable as the basis of law, while its authority is directly attributable to "his unique position as the leader of the most massive revolution in the late 20thc…only Khomeini in fact had the combined religious and political authority that would translate his…ruling into law" (Najmabadi, 2014, 174). Countering the legal obligation to enforce SRS in all found cases of transsexuality, the state fully covers only the costs of hormones not SRS and thus the obligation to pursue surgery is unenforceable, while enforcement itself would be unpopular with a number of conservative religious jurists.

Reassignment also highlights personal narratives and an informal register of social chatter and cultural production in the particular forms of self-narration that support the medical and legal assessment of bodies and subjects. A dialectical pair emerges in the surfeit of a new confessional apparatus: the same-sex player (*kuni*, which is only unevenly described as "gay" and never as "lesbian") and the transsexual (and in particular MtF persons), whose mutual self-definition highlights the entanglement of two seemingly incompatible models of subjectivity: the psychological, deep subject of self-reflection and the contingent self-in-conduct, who finds themself in litanies of action and surface appearance. Intertwined by law, medicine, parties and home, this couple poses fundamental questions for postcolonial critiques of psychoanalysis and transnational accounts of subjectivity.

On the subject of psychoanalysis and its other lives in the global south or east, I will be tacking only lightly into the fabric of a project that is a major preoccupation for me, but in addition to noting that the elaboration of psychiatry, psychology and psychoanalysis in the region is co-eval with its development in Europe, I have been following along the lines of Jean Laplanche's model of sublimation and fantasy to think through the multiple ways that homosexuality and transsexuality are co-defining in communities and by individuals equally exposed to gossip and public opinion, forces that not only shun sexual dissidents or exclude them but also accept the transsexual transfigured by juridico-ethical and religious sanction. Earning the state's certification that one is indeed in need of SRS opens the self and its narration to subjection via medicalization while also authorizing a spiritual actualization self-endorsed by the state. Spiritual, religious and moral truth of one's gender and sexuality is laced through the impersonal materiality of a documentary archive required for certification, one that is to be *made* rather than found for it is created in tandem with a casting away of any similarity with the morally despised role of *kuni*. This negative determination is produced only in close proximity and intimate knowledge of the refused role and the negative path of determination for legal approval and state sponsorship of SRS must pass through the knotted relation to and distinction from same-sex playing even if at some level same-sex playing is a matter of one's transsexual everyday practice.[2] This is to say that the state can and does permit the transsexual in pursuit of trans certification and SRS approval to practice a sexuality that is not otherwise so sanctioned. Thus, in the process of becoming – a becoming that may extend indefinitely – the transsexual in a male body may continue to live and be loved by her man, all under the watchful eye of institutional authority. This material reality along with overlapping social cliques and public meeting places draws same-sex players and transsexuals into close and continuous knots of becoming and self-definition. In short, the Revolutionary Islamic State creates spaces of emergent subjectivities, as Najmabadi puts it, "safe havens" for gays and lesbians because of the unusual state sanction of transsexuality.

Contemporary medical notions of psychology, pharmacology and cognitive therapies do not constitute a foreign or "western" scientific matrix, though their implantation has necessarily evolved in tandem with the currents of local culture and taken up vocabularies of self and other that reflect regional, sedimented and linguistic as well as religious inflections of place and people (Bennani, 2008; El Shakry, 2017; Homayounpour, 2012; Keller, 2007; McCulloch, 2009; Pandolfo, 2018). Let this fact serve as an example of the uncanny memory of a forgotten archive well-documented in Middle East histories of colonial science and medicine but unable to materialize as "*savoir*" or common sense for most Western publics, even academic ones concerned to do good to the other, here the African, Arab and Persian. When trying to think with the archive of colonial medicine from Africa to west Asia and not only from its political, social and historical sediment but also in the spectral forms materialized as psychic traces of relations of violence and loss ranging from the brutal to the passing and delicate, the figure that has seemed most adequate and compelling to me has not been that of a foreclosure on lost affect, a closed door, a secret chamber of lost knowledge or a failure to recall the knowable, but a loose tacking back and forth, up and down the sliding ladder of value, knowledge, past and future becoming. The earliest evidence of knitting originates *fil shat al-arab*/on the Arab river or confluence of the Euphrates and the Tigris, also known in Farsi as *arvand rud* and which draws the border between yesterday's Iraq and Iran. A "swift river", the fish must have run it faster than hooks could catch their gills; much easier to drive them into openwork nets light or heavy, made by bone needles with flax and knotted sinkers. The production of vitality and daily practice from a knotted mesh of gathered fibers is both apt and evocative as an image for the Iranian modernity described in *Professing Selves* where no single explanatory narrative or psychic model dominates the self-understanding of the persons at stake.

Knitting the New Self

By way of illustration a vignette: in the office of the resident clinical psychologist at the Navvab Safavi Emergency Center of the Office for the Socially Harmed of the Welfare Organization, the weekly transsexual support meeting is underway.

> The previous week, … Asadbaygi [the physician] had talked about the importance of 'knowing oneself' (*khaudshinasi* – literally 'selfology') and had asked everyone to contemplate that topic for the following week's conversation. He opens the day by asking if the group members had engaged in 'knowing oneself.' He is dismayed to see that his proposition had not been taken seriously. S., an MtF, blurts out that she had had no time for it. What was she doing then? "I was busy with my boyfriend, cooking, making sure I make myself up in the style he likes." [The physician] is clearly annoyed, "are you that dependent on him?" S. is not fazed, "of course, I am really in love with him.".… Y., also an MtF, who was there the previous week in a black chador but on this day has shown up in his/her army uniform, is expected by the group to explain [the change of dress as change of gender habit]. "Yes, I do consider myself MtF, I do want to go for SRS, but I am also prepared to take my time. Once I change sex, I won't be able to pursue some of my ambitions. In any case, when I am in masculine clothes, I enjoy doing manly things; when I am in feminine clothes, I like to do womanly things".
>
> (Najmabadi, 2014, 280)

These avowals suggest a recoil from the depth model of self-reflection that frames the clinical setting and a dispersal, but also a holding, of the trans subject in the agency of conduct. Najmabadi calls this dispersed subject the "subject-of-conduct" and shows convincingly that both models of conduct and deep interiority are interlaced through the trans and same-sex playing community.

"M., another MtF" challenges Y.'s commitment to their shared identity as transsexual only to face a pileup of other criticism as H. and S. expand on the topic of the necessity of flexible gender habit to accommodate changeable work opportunities and the ups and downs of romance. "Yes, if my current relationship doesn't work out and I have to go back to work, I'd switch clothes to be able to get better jobs" (Najmabadi, 2014, 281).

Yet none of these SRS potentials would consider themselves gay or same-sex players and this without necessarily sharing in a homophobia of aversion, though certainly some do voice extreme discomfort or shame at being "mistaken" for *kuni* or even about sex had under the assumption that both partners were of the same sex or, in a more extreme case, when a husband and wife had sex, though the wife felt herself to be male, and others, including both female intimates and male friends, saw her as male identified. Trans identity in becoming is neither forced into a single path nor is it frayed or worn thin by the necessity to present as the "wrong" gender habit. Each member of the support group capably calculates with that necessity and risk of disapproval while also refusing the judgment of others who so calculate. This flexible sensibility loops back upon itself to escape the exposure of gossip and shame by avowing and embracing the potential "realities" of unpredictable fates, including the surprising evidence of God's "creativity" in creating the transsexual as one testimony puts it.

These vignettes of talk among transsexuals and same-sex players in Tehran in the last decade echo, affirm and elaborate a shared activity of weaving in the spaces traversed by revolutionary subjectivity, juridical status and medical diagnosis. A similar weave of countervailing forces preoccupied Michel Foucault in his final lectures and of interest for transgender studies, I single out two interlaced themes in the late Foucault, found in the 1981–1982 lectures at the College de France entitled "The Hermeneutics of the Subject, 6 January and 10 February 1982". In these lectures, Foucault follows the trail of discussions of "truth" as grounded in "the subject" from ancient Greek care of the self to the Christian pastoral tradition and thence to our modern epoch. At stake is a strange turn in the genealogy of the subject and truth, where he locates the emergence of truth as a duty to care for and guide others by cultivating a soul-searching interiority. Directing others to have right conduct toward their fellows and to themselves forms the basis of a religious reflection on the true self, as we might expect; yet, it is more difficult to explain how and why right conduct becomes central to both revolutionary Marxism *and* psychoanalysis, as it differentiates itself from medical considerations of pathology to develop a critical diagnosis of psychic life and the appetite for power. Foucault speculates that this prehistory to biopolitical technologies of subjectivity takes a detour in the 1830s and 1840s as the revolutionary subject is born behind the barricades.

> We cannot understand the revolutionary individual and what revolutionary experience meant for him, unless we take into account the notion or fundamental schema of *conversion* to the revolution…the problem is to see how this element of technology of the self, was plugged into this new domain and field of political activity…[and] linked to the revolutionary choice, to revolutionary practice.
>
> (Foucault, 2005)

There are several reasons to recall this work on the genealogy of shifting conditions of truth and subjectivity as conditioning the revolutionary character and further, as a context for the discussion of transsexuality in post-revolutionary Iran. Crucially, the lectures of 1981 until shortly before his death in June of

1984 were preoccupied with teasing out a genealogy of shifting conditions of truth that have shaped today's technologies of the self and enabled their emergence out from under the heavy burden of the deployment of sexuality. In the consideration of conversion to the true self as a condition of the revolutionary character, this work returns to the question of spirituality. While adhering closely to a Mediterranean and Christian basis, Foucault's reflections on the historically mutable understandings of "truth" in interrogating life and self become newly legible if we recall the seismic effect of the Iranian revolution of 1979 on intellectual currents of the 1980s during a period of the exhaustion of political militancy in Europe generally. Foucault's writings on Iran in this period identify "political spirituality" as a motive force that could perhaps inspire a resurgence of utopian drives in Europe. Certainly, his attention to topics like truth, sincerity, morality, belief and fantasy is out of joint with the prevailing sentiment of 1980s cynicism, and with the infinite forms of decadent irony through which many in the "west" thrived and survived. To read Najmabadi's map of the knitting together of trans and same-sex desire in post-revolutionary Iran into Foucault's final lectures is to ask what conditions of truth were obtained for *him* when he was led to pause in his disquisition on first and second century C.E. to distinguish the nineteenth-century commitment to revolution from religiosity while retaining the force of conversion:

> ...this notion of conversion, of the return to the self, of the turning around towards oneself, is certainly one of the most important technologies of the self the West has known...we cannot understand the revolutionary individual and what revolutionary experience meant for him, unless we take into account the notion or fundamental schema of conversion to the revolution...the problem is to see how this element of technology of the self, was plugged into this new domain and field of political activity...[and] linked to the revolutionary choice, to revolutionary practice.
>
> (Foucault, 2005, 208–209)

Earlier in the 1982 lecture, he comments on the need to think beyond Marxism and psychoanalysis so as to recognize that each had in its own way incorporated elements of prior spirituality. Key among these elements is the concern for "what is at stake in the subject's being...and what might be transformed by virtue of his access to the truth" (Foucault, 2005, 29). Class position, group identity and institutional membership: these social forms of belonging and identification condition not only a subject's being but also their "preparedness for truth" and truth not as a property of knowledge but as a condition that rebounds upon the subject in the social scene of its discovery or production.

And this leads him to a curious admission: the spiritual *insecurity* of the subject, a crucial topic of the genealogy forgotten by organized dogma (religious, Marxist, psychoanalytic), returns in the practice of Jacques Lacan, who Foucault says is the only one to have posed the "specifically spiritual question: that of the price the subject must pay for saying the truth and of the effect on the subject of the fact that he has said, that he can and has said the truth about himself" (Foucault, 2005, 30). Carried forward in the stream of psychoanalytic thinking since Freud, this concern for the truth of the subject arrives at a paradoxical agency of the subject, one which is materialized only in an address that reflects back upon him, binding him in a scene of agency as a social process of speaking a truth with consequences.[3] Spiritual precarity, the other side of "political spirituality", opens the subject to the social risk of being undone in the political project of announcing one's truth.

The Corpse Washer

In the early pages of *Professing Selves*, Najmabadi presents us with her regretful realization that she could not in good conscience write an ethnography of the contemporary trans community in Tehran. This insight came early in the 12-year project, as she began to frequent trans support groups, activist spaces and clinic and court archives. She resolves her conundrum by steering between the patterning of ethnography and an impersonal history of law and institution all the while narrating snippets and fragments of stories told to her over a decade of conversation and careful listening. As fragments of an archive of encounter, they have the uncanny effect of unweaving the categorical order of the state and dissolving the analytic lexicon of medicine and academic studies. Words like "transgender", "gay" and "lesbian" were the first casualties of listening attentively to the transgender and same-sex desiring people, who met in the group therapy described above but also regularly in public places like urban mall eateries to talk about sexuality and gender performance. A further knot extends the net: religious themes are not uncommon in the dreams and fantasies that Najmabadi reports. Several of these bear out what still other trans individuals reveal; namely, that for many their motivation or inspiration for transitioning is best expressed in a vision of their own body in death.

"When my body is being washed for burial, I want the [corpse] washer (wo) man to see a (fe)male body/I want the corpse washerman to see a male body" (Najmabadi, 2014, 245). Proffered as an explanation for pursuing SRS even after legal reassignment has been achieved, this imaginary scene attests to a desire in excess of state law, community norms and religious dogma. Laplanche and Pontalis's famous 1964 essay on fantasy contains the oft-cited claim that the subject is dispersed in the scene setting of the fantasy rather than represented in a single element or character (Laplanche, 1968). The corpse washer fantasy may indeed be such a syntax for the desire of the SRS aspirant, but another, later formation of fantasy enables a reading of the fantasy as a particular form of sublimation of what Laplanche calls the enigmatic message as it is carried and repeated in an ongoing address to and from the other, who presents the enigma of gendered embodiment and desire (Laplanche, 2014).

In 1999, Laplanche returned to Freud's metapsychology to argue that the seduction theory holds the kernel of "human sexuality" insofar as the infant is the recipient of nurturing care, suckling and caresses, which communicate the sexual unconscious of the caregiver and inscribe this enigmatic message as a mystery or enigmatic signifier. The mystery of the other's desire has many psychic destinies but includes sublimation, which Laplanche associates with symbolization. The enigmatic message marks the irreducible dimension of otherness for which the forms of translation (repression, sublimation, etc.) are "process(es) of closure to the other's address ... an enigmatic... seductive ... sexual address" in the service of a primary drive to "know" by resolving the enigmatic message in flattening sublimations that bind the drive or by opening up to otherness as traumatic enigma. Far from signaling a freedom we associate with creativity, symbolization contains mystery and shuts down unbound energy. As a counterpart to binding, inspiration is an orientation of openness to trauma that "drives" the subject to seek further expression or find new symbols.

Gender is part of the message and positioned prior to sexuality insofar as the sense made of the enigma (in touch, silence, gesture and signs between adults) arrives as already gendered and to be translated, repressed or foreclosed as the advent of sexuality through fantasy. Among the overwhelming priority of unconscious signifiers is the question of gender as a mysterious imposition of the other's desire and iterative closure to the other's address or as responses to a goad. "Laplanche's view is that we rethink gender assignment as an unconsciously transmitted desire, a view with implications for current sociological and legal approaches to questions of gender assignment and reassignment" (Butler, 2014, 126–127). The corpse washing fantasy, as an answer to the question, "Why Surgery?", with the implication of "when the signs could be enough", engages the enigmatic other by repeating the gestures of intimate care and implantation in a fantasy of last rites.

The Muslim burial rite makes few demands but among them, the body must be washed and wrapped in a clean cloth to be buried within three days. Beyond that, simplicity is the rule and variation the reality. Even the prayers may be brief. Thus, the extension and suspension of time in the fantasy – its "time of fantasy" – which imagines the preparation of remains for burial when the aspirant is still living, are itself both reflective of the character of Muslim rites and a violation of the simplicity and "letting go" that this simplicity serves. Practices vary; it is of interest to note that among the general rules, the eldest relative of the same gender washes the body and so, the corpse washing fantasy carries the kernel of familial care and gender decorum in the scene of after death where the encounter between the caregiver and the self stages only serenity. The silent labor of the corpse washer, who looks but sees that there is nothing to see, affirms the symbolic recuperation of the subject in an imaginary form. As Laplanche puts it, contra "a certain Lacanianism", "the 'symbolic' as well as the 'imaginary' are both in the service of the ego – and thus caught up in the almost inescapable position of 'Ptolemaic' reclosure" (Laplanche 2014, 91). Here, in the corpse washing fantasy, the symbolic reinscription and redemption of the body and its true, preferred, sensed and perceived gender work in tandem with the imaginary by "binding through the narcissistic image" (Laplanche 2014, 91).

This fantasy is also legible as an imaginary address to the enigma of the other, Laplanche's primary other, who is not represented in the scene, neither washer nor the washed but who is dispersed throughout the fantasy. Fundamentally a dramatization of the awakening of the subject to "new life" and "new sexuality", the scene conveys an image of passive receptivity or originary helplessness. What awakens here is the body as the true body, appearing in the guise of ego ideal or that which I wish another to see in me; yet, it materializes without authority for the agency of the scene lies with the washer's caring hands and neutral vision. As Laplanche puts it, "inspiration is conjugated via the other. Its subject is not 'the subject' but the other" and "in its resonance with the originary adult other, this other comes to re-open at privileged moments the wound of the unexpected, of the enigma".

The fantasy of finitude (expressible as "death comes despite my life") is also a fantasy of fatality ("my death as condition and evidence of new life"); this transitive fantasy or transitivity of the fantasy can be understood as a radical exposure or as Laplanche puts it, the re-opening and unbinding of the wound of the primary other's incursion. In this way, the narcissistic image is already undone by dint of its social blocking or staging through the neutral gaze of the washer. This scenario of spiritual insecurity resolved by an evident truth, even in fantasy, converts the revolutionary self to themself without returning us/ them to a singular body or self.

And finally, the fantasy of one's own death, legible as an imaginary address to, in Laplanche's terms, the enigma of the primary other, inspires particular trans subjects to pursue a more sincere and authentic embodiment of themselves. Here, the bodily ego imagines a scene of its ideal body, the one seen by the corpse washer as only a body without surprises, as expected, indeed a body mirroring their own.

The trans fantasy of the corpse washer evokes a religious rite and spiritual devotion as a symbolization and sublimation of new life. To become the ideal body, the cis-gendered body must die. Does the fantasy imagine the self as newly cis or transsexual? Does the accomplishment of SRS serve the function of erasing the labor of living conduct to replace it with the calm repose of indisputable gendered bodily form in deathly matter? Has the difference between cis and transsexual become indistinct and immaterial before the materialization of the new body, now only imaginable as lacking the animating soul? If the meaning of the religious ritual is not otherworldly but fixed on the experience of the washer after the self-in-conduct has relinquished the self, does it also carry a trace of ambivalent mourning for that unwanted body, who had to die so that they might live? Along the lines proposed by Laplanche and Freud that we imagine our own death through the death of the person "close to us", I am suggesting that the trans-ness of the fantasy depends upon this translation or trace of the unwanted and mistaken body, while the inspiration allows the other, here the corpse washer in the "right" body, to re-appear, to re-open the wound of the traumatizing message. In Laplanchean terms, this is to read a fantasy of originary seduction and implantation of the enigmatic message of and as sexuality while also understanding it as a making oneself available to the "other, who comes to surprise me". Serenity of the death rite is the language of this surprise.

The self-in-conduct continues its practice as, paradoxically, commitment to SRS might also act as a goad to linger in the group therapy where conduct is schooled and adjudicated and where the liberty to assert new forms of the self not following from the prescriptions of one's fellows is upheld through the very elastic and tangled course of conversation and cultural elaboration. But this self-in-conduct conflicts with the desire of the fantasy for a radical conversion to its revolutionary self in the serenity of the true self committed to a *vita nuova* for our time.

Notes

1 Najmabadi uses the vernacular Farsi tara-jinsi which translates as transsexual rather than transgender, the preferred term in North America. The jinsi in tara-jinsi is itself a trace of the deployment of sexuality that invents the word "sexuality" in Arabic and Farsi on the Latin gens.
2 "Same sex playing" is the term used in context to denote a pejorative homosexuality often structured around differences of age or income, in contradistinction with the term for same-sex orientation, which holds the promise of romantic equality. See Najmabadi (2014, 122).
3 Spiritual insecurity refers to the anxious precarity of speaking one's truth about oneself and is related to though distinct from the explicit use of "political spirituality" in Foucault's writings on the Iranian revolution. This precarity is a political one and subjects speakers and selves to the instability of a truth whose force rebounds upon the speaker, the spiritual crisis of the revolutionary character. For an account of the relationship between al-Shariati and Foucault on the problem of political spirituality, see Ghamari-Tabrizi (2016).

Bibliography

Bennani, J. (2008). *Psychanalyse en terre d'islam, Introduction à la psychanalyse au Maghreb*, Paris: Arcanes-Erès.
Butler, J. (2014). "Seduction, Gender and the Drive," in *Seductions & Enigmas: Laplanche, Theory, Culture* (pp.118–136), ed. J. Fletcher and N. Ray, London: Lawrence and Wishart.
El Shakry, O. (2017). *The Arab Freud: Psychoanalysis and Islam in Modern Egypt*, Princeton: Princeton University Press.
Foucault, M. (2005). *The Hermeneutics of the Subject: Lectures at the Collège de France 1981–1982*, ed. F. Gros, F. Ewald and A. Fontana, trans. G. Burchell, New York: Palgrave Macmillan.
Ghamari-Tabrizi, B. (2016). *Foucault in Iran: Islamic Revolution After the Enlightenment*, Minneapolis: University of Minnesota Press.

Homayounpour, G. (2012). *Doing Psychoanalysis in Tehran*, Cambridge: MIT Press.

Keller, R. C. (2007). *Colonial Madness: Psychiatry in French North Africa*, Chicago: University of Chicago Press.

Laplanche, J. (2014). "Sublimation and/or Inspiration," in *Seductions & Enigmas: Laplanche, Theory, Culture* (pp.77–106), ed. J. Fletcher and N. Ray, London: Lawrence and Wishart.

Laplanche, J. and J. B. Pontalis (1968). "Fantasy and the Origins of Sexuality." *The International Journal of Psychoanalysis*, 49(1), 1–18.

McCulloch, J. (2009). *Colonial Psychiatry and the African Mind*, Cambridge: Cambridge University Press.

Najmabadi, A. (2014). *Professing Selves: Transsexuality and Same-Sex Desire in Contemporary Iran*, Durham: Duke University Press.

Pandolfo, S. (2018). *Knot of the Soul: Madness, Psychoanalysis, Islam*, Chicago: University of Chicago Press.

Chapter 15

Lacanistas in the Stalls

Urinary Segregation, Transgendered Abjection, and the Queerly Ambulant Dead

Calvin Thomas

Aggressively Abject Abstract

This essay considers how certain formulations found in Lacanian theory shed light on the frequently lethal transphobic logics that pervade anti-LGBTQ ideologies.[1] The formulations in question—which sometimes participate in what they illuminate (though that's an old sad story in psychoanalysis)—are all clustered around Lacan's conflation of "sexual difference" with linguistic difference for the human subject as such. On Lacan's view, language, or the symbolic order, orchestrates our constitutively human difference from "the Real" as "sexual difference," and conflates the so-called "Real of Sexual Difference" (Žižek) with *our* linguistic difference from "the Real" (Žižek, 2019, 247–268). In other words, the "symbolic order" *qua* "order to symbolize" compels the *parlêtre* not simply "to be" but "to mean"—and never "to mean" simply but always to make meaning *as* "a man" *or* "a woman" as per "the laws of urinary segregation" imposed by the twin bathroom doors famously illustrated by Lacan in *Écrits*, and as per what Lacan calls the "order[s] and norms [that] must be instituted which tell the subject what a man or a woman must do" (Lacan, 2006, 720). The cross-identified subject who doesn't follow the(se) heteronormative symbolic order(s), who breaks, questions, transgresses, or otherwise attempts to repeal the laws of urinary segregation, that criminal pisser who, like Kristeva's abject outlaw, "doesn't respect borders, positions, rules" (Kristeva, 1982, 4), who dares "to be" *and* "to mean" as "a man" *and* "a woman" at the same time, appears to abolish the merely *symbolic* distinction between the *really* identical bathroom doors, and hence to shatter the *fictional* but constitutively humanizing difference between the Symbolic and the Real, to blur the line between signifier and signified, to signify psychic dissolution as such, to signify the end of significance itself.

And then it gets worse. In the transphobic imaginary, the transsubject who dares to "go" through the "wrong door" seems not only to threaten vaunted heteronormative notions of privacy (and to provoke reactionary child-protective fantasies according to which bathroom invaders are going in there to take not leaks but kids) but also to erase distinctly hygienic lines between

DOI: 10.4324/9781003284888-19

properly socialized bodies and all the actually ungendered waste matters, fluid or solid, deposited on the other side of any door gone through. Here, indifference to urinary segregation, indifference to the difference between one door and the other, suggests indifference to the difference between the "clean and proper" and the abjectly "other" side of any designated bathroom door. And so, given that the *human corpse* is "the utmost in abjection" (Kristeva, 1982, 4), the transgendered subject seems to unsettle the boundary between the quick and the dead, to sully "the limit between life and death" by immigrating across the border between female and male. In this murderously "mistransisist" logic, the immigrant "tranny" gets figured as abject "zombie," as ambulant excrement, and thus as a perfect target for (typically male) political violence. For as Oren Golan observes, "the bathroom is not just a place of satisfaction [of real bodily needs] but also a place of frustration and hate where excrements represent both abjection and aggression" (Gozlan, 2017, 455). And as Sheila Cavanagh puts it, "Identity-based borders, like public toilets, are frantic zones of aggressive projection whereby one person's disavowed difficulties with gender get projected onto others, often in aggressive ways" (Cavanagh, 2017, 330).

This essay, then, will attempt to do what Kavanagh calls the "shitty work" of "countering transphobia." Enacting its own sort of aggressive abjection, the essay will take a massive dump, so to speak, on pathologizers of all stripes who strain themselves to drop transsubjects back into "the Real" and to leave those subjects lifelessly behind, "'outside of language, outside of meaning, outside of the symbolic, outside of relation, outside of desire'—in a space of 'radical abjection and death.'"[2]

If certain Lacanistas (like Catherine Millot and Slavoj Žižek) have helped construct these unlivable "outsides" for transsubjects world-wide, this essay will operate in the spirit of those, like Cavanagh and Gherovici, who "have not only critiqued the reduction of trans* to pathology but also effectively used [Lacanian] psychoanalytic theories to advance a nonpathologizing understanding of trans* identification" (Cavanagh, 2017, 327).[3] In the writing that follows, I will use and abuse Lacan to make as big of a trans-affirmative mess as a more-or-less cisgendered straight white male queer theorist can possibly make.

But I'll begin with an abrasive question.

What the Fuck Happened to "the Real"?

Lacan is said to conflate "sexual difference" with "linguistic difference." But what does that "really" mean?[4] And what might it mean to translate, as I have above, Žižek's "the Real of Sexual Difference" into *our* linguistic difference from the Real"—with the emphasized ungendered possessive pronoun here serving to represent a queerly universal "all of us" who are *all* ontologically *lacking*, who are all *not all*, no matter what?[5]

First question first: What does it "really" mean to conflate sexual with linguistic difference? To use Judith Butler's words, Lacanian theory concerns "the emergence of the speaking subject through sexual differentiation." There is, Butler (1994, 69) writes, a strong Lacanian imperative "to understand sexual difference as coextensive with language itself," so that there seems to be "no possibility of speaking, of taking a position in language outside of differentiating moves," the *primary* move or movement supposedly being that "differentiation from the maternal which is said to install a speaker in language for the first time."

But is it really "the first time"? And does this *singular* phrase "differentiation from the maternal" adequately account for what Lacan calls "the effects of symbolization in the child" (Lacan, 2006, 202) *if* those effects can be thought, as Lacan here seems to think them, in the *plural*? Does this phrase adequately address the question of "what was excluded at the *first* moment of symbolization"? (Lacan, 2006, 320; emphasis added). And even if Butler (2019, 244) is correct (as of course they are) in saying that "discrete genders are part of what 'humanizes' individuals within contemporary culture," does "differentiation from the maternal" fully account for the question of subjectivization as discretely gendered humanization or, to use Lacan's word, "hominization"? (Lacan, 2006, 572). Or the question of what "really" gets constitutively expelled from this hominized subject, of what "constitutes the real insofar as it is the domain of that which subsists outside symbolization"? Or of "the primal expulsion, that is, the real as outside the subject"? Of "the real—as that which is excised from the primordial symbolization" (Lacan, 2006, 324), etc.? And anthropogenetically speaking, how exactly do we square either "differentiation from the maternal" or "the real of sexual difference" with what Žižek calls "Lacan's thesis that [the] animal became human the moment it confronted the problem of what to do with its excrement" (Žižek, 1994, 179)?

What if the realest question of "the real of the difference supposed to be sexual" is not "how are the sexes different?" or the hysteric's "what sex am I anyway?" but rather *what the fuck happened to the real?* Initially, I think, this question could have little enough to do with "sexual difference" *qua* the question of "man" or "woman" or how they do or don't or will or won't end up fucking. Initially, I think, the question isn't yet homologous with such readily Oedipalized inquiries as where's mummy, where's my or mummy's dick, where should I be in relation to her lack, what must I be (*no*) or have (*sorry*) or say (*bingo!*) to register in the big Other's desire, etc. To be sure, the *initial* question—what happened to the real?—will *eventually* or *retroactively* be caught up in these all too Oedipal questions, the questions of the phallus, sexual difference, man, woman, and the motherfucking fuck. But just as the emphatic question *"what the fuck?!"* is rarely raised in the midst of real fucking (unless something has gone quite horribly wrong), so the initial question of "the primal expulsion, that is, the real as outside the subject . . . as that which is excised from the primordial symbolization" (Lacan, 2006, 324) might be productively isolated from the question of sexual difference as the "traumatic cut" between (the) M and (the) F.

If the *real* question of "the real of sexual difference" is the question of what happened to the real, then this question can be diachronically divided: not simply *what happened to the real* at the expulsive moment of primordial symbolization, but *what is still happening* to the real here and now as the *parlêtre* continues (self-expulsively) to speak, so to speak? For the real, both temporally *precedes* and synchronically *exceeds* the primary differentiation that installs "all of us" into positions as speaking subjects. The real involves, among other things, what Lacan calls "the very young child's experience of itself," which "develops on the basis of a situation that is experienced as undifferentiated" (Lacan, 2006, 91). The real is that "oceanic" *whatever* that resists symbolization, that "all of us" lose/are lost from, thanks to "castration" whenever *that* term is used to designate or "taxonomize" what happens "when a polymorphous lack of differentiation gives way to differences and taxonomies" (Roof, 2016, 59–60).[6]

But what if we don't use *that* term? What if we don't reduce what Lacan (2006, 339) calls "the preoedipal mess" of the real to what Žižek (2000, 257) calls "the pre-symbolic *incestuous* Real Thing"? What if we refuse to reduce the "traumatic cut" between the symbolic and real to a "sexual difference" that *must* end up only ever *Oedipally* meaning man/woman/the fuck, so that the universal emptiness that Lacanian theory consistently reveals must forever be filled with the same fucking contents?

For some of us, the Lacanian conflation of *linguistic difference* with *sexual difference* seems to keep rebirthing a heteronormatively formalist fantasy that *symbolically* weds grammatically correct *linguistic completion* to *socially* sanctioned *sexual completion*. By marrying the inevitable "fact of the signifier" to the *nom/non du père* prohibiting incest, by mapping a symbolically ordered passage through "the defiles of the signifier" (Lacan, 2006, 525) that is universally necessary for "all of us" human subjects onto a particular church-and-state-sanctioned march "down the aisle" that is available only to some, straight Lacanistas seem to reproduce the historical contingencies of heterosexual "family life" as a single, universally necessary structure, making hetero-procreative fucking the only eternally valid answer to the question of what the fuck happened to the real.

Take This *Jouissance* and Shove It!

And yet, for a little *coitus interruptus*—or perhaps a *petit a*bortion—we might ask what happens when the symbol, pried loose from our pre-Oedipal mess, is *not* mapped onto the question of sexual difference. What if what's at issue "at first" is *only* symbol's "freedom" from a real that it primordially expels? What if all it *initially* means to initialize meaning is to lose/be lost from the real, to consent to the so-called "castration" and let our oceanically "polymorphous lack of differentiation give way to differences and taxonomies" that, like the overly taxing taxonomy "castration" itself, are "'multiple,' provisional, and subject to change"?[7] What if all Lacan ever meant by "order[s] and norms [that] must be instituted which tell the subject what a man or a woman must do" is that *all* human orders and norms whatsoever *must indeed be instituted*, don't grow on trees or fall out of the sky, are only ever produced through human labor, and are therefore necessarily contingent, multiple, provisional, and subject to change?

What arguably *isn't* subject to change for Lacan is the fact that "It is the world of words that creates the world of things—things which at first run together in the *hic et nunc* of the all" (Lacan, 2006, 229). What doesn't change for Lacan is the utterly ungendered fact that "the symbol first manifests itself as the killing of the thing, and this death results in the endless perpetuation of the subject's desire" (Lacan, 2006, 262). What never changes for Lacan is the fact that "all of us" human subjects are effects of the signifier, of which Lacan says that "we cannot say of [it] that, like other objects, it must be *or* not be somewhere but rather that, unlike them, it will be *and* not be where it is wherever it goes" (Lacan, 2006, 17)—all of which *goes* to show that "all of us" *parlêtres* will perpetually be and not be, are always ontologically lacking, something real forever missing from us, wherever we go, even if thanks to whatever "laws of urinary segregation" still prevail we all must line up to go through *one* door *or* the other, Ladies *or* Gents, M or F, whenever we really *really* have to go, and even though once we're through those doors and situated in our respective stalls, we all end up "doing" the same pissy and shitty things, which all really "run together" again in the cloacal/oceanic *hic et nunc* of the all.

But what if anything do all these "same things" have to do with the "this death" mentioned above, with the symbol's fundamental *killing* of the thing via the primordial *expulsion* of the real that situates the generic *parlêtre* in perpetual desire? How does symbolic *reicide* play into the idea that "all of us" *parlêtres* get to be *and* not to be wherever we go but that some of us must (still) go through one door *or* the other lest we risk re-appearing as the return of the primordially repressed, as provocatively real "things" or abject "its" that "the symbol" somehow neglected to kill or waste (a murderous service that really reicidal trans-assassinators are all too anxiously happy to provide)? And how do we account for the analytical/theoretical/political anxiety on some of "our" parts that the eradication of the *fictional* difference between the same two real doors, or the *technological* drive to "deny the difference of the sexes," or the actual *surgical* transformation of one sort of sexed body into another, would result in somebody's (or the whole world's) really shitty death and/or psychic dissolution? How do we account for the conclusion, as per the epigraph from Luce Irigaray above, that there *must* be "sexual difference" as heteronormatively understood or else "we are [all] dead"? How do we account for the desire (of certain analysts) to jettison some of "all of us" out the door or down the hole, to some unlivable dumping ground "'outside of language, outside of meaning, outside of the symbolic, outside of relation, outside of desire'—a space of 'radical abjection and death'"? How, in other words, do we account for and counter that pathologizing set of diagnostic equivalences in which transsex=*horsexe*=silence=death?

I of course refer to Catherine Millot's *Horsexe: Essay on Transexuality*. Millot notoriously holds that while "gender dysphoric" subjects petitioning for actual surgical transition may *consciously* think that they want to change from one sex to another, what they really *unconsciously* desire is not to be "the other sex" but to be "other than sex" altogether—*horsexe*, outside "sex" understood as the real of sexual difference. But if real sexual difference coincides with linguistic difference from the real, then to *be* outside sexual difference means to *be* outside the difference between meaning and being, the killing symbol and the murdered thing. Millot, in other words, translates the desire to transition as the desire to be *horsexe*, to occupy all the stalled "outsides" already repetitively mentioned, to be outside language, meaning, the symbolic, relation, and desire itself. The surgically successfully *horsexual* subject would no longer be "one of us," a spectral *parlêtre*, a presence made of absence—a real-loser, a hungry ghost gnawing its self-alienating way along the links of the signifying chain like every other animal at language's mercy—but would be the completely self-identical, fully self-satisfied subject *qua* "unimpeachably real" thing. For Millot, says Charles Shepherdson, the subject who would be *horsexual* is "engaged in a fantasy of totalization" and is *really* aspiring to expire, frantically/thanatically struggling to occupy "a position from which (if it could only be occupied) nothing more would need to be said," the terminal position or absolutely real object/objective of "what Freud called 'the silence' of the death drive" (Shepherdson, 2000, 112).

But do Millot and her confederates actually trust in their pathologizing belief that the post-operative transsexual, having successfully become *horsexual*, will have actually "lost" not only the unwanted genitals but, along therewith, the desire (if not the actual capacity) to speak, to mean—that, having "overcome" the real of sexual difference, having "nothing left" of the undesired dysphoria-genic genitals, the happily destitute post-surgical subject would have "nothing more" to say and nothing more to do than simply (shit itself and) roll over (in it) and die?

Or, to make short work of Millot and jump/cut abruptly from theoretical/analytical to cultural/cinematic pathologizations, let's ask a different sexual question about the real of sexual difference: how does the *horsexual* figure supposedly wanting to embody "what Freud called 'the silence' of the death drive" end up (quite deservedly) *dead* at the tail end of *The Silence of the Lambs*? In Jonathan Demme's 1991 film, Buffalo Bill (Ted Levine) is a serial killer and all-too-real gender-bender who "wears" the skins of his female victims. He also sports lipstick and eyeliner and poses "self-castratedly" naked in front of a mirror, penis tucked between his legs, etc. When FBI agent Clarice Starling (Jodie Foster) ventures, phallic firearm drawn, into the killer's basement, she obeys the cinematic convention that misreads *un*conscious as *sub*conscious and compels the protagonist to visibly enter some cloacal subterranean hole or another in order to confront her own unacknowledged fears and desires. And what the pistol-toting Starling finds in the cellar is a startling scene of sexual undifferentiation, an abject place where meaning has collapsed because the primordial "cut" separating the symbolic from the real, life from death, M from F, has been inhumanly sutured. The money-shot of this sequence comes when Clarice beholds a bathtub filled with some "unspeakable" dark gunk, from which protrudes what appears to be the "iceberg" tip of a submerged human skull. This anamorphic tank is apparently the acid bath in which Buffalo Bill dissolves the last remains of his victims. A good cinematic example of the bad oceanic feeling, this cloacal tank is the last hideous "thing" Clarice sees before the lights go out and she loses herself in the dark. Shooting blindly, Clarice manages to shatter a transom window, which lets in sufficient light for her to take aim and shoot a few little *fenêtres* into the breast-less chest of the approaching Buffalo Bill. Bill is then shown lying face-up in the dirt of his own rectal grave, soon to be no longer a *parlêtre* but a real (dead) thing with nothing left to say, the blood gurgling up from his throat and spreading slowly across his lips fatally literalizing the merely cosmetic red gloss we'd earlier seen there applied. All that's missing, were *Silence* a far stupider film, would be for agent Starling to go all Dirty Harry on the dying villain's ass and quip something vicious like "You wanted to wear some lipstick, killer? *There's* your lipstick."

But *Silence* isn't a *stupidly* transphobic film, any more than Catherine Millot, I don't guess, should be called a viciously transphobic psychoanalyst. However, there's pretty clearly an ugly correspondence between diagnostic theories that situate the transgendered in abjectly undifferentiated spaces between life and death and cultural representations that figure transsubjects as silent killers, murderous turds who deserve to be wasted. And this correspondence is, if not complicit with, at least a condition of possibility for our general global climate of punitively abjecting and frequently lethal anti-trans* violence.[8] The question I'll turn to now is whether this very "correspondence" can be *rewritten* in a queerly trans-*affirmative* way that would not only "advance a nonpathologizing understanding of trans* identification" but also participate in the "shitty work" of impeding (or perhaps radically redirecting) *our* death drive's abjectifying violence.

On the analytical/theoretical side of this rewriting, a brief case in point: the line from Patricia Gherovici's *Transgender Psychoanalysis* included as an epigraph to this essay would seem at quick glance to be compatible with the lines from Irigaray and (the early) Lacan between which hers is sandwiched. Her line would seem to line all the man/woman/living/dead/questions/matters up along the same fraught "same/other" lines as theirs, and this line-up might be considered complicit with the potentially violent/lethal "correspondence" mentioned in the paragraph above. But *unlike* Irigaray and early Lacan (or, for that matter, Millot), Gherovici raises these questions (from the dead) in order to trans-affirmatively champion gender's always aesthetically embodied *plasticity*, to let gender transitioning be *both* a matter of life and death *and* a radical "practice of creativity,"[9] a question of *écriture*. The most concise way (for me) to describe Gherovici's strategy in *TP* is to say that she taps into the *late* Lacan's notion of the *sinthome* in order to *sinthomize*, rather than pathologize, trans* identification. Space (and, frankly, intellectual) limitations prevent me from explaining the late Lacan's *sinthome* any further or better here than to say that it involves the way Lacan thinks James Joyce saved himself from psychosis by writing *Finnegans Wake*. And so, given my limits, and turning back to other matters in (or on) Gherovici's *TP* that are more in my cognitive ballpark, I'll simply add that, with chapter headings such as "That Obscure Object: from beauty to excrement" and "Freud's Scatolog," Gherovici aligns her analysis with what Tim Dean's epigraph reminds us about Lacan's most fundamental "model of subjective loss" and thus helps prod "all of us" who are invested in "the futures of trans-affirmative Lacanian psychoanalysis" to get on the same page, if not in the same stall, and to do our shitty work of countering transphobic logics together.

On the cultural/cinematic side of this rewriting, a much longer case in point: so far in this essay, I've worked to identify fatal/fecal transphobic logics in a few "frantic zones" of theory and culture. I would now like to start ending the essay by examining that logic's queer *inversion*, its explosive or "terrorist" *celebration*, in *V for Vendetta*, the 2005 film written and produced (but not directed) by then Larry/now Lana and then Andy/now Lilly Wachowski—a sublime cinematic shit-show that arguably set(s) the stage for *their* subsequent transition(s) and figuratively fights back from the very space of "radical abjection and death" to which its multiple queer protagonists have been politically consigned.[10]

LGBTQ/POV/*V for Vendetta*: or, How to Blow Up the Heterosexual Matrix

There's a little trick I play on the Wachowski's 1999 film *The Matrix* when I teach it in my pop culture class. We're at the end of the film; Neo (Keanu Reeves) has finally and firmly been established as "the One" (the quasi-Christified savior-figure destined to lead the charge against the inhuman agents of oppression working for/as the system known as "the Matrix"); we see the words SYSTEM FAILURE spread across the screen, and as Neo's change-is-gonna-come voice-over promises us "a world without rules and controls, without borders or boundaries, a world where anything is possible," the camera tracks in toward and moves through the space between SYSTEM and FAILURE, passing into the greenish digital void beyond.

But here's the trick: if we hit PAUSE at just the right point in the camera's journey, at the last moment before the fantasy of SYSTEM FAILURE is traversed, what we witness filling the screen are the two great big honking letters:

M F

Now, students are usually pretty quick to get the point of this tricky PAUSE, particularly if they've been paying attention to what we've been discussing about *The Matrix*'s more conspicuously heteronormative narrative gestures, most notably its "neutralizing" treatment of the character Trinity (Carrie Moss), who begins the film resplendently kicking (predominantly white male) ass, hacking into military computer systems with such serious skills that most people (including Neo) have assumed her to be a man, maybe even hooking up with the butchier bleached-blonde character Switch (Belinda McClory), but who ends up no longer kicking or hacking or Switching but occupying the ancillary position of caring kissing shielding protectress of Neo's white hetero-masculinist, love-resurrected "One." In other words, what my stalling of the camera's movement through the words SYSTEM FAILURE at the point be-tween the still-visible signifiers M and F suggests is that the film, even while asserting the coming collapse of all borders and boundaries, has still left erected a few of its own: if only for a passing moment, the gendered binary of the M and the F is left standing, like segregating insignia on twin bathroom doors, side-by-side, but with "the One," M, taking syntagmatic priority over the other, F. The sex/gender SYSTEM, it seems, has not yet been brought to FAILURE in or by *The Matrix*.

Of course, this trick against the film's logic works only if we assume M and F to stand for Male/Masculine and Female/Feminine. Things get trickier, maybe even trans*ier, if we crisscross some borders and boundaries and let M F stand for the "monstrous[ly] transsexual" conglomeration Male-Mother/Female-Father.[11]

Cut to the closing scene of *V for Vendetta*, V (Hugo Weaving, who played not only Agent Smith in *The Matrix* but also Tick/Mitzi in the 1994 film *The Adventures of Priscilla, Queen of the Desert*) is dead, but his "truth" is marching on. That is to say that Evey Hammond (Natalie Portman) has magnificently executed V's plot to blow up the Houses of Parliament (with a massive *fertilizer* bomb composed, we note, of 100% British excretion). We hear fireworks and the booming finale of queer composer Peter Tchaikovsky's *1812 Overture*, and we see the shaven-headed Evey standing with politically suspect (because Irish) Inspector Eric Finch (Stephen Rea, who played Fergus in Neal Jordan's 1992 *The Crying Game*) on a balcony overlooking the explosive/anarchic celebration. To Finch's question about V's true identity, Evey responds with a fiction and says that he was Edmund Dantès.[12] Then she goes on to say that V was her father, her mother, her brother, her friend, you, me, and all of us.

The camera then starts to show all of us to all of us, to show us (the film's viewers) the multitudinous all of us who have mutinously marched down Whitehall from Trafalgar Square, all wearing the mass-produced Guy Fawkes masks V has provided—the very mask which we Viewers *of* the film, much earlier *in* the film, have ourselves put on and peered through in order to briefly see *ourselves as* V.[13] We are, I think, all there to witness not just an historico-political monument's demolition but the figurative collapse of the heteronorma-tively understood "real of sexual difference" itself, not only an "ethical act" of suicidal terrorism but the utter destruction of the "vital" distinction between the M and the F, the quick and the dead, a radical shattering of all the segre-gations that support and maintain transphobically heteronormative "meaning" as such. For among the oceanic sea of faces that Viewers of/as V see when the anonymous multitudes start taking off their masks are some figures we've all seen before, characters we recognize, subjects who *we have taken to be queer* (because we've seen them being "taken away" for being queer) and who *we know to be dead* (because we've seen more than a few of them being murdered for being queer) but who we now clearly envision as living. These are the queerly ambulant dead of this essays' title.

One such ambler, the closeted TV comedy producer Gordon Dietrich (played by openly gay and vocally atheist actor Stephen Fry), we know to have been murdered outright by the explicitly xenophobic, homophobic, white-nationalist, kleptocratic, theocratic, and neo-fascist regime headed by Adam Sutler (John Hurt), along with greedy henchman Creedy (Tim Spigott-Smith) and other political, military, medical, cultural, and clerical/evangelical enablers. But at film's end, just before we see the known-to-be-murdered Gordon take off his Fawkesian mask and out himself as among the living, we see an unmasked Male and Female who to me suggest the very figures Evey has just identified as being V—i.e., her own politically murdered Mother and Father. The IMDB doesn't help me out here, since the M F couple shown to us don't appear to be the actors Selina Miles and Carston Hayes, who actually play Evey's mum and dad; nonetheless, the camera's cut from this conspicuously parental-looking pair to the revealed revitalization of the queer Gordon Dietrich allows us to "remember" not the 5th of November but some earlier coincidences/convergences in the film.

When Evey first leaves V's hideaway and seeks refuge with Gordon, who had been her employer, he cooks her up some eggies in the basket, made just the way his mum used to make them. Evey is disturbed by and comments upon on the strange coincidence that V himself (having donned a *hausfrau*'s apron) had earlier made her just such eggies. Gordon "comedically" offers Evey the following explanation for this unsettling convergence: he says that he himself is V. Though Evey isn't amused and of course doesn't believe him, I believe that the film's final shot of Gordon's upturned unmasked face, illuminated by anarchic fireworks, suggests that he has indeed been telling some serious truth after all, that a real revolution, a revolution of the real, lives on in him, that he, like/as "all of us," really *is* the "terrorist" V.[14]

Now, if Evey is really "right" to say that V is her father and her mother, then Gordon's turning out to be telling the truth about his really being V *turns* him into Evey's mum. *NB*: V makes Evey eggies just like Gordon makes Evey eggies, and Gordon serves up these *ova* just like *his* mum did, which makes *her* like V, who makes *them* the same way, which *again* turns Gordon into V and V into Evey's mum. And, speaking of repetition, the scene of Evey's actual activist mother (Selina Miles) being dragged away by the fascist regime, which Evey as a young girl views in terror and tears while hiding under her bed, is served up in exactly the same way, from the same POV, as the scene of Gordon's being extracted from his flat by Creedy's squad of goons. Evey's mum's face and Gordon's are *framed* the same way and *occupy the same space* in both shots.

We'll return to that strange coincidence. But first there's another living/loving unmasked face in the final mass of ambulant dead witnesses that we Viewers of *V for Vendetta* need to consider: that of Valerie (Natasha Wightman), the "out" lesbian film actress who, when Sutler's regime takes power, gets rounded up with the rest of the masses and extracted to/experimented upon/exterminated at Larkhill, the regime's "resettlement" concentration camp, where they specialize in "radical abjection and death" for various representatives of variety, for all the dark-skinned and/or deviant, not excluding those Lewis Prothero (Roger Allam) disgustedly calls "immigrants, Muslims, terrorists, [and] homosexuals"—it's Tuskegee with a dash of Dachau and more than a hint of HIV/AIDS hysteria.[15]

Now, it turns out that for a time Valerie and whoever/whatever V was before becoming fully V had occupied side-by-side cells at Larkhill (she was in IV, or maybe VI: he was definitely in V). It also turns out that, before having her lifeless body dumped into a mass grave with all the other others, Valerie had inscribed her life-story on *toilet paper* and had passed that narrative to V through the rat's passage which connected their cells, the metaphorical glory hole connecting their stalls.

Later on, V, pretending to be one of Creedy's goons, captures Evey and subjects her to a quasi-simulated Larkhillian imprisonment, to "fake" incarceration but real torture—shaving her head, steam-hosing her like contaminated cattle, shoving her face into a toilet, relentlessly threatening her with death if she doesn't give up the identity of the terrorist V. What the terrorist V arguably intends is (to put it in roughly Žižekian Lacanese) to liberate Evey from her fantasy of herself, to prod her to traverse that fantasy, to reduce Evey to a state of "subjective destitution" so that she might eventually get in on V's suicidally "ethical act" of blowing up the Houses of Parliament. And the trick works: Evey, by opting for death before disclosure, by refusing to give up V's "identity" to the big Other, radically discards the limitations of her own.

In the course of orchestrating her radicalization *qua* subjective destitution, V quasi-rectally retransmits scraps of the murdered Valerie's *poubellications* to Evey, on the same crappy medium and through the same abject hole, "speaking" to Evey from Valerie's former position just as Valerie had spoken to V, writing on t.p. to Evey *as* Valerie *as if* Valerie were still alive and kicking in the adjacent stall/cell. Conspicuously, Evey keeps what she supposes to be Valerie's screeds wrapped in plastic and tucked under the rim of the same toilet in which we've seen her own face framed (we see, that is, her submerged face from the *toilet's* POV). After V outs himself as her captor/torturer and as the *real* courier/carrier of Valerie's viral *écrits*—including her ultimate message of anonymous universal love indifferent to the real of sexual difference—V leads Evey to Valerie's shrine, a large framed publicity poster for her film *The Salt Flats*, which image V stands beside as he explains to Evey the universally loving intent behind his particularly cruel treatment.

But what's crucial here is the way V's self-explanatory discourse is visually framed. From Evey's POV, we Viewers see the life-sized image of the murdered muted lesbian Valerie side-to-side *and in visual equivalence/contiguity* with the inanimate visage of the living speaking "killing machine" called V. In this gender-blending syntagmatic visual alignment, we see a sort of interpenetration between the killed and evidently *female* Valerie and the *presumably* male but definitely dangerous killing machine called V. To my eye, at least, this coupling of Valerie with V in and as one framed shot, as if they were a very queer sort of mum and dad (who never "really" ever procreatively fucked), effectively *condenses* the two separate or segregated shots described above, the shots that repeat the abduction of Evey's mum *as* the extraction of Gordon Dietrich. And—again, from my limited POV—this metonymical *contiguity*/metaphorical *condensation* of Valerie with V invites "all of us" Viewers to envision something like a Valerie to V/V to Valerie *transition*, and thus to do the productively shitty dream-work of remembering V as something like a trans* action hero and affirming *V* as a trans-affirmative film.

V (?)

But *should* we think (well) of V as a trans*action figure? Should we smile on *V* as a trans-affirmative film? Doesn't making V a throat-slashing "monster," a "dangerous killing machine" throwing knives and launching excremental bombs, dangerously align this "terrorist" with *Silence*'s Buffalo Bill and countless other murderous turds (including the sewer-dwelling killer clown in the most recent film adaption of Stephen King's *It*)? Doesn't making V a sort of gender-blender-killer-diller align him with that transphobic logic described above, the Millotian logic that reads the transsubject as *horsexual* wanting nothing more than to be outside of language, wanting to occupy the position of "the silence" of the death drive, a position from which there's supposedly nothing left to be said? Well, one problem with that last alignment is that V never seems to be at a loss for words (particularly words that begin with the letter V). Even though V's face is uncannily inanimate, even though we never see the lips of the Fawkesian mask moving, we know that V believes in the art of the sentence; we know that he believes in the power of language; we know that he keeps relentlessly *speaking*. After all, if V stands for anything at all, it's virulent virtuoso verbosity. There's really no shutting his ass up.

But here's another question about V. Not so much Finch's "who was he?" as *"what* was he?" or maybe "was V really a *he?"* Before addressing that question, I would just like to say, taking another swipe at *The Matrix*, that whoever/whatever V is/are, V *isn't* "the One." V's being "all of us" pretty clearly/queerly precludes his/their being "cross-identified" as "the One" true slain and resurrected savior. Granted, there are copious quasi-Christological gestures, intimations, and exclamations packed into *V for Vendetta*, including (to mention only one) the military commander's blurting out the words "Jesus Christ!" when he beholds the multitudes marching down from Trafalgar. But I would prefer to cut the Christ and keep things universally queer here.[16] And so let's all of us go back to the question of V's sex-which-is-not-(the)-One.

Is V a he? Maybe not so much. Near the film's end, when Evey finally quasi-romantically/sexually kisses the lips of V's mask, V says "I can't" and turns away. This admission of incapacity could mean a number of things, but one could be something like "I can't engage in standard rom-com action-hero hetero-genital intercourse with you because I no longer have the physical means to do it." We find some support for this interpretation of V's "I can't" (if we need or want it) by turning to a detail in the story that Dr. Delia Surridge (Sinéad Cusack) tells about the explosion at Larkhill that first "created the monster" V. As we listen to Delia's voice-over, we see the big explosion, and we behold the radically burned but now superhumanly empowered figure that we take to be V emerging from the flames and raising his mighty arms into V-formation and ferociously roaring. Describing this flesh-melted dis-figure, Delia intones that she couldn't see the eyes because there were no eyes. Now, since we know that V has vision, is indeed a visionary, we might assume that V in fact has a set of operative *eyeballs*. So we might also assume that by "there were no eyes," Delia might be taken to mean something other than what she says. And we might "remember" the old Freudian/Lacanian line that takes Oedipus's using the famous brooches to stab out his own eyes and translates that tragic act into punitive self-dismemberment, a cutting off of his own gaze. So then maybe we re-hear Delia's line as "I couldn't see any genitals. There were no genitals" and we go back and View V's flaming emergence again and note that, sure enough, we can see that we can't see anything in the way of M genitals on that transmogrified naked torso either. We can pretty clearly see that there's "nothing to see" there.

Now, I'm not saying that this "nothing to see" is by itself adequate grounds for reading V as "monstrous [M2F] transsexual" or super-heroized trans*action figure. I'm not indifferent to the difference between, say, the real Wachowski's purely elective gender-transition surgeries and *one* of their cinematic characters involuntarily having *their* junk burned off in a chemical explosion at a fictional fascist death camp. V's having possibly lost his Johnson at Larkhill is just *one* detail in the case I've been making here for thinking of *them*—V and V—as trans-figuratively trans-affirmative.

But it's only one detail among many others. It isn't the "One" detail that really makes "our" case. And it certainly isn't the most important "One."

Because there isn't—and never has been, and never will be—a most important "One."

Or so say "all of us."[17]

Notes

1   This essay originally began with a set of epigraphs from Lacan, Gherovici, Irigaray, Tim Dean, and Sheila Cavanagh. First, from Lacan: "It is an experiential truth for psychoanalysis that the question of the subject's existence arises for him ... as an articulated question—'What am I there?'—about his sex and his contingency in being: namely, that on the one hand he is a man or a woman, and on the other that he might not be, the two conjugating their mystery and knotting it in symbols of

procreation and death" (2006, 459). Second, from Gherovici: "Gender transition is more about mortality, the limit between life and death, than about sexuality, the border between male and female" (2017, 106). Next from Irigaray: "The human spirit already seems subjugated to the imperatives of technology to the point of believing it possible to deny the difference of the sexes .... But as long as we are still living, we are sexually differentiated. Otherwise, we are dead. The question of whether language has a sex could be subtitled: Are we still alive?" (1993, 107). Then there's Tim Dean: "Lacan's model for subjective loss is not the phallus but feces, an ungendered object. In the face of *this* object-cause of desire, the controversy over the concept of the phallus pales into insignificance, since whether or not we're all—men as well as women—missing the phallus, certainly we've all lost objects from the anus" (2000, 264). And finally, Sheila Cavanagh: "Countering transphobia is shitty work" (2017, 330).

2 Most of this quotation is from Salamon (2010, 41). But the larger quotation is to be found in Coffman (2017, 472–496). The full quotation included below is clunky but informative:

> Underscoring the dangers of [Jay] Prosser's insistence [in his 1998 Columbia UP book *Second Skins: The Body Narratives of Transsexuality*] "that the transsexual body is 'unimpeachably real,'" Salamon charges that this claim "ends up landing him squarely in the Real," in all its "plenitude and fullness"—a positioning that is problematic because it leaves the transsexual "outside of language, outside of meaning, outside of the symbolic, outside of relation, outside of desire"—in a space of "radical abjection and death"
>
> (478)

3 Cavanagh (2016) and many others have complained about the way "contemporary Lacanian psychoanalysts over rely on Catherine Millot's (1989) *Horsexe*, a book that establishes a metonymic link between trans* feminine subjects and psychosis" (326), and I will be saying bad things about Millot later on in this essay. As for Žižek, don't get me started: just see Coffman (2017).

4 Much of what follows in the second and third sections of this essay rehearses/condenses/updates a longer discussion in my ill-titled *Masculinity, Psychoanalysis, Straight Queer Theory: Essays on Abjection in Literature, Mass Culture, and Film* (2008, 19–62).

5 Madhavi Menon (2015, 19) helps "all of us" considerably when she writes that

> queer universalism undertakes the refusal of identity outlined by Lee Edelman when he notes that 'queerness can never define an identity; it can only ever disturb one' ... What is universally queer is the ontological impossibility of self-identity. Everything is queer because no-thing—peoples, events, desires—can achieve ontological wholeness.

6 It occurs to me that these two questions—"what the fuck happened to the real?" and "what happens 'when a polymorphous lack of differentiation gives way to differences and taxonomies'?"—are pretty much the same question.

7 That's the already-cited Judith Roof quote about castration again, as it appears in the place I actually found it: Coffman's (2017) "Žižek's Antagonism" (476).

8 For the latest dismal figures, see the Human Rights Campaign website: https://www.hrc.org/resources/violence-against-the-transgender-community-in-2018.

9 Cf. Foucault (1997, 262):

> I think that from the theoretical point of view, Sartre [rightly] avoids the idea of the self as something that is given to us, but through the moral notion of

authenticity, he turns back to the idea that we have to be ourselves—to be truly our true self. I think the only acceptable practical consequence of what Sartre has said is to link his theoretical insight to the practice of creativity—and not to that of authenticity. From the [salutary] idea that the self is not given to us, I think there is only one practical consequence: we have to create ourselves as a work of art.

10 *V* was directed by James McTeigue. For the details of the Wachowskis' transitions, and an analysis of their oeuvre, see Keegan (2018). I regret and apologize for the fact that Keegan's work appeared too late on the scene for me to learn anything from it in writing mine.

11 Cf. Gozlan's (2017) speculation:

> I'm putting forward the idea that the entrance of a gender-ambiguous person into the bathroom may activate primitive superego defenses in response to perceived threats to the self's imagined gender coherence.... For the bathroom police, the "monstrous transsexual" could be easily identified with the combined parental couple, an imagined fused figure of the parents—and the genders— that confuses, excludes, and distresses. The combined parental couple, joined in coital jouissance, reminds the child of the pain of exclusion: "you cannot come in here," "we are complete without you." From this perspective, we could imagine the expelling of the gender-ambiguous other as a reversed enactment of the pain and anger of infantile exclusion, as a repetition of the primal scene from an active and empowering position that turns "I can't come in" into "you must stay out." If ... the transsexual subject is perceived as dangerously fusing two genders ... aggression against this combined figure would help to keep objects apart and differentiated—so that genders remain whole and known.
>
> (459–460)

12 Evey has watched V watching and identifying with the character Edmund Dantès in the 1934 film *The Count of Monte Cristo*, which is of course based on the novel by Alexandre Dumas, and Alexandre Dumas—as Dr. King Schultz (Christof Waltz), points out to slave-plantation commandant Calvin Candie (Leonardo DiCaprio) in Quentin Tarantino's 2012 film *Django Unchained*— "was black." Dr. King points out Dumas's blackness to Calvin because Calvin has assigned the name D'Artagnan to a re-captured runaway slave (Eno Assandoh) whom he, Calvin, finally orders to be torn apart by a pack of dogs. Now, my point in letting a black or "mixed-race" Dumas be a point of intersection between *V for Vendetta* and *Django Unchained*— and between V and Django (Jamie Foxx)—is to underscore V's anti-racist as well as its trans-affirmative interventions. After all, both films end with their heroes dynamiting the institutional sites of their oppression—Parliament and Candyland, respectively—though Django, unlike V, doesn't, I admit, really seem to have much to tell us about trans*.

13 In a complicated early sequence that sets up a load of associations and cross-identifications, we get our first sight of Evey, looking into a mirror and putting on her make-up, evidently preparing to "go out." The camera then takes us "around" Evey's mirror and into a seemingly adjacent and opposing room in which we see V also situated in front of a mirror, which would seem to be the other side of Evey's mirror, so that if it were all a clear glass window or open portal, they would both be seeing each other's faces face-to-face. At a certain point in this crisscrossed "reach-around," the camera, and hence we, assume(s) V's POV, and what we now see is the interior of the Guy Fawkes mask just as it covers "our" face, which is what allows us to peer through the mask's eyeholes and see ourselves as V in the

mirror that "all of us" are now facing. And as if all these visual cross-identifications weren't enough, "all of us"—Evey, V, and we—are having to listen to the
government's official radio station blaring the hate-speech of self-designated Voice
of England Lewis Prothero (Roger Allam), who is going garrulously on about
the USA as the Ulcerated Sphincter of Arse-erica and ranting about the threat
posed to white Christian Anglo-nationalist coherence by immigrants, Muslims,
terrorists, and homosexuals, all of whose undesired presences he chalks up to the
overarching plague of godlessness. It's interesting to compare Prothero's rant to the
following from Donald Widmon, not a voice of England but, reports Lee Edelman,
the "founder and head of the deeply reactionary American Family Association."
Widmon opines that

> Acceptance or indifference to the homosexual movement will result in society's
> destruction by allowing civil order to be redefined and by plummeting our-
> selves, our children and grandchildren into an age of godlessness. Indeed, the
> very foundation of Western Civilization is at stake.

Prothero's blather apes Widmon's so well it's as if the screenwriting Wachowskis
had based the one upon the other; moreover, one might speculate that one Wachowski or the other first saw Widmon's homophobic jeremiad in the text from
which I've drawn it, a text anyone invested in "the futures of trans-affirmative
Lacanian psychoanalysis" should get to know, Edelman's *No Future: Queer Theory and the Death Drive* (2004)—or, more precisely, Edelman's 1998 "The Future is Kid Stuff: Queer Theory, Disidentification, and the Death Drive" (1998)
reprinted (guess where?) in *Adventures in Theory: A Compact Anthology*, edited
by Calvin Thomas (2019, 269–284). You'll find "the Donald" in *Adventures*
(275–276).

14 I should briefly point out another conspicuously queer coincidence linking the "terrorist" V to Gordon—namely, the latter's covert and lethally illegal ownership of a
copy of the Koran, which has been banned by the regime, and which Gordon keeps
not because he's a practicing Muslim but because he appreciates the text's poetic
beauty. The Koran gathers Gordon into Prothero's deadly rhetorical grouping of
"Muslims" together with immigrants, terrorists, and homosexuals, while his aesthetic (rather than fundamentalist) appreciation of the sacred text aligns him with
V as a lover of art (V's lair is filled with artworks stolen from Suttler's antiseptically
anti-aesthetic regime). I speculate, for what it's worth, that Gordon has also been a
lover of the man who will eventually become V.

15 In his introduction to his graphic novel *V for Vendetta* (1988), Alan Moore provides
"the historical background" of the story. Lamenting his native England's nudging
itself "towards fascism," Moore writes:

> It's 1988 now. Margaret Thatcher is entering her third term of office and talk-
> ing confidently of an unbroken Conservative leadership well into the next cen-
> tury.... [T]he tabloid press are circulating the idea of concentration camps for
> persons with AIDS.... The government has expressed a desire to eradicate ho-
> mosexuality, even as an abstract concept, and one can only speculate as to which
> minority will be the next legislated against.
>
> (6)

16 I love Madhavi Menon's *Indifference to Difference* (see note 5) for the way she wrests
universalism from Žižek's and Badiou's crusty Christian clutches and claims it for
the queer.

17 Just for good measure and/or the hell of it, see Beredjick (2017).

Bibliography

Beredjick, C. (2017). *Queer Disbelief: Why LGBTQ Equality is an Atheist Issue*, Friendly Atheist Press.

Butler, J. (2019). "From Interiority to Gender Performatives," in *Adventures in Theory: A Compact Anthology* (pp. 239–246), ed. C. Thomas, New York: Bloomsbury.

Cavanagh, S. L. (2010). *Queering Bathrooms: Gender, Sexuality, and the Hygienic Imagination*, Toronto: University of Toronto Press.

Cavanagh, S. L. (2014). "Gender, Sexuality, and Race in the Lacanian Mirror: Urinary Segregation and the Bodily Ego," in *Psychoanalytic Geographies* (pp. 323–338), ed. P. Kingsbury and S. Pile, London: Ashgate.

Cavanagh, S. L. (2017). "Transpsychoanalytics." *TSQ: Transgender Studies Quarterly* 4(3–4) (November), 326–357.

Coffman, C. (2017). "Žižek's Antagonism and the Futures of Trans-Affirmative Psychoanalysis." *TSQ: Transgender Studies Quarterly* 4(3–4) (November), 472–496.

Dean, T. (2000). *Beyond Sexuality*, Chicago: University of Chicago Press.

Edelman, L. (2004). *No Future: Queer Theory and the Death Drive*, Durham: Duke University Press.

Edelman, L. (2019). "The Future Is Kid Stuff: Queer Theory, Disidentification, and the Death Drive," in *Adventures in Theory: A Compact Anthology* (pp.269–284), ed. C. Thomas, New York: Bloomsbury.

Foucault, M. (1997). "On the Genealogy of Ethics: An Overview of Work in Progress," in *The Essential Works of Foucault, 1954–84, Vol I: Ethics, Subjectivity and Truth* (pp.253–280), trans. P. Rabinow, trans. R. Hurley, New York: The Free Press.

Gherovici, P. (2017). *Transgender Psychoanalysis: A Lacanian Perspective on Sexual Difference*, New York: Routledge.

Gozlan, O. (2017). "Stalled on the Stall: Reflections on a Strained Discourse." *TSQ: Transgender Studies Quarterly* 4(3–4) (November), 451–471.

Irigaray, L. (1993). *Sexes and Genealogies*, trans. C. Porter, New York: Columbia University Press.

Keegan, C. (2018). *Lana and Lilly Wachowski: Sensing Transgender*, Urbana: University of Illinois Press.

Kristeva, J. (1982). *Powers of Horror: An Essay on Abjection*, trans. L. S. Roudiez, New York: Columbia University Press.

Lacan, J. (2006). *Écrits: The First Complete Translation in English*, trans. B. Fink, New York: Norton.

Menon, M. (2015). *Indifference to Difference: On Queer Universalism*, Minneapolis and London: University of Minnesota Press.

Millot, C. (1989). *Horsexe: Essay on Transexuality*, trans. K. Hylton, New York: Autonomedia.

Moore, A. (1988). *V for Vendetta*, New York: DC Comics.

Prosser, J. (1998). *Second Skins: The Body Narratives of Transsexuality*, New York: Columbia University Press.

Roof, J. (2016). *What Gender Is, What Gender Does*, Minneapolis: University of Minnesota Press.

Rubin, G. S. with J. Butler. (1994). "Sexual Traffic." *Differences: A Journal of Feminist Cultural Studies* 6(2/3), 62–99.

Salamon, G. (2010). *Assuming a Body: Transgender and Rhetorics of Materiality*, New York: Columbia University Press.

Shepherdson, C. (2000). *Vital Signs: Nature, Culture, Psychoanalysis*, New York: Routledge.

Thomas, C. (2008). *Masculinity, Psychoanalysis, Straight Queer Theory: Essays on Abjection in Literature, Mass Culture, and Film*, New York: Palgrave Macmillan.

Žižek, S. (1994). *Metastases of Enjoyment: Six Essays on Woman and Causality*, New York: Verso.

Žižek, S. (2000). *"Da Capo senza Fine,"* in *Contingency, Hegemony, Universality: Contemporary Dialogues on the Left* (pp.213–262), ed. J. Butler, E. Laclau, and S. Žižek, New York: Verso.

Žižek, S. (2019). "The Real of Sexual Difference," in *Adventures in Theory: A Compact Anthology* (pp.247–268), ed. C. Thomas, New York: Bloomsbury.

Chapter 16

Becoming Being
Chance, Choice and the Troubles of Trans*cursivity

Dany Nobus

Introduction

Of all the ostensibly infinite permutations that characterize the human lived experience of sexuality, public interest has become increasingly directed over the past couple of years toward instances of gender-nonconforming, and especially toward the question of trans*.[1] The June 2014 cover story of *Time* magazine, featuring a glamorous and defiant image of the American trans actress Laverne Cox, referred to a "transgender tipping point," whereas the January 2017 special issue of *National Geographic* explored "the shifting landscape of gender" and the "gender revolution," with a subscribers' cover showing a nine-year-old against the caption: "The best thing about being a girl is, now I don't have to pretend to be a boy" (see Steinmetz, 2014). There is a talk that Western society is currently living through a "trans-moment," whose implications are much more far-reaching than any of the discussions around sexual orientation from the 1970s and 1980s. How are we to account for the fact that trans*, perhaps more than any other human sexual configuration, is now receiving so much more scholarly, political and media attention, and why has it taken so long for the T in LGBTQ+ to shed its reputation as the forgotten stepchild of sexual nonconformity, and for it to be studied with the same vigor and intensity as the other components of the initialism?

These two questions are evidently related; yet, I believe that they should be considered separately, if only because the first one invites a more strictly historical analysis of key social developments within Western sexual identity politics. In the first part of this chapter, I shall therefore briefly reflect upon how the question of trans* rose to prominence over the past decade, and how current socio-cultural debates around sexual identity converge with prevailing political agendas on individual liberty and freedom of choice. Drawing on some facts and figures, and various mediatized versions of the contemporary trans* culture, I will argue that trans*activists, in their campaign for the socio-political recognition of the voluntarist shaping of sexual identity as an ontological right and command, i.e. as a "necessary affirmation" of being irrespective of the "accidental" biological sex at birth, have in fact gained tremendously from the forces of

DOI: 10.4324/9781003284888-20

securitization and productivity that animate the individual liberties advocated by contemporary neo-liberal ideologies. Extending Jasbir Puar's argument, in her ground-breaking and widely acclaimed *Terrorist Assemblages*, I shall propose that the trans* identity has been insidiously included in a neo-liberal ideology of trans*nationalism, where it operates as a politicized site of individual power, self-governance and psycho-social freedom (Puar, 2017). In the second part of the chapter, I will then open a critical perspective on these trans* identity politics, in parallel with provocative contributions to the debate by Slavoj Žižek and Jacqueline Rose, and argue that the sexual subject can only purchase the radical freedom to desire and to become whom they believe themselves to be—in what I shall designate as a trans*cursive enunciation—at the expense of accepting certain discursive constraints, and that this principle applies to trans* and cis-sexual people alike. Finally, I shall point out that, despite a growing trend among mental health care professionals to present themselves as trans-friendly or trans-positive, a trans-affirmative psychoanalysis is a contradiction in terms, because psychoanalysis does not *a priori* corroborate *any* type of sexual orientation and sexual identity.[2] Sadly, this foundational principle of psychoanalytic clinical practice, which implies that all the constitutive components of human sexuality must remain open to questioning as they enter the analytic process, has been used and abused by psychoanalytic institutions within a hetero- and repro-normative ideology, resulting in numerous instances of exclusion and conversion of sexually nonconforming patients.[3] Yet, the long overdue psychoanalytic de-pathologization of non-normative expressions of gender and sexual orientation cannot coincide with an uncritical, axiomatic re-affirmation of these expressions, because this would run counter to the main purpose of a psychoanalytic process, as a prolonged journey of persistent self-questioning and dis-identification, toward what Lacan at one point designated as a state of subjective destitution (Lacan, 1995, 8).

The Trans*moment(um)

It cannot be disputed that the Western world became progressively more inclusive during the 1990s and the first decade of the twenty-first century, with many countries also gradually embracing the values of social integration, equality and diversity in the realm of human sexuality. However, until recently, attention was largely focused on the civil rights of lesbian, gay and bisexual people, as reflected in the conceptual deconstruction of hetero-normativity, the de-pathologization of "alternative" modalities of sexual orientation and the opening up of traditional social institutions, such as marriage, to non-heterosexual people. It is no doubt telling, in this respect, that in the original edition of their hugely influential *Gender Trouble*, Judith Butler (1990) devoted just one single paragraph to transsexuals [*sic*], notably in order to illustrate the imaginary status of desire, despite their entire volume being dedicated to how sexual identity can become subverted, and despite their articulating a sustained argument in favor of gender as sexual performativity (Butler, 1990, 70–71).[4] It is equally striking that in Butler's follow-up collection *Bodies that Matter* (1993), transsexuality was not mentioned at all, despite the book's protracted critique of culturally established conceptions of the sexed body, and their rekindling of the ancient idea that matter is synonymous with potentiality, temporal change and transformation (Butler, 1993, 31). Butler's first extended engagement with the issue of transsexuality did not appear until 2001, when they applied their theory of gender performativity to the tragic case of David Reimer, whose troubled life history had made the headlines a few years earlier and who would eventually commit suicide in 2004 (Butler, 2001).[5]

Yet as Galadriel, the sibylline Lady of Light, put it so eloquently in Peter Jackson's film adaptation of J. R. R. Tolkien's *Lord of the Rings*: "*I amar prestar aen. Han mathon ne nen*"—"The world is changed. I feel it in the water." In recent years, the question of trans* has pretty much overtaken all other "non-standard" configurations of human sexuality as a new area of investigation for philosophers, cultural critics, mental health care practitioners, policy makers and media pundits. Although reliable statistics are difficult to obtain, it is estimated that about 3% of the American population (some 700,000 individuals) now identify as trans*.[6] With the advancement of medical technologies and the development of more rigorous treatment protocols, an increasing number of people are now also having access to what has been re-branded as "gender confirmation surgery," many of whom openly testifying to their transitioning experience in candid and often harrowing autobiographical narratives (see, e.g., Bornstein, 2012; Jacques, 2015; McBee, 2018). Over the past ten years, there has been an exponential increase in people transitioning socially, opting for top and/or bottom surgery, or (in the UK) seeking a referral to a specialized Gender Identity Clinic for what, in the psychiatric nomenclature, is still called "gender dysphoria" (see American Psychiatric Association, 2013, 451–459).[7] As Tricia Romano, the then "Fly Life" columnist for the New York *Village Voice*, reported back in 2007: "Transsexual people are the fastest growing population" (Romano, 2007). This may be (deliberately intended as) a hyperbole; yet, it is nonetheless true that more people than ever before come forward for an initial assessment, that more confirmation surgeries are being performed on a daily basis and that the trans* community is also becoming younger and younger. In 2018–2019, Great-Britain's only Gender Identity Development Service, which was established in 1989, received 2,560 referrals for children under the age of 18—compared to just under 100 in 2009–2010—including 10 for children as young as 3 and 4.[8] This may still seem a relatively small figure, but the numbers are rising—so much so that the service cannot cope with the unprecedented surge in referrals, and the waiting time for a first assessment has now increased to at least 18 months—while more and more children and teenagers also decide to transition socially, living full-time with their declared gender.[9] Although we need to be mindful of the possibility that these figures may not constitute a real increase in trans* but rather an accelerated form of "coming out," which might in itself be conditioned by higher degrees of acceptance among parents, educators and the general public, the past decade has witnessed a veritable explosion of trans* in all layers of Western society.

When it comes to considering possible explanations for this trans*moment(um), one cannot ignore the impact that virtual environments, and social media platforms in particular, have had on enhancing public awareness, building cross-cultural communities, garnering large-scale support and boosting the confidence of "gender outlaws"—as Kate Bornstein (1994) famously called them—to express themselves. As a result, trans* has become more visible and less elusive, more tangible and less marginal, more consistent and less isolated. In addition, the growing social recognition of trans* may have also capitalized on our ineluctable obsession with celebrity culture and media sensationalism. I am thinking, here, of the widespread reportage accorded to high-profile trans* people, such as Caitlyn Jenner, former Olympic gold medalist and stepfather of Kim Kardashian, and Kellie Maloney, quondam boxing promoter and former UKIP politician. Some trans* people may have serious doubts as to how a reality-TV star's coming out as transgender, and subsequently adding to her already substantial fortune by appearing on the cover of *Vanity Fair* in a very stereotypical, clichéd pose of femininity, could advance their cause; yet, we cannot deny that whenever a famous face appears on, or behind an issue of human interest, public opinion is being shaped (Bissinger, 2015). In the case of Caitlyn Jenner, the responses have been extremely mixed, including from within the LGBTQ+ community, despite the fact that she has capitalized on her celebrity status to facilitate socio-political debates about improving the lives of trans* people. Jenner is being seen by many trans*activists as distinctly unrepresentative of the trans* community, partly because she has simply "crossed over" from one side of the binary to the other, postponing pursuing full gender confirmation surgery, partly because in her new gender identity, she has reinforced the traditional image of a successful, materially secure "feminine woman," thus re-confirming the binary rather than challenging it.[10] Some trans* people may recognize themselves in how Jenner appears in her TV series, yet many do not, because what they aspire to is precisely a blurring, questioning and "transcending" of the conventional dichotomy between masculinity and femininity. Although younger people with "gender dysphoria" often express a desire to be socially acknowledged in accordance with their discerned gender identity, which they experience as the exact opposite of their biological sex, many trans* people do not identify in this "other-categorical" way at all. The range of identifications among trans* people is much more diverse, much more flexible and seemingly limitless. Common terminologies include, but are far from restricted to, gender-fluid, gender-variant, non-binary, a-gender, gender-neutral, gender queer, third gender, pandrogynous, trigender, bigender, demigender, demiflux, etc.[11] Caitlyn Jenner subsequently also appearing on the cover of the LGBTQ+ magazine *The Advocate* (2016) with the caption "I can handle anything" seems very far removed, then, from how many trans* people "handle" or indeed refuse to handle traditional gender categorizations.

The last reason I would like to adduce for our contemporary Western concern over the fate and (mis)fortunes of trans* people is probably less self-evident and more insidious; yet, all the more important for that. Much like the early twenty-first century witnessed the Western normalization of homosexual relationships within and partly owing to the ascendancy of a neo-liberal economic bio-politics, resulting in what Jasbir Puar has designated as an ideology of homonationalism or "homonormative nationalism," the principle of T in LGBTQ+, as a distinct form of human sexual expressiveness deserving of equal social recognition as its non-normative companions, has been co-opted by and recuperated within the neo-liberal rationalities that undergird our Western socio-economic living conditions, which emphasize, create and commodify individual choice and personal enterprise as the highest good, and the necessary precondition for happy citizenship (Puar, 2017, 38–39; on the homonationalist sexual identity politics of neo-liberalism, see also Duggan, 2002, 175–194). By virtue of some trenchant critiques of the various ways in which the neo-liberal ideology has surreptitiously transformed the social sphere into a profitable pantheon of customers, consumers and consumables, we are starting to understand how the growth imperative is infiltrating and ruling such constituent sectors of society as public administration, law enforcement, social justice and higher education, in which aims have been replaced with performance indicators, objectives have been exchanged for credit ratings and learning outcomes have been turned into educational gains (see, e.g., Brown, 2015). However, one area of study which may not have received just yet the detailed attention it deserves is the neo-liberal bio-politics of the sexual and sexualized human body, as it operates within a complex bio-psycho-social milieu of internal and external, real and virtual interactions.

One of the hallmarks of neo-liberal rationality is that choice equals freedom, and that self-governance is synonymous with personal growth. Vice versa, not being able to choose, or being constrained in one's choices is tantamount to disempowerment, whereas any imposed reduction in one's ability to exercise full control when it comes to making decisions creates dependency, feelings of disenfranchisement and ultimately unhappiness. This is the rationale, for example, behind the British government's idea that students in higher education should be placed in the driver's seat, at the heart of the educational system, fully entitled to make their own informed choice of service provider, with institutions now being obliged to release "product specifications" in the form of a Key Information Set, while also being held accountable by the Competition and Markets Authority in terms of recruitment and pricing strategies. However, aside from the improvement of freedom of choice and the enhancement of self-governance in the retail, entertainment, educational and professional arenas, the ultimate, as yet largely uncharted and unregulated territory of in-dividual liberty, must be the site of the human body, if only because it is invariably associated with nature—not just the natural environment in which we live, but the natural environment that purportedly determines us, and in a much more fundamental way than any other system of control. Actively creat-ing and positively advancing new opportunities for people to reshape, restyle, "customize" their bodily nature, be it with the assistance of endocrinologists and a specialized team of surgeons, giving people the choice and the chance to modify the unmodifiable, to recreate creation, to take personal control of the uncontrollable, for the purposes of substantially improved psycho-social well-being and eventually a higher degree of productivity, must be the su-preme neo-liberal value—the furthest stage of self-governance and voluntarist self-fashioning, bar none.

At this point, I need to emphasize that I am by no means insinuating, here, that all trans* people are *de facto* champions of neo-liberal rationality, even less that the full social recognition of trans* will only be accomplished under conditions of neo-liberalism. What I am arguing is that the current Western socio-political interest in and support for trans* rights and trans* equality conforms with how a neo-liberal ideology would always underscore the importance of individual enterprise, especially when it is being seen as promoting well-being, because this may subsequently serve the production process, and contribute to economic growth. In other words, the homonorma-tive nationalism Puar identified as a staple of Western neo-liberal bio-politics during the first decade of the twenty-first century has been extrapolated to include what I can only designate as an ideology of trans*nationalism, and this trans*nationalist political agenda is all the more significant for Western neo-liberal policy makers, because it revolves explicitly around the questions of identity and self-governance. While some trans* people may feel very un-comfortable about someone merely crossing over in order to then reaffirm traditional gender stereotypes, the neo-liberal ideologist will not care all that much about where someone is situated and identifies within the gender spectrum—in one of the two conventional categories, somewhere in between, or above it all—as long as the person feels good enough about themselves to enter the workforce. Hence, while in reality, an individual's declaration of being trans* entails an immensely complex and often painful navigation of desires and identifications, its presentation as an ontological claim and a right to self-governance, including the concurrent appeal for social welfare and individual happiness, chimes perfectly with the neo-liberal imperative of unrestrained enterprise. This is not to say that Western trans*nationalism, as a bio-political representation of sexual identity, captures the essence of trans*, whatever that may be; yet, it has contributed extensively to the discursive construction and social legitimacy of trans* as a normative site of sexual ex-pressiveness and civil liberty.

The Troubles of Trans*cursivity

Back in 2002, the British philosopher John Gray wrote in his highly acclaimed *Straw Dogs*:

> For us, nothing is more important than to live as we choose... [W]e have identified the good life with the chosen life... The cult of choice reflects the fact that we must improvise our lives. That we cannot do otherwise is a mark of our unfreedom. Choice has become a fetish; but the mark of a fetish is that it is unchosen.
>
> (Gray, 2002, 109–110)

A full 20 years down the line, I think it is fair to say that in some quarters of life, the cult of choice has become a veritable tyranny of choice, in a radical reversal of Kant's (1997, 28) categorical imperative, which made personal autonomy and rational freedom dependent upon the unconditional injunction of moral duty. With the gradual ascent and seemingly unstoppable proliferation of neo-liberalism, citizens are effectively being forced to choose, quite simply because the options and opportunities are there, including the ultimate option of having the chance to design one's own option.

Much as these newly created freedoms can be seen as playing into the hands of trans* people, insofar as they explicitly reclaim the civil right to turn chance (in this case, the "accident" of biological sex) into choice (personal autonomy and self-customization)—with the important caveat that choice itself is presented as a necessary "affirmation of being"—the logic is unfortunately far less emancipatory than it appears. For one, neo-liberal rationalities only value and encourage choice if and only if it leads to a sense of identity, and if this (newly acquired) identity releases individual agency, psycho-social well-being and economic productivity. Caitlyn Jenner might fit this pattern quite well, but many trans* people probably do not, partly because they do not aim for a re-embodied subjectivity, nor for a relatively stable reintegration of body and mind, partly because their journey, regardless of its aims, is more often than not fraught with terrible agony and prolonged suffering. In other words, the neo-liberal tyranny of choice may be liberating for those who seek to re-identify and for whom re-embodiment equals the opening up of previously inaccessible sources of subjective power, as in Caitlyn Jenner's battle-cry to *The Advocate*, but it may push those who see trans* as a radical call for dis-identification and de-categorization further out of the allegedly inclusive value system of cultural acceptance and social integration. Some of the most outspoken trans*activists, such as Patrick Califia, Kate Bornstein and Susan Stryker, have responded to this issue by arguing in favor of sexual identity as something that should be completely stripped of any form of identification, unless it is the paradoxical identification of ambiguity, variability, provision and fluidity—in short, non-identity. What informs the transitioning process, here, may still be a choice *qua* ontological claim; yet, the choice is directed toward maintaining a state of transitionality rather than a new identity, and toward creating what I would call a logic of trans*cursivity, as opposed to the conventional logic of discursivity, which is driven by categorical binaries, dichotomies and oppositions. Hence, although voluntarist self-fashioning in the realm of trans* may stand to profit from the neo-liberal imperative of free enterprise, trans*cursivity runs counter to how citizens are expected to operate, as confident self-governing economic agents, in a neo-liberal ideology. The latter only tolerates diversity within (a categorical norm of) identity, and does not accommodate rhizomatic multiplicity, because it is associated with chaos, rebellion and anarchy.[12]

The contemporary tyranny of choice, which relies on the availability of an endless array of freely combinable products and services, also tends to reduce the intrinsic significance of the object of choice—priceless as it may be in the fantasy of the choosing agent, especially when it is self-designed or customized —partly because the object is merely there to provide the citizen-consumer with the illusion of choice, partly because in the endless panoply of choice-objects the difference that would allow objects to become clearly distinguishable (and distinguished) is often reduced to the smallest unit of differentiation in shape or size. The upshot is that the process of choice itself becomes simultaneously trivial and frightening. It becomes frightening, because the illusion of complete freedom that is generated by the limitless series of mutually compatible options makes people feel lost and cast adrift, confronted as they are with the need to square their desire—as if they are supposed to know what they want. It becomes trivial, because the fact that the options are not all that different from one another and tend to represent just minimally divergent variations on the same overarching theme (the tolerable margin of diversity within the norm of identity), transforms the choice from a strong subjective commitment to a no-strings-attached, casual selection—the latter obviously reinforced by money-back guarantee and other return policies.

Applied to trans*, this mechanism can make people feel more anxious than ever before, because they may feel that they are being surreptitiously forced to make a clear, unambiguous decision about what they want. Yet more worryingly, it may falsely present the transitioning process as just another consumerist choice, as a choice among others, thus giving the impression, if not to the trans* people themselves at least to the general public, that the sexed body (its biological as well as its legal inscription) is readily available for reconstruction and customization, in accordance with the wishes of its alternatively gendered denizen. In January 2016, the journalist Melanie McDonagh wrote a controversial opinion piece entitled "Changing sex is not to be done just on a whim," in which she took issue both with the suggestion that anyone over 18 should be given the right to change their gender on the basis of a simple application form, and with the proposal to create gender-neutral passports, on the grounds that "the boy-girl identity is what shapes us most." This eventually led her to conclude: "[T]he notion that you can simply put on a gender the way you change your contact lenses is, I think, symptomatic of a worrying indifference to a basic question of what makes us ourselves" (McDonagh, 2016). As many respondents to the piece highlighted, it is quite simply untrue that trans* people decide to change their sex "on a whim". Yet the fact that this is how it is commonly perceived, including by presumably well-informed journalists, is in itself symptomatic, not of a "worrying indifference to… what makes us ourselves"—indeed, the proposals under review are expressly designed to ensure that we can coincide with ourselves—but of a worrying side-effect of the neo-liberal tyranny of choice, i.e. the trivialization of the transitioning act as a function of simple consumerist selectivity. And this may not advance the cause of trans* people at all, let alone alleviate their anxieties and protect them against discrimination.

At this point, I wish to rekindle the second question I formulated in the introduction of my essay and reflect upon the reasons as to why trans* took so much longer to appear on the scholarly and political radars than the other non-normative permutations of human sexuality in the LGBTQ+ initialism. It goes without saying that I cannot possibly offer, here, a comprehensive analysis of the social history of trans*.[13] And so I will restrict myself to some fairly general observations, which may nonetheless inform a new series of questions concerning the contemporary challenges posed by the presence of the trans*body and the status of trans*cursivity in Western society. The first thing to note, when comparing T to L, G and B is that T does not belong to the three-partite cluster preceding it or, to put it more precisely: T is not the fourth alternative in the series. It exists both outside the LGB spectrum, and potentially resides within it, for the simple reason that LGB refers to instances of human sexual orientation, whereas T reflects human sexual identity or—were we to employ the classic, and to some extent obsolete distinction between (anatomo-physiological) sex and (psycho-social) gender—it signifies a certain relationship, and a consciously experienced incongruity not between people, but between the sexed body and the gendered mind of one and the same person. Although some nineteenth century sexologists were firmly of the opinion that male homosexuals act upon a male body that provides shelter to a feminine soul (*anima muliebris virili corpore inclusa*), we now know that human sexual orientation is not in any consistent way determined by a certain (incongruous) combination between sex and gender.[14] As the writer and trans*activist Jennifer Finney Boylan put it: if sexual orientation is about who you want to go to bed *with*, transgender is about who you want to go to bed *as* (Boylan, 2011). And the latter definitely does not condition the former, or the other way round for that matter. Not all gay people are to some extent trans*, and not all trans* people become gay after socially transitioning, or after gender confirmation surgery. From a psychoanalytic perspective, one should also add the further complication that even if someone believes to know who they go to bed *with*, their knowledge of who they go to bed *as*, both for the person they go to bed with and for themselves, remains forever fractured and precarious.

Because the question of trans* affects human sexual identity rather than human sexual orientation, it is much more fundamental and potentially much more disruptive than any of the other non-normative configurations, if only because it forces us to rethink who we are, what we represent in terms of our identifications and gender performances, and whether the traditional, purportedly natural "boy-girl distinctions" should be maintained. In addition, the question of trans* does not just interrogate the significance of human biology and the importance of the gendered mind, or indeed the relation between both in the context of a given socio-cultural and historical discursive practice, with its specific norms and values, but also the legal and administrative status of sexual citizenship and, perhaps most critical of all, the symbolic structure of language, in which (binary) gender categories are constantly employed as personal pronouns and grammatical inflections. For those trans* people who have anatomically and/or socially crossed over to a new, post-transition identity, the established gendering of language is generally not a problem, provided that they are being addressed with the correct pronoun, i.e. insofar as they are not being misgendered. However, for those who take the question of trans* to index a radical challenge to normative sexual identity politics, nothing less than a de- or re-gendering of language is deemed acceptable. This dismantling of established discursive structures and their associated gender binaries is also a necessary precondition for what I designated earlier as trans*cursivity, and it has manifested itself primarily in the emergence of the so-called neopronouns. To give but one example, in September 2015, the Harvard Faculty of Arts and Sciences passed a motion approving the use of an alternative set of gender-neutral pronouns by students, including *ze, sie* and *hir,* alongside the already common practice of gender categories being avoided through the plural pronouns *they, them* and *their.* Although it is to be expected that these initiatives will spread, they remain hugely controversial, and have sparked outrage among state senators and English grammarians alike. Irrespective of the perceived damage done to the good old English language, one may also wonder how well the new pronouns reflect gender-neutrality, and whether allowing for gender-neutrality is the best way to recognize non-normative, gender diversity.

The main problem, of course, is that once conventional symbolic categories become destabilized, and discursivity is replaced with trans*cursivity, what appears is an infinite variety of options, to which no new, allegedly more inclusive system of (non-)classification would ever be able to do justice. Critically reflecting upon the so-called "toilet wars" in the United States, Slavoj Žižek has argued that the only solution to this "deadlock of classification" would be the one adopted by environmentally friendly councils when they try to encourage citizens to correctly prepare their waste for recycling. When nothing really fits into any of the designated bins, or the waste object is a compound that cannot be disassembled, it can always be thrown into the "general waste" container (see Žižek, 2017a, 208; and 2017b, 137). Another, slightly more elevated example of this principle, which Žižek fails to mention, is of course to be found in the pages of the *Diagnostic and Statistical Manual of Mental Disorders*, including in its current fifth edition, in which, when all is said and done, those patients who do not fit diagnostically into any of the distinct categories can still be categorized, and thus clinically "processed," because they can still be allocated to the "unspecified" category. Within the gender dysphoria section of the manual, there are now even two such "general" categories, one called "Other specified Gender Dysphoria" and the other called "Unspecified Gender Dysphoria," the difference being that although in both cases patients do not meet the full criteria for gender dysphoria in the latter case the clinician "chooses *not* to specify the reason that the criteria are not met" (American Psychiatric Association, 2013, 459).

Trivial as these analogies may be, they do indicate how penetrating and politically sensitive the question of trans* is. With his perceptive eye for the counterintuitive observation, Žižek (2017b, 209) goes on to point out that the "deadlock of classification" is actually not conditioned by the

> empirical wealth of identities that defy classification but, on the contrary, [by] the persistence of sexual difference as real, as 'impossible' (defying every categorization) and simultaneously unavoidable. The multiplicity of gender positions... circulates around an antagonism that forever eludes it.

Žižek's argument, here, goes straight to the heart of the matter: in transcending normative dichotomies of gender and celebrating the multiplicity of gender positions, trans*cursivity both de-stabilizes and confirms the irreducible tensions that run through sexual identity politics. The question of trans* thus demonstrates that identification is both impossible and necessary. Even the ultimate identification with non-identity—with the general wastebin, the "other specified" or "unspecified" conditions, or the "gender neutral" pronoun—is still a type of identification which positions itself *vis-à-vis* the normative categories. In other words, the radical freedom to self-customize in an act of trans*cursivity can only be obtained at the expense of acknowledging, consciously or unconsciously, the established symbolic dichotomies. Trans*cursivity cannot cancel out discursivity; normative discursivity will continue to operate, albeit as the "repressed" dialectical underside of trans*cursivity. In his *Anti-Oedipus Papers*, Guattari put it as follows: "The subject of transcursive enunciation is the damned double of the subject of the law. It is its doublet. It exists in counter dependency to the law" (Guattari, 2006, 36). The sexual subject can thus only be the sovereign master of its ontological fate in opposition to and by virtue of an ongoing exposition of the discursive practices that prevent *hir* from being so, which implies that absolute sovereignty must remain impure, since it is invariably contaminated by the dependency upon categorical discursivity.[15]

What the question of trans* elicits here, for trans* people and cis-sexuals alike, is the impossible necessity of human beings having to identify sexually, of thereby having to accept that something will be irretrievably lost (whatever it is that we fantasmatically attribute to the other positions), and of the endless and hopelessly meandering quest for sexual self-fulfillment. In an exceptionally thoughtful piece on trans* for the *London Review of Books*, Jacqueline Rose (2016, 10) captured the issue with the following words:

> [T]he process [of transitioning] opens up a question about sexual being to which it is more often than not impossible to offer a definitive reply. This is of course true for all human subjects. The bar of sexual difference is ruthless but that doesn't mean that those who believe they subscribe to its law [the cis-sexuals] have any more idea of what is going on beneath the surface than the one who submits less willingly [the trans*individuals].[16]

Unfortunately, trans*cursivity is often promoted by radical trans*activists as the only valid way forward, whereby conventional discursivity is rejected altogether as an inherently restrictive and trans*phobic symbolic system, in an attempt to preserve the (imaginary) purity of trans*cursivity, with all kinds of symptomatic effects.[17]

Conclusion

By way of conclusion, and without wishing to integrate the various points I have made into a succinct synthetic summary, I would like to articulate the key social and clinical challenges posed by the question of trans*. First of all, from the perspective of social policy making, and drawing on the values of inclusivity, social integration, equality and recognition of diversity, trans* is a much more demanding issue to address than sexual orientation, partly because it is more inherently visible, partly because it is much more encompassing, partly because it is much more varied. And because the normative opposition between male and female is so pervasive in Western society, ensuring equality and preventing discrimination is an infinitely more taxing task than it ever was with regard to sexual orientation. It will have to involve a review of the criminal justice system and the prison service, of educational settings and general learning provisions, of employment policies and the workplace environment, of sports event management, of media regulations, of health care policies, and potentially of the public sphere as a whole, up to and including the symbolic structure of language. In terms of health economics, the progressive "democratization" and emancipation of trans* will not reduce the costs of the transitioning process, especially when it involves gender confirmation surgery.

For mental health care practitioners in particular, the question of trans*, which has now been de-pathologized, at least in many Western countries, at the point where a person's declared incongruence between their sex assigned at birth (AFAB or AMAB) and their gender is no longer regarded as *de facto* indicative of a mental health problem, requires a robust review of diagnostic criteria (it clearly is no longer appropriate, for instance, to refer to co-morbidity when a patient presents with allied mental health issues), and of clinical treatment protocols, especially when they involve decision-making processes regarding the prescription of puberty blockers and cross-sex hormones to young people. In her article for the *London Review of Books*, Rose also averred that trans* people persistently have to oppose the lingering stigma according to which their specific type of gender-nonconforming constitutes an intrinsic, pathognomonic sign of psychopathology, because this type of troubling, "ego-dystonic" experiential account "is likely to disqualify them from surgery, where the only narrative that passes is the one that confidently asserts that they have always known who they really are" (Rose, 2016). In a letter to the editor in the subsequent issue of the *London Review of Books*, a representative of the British Association of Gender Identity Specialists pointed out that, although gender dysphoria is not in itself regarded as a mental disorder—so what is it still doing in the *DSM*, one may ask—its association with mental and/or physical disorders does not exclude anyone by definition from gender confirmation surgery.[18]

If Rose is right, then the latter part of this statement will be particularly challenging for practicing psychoanalysts, many of whom now present themselves as trans-friendly, trans-positive or trans-affirmative.[19] It is challenging, because it goes against the grain of what psychoanalysis, as a clinical process, has always stood for, or has at least pretended to stand for, i.e. neutrality and unconditional acceptance, and what it continues to offer, even in the literal sense of "an analysis of the psyche." Beyond all considerations of psychopathology, and away from all distinctions between neurosis, psychosis, perversion and borderline, the psychoanalytic process (and this is what Lacan famously designated as the ethics of psychoanalysis) neither starts nor ends with the acceptance or the affirmation of subjective authenticity, i.e. the truthful knowledge of who one is, the becoming or identification of being (see Lacan, 1992, 1–15). If anything, psychoanalysis creates the space and the opportunity for a subject to question, explore and traverse (in the sense of moving backward and forward within) the fantasmatic narratives they have constructed about themselves, and it operates on the basis of the analyst's implicitly extending an open invitation to the analysand to articulate, formulate and re-formulate a response to the impossible question of "Who do you think you are?" More concretely, this principle implies that whatever the analysand brings to the analytic process by way of a symptom is not addressed directly, but only ever taken as a point of departure for a carefully guided journey of self-unraveling, of prolonged and intensive subjective deconstruction and reconstruction. It also implies that nothing of the analysand's life history can remain, as a matter of principle, untouched or untouchable, because normative psycho-sexual arrangements, allegedly "mature" object-relations and conventional attachments are as problematic and questionable as their non-normative variations. Hence, if there is a direction to the psychoanalytic process, then it never serves the purpose of the crystallization of a "confident narrative," but almost envisages exactly the opposite: the dis-integration of the subject's narratives, what Lacan dubbed "subjective destitution," with a view to their acceptance that true self-knowledge and full meaning will always continue to escape (Lacan, 1995, 8).

As such, trans*affirmation and trans*friendliness (if the latter is held to mean that the subject's trans* identity will not be touched, let alone questioned) are incompatible with one of the foundational principles of the psychoanalytic process, notably that confident self-affirmation is intrinsically problematic, for cis- and trans* people alike. In other words, there is no such thing as a trans*-friendly analyst; the extent to which an analyst presents as trans*friendly is but a measure of their willingness to abandon their analytic profession for a spurious emblem of social recognition. However, viewed from the angle of trans*cursivity, which promotes a radical "de-territorialization" of all established structures, without its being able to fully relinquish the laws and categories of discursivity, the psychoanalytic process, as a journey of dis-integration, may be inherently more trans*oriented than many are prepared to accept. For if trans*cursivity, as I have endeavored to argue, involves the de-stabilization of inherently hierarchical discursive structures and the binary oppositions that run through them, the foundational linguistic practice upon which psychoanalysis rests, and which Freud designated as "free association," constitutes in and of itself a trans*cursive act, which does not provide any stable points of identification, but which precisely equips the analysand with the tools to carve out a transitional or translational space between and beyond identification, which is simultaneously a space of subjective freedom and a space of limitless opportunity.

Notes

1 Preliminary versions of this essay were presented as a Grand Rounds Lecture at the Mayo Clinic in Rochester MN on 16 November 2016, and as a paper for the International Conference on "Transgender, Gender and Psychoanalysis," organized by The Site for Contemporary Psychoanalysis at the Freud Museum London on 12 March 2017. I am grateful to Magdalena Romanowicz and to Dorothée Bonnigal-Katz for inviting me to speak. A detailed report on the Conference was subsequently included in a special issue of *Transgender Studies Quarterly* (Osserman, 2017). In its present form, the essay has benefited enormously from Patricia Gherovici's and Manya Steinkoler's constructively critical and invariably insightful comments on an earlier draft, which not only prompted me to improve the overall clarity of the text, but also encouraged me to rethink substantial parts of the argument.

2 As Freud (1953, 146 [note]) stated in a 1915 addition to his *Three Essays on the Theory of Sexuality*:

> [F]rom the point of view of psycho-analysis the exclusive sexual interest felt by men for women is also a problem that needs elucidating and is not a self-evident fact based upon an attraction that is ultimately of a chemical nature.

3 The exclusion of homosexuals from the psychoanalytic profession was first suggested by Ernest Jones in 1921, when it attracted a vehement rebuttal by Freud and Otto Rank. However, Jones' position in the International Psycho-Analytic Association allowed him to turn this suggestion into an unspoken rule, which prevailed until well into the 1980s. Not until May 1991 did the American Psychoanalytic

Association (APA) issue a statement opposing discrimination against gay men and lesbians as members of its affiliated institutes. Not until April 1992 did the APA acknowledge that homosexual analysts should also be given the opportunity to advance to the most highly ranked positions of Training and Supervising Analyst. Not until June 2019 did the APA issue a formal apology for their historical role in the stigmatization, discrimination and traumatization of sexually nonconforming people. I am still waiting for the British Psychoanalytic Council to follow suit, and I have been waiting for over two decades now for the Lacanian movement to admit to its own historical hetero-normativity, and for them to issue some form of apology. See Wittenberger and Tögel (2001, 297–304), Isay (2009, 147) and Puckett (2019, 45).

4 To the best of my knowledge, nobody has ever taken issue with Butler's comments on transsexuals here; yet, I would not be surprised if their mildly dismissive tone and the implicit reification and homogenization of transsexual desire in her unusually brief reflections constitute a sufficient reason for her to be considered trans-phobic or a Trans-Exclusionary Radical Feminist (TERF).

5 Butler's essay was reprinted in her 2004 volume *Undoing Gender*, with a short epigraph on the recent death of David Reimer. For more details on Reimer's story, see Colapinto (1997, 2000).

6 Although estimates for European countries vary considerably, they represent a significantly smaller proportion of the general population, which may simply be the result of a lack of accurate measurements. In the UK, for example, it is estimated that the trans* community counts no more than 3,000 individuals, i.e. a mere .0005% of the population.

7 Interestingly, the constantly updated web pages of the *DSM* now feature a statement in which it is said that the *DSM-5* includes gender dysphoria as a "nonmental disorder diagnosis," without specifying how this should be understood, or what that may be. See, in this respect, https://www.psychiatry.org/psychiatrists/cultural-competency/education/best-practice-highlights/working-with-lgbtq-patients (accessed on 12 August 2019).

8 See http://gids.nhs.uk/number-referrals. The 2018–2019 figure represents a 33% increase on the 2016–2017 referrals and almost a quadrupling of the 2014–2015 figure. Of the 2,560 referrals, the vast majority was for young people Assigned Female At Birth (AFAB), which contradicts the still popular belief that most trans* people are Male-to-Female (MTF).

9 I am deliberately avoiding the notion "preferred gender," because it might suggest that trans* is a matter of choice, which is what many trans* people refute on the grounds that their intimately felt sexual identity is not in doubt, and that it was present from early childhood, thus suggesting that it is inborn rather than constructed. Of course, this does not cancel out the fact that the transitioning process involves a great many choices, and that these choices are both life-changing and political.

10 In a new memoir, Jenner (2018) revealed that she did undergo gender confirmation surgery in January 2017.

11 Slavoj Žižek (2017b, 135) reports how New York City now offers its residents 31 categories for describing their sexual identity, without this list being regarded as exhaustive. It is precisely on account of this open-ended series of options that an asterisk * has been attached to the word trans, so that trans* includes all the possibilities on the widely diverse spectrum of unconventional sexual identifications, i.e. everything that falls outside the norm of mainstream, cis-sexual masculinity or femininity. The principle itself is derived from the use of * as a Boolean operator, in order to ensure that all permutations of a particular term are being included in a database search.

12 The notion of "transcursivity" appears on various occasions in Félix Guattari's *Anti-Oedipus Papers*—a series of notes and journal entries the French philosopher and psychoanalyst made while working with Gilles Deleuze on *Anti-Oedipus*. Although Guattari's writings, here, have no direct bearing on the question of transgender, and he never offers a clear definition of transcursivity, in his conception of it, a transcursive enunciation is characterized by free-floating, polyvocal and unpredictable connections between fluctuating singularities, by contrast with its discursive counterpart, which is categorical, hierarchical and mechanistic. See Guattari (2006) and Deleuze and Guattari (1983). For an excellent explication of Guattari's theory of the transcursive, see Watson (2009, 156–158).

13 As of August 2019, a comprehensive scholarly social history of trans* remains to be written. Two books that cover a lot of ground, despite their historical and cultural constraints, are Feinberg (1997) and Stryker (2017).

14 For the idea that male homosexuality is conditioned by a feminine soul in a male body, see Numa Numantius (1898).

15 As Maurice Blanchot observed, a similar incongruity runs through the ideology of the Sadean libertines, i.e., the fictional band of brothers and sisters who desperately want to liberate their desires from all social constraints in order to commit the mother of all crimes: their "sadistic" acts remain forever impure, because they can only perform them by virtue of identifying and immolating virtuous victims, or on account of their transgression of an accepted social or religious command. This is also why, in "Kant with Sade," Lacan (2006) could argue that it is impossible for desire to free itself from the symbolic law or, alternatively, that the symbolic law is a necessary precondition for desire to manifest itself, as a result of which it is never pure. See Blanchot (2004, 7–41).

16 Žižek does insinuate that, in campaigning for the abolition of the Real of sexual difference, trans- or gender-fluid people simultaneously reject symbolic castration, which would be sufficient for many a Lacanian to conclude that they must operate indiscriminately within a psychotic structure. Thankfully, by virtue of Patricia Gherovici's (e.g. 2017) seminal work on transgender (Lacanian) psychoanalysis, this pathologizing view of trans* is slowly beginning to change.

17 One relatively innocuous, symptomatic instance of this illusory project of trans*purity occurred during the discussion after my second presentation of some of the ideas in this essay, on the occasion of the Site Conference on "Transgender, Gender and Psychoanalysis" in March 2017. An extremely disgruntled trans* delegate first responded to my paper by saying that my intermittent address of the audience as "Ladies and Gentlemen"—consistently employed with more than a touch of rhetorical irony that neither the delegate in question nor the obsequious conference reporter in *Transgender Studies Quarterly* managed to grasp, let alone appreciate—was clear evidence of my being trans*phobic, given the insistence of the binary oppositions, and then proceeded to ask: "So where do you stand with regard to trans*? For or against?" Much more serious instances of what can only be described as the trans* wars have taken place in the wake of scholarly attempts at bridging the gap between transgender and transrace—the most disturbing example being the 2017 radical character assassination of the young academic philosopher Rebecca Tuvel, following the publication of her paper on transracialism in the feminist journal *Hypatia*—and are happening on a daily basis within the trans* community itself, where people are regularly being ostracized as trans*trenders, i.e. fake trans*, and in which the definition of trans*phobia is forever expanding, each and every move being constantly scrutinized for its surreptitious trans*phobic meaning. Indeed, in some trans* corners, the asterisk has now also been abandoned as a reprehensible trans-phobic sign, partly because

it allows for transracial people to join the trans community, partly because it was allegedly suggested by a hetero-normative cis-sexual … (see Tuvel, 2017 and Singal, 2017). For a balanced sociological perspective on the confluence of transgender and transrace, which has nonetheless also attracted vitriolic criticisms from trans*activists, see Brubaker (2016).

18 See Barrett (2016).

19 The issue as to when and how a trans*person comes to know that they were born in the wrong body, or assigned to the wrong sex at birth, despite their internal and/or external genitalia, is hugely complex and would warrant detailed consideration in its own right on the basis of a careful study of memoirs and personal testimonies. Patricia Gherovici kindly enriched my own lack of insight into the matter with the disclosure that, in her experience, the trans* knowing or trans* "realization" often entails a retrospective reconstruction of the person's past, of which trans* people are well aware, which then provides direction for the future. Gherovici also informed me that trans* people often know very well that they need to construct a solid, coherent autobiographical narrative in order to qualify for gender confirmation surgery, yet that they are rarely duped by this process of utilitarian self-construction.

Bibliography

American Psychiatric Association (2013). *Diagnostic and Statistical Manual of Mental Disorders. Fifth Edition (DSM-5)*, Washington and London: American Psychiatric Publishing.

Barrett, J. (2016). "Trans." *London Review of Books*, 38(10) (May 19), 4.

Bissinger, B. (2015). "Caitlyn Jenner: The Full Story." *Vanity Fair* (July), https://www.vanityfair.com/hollywood/2015/06/caitlyn-jenner-bruce-cover-annie-leibovitz.

Blanchot, M. (2004). "Sade's Reason," in *Lautréamont and Sade* (pp.7–41), trans. S. Kendall and M. Kendall, Stanford: Stanford University Press.

Bornstein, K. (1994). *Gender Outlaw: On Men, Women, and the Rest of Us*, New York: Vintage.

Bornstein, K. (2012). *A Queer and Pleasant Danger: The True Story of a Nice Jewish Boy who joins the Church of Scientology and Leaves Twelve Years Later to Become the Lovely Lady She Is Today*, Boston: Beacon Press.

Boylan, J. F. (2011). "We Want Cake, Too." *The New York Times*, August 11. https://www.nytimes.com/2011/08/12/opinion/wewant-cake-too.

Brown, W. (2015). *Undoing the Demos: Neoliberalism's Stealth Revolution*, New York: Zone Books.

Brubaker, R. (2016). *Trans: Gender and Race in an Age of Unsettled Identities*, Princeton and London: Princeton University Press.

Butler, J. (1990). *Gender Trouble: Feminism and the Subversion of Identity*, New York and London: Routledge.

Butler, J. (1993). *Bodies that Matter: On the Discursive Limits of "Sex"*, New York and London: Routledge.

Butler, J. (2001). "Doing Justice to Someone: Sex Reassignment and Allegories of Transsexuality." *GLQ: A Journal of Lesbian and Gay Studies*, 7(4), 621–636.

Butler, J. (2004). *Undoing Gender*, New York and London: Routledge.

Colapinto, J. (1997). "The True Story of John/Joan." *Rolling Stone*, 775 (December), 54–97.

Colapinto, J. (2000). *As Nature Made Him: The Boy Who Was Raised as a Girl*, New York: HarperCollins.

Deleuze, G. and F. Guattari (1983). *Anti-Oedipus: Capitalism and Schizophrenia*, trans. R. Hurley, M. Seem and H. R. Lane, Minneapolis: University of Minnesota Press.

Duggan, L. (2002). "The New Homonormativity: The Sexual Politics of Neoliberalism," in *Materializing Democracy: Toward a Revitalized Cultural Politics* (pp.175–194), ed. R. Castronovo and D. Nelson, Durham and London: Duke University Press.

Feinberg, L. (1997). *Transgender Warriors: Making History from Joan of Arc to Dennis Rodman*, Boston: Beacon Press.

Freud, S. (1953). *Three Essays on the Theory of Sexuality*, in *The Standard Edition of the Complete Psychological Works of Sigmund Freud, Vol. 7*, ed. and trans. J. Strachey, London: Hogarth Press.

Gherovici, P. (2017). *Transgender Psychoanalysis: A Lacanian Perspective on Sexual Difference*, London and New York: Routledge.

Gray, J. (2002). *Straw Dogs: Thoughts on Humans and Other Animals*, London: Granta.

Guattari, F. (2006). *The Anti-Oedipus Papers*, trans. K. Gotman, New York: Semiotext(e).

Isay, R. A. (2009). *Becoming Gay: The Journey of Self-Acceptance* (rev. edn), New York: Vintage Books.

Jacques, J. (2015). *Trans: A Memoir*, London and New York: Verso.

Jenner, C. (2018). *The Secrets of My Life: Bruce to Cait*, New York: Grand Central Publishing.

Kant, I. (1997). *Critique of Practical Reason*, trans. M. Gregor, Cambridge: Cambridge University Press.

Lacan, J. (1992). *The Seminar. Book VII: The Ethics of Psychoanalysis (1959–60)*, trans. D. Porter, New York: W. W. Norton.

Lacan, J. (1995). "Proposition of 9 October 1967 on the Psychoanalyst of the School," trans. R. Grigg, *Analysis* 6, 1–13.

Lacan, J. (2006). "Kant with Sade," in *Écrits* (pp.645–668), trans. B. Fink, New York: W. W. Norton.

McBee, T. P. (2018). *Amateur: A True Story of What Makes a Man*, Edinburgh: Canongate Books.

McDonagh, M. (2016). "Changing Sex Is Not to Be Done Just on a Whim." *The Evening Standard* (London), January 5, p. A15.

National Geographic—Gender Revolution Special Issue: The Shifting Landscape of Gender (January 2017).

Numa Numantius [Karl Heinrich Ulrichs] (1898). *Forschungen über das Rätsel der mannmännlichen Liebe*, Leipzig: Spohr.

Osserman, J. (2017). "Report of SITE Transgender, Gender, and Psychoanalysis Conference." *Transgender Studies Quarterly*, 4(3–4) (November), 662–667.

Puar, J. K. (2017). *Terrorist Assemblages: Homonationalism in Queer Times*, 10th Anniversary Edition, Durham NC and London: Duke University Press.

Puckett, L. (2019). "American Psychoanalytic Association Apologizes for Previously Treating Homosexuality as an Illness." *The Independent* (June 22), 45.

Romano, T. (2007). "Bye, Bye, Boobies: Fundraising Parties for Trans Surgery Are All the Rage." *The Village Voice*, 51(24) (June), 20–26.

Rose, J. (2016). "Who Do You Think You Are?" *London Review of Books,* 38(9) (May 5), 3–13.

Singal, J. (2017). "This Is What a Modern-Day Witch Hunt Looks like." *New York Magazine* (May 2), https://nymag.com/daily/intelligencer/2017/05/transracialism-article-controversy.html.

Steinmetz, K. (2014). "America's Transition." *Time*, 183(22) (June 9), 38–46.

Stryker, S. (2017). *Transgender History: The Roots of Today's Revolution* (rev. edn), New York: Seal Press.

Tuvel, R. (2017). "In Defense of Transracialism." *Hypatia*, 32(2), 263–278.

Watson, J. (2009). *Guattari's Diagrammatic Thought: Writing Between Lacan and Deleuze.* London and New York: Continuum, 2009.

Wittenberger, G. and C. Tögel (eds) (2001). *Die Rundbriefe des "Geheimen Komitees,"* Band 2, 1921, Tübingen: Diskord.

Žižek, S. (2017a). *The Courage of Hopelessness: Chronicles of a Year of Acting Dangerously,* London: Allen Lane.

Žižek, S. (2017b). *Incontinence of the Void: Economico-Philosophical Spandrels,* Cambridge MA and London: The MIT Press.

Chapter 17

Just Kidding

Valerie Solanas's *SCUM* and Andrea Long Chu's *Females*[1]

Elena Comay del Junco

Jokes can go wrong in a number of ways. Here are two of them. When a joke is told too often, it stops being funny. The punch line relies on the unexpected or at the very least incongruous, and once you've seen or heard something for the tenth time, it's usually no longer surprising. Second, when one tries to explain the mechanics of a joke, it has already failed. If the audience didn't get it the first time, it won't do much good trying to present an argument for why it is supposed to be funny. Explaining your own jokes has the same aura of desperation as the other comedic sin, laughing too hard at them. There are, of course, other ways that humor can go wrong. We flatter ourselves in thinking that offensiveness is a uniquely contemporary malady, but the real problem with offensive jokes isn't that they are not funny; it's that they are too funny. Their issue is, as it were, external to their humor.

Valerie Solanas, the writer, playwright, and activist best remembered for shooting Andy Warhol, was something of a humorist. In the *SCUM Manifesto*, her one piece that people read, her most intense scorn is reserved for failing to have fun or, in other words, for being tedious. More than the rank injustice of patriarchy, it is our society's aesthetic failure that bothers Solanas the most. Life in this society is, she tells us, an "utter bore." It has fed us the lie that the female function is to reproduce the species while it is actually to "groove, love and be herself, irreplaceable by anyone else ... to explore, discover, invent, solve problems, crack jokes" (Solanas, 2004, 9).

In almost killing the most famous artist of the day, Solanas didn't make it easy to see the extended joke that is her manifesto. This is not to say she's not serious, either in her critique of men or in her proposal to eradicate not just the male sex, but death itself. Comedy usually is, at bottom, deadly earnest.

Like Solanas, who is something of an intellectual hero for her, Andrea Long Chu is also interested in jokes. Chu is a writer of essays and criticism who has amassed a large following and a high profile in the last couple years for a series of essays in which she used the narrative of her own transition to overturn some of the basic tenets of what we think it means to be trans. In her debut essay, "On liking women," published in *n* + 1 in early 2018, she argued for a shift in our understanding of transition: instead of thinking of transition as the

DOI: 10.4324/9781003284888-21

expression of true identity – innate or otherwise – we should think of it as the fulfillment of a desire. If the thesis seems serious, that's because it is. But to leave it there would be to ignore the undeniable fact that much of Chu's success rests on her style and, more specifically, on her sense of humor. (The subtitle of "On liking women," in a nod to her hero Solanas: "The Society for Cutting Up Men is a rather fabulous name for a transsexual book club.")

Chu has also made a name for herself as a book critic, specifically the author of the kind of unsparing book reviews whose death has been pronounced every few years since 1959, when Elizabeth Hardwick inaugurated the "decline-of-book-reviewing" genre. Chu's review of *She Wants It*, by the creator of the television show, *Transparent*, Jill Soloway was particularly savage and often particularly funny: "Soloway introduces deep-sounding quotes from other authors like a middle-schooler phoning in a Kate Chopin paper" (Chu, 2018a). But at other times she is able to put humor in service to straightforward polemic. Her *New York Times* op-ed, published under the absurd title, "My new vagina won't make me happy," called for reframing trans healthcare to foreground patients' autonomy rather than doctors' notions of "good outcomes" (Chu, 2018b). The essay form works well for Chu and shorter forms better still. The Soloway review, which appeared online in *Affidavit*, was pieced together from a long thread of tweets posted as she read the book, offering her – incontrovertibly funny – comments page by page in real time. Her many Twitter followers are well deserved.

Chu has now come out with a first book, *Females*. Her essays and reviews derive much of their satisfaction from a kind of manic rush between literary analysis, direct theorizing, and personal anecdote that never gets resolved into a single thesis; what we get is the satisfaction of associative thinking at its best and the fun of making seemingly improbable connections. Chu presents *Females* as an argument for a single thesis, namely that "everyone is female, and everyone hates it" (Chu, 2019, 11). As with her most successful writing, to say that this is a joke is neither an insult nor a dismissal. Nor is it to suggest that it is also not meant in earnest.

In her admittedly idiosyncratic – she proudly calls it "wildly tendentious" – definition, "femaleness" is neither biological (sex) nor cultural (gender). It is what she calls the "ontological" state or "universal existential condition" shared by all humans of being subject to another's desire (Chu, 2019, 12). *Females* is written under the sign of Solanas, whom Chu renders an avatar for her account about not just what it means to be transgender, but what it means to have a gender at all. Her contention, picking up on Solanas's line that men live in terror of "the discovery that males are females," is that we are all, men and women, cis and trans, female.

Besides being a comedian, however, Chu is also an academic at heart and so puts in some work to make the statement coherent. Which means she wants to have her joke and explain it, too. The argument would go something like this: at base, we are all dependent on others, subject to their passions, at risk of being swallowed in our attempts to satiate their demands. And so if this is what we mean by the term "female" – it isn't, really, and Chu knows that – we are all female and no one more so than cis, straight men, who have the furthest to fall when the approval of others is withheld. Hence the ubiquity of the phrase "fragile male ego" and so on.

Or, in the theoretical register Chu employs most frequently the focus on castration as fundamental to the psychic structure of females and, even more so, males. There is a satisfying, funhouse-mirror effect to taking logic to its breaking point. Chu cites Solanas copiously, but not much else, which is not a criticism, since her theoretical debts would be clear enough even without the glancing reference to Freud's *Three Essays*. Freud's claim that a castration complex lies at the roots of both male and female sexualities is a clear – however distant – ancestor of Chu's central thesis. (Perhaps it is intolerably pedantic, though, given the sensibility of her project, to note that castration is above all a *male* phenomenon.)

The Freudian roots of Chu's essay are, perhaps unsurprisingly – given both her vocabulary and her academic formation – mediated through Lacan, though he is never mentioned by name. The degree to which Freud himself believed his account of sexual difference to be rooted in biology is of course a matter of extreme contention, but not one that matters here. Lacan's categorical rejection of a biological basis for sexual difference is one thing. But his location of such difference in the realm of logical form – as opposed to, for example, socially contingent, if durable and harshly enforced, roles – is quite another. We do not need to make sense of the Lacanian position in order to see how Chu's thesis that "femaleness" refers neither to biological sex nor to social gender is its direct descendant.

But interesting as tracing this lineage may be, it can only take us so far. For the obvious question is: why call this state of universal dependence on others "female"? (Even Lacan didn't.) Chu's own answer is that "everyone already does." Obviously, this is not literally true, and to take Chu to task for that would be failing to recognize that her entire claim is, at some level at least, a joke. But we can ask why the joke works at all, and the answer would be that it seems to rely on the longstanding equation between femaleness (in the usual sense) and passivity. Whether subordination is integral to what it means to be a woman, or it is a contingent – if pervasive – fact that women are subordinated, the link between "passive" and "female" is surely not arbitrary. But Chu takes things a step further. By claiming that *everyone* is dependent, passive, unfree, and calling this state "female," Chu has built the equation between women and passivity into the very core of human nature.

I understand why many readers have found themselves uneasy, and many others have taken offense at Chu's equation of femaleness and passivity. According to many of her critics – both on social media and in reviews – Chu doesn't just flirt with, but entirely embraces the anti-trans commonplace that trans women's conception of and desire for womanhood amounts to nothing more than fetishized tropes and symbols of traditional femininity. Chu's anticipatory defense is that this does not characterize trans women's desire, but human desire generally. ("We're all dumb blondes.") That is, she isn't attempting to make certain offensive strains of trans exclusionary thought palatable; rather, Chu is trying to show that the allegedly specifically transsexual experience of gender is, in fact, universal. Everyone's experience of gender – be it their own or the opposite – is constituted by wanting things that are bad for them.

But the problem I'm interested in is not potential offensiveness (anything so calculated cannot, really, be offensive) but the fact that by the time the claim of universal femaleness has been not merely asserted, but explained, it has lost whatever force, shock value, or provocation it initially possessed. Chu has come up with a moderately good one liner, but even to fill a book as short as *Females,* she has to first repeat it many times and then, for good measure, explain it. In short, it is no longer funny.

***

Let me try to be fair. *Females* is a book born out of exasperation at the hollowness of a vision of gender as simply a matter of identification, the feel-good slogan that you are who you say you are. Chu is right when she insists that what other people see and think matters, and nowhere is that more evident than in the project of transitioning. If gender were a matter of pure interiority, none of the costly, physically painful, and, most importantly, socially precarious risks entailed by coming out would be worth taking. At risk of putting too Hegelian a point on it, it is a fact of human life that we all require recognition, that recognition is unequally distributed, and trans people too often get a particularly raw deal.

It would be unfair to Chu to simply say that she is *simply* pushing back against a straw man. There is certainly a strain of gender theory – though it hardly merits even the dubious legitimation afforded by that term – which says, in effect, that you are who you say you are, no further questions. To say, as Chu does, that "When people today say that a given gender identity is 'valid,' this is true, but only tautologically so" (Chu, 2019, 38) is quite obviously right. Whom, though, is she criticizing here? Perhaps Chu's most obvious target is the discourses proliferated on sites like Tumblr in the last decade or so. This was a prime source for the dissemination of the term "valid," which Chu is quite correct in finding insufferably vapid and simplistic, as well as moralizing and Manichaean, and repeated in public awareness campaigns that emphasize, as such a genre always does, simple and easy-to-digest slogans. These are undeniably sentimental and intellectually vacuous, at least if we look to them for an adequate theory of gender. (Though one might rightly ask if that is really what we should be looking to them for.)

After contending, again correctly, that "gender is something other people have to give you," she suggests that the entire notion of "validity" is "At best …

a moral demand" (Chu, 2019, 38), that is, a demand for recognition. This, once more, is correct. But if Chu is demanding a shift from thinking of first-person gender claims from the epistemic to the ethical, she is on well-trodden territory.[2]

Chu, however, does not simply point to the universal need to be seen by others. If that were all, it would, once again, be a strange use of the term "female," and the claim itself would hardly be remarkable. The problem is that in Chu's world, there is nothing to be done about the expectations of others: meet them, or else. It's not a matter of nihilism, as has been charged, but of fatalism; social change is attempted at one's own peril (Gabriel, 2019). Tragically, Chu ends up falling into the same degree of simplemindedness that she accuses proponents of gender-as-inner-feeling. Feeling like a woman (or a man, or whatever) is substituted for *wanting* to be a woman, but the situation is still treated as something one can't do anything about. Submit, or else.

There is no questioning the origins of our desires, nor how we want to relate to them. They are brute facts or, in Chu's terms, "ontological" (Chu, 2019, 12). And calling something ontological is, it turns out, just another way of saying that there is nothing to be done about it. To take the most obvious example, it is easier to make one's appearance conform to gender norms than it is to change those norms to accommodate one's appearance. Any trans woman who has given thought to facial feminization surgery, in particular, will be familiar with the dilemma. (I am writing this while traveling to a plastic surgeon's office.) But this insight is hardly limited to this demographic. And because Chu's notion of femaleness has nothing to do with gender, this dilemma is not specific to trans people, but is one of politics generally.

The responsible answer is that we need to approach this from both ends. In the case of trans people – the only end in which Chu actually seems interested – this means we need to, on the one hand, radically increase access to healthcare, especially for procedures deemed "cosmetic," which are ironically the ones most legible in the public sphere. And on the other, we need to transform the vision of what it means to have a gender, to place less emphasis on passing, on conforming, on having the right kind of body, voice, behavior, and so on. If it sounds like these goals are in tension, even contradictory, it's because they are. It is a situation that requires thinking, to use an old term, dialectically.

I have already said that Chu is a comedian but that she also wants, in *Females* as in her earlier essays, ultimately to be writing social theory. It is unclear if she can do both. The only real motivation for calling the universal position of being subject to other minds "female" is, as far as I can tell, to set up the joke whose thrilling punch line is the claim that, since heterosexual masculinity is, as everyone knows, the most fragile of psychic states, straight cis men are the most female of all. But the result of wanting to be funny and serious at the same time is that, rather than playing humor and theory off one another, Chu ends up achieving neither. The joke falls flat, while the theoretical machinery brought in to back it up provides, at best, a meager philosophical payoff.

Solanas, in contrast to Chu, does not really seem particularly intent on being funny, though the outrageousness of her propositions is certainly amusing. As a result, she often stands accused of having a depressing, Manichean worldview. At one level, this is true. But she is also nothing if not an optimist, albeit of a strange sort. Not only does she think that the male sex can be made obsolete if scientists just worked harder, but that immortality itself is within reach. Maybe it's because she was writing during a more optimistic historical moment. Solanas never really refers to the historical situation in which she writes, but it seems she – and others, Shulamith Firestone most notably – absorbed some of the ideology of progress. The Apollo program may have been the masculinist product of Cold War imperialism, but it was surely an inspiring monument to human ingenuity. And Solanas, for her own part, extols the possibility of phasing out "natural" reproduction by means of technological advances then coming into their own (Solanas, 2004, 3).

Chu is not entirely to blame for the fatalism of her message. We do, after all, seem to have rather little to hope for. Far from cracking the secret to immortality, we seem increasingly incapable of getting it together to last even a few more generations. Nevertheless, dark times can generate ameliorative humor; they can also produce good philosophy. Perhaps they can't do both at once.

Notes

1 This is an expanded version of a review which appeared as "Killing the Joke" in *The Point Magazine*, 13 February 2020. My thanks to Camille Gilchriest, Rami Karim, Gal Katz, and Quinn Roberts for their comments and discussion.
2 I have in mind in particular Talia Mae Bettcher's (2009, 98–120) account of an ethical first-person authority as grounds for self-determination over one's gender.

Bibliography

Bettcher, T. M. (2009). *"You've Changed": Sex Reassignment and Personal Identity*, trans. L. Shrage, Oxford: Oxford University Press.

Chu, A. L. (2018a). "No One Wants It." *Affidavit*, 5 November, https://www.affidavit. art/articles/no-one-wants-it

Chu, A. L. (2018b). "My New Vagina Won't Make Me Happy, and It Shouldn't Have To." *The New York Times,* 24 November, https://www.nytimes.com/2018/11/24/opinion/sunday/vaginoplasty-transgender-medicine.html

Chu, A. L. (2019). *Females*, London and New York: Verso.

Gabriel, K. (2019). "The Limits of the Bit." *The Los Angeles Review of Books,* 25 November, https://lareviewofbooks.org/article/the-limits-of-the-bit/

Solanas, V. (2004). *SCUM Manifesto*, intro. A. Ronell, London and New York: Verso.

Chapter 18

Transgender Quarrels and the Unspeakable Whiteness of Psychoanalysis

Yannik Thiem

Gender is not a settled matter. For none of us. As the trans community becomes more genderqueer and variegated, trans individuals are bringing to the fore aspects of the ongoing unsettled nature of gender development that affects all of us, even though not all of us experience this ongoing negotiation with the same intensity. What makes trans individuals so "challenging" to many analysts, therapists, and society at large is not that we are so different, but that we are quite similar to cis people after all. Interactions with transgender individuals often (and especially, but by no means only, in analysis) become occasions that heighten the intense experience for analyst and analysand of the ongoing unconscious relational processes of being bodily addressed, elaborating upon all vectors of embodiment. However, as long as we and those around us adhere to the socially settled scripts sheltered by cisnormativity and whiteness, we remain unaware of these complex negotiations.[1]

One of the paradoxes of gender is that we experience it as immediate self-knowledge, while at the same time we all are aware that gender development is relational, historical, and mediated. Gender embodiment is constantly developing over time in relation to changing body morphology, familial constellations, social and cultural images, and to community norms and cultural milieu. The paradox is that once assigned and taken up, gender is presumed to be relatively stable, and our everyday mostly unconscious negotiations tend to revolve around "What *kind* of a woman, man, person do I want to be in relation to the models of similarity and difference around me?" Transgender individuals, however, especially ones embarking on transitioning, ask, "Am I a woman; am I a man; am I a person of another or any gender altogether?" Because of the thorough, ongoing relational negotiation of gendered embodiment, trans individuals also inevitably challenge cis individuals to ask themselves, "How do I actually know my own gender in the first place?"

It may seem that this question is primarily one of gender, but as I explore in this chapter, the trans experience reveals how racialization is a medium of negotiating gender, and vice versa. In some ways, the connections between transgender embodiments and race are all too obvious. How could we not attend to the dynamics of race and racialization when we talk about transgender questions?

DOI: 10.4324/9781003284888-22

Transgender people of color and especially Black and brown trans women are among the most precarious populations facing, among other issues, exceptionally high rates of violence: discrimination in employment, housing, healthcare, and even murder. So how is it that so often the relation to race and racialization gets neglected in psychoanalytic inquiries into transgender embodiments? Even though in our live experience and in society at large the interrelation between race and gender seems rather obvious, when we try to grasp the deep conceptual structures, the entanglements of race and gender as mediums of embodied development and experience are anything but obvious. Gender transitions confront us with the tense entanglements of and divergences between race and gender as categories, psychic and social structures, and experiences.

The understanding of gender and gender development in psychoanalytic theory and practice has been shifting, especially as more and more people inhabit openly, visibly, audibly, perceptibly non-binary variations of genders.[2] Equally, English-language psychoanalytic contributions over recent years have been increasingly reckoning and wrestling with the lacunae of theorizing race and particularly whiteness.[3] But despite the broad acceptance of this intersectionality, it is not taken for granted that psychoanalytic reflections on gender and on transgender in particular take race into account.[4] In this chapter, I would like to trace some of these uneasy entanglements to explore the still common psychoanalytic rendering of racialization as secondary to the presumed more primary vagaries of psychosexual development. The theoretical wager here is that this particular severing of sex and gender from race within twenty-first-century Euro-Atlantic contexts points to how whiteness continues to be encoded and rendered imperceptible in our theories of desire, embodiment, and individuation.

Various aspects of difference, such as race and gender, always inflect each other; we never experience them as distinct. My analysis, however, is less concerned with these lived, concrete mediations. Instead, I am focusing on examining how racialized frames of reference are embedded within psychoanalytic understandings of gender, sex, and sexual difference at the conceptual level. In other words, we cannot simply add race to our existing analyses of sex and gender. Rather, incorporating attention to race and racialization at the conceptual level will also require undoing and reconstituting how we think about sex and gender in the first place.

Trans Theorizing: Points of Pressure, Pain, and Provisional Exploration

The lived realities of trans people and their experiences of transitioning heighten our sensibilities for all kinds of intersectional mediations of gender—to class, bodily and cognitive ability, age, body shape, and, of course, also race. Nobody gender-transitions in the abstract, separated from other dimensions of lived experience of embodiment such as race, body shape, age, and disability. Consider, for example, a transmasculine person who is being perceived as a Black male. This experience imposes a precarity and danger quite different from transitioning and navigating the world as a transmasculine person perceived as a white male. For a white person, gender-transitioning can or at least maybe should make one realize that whiteness, as a non-experience, functions as a transparent or seamless medium when negotiating gender, even when one occupies a minoritarian gender position.

For the white person writing this chapter, who has settled into a more or less permanent transition from Germany to the United States, embarking on a journey of gender explicitly in transit meant that whiteness became as much, if not more, of an issue as did gender, and inseparable from how gender and whiteness inflect and specify one another. Having been assigned the gender marker female at birth and having lived most of my adult life as a visibly queer woman, the question of transitioning concerned what it would mean to be perceived not just as male, but specifically as a *white* male person. From there, it became impossible for me not to wonder to what extent being read as a woman and being visibly queer had worked as an unconscious "carbon-offset" for my whiteness and my access to the privileges that whiteness affords. I ask myself how and under what circumstances do some transgender identifications coalesce with and support continued desires to disown one's inheritances of whiteness and refusals to let go of investments in whiteness?[5]

I write the preceding paragraph only with great trepidation. Trans-antagonistic argumentations readily and viciously marshal a certain white-washed version of these arguments against gender transitioning. According to them, trans people seek only either to access male privilege or to appropriate female oppression. To the trans-antagonists, gender transitions are nothing but a ploy, an attempt at getting out of the specific complexities that come with the gender assigned at birth.

The difference between wondering about how transgender identifications may be animated by and displace other investments and these trans-antagonistic accusations is that the latter work precisely by putting the intersectional dynamics of the former questions under erasure. Anti-trans arguments champion a reductive genital anatomical version of sex as the all-determining dimension of embodiment. The transmisogynist accusation that trans women appropriate "female oppression" and "disavow male privilege" prioritizes and universalizes "female oppression," which, in turn, renders race, class, disability, and other dimensions shaping embodiments and experience as secondary, if not mostly irrelevant. The clamor of gender allows trans-antagonists to absolve themselves from their silence on their own complex complicities in hegemonic whiteness.

In this context—at this time in the United States—it is probably also impossible to write about transgender and race without a note on racial crossings and in particular on white individuals identifying as Black. Racial crossings, also known as racial passing, are not new phenomena, nor is the impossibility for some to pass or even tentatively cross the color line. While it may therefore be tempting to see race and gender as analogous categories, there is a crucial divergence between the normative conceptions anchoring gender and race, namely, between cisnormativity and normative whiteness.[6] Cisnormativity is inherently binary, whereas normative whiteness is, as Kalpana Seshadri-Crooks (2000) and Dorothy Holmes (2019) have argued, an imagined oneness or wholeness.[7] Altman (2006b) shows that in this oneness and omnipotence fantasy, whiteness has the structure of pathological narcissism.[8] Whiteness as a norm relies on othering and repressing difference and is experienced as not raced. Conversely, normative cisgenderedness is experienced as being of one or the other sex, anchored in an assumed irrefutable physiological binary. Racialization, as Seshadri-Crooks (2000) argues, "is fundamentally a regime of looking, although race cannot be reduced to the look…. [I]dentity is a question of 'heritage,' not skin color. Once claimed, however, heritage is ultimately marked by the body" (2).[9] As far as the connection to heritage is concerned, cisnormativity and normative whiteness operate with different temporalities and assumptions regarding how they are passed on. With respect to sex and gender, the parents' sex and gender are not assumed to give any prediction regarding the child's sex and gender. With respect to race, however, parental and communal racial identities do determine a child's racial position. Moreover, the binary of sexual difference is assumed to be stably reproduced throughout the generations, but the assumption about race is that racial mixing happens over generations.[10] These divergences between normative cisgenderedness and normative whiteness that underlie how gender and race currently function mean that race and gender cannot be considered as analogous, especially not with respect to crossings and transitions.[11]

This chapter is intentionally not adjudicating any claims to transitions and especially not to racial crossings.[12] Not only is that latter issue not in the purview of this chapter, but it is a question of intellectual and scholarly ethics to hold off writing on that question, since I am neither a member of the communities most affected nor a clinician working with and embedded in these communities. Consequently, my role is to listen to members of the trans community of color, the Black queer community, and the Black community as they interrogate questions of identifications across racial lines, including white individuals' identifications with Blackness. Thinkers such as Marquis Bey (2017), Kat Blaque (2015), Kai Green (2015, 2016, 2017), Dorothy Holmes (2016a), Matt Richardson (Ellison et al 2017), C. Riley Snorton (2017), Kris Sealey (2018), and Treva Ellison et al. (2017), among many others, who are differently positioned within these communities, have already contributed significant and divergent analyses and reflections on the complexity of these issues. To be clear, I am not arguing that members of marginalized communities have a responsibility to take the lead or need to educate those who are outside these communities. Rather, my point here is to give communities the space to explore these questions. If one seeks to enter the conversation, one needs to take time and care build the relationships and the trust that enable one to theorize out of and in intimacy, as trans philosopher Talia Mae Bettcher (2017) puts it. But sometimes as scholars, it may also simply be our task to postpone publishing—not to add our own voices right away, but rather to make the time and listen, read, learn, and engage.[13]

In this chapter, I seek to examine how within psychoanalytic theorizing, prompted by rethinking gender through transgender embodiments, we might understand sex, gender, and race as intertwined at the structural and theoretical level, beyond the identities of the individuals in the room. There is a growing body of literature on transgender psychoanalysis, but this work has rarely engaged with psychoanalytic theorizing on race, in which the longstanding pattern has been that race is only thematized when at least one part of the analytic dyad happens not to be white.[14] In much of psychoanalytic theorizing, sex and gender are still largely considered unquestionably foundational to the development of patterns of desires, identifications, and self-differentiation, while racialization does not seem to be considered equally foundational. In this regard, there has been very little uptake of Judith Butler's (1993) argument in *Bodies That Matter* that "[T]o claim that sexual difference is more fundamental than racial difference is effectively to assume that sexual difference is white sexual difference, and that whiteness is not a form of racial difference" (135). As Adrienne Harris (2019) observes in "The Perverse Pact: Racism and White Privilege," even when race plays a role in psychoanalytic inquiries, still gender and sexuality are foregrounded. Race is reinterpreted as surface phenomenon and gender and sexual dynamics as core "actual" deeper truth.[15] Moreover, the structural interrelations of sex, gender, and race beyond individual experiences remain largely undertheorized in psychoanalysis.[16]

Some inroads into repositioning the relationship among race, gender, sex, and sexual difference are offered by Seshadri-Crooks and Sheila Cavanagh. Cavanagh (2019) asks, "Who says that racism is not one formulation of sexual difference (where, for instance, Black men are feminized and White male hetero-masculine virility exaggerated), and that there is not ... a colonization of psychic space?" (227). In *Desiring Whiteness,* Seshadri-Crooks (2000) details whiteness as a structure of fantasmatic wholeness that depends on and supplements sexual difference's constitutive lack. For the individual's path of development, according to Seshadri-Crooks' account, race and gender are coeval and mutually implicated dimensions. However, conceptually Seshadri-Crooks retains sexual difference as the primary structure to which racialization and whiteness are supplemental. Similarly, in Cavanagh's (2019) question, sexual difference precedes its transposition and formulation in racial terms. Above all, I take these struggles as indicative of the difficulty of theorizing the mutual implication of race, gender, and sex at the conceptual level. My aim here is to show how our conception of "sex" is already suffused with illegible racialized meanings and histories of normative whiteness. Consequently, race does not just intersect with gender at the level of concrete lived embodiments, but it is also inscribed at a deeper structural and collective level where racializations and normative whiteness have enabled and fixed the naturalized and anatomized inflections of sex and sex differences.

Taking up transgender questions in psychoanalysis seriously compels us to reexamine sex, gender, and sexual difference and also forces us to reflect on the differences and intersections between gender and race. If we can expand our understanding of how gender and sex are implicated in normative whiteness, then the rethinking of gender that transgender has set in motion can also provide us with gender as a site for making tangible, exploring, and possibly even fracturing and working through attachments to whiteness.

Transitional Differences: Emergent Formations of Gender, Sex, and Sexual Difference in Psychoanalysis

"Everyone is duped by gender's apparent obviousness," Oren Gozlan observes while considering trans children's gender development (2018a, 6). Transgender individuals and their journeys disrupt this obviousness of gender for everyone involved. Our thinking about gender in general needs to change, as Gozlan argues, and psychoanalysis in particular needs to analyze its attachments to its ideals framing gender development, which come under pressure when working with trans individuals. Gozlan argues that psychoanalysis needs to let go of its attachments to the ideals of an "authentic" or a "true" gendered self, of an alignment between body and psyche, and of a bodily developmental continuity with a "natural" destiny.[17] Drawing on Donald Winnicott, Gozlan proposes understanding gender in general as a "good-enough placeholder" for negotiating and embodying differences in relation to oneself and others.[18]

Gozlan (2018a) arrives at this recasting of gender by way of analyzing how anxieties around transgender children are inseparable from the gender anxieties and fantasies of the adults around the children. "Gender embodiment," Gozlan (2018a) writes, "is always already enveloped by transgenerational meanings and investments, and … this inheritance, which is also unconscious, makes the body something more and other than a natural, given thing" (11). In this emphasis on the transgenerational constitution of gender embodiments, Gozlan takes up the rethinking of sex, gender, sexuality, and processes of differentiation via the concept of enigmatic messages, as introduced by Jean Laplanche. Caregivers and others tending to the infant involuntarily communicate "enigmatic messages," because all relating to the infant is suffused with desires, wishes, fantasies, and other unconscious material, which radically exceeds the infant's capacity to make sense. These enigmatic messages are, as Laplanche (1999) argues, both stimulating and overwhelming and in response the infant "translates" and assimilates as much and as best as it can repressing the untranslatable rest. One's sense of self, one's body, and one's desires are shaped by these translations, transpositions, decompositions, and retranslations over time.[19]

In "Gender, Sex, and the Sexual" (2007), Laplanche responds to and incorporates feminist insights and critiques of psychoanalytic theories of gender formation, in particular those of Judith Butler. Laplanche opens his essay by proposing to hold three aspects in play when we theorize psychosexual development: (1) gender is social and plural and, importantly, precedes sex; (2) sex is dual; and (3) what he calls "the sexual" is polymorphously multiple and constituted by repression, which happens as the enigmatic messages suffused in gendered meaning are being metabolized and symbolized by sex (pp. 201–202). In the ensuing account of gender identification, Laplanche emphasizes that it is not the infant who identifies with a gender or sex; rather, gender comes to us through assignment by those who care for us. It is not "society" at large or its norms that ascribe gender to us, even though social norms and expectations are of course part of the caregivers' messages:

> [C]ommunication does not only pass through the language of the body, of bodily caretaking; there is also the social code, the social language; there is also the message of the socius; these messages are especially *messages of gender assignment*. But they are also carriers of many "noises," all those brought by the adults who are close to the child: parents, grandparents, brothers and sisters. Their fantasies, their unconscious or preconscious expectations.
>
> (Laplanche, 2007, 215)

Notably, Laplanche introduces the plurality of gender in two dimensions here that change how much of psychoanalysis has conceptualized and continues to conceptualize gender formation. Neither a "mother" nor a "father" nor any parental unit has a conceptual primacy of place. Gender comes to us through many forces surrounding us as infants. What the relevant constellations look like depends on the community structure and the care networks through which an infant grows into this world. The developmental path and conceptual challenge that Laplanche charts out is one of varied and complex constellations. The cultural, social, and intergenerational dimensions of gender formation are inevitably entangled with a wide variety of affective messages that are communicated to the infant, because, as Laplanche explains, handling the infant cannot but reactivate the remnants of the adults' metabolizations of their own infantile sexuality.

In "Seduction, Gender, and the Drive" (2014), an essay responding to Laplanche, Butler applauds the rearticulation of sex and gender for psychoanalysis and how Laplanche opens paths for understanding novel and emerging gender constellations. Butler writes, "Laplanche takes up the position that gender *precedes* sex, and thus he suggests that gender … precedes the emergence of the 'sexually and genitally differentiated body image'. Needless to say, I agree with this point" (128). Butler emphasizes that gender formation should be understood in terms of its assignment and development via the scrambling and ongoing metabolizing of enigmatic messages. However, Butler sidesteps Laplanche's refusal of the idea that if gender precedes sex, gender must also structure sex. Laplanche actually emphatically insists that "sex organizes gender" and seems committed to arguing not only that sex but specifically the *duality* of sex organizes gender. Laplanche's essay (2007) opens with the stipulation that "sex is dual" and it is so "by virtue of sexual reproduction and also by virtue of its human symbolization, which fixes and consolidates the duality" (202). It is hard not to read these claims as a disappointing and all-too-familiar return of psychoanalysis to some anatomical destiny that, while making some room for gender plurality, nevertheless tells us that in the end, we are stuck with a binary imposed by a biological reality grounded in reproduction.

If that duality organizes gender, then gender may precede sex developmentally for the individual, but the sex binary appears once again as an inescapable ultimate reality. If that is how we read Laplanche, it makes sense why Butler, as well as others who have taken up Laplanche in trans-affirmative accounts of gender, would remain agnostic regarding Laplanche's brief and somewhat cryptic claim that the duality of sex organizes gender.[20] However, I would like to explore this point by Laplanche as an important stumbling block that does not mean championing sex difference as an inescapable and unalterable symbolic and material binary.[21]

In particular, I would like to suggest that Laplanche's hard-to-digest remark is actually helpful for transgender psychoanalysis and, less obviously, for rethinking the relationship of psychoanalytic key concepts to structural whiteness. The remark stages how gender and its plurality challenge—but also run up against—the strange weight of somatic differences and a strangely tenacious duality bearing on gender. As Laplanche positions it, sex and its duality exert a force shaping gender and the polymorphous nature of desires. At the same time, we would be mistaken to assume that sex and its duality are given absolutely and unchangeably. For Laplanche (2007), the duality of sex, while referring to sexual reproduction, would not be as salient as it is, *except for its consolidation by human development and symbolization*: "[T]he sex entering into a relation of symbolization with gender is not the sex of biology but to a great extent the sex of a fantasmatic anatomy profoundly marked by the condition of the *human* animal" (208, fn 10). Laplanche continues to explain that in an upright animal, the genitals are neither directly visible nor olfactorily perceived as such; hence, "the *perceptible difference of sex*, as sign or as signifier, has *practically nothing to do with the biological and physiological* male/female difference" (217, emphasis added). Sex is a duality that stems from a long history of humans coding or symbolizing biological and physiological differences in relation to genitalia and reproduction. This duality is fantasmatic and material at the same time. However, even the materiality in question here is not biology or anatomy, but rather material human culture over time.

Butler and Laplanche actually agree that, as such, there is no absolute sexual bimorphism. But the emphasis of their subsequent questions about sex as bimophic resides in different, but—as I am trying to show—compatible registers. Butler (2014) asks, "[A]re there conditions under which 'sex' understood as sexually differentiated morphology, comes to appear as a 'given' of experience, something we might take for granted, a material point of departure ... for any further understanding of gender acquisition?" (29). Butler takes sex's organizing function as something that only appears to us as self-evident in its material facticity because we cannot grasp the primacy of gender as assignment, since gender is part of what precedes and exceeds our conscious sense of ourselves and what always remains enigmatic, partially unconscious, unlike somatically differentiated sex.[22] The affectively charged messages and desirous trajectories of gender stemming from others come to condition how the individual and others map, symbolize, and make sense of one's body, which then attains a kind of clarity and stability when it is grasped as a determinately sexed body. Butler's focus is on how individual gender development involves forming a sense of somatic sex and how its "givenness" can come to appear to be so inescapable. It is in terms of that "givenness" that Laplanche's claim about sex organizing gender refers to an additional historical trajectory, namely, a long evolutionary arc that is at the same time both physiological and cultural.

Regarding the individual, Laplanche appears to agree fully with Butler's conclusion, since he emphasizes that taking gender as assignment seriously for infantile development means "to call into question the primacy of sexual difference as a foundation" (172).[23] There is plurality before there is anything else. Laplanche, like Butler, turns the tables on psychoanalysis and asks analysts to analyze their own investment in sexual difference as primary. However, Laplanche also holds firm to keeping in mind collective development that extends over multiple generations, structuring gender by the sedimented symbolizations of sex that are grafted onto "anatomy."

In our gender transitions, explorations, and experimentations, trans individuals challenge not solely gender assignments, but also the sex binary itself—its meaning, its primacy, and its settledness. Sex as dual is questioned precisely not because it is meaningless for trans individuals, but because transitioning involves intense renegotiations of the category "sex," running up against its limits, symbolizations, and meanings, as well as how it inflects desires. Some trans-antagonistic worries may even be picking up on exactly this nuance that the sex binary is not absolute but is a sedimentation over time and consequently changeable and that trans people rework not only gender, but also the very meaning and symbolizations of sex and sexual difference. To date, there has been little psychoanalytic literature written on that aspect of the complicated labor involved in transitioning, which includes renegotiating one's body as an erotic and sexual body.[24] When transphobic clinicians suggest that trans individuals are psychotic and deny the reality of sexual difference, sometimes we may want to answer, "We wish!" If we were psychotic, we could replace the existing reality with an alternate version. But even neurotic disavowal is less enjoyable at a certain point than it may at first sound. The renegotiations underway are exactly, as Laplanche emphasizes, not only the doings of individuals, but also a matter of collective embodiments, desires, fantasies, and experiences—and possibly therefore extremely threatening to some. The collective task in progress is negotiating plurality, including at the level of sex and genitality. Some women have a clitoris that is not only significantly larger than most women's, but that can also ejaculate; some might enjoy calling this clitoris their penis, while others do not; some might delight in other terms. Yet others may find themselves in entirely new re-combinations and conceptualizations of sex and gender altogether.

Among many other aspects, what these renegotiations bring to the fore in attempts to theorize gender formation is that there are (at least) two intertwined conceptual dimensions to the relationship between gender and sex. There is the individual experience of body as sexed, where, if we follow Laplanche, Butler, Gozlan, and others, the assignment of gender precedes the emergent experience of the body as sexed. But at the same time none of these assignments of gender are inherited in a vacuum. Rather, every assignment also transmits the culturally and historically shaped meaning of sex as a fantasmatic anatomy that organizes gender on the level of the collective unconscious. The plurality of gender is delimited and ordered by what is inherited through "sex," where the material force of meaning is shaped over many generations. Trans experiences call attention to the fact that gender and sex are neither reducible to each other nor completely separate—nor can one supplant the other. Instead, diverse gender embodiments also entail struggles of forging new relationships to what sexual differentiation and the body as sexed mean.

Both gender and sex are material and historical, but the trajectories and temporalities of their reshaping differ. The symbolization of sex as duality in relation to sexual reproduction undergoes a slower remaking than gender imaginaries and embodiments. Laplanche (2007) refers to the evolutionary history of upright clothed presentation as the ground for shaping the sense of "the contingent, perceptual, *illusory* nature of the anatomical difference of sex" as "the true destiny of civilization" (219, emphasis in the original). This "destiny" is not biologically determined, but a matter of cultural developments. The sedimented meanings of anatomical difference in terms of the duality of sex and of reproduction are historical, cultural trajectories that have also been mediated by racialization and coloniality. When we consider the interrelation of sex, gender, and race in psychoanalysis, this consideration needs to extend beyond experiences, bodies, and lives as shaped by the interplay of various dimensions of embodiment and social life. We also need to rethink the conceptual frameworks to take into account how racial and colonial histories have been encoded, naturalized, and dissimulated in our categories for thinking gender formation and psychosexual development.

White Noise of Gender

Within psychoanalytic theories, certain longstanding assumptions for gender formation and psychosexual development still prevail, such as the duality of sex, the foundational role of sexual difference, and a parental (mostly heterosexual) couple as key context and reference structures. As transgender experiences and embodiments become more variegated, they challenge the fixity of the binary of sex difference and narratives of an "authentic" gender that must be discovered, established, and kept in place. Developing trans psychoanalysis therefore requires, as Gozlan (2018a) argues, an unclenching of psychoanalysis' attachments to core tenets, such as "to its naturalized understanding of development, to the presumed alignment between body and psyche, and to the primacy of the heterosexual couple" (27). As I show in this section, the tenets of the duality of sex, the nuclear family structured by the (heterosexual) couple, and the primacy of sexual difference are also intricately bound up with now disavowed histories of coloniality and structural whiteness.[25] Consequently, the challenges that transgender desires and trajectories pose to psychoanalysis also provide the opportunity to take up the urgent work of uncovering and working through the inheritances of racializations and hegemonic whiteness as they are embedded in and continue to structure concepts and dynamics for theorizing psychosexual development.

In *Queering the Color Line*, Siobhan Somerville (2000) demonstrates that the original understanding of sex duality, which sexology and psychoanalysis further elaborated, took up "insights" about sexual differentiation that race science had been developing since early European modernity. Derived from the Darwinian model, the concept of increasing sexual anatomical differentiation was taken to be a measure indicating higher civilizational and developmental accomplishment (Somerville 29). Scholars and public discourse in the late-nineteenth and early-twentieth centuries understood sexual ambiguity, in particular the purported ambiguity of Black women's genitalia and reproductive organs, as confirmation of the inferiority of Black people. Historian of psychoanalysis Sander Gilman (1985) underscores, "[A]ny attempt to establish that the races were inherently different rested to no little extent on the sexual difference of the Black" (112).[26] At the same time, racial difference also deepened a visceral sense of the stakes of differentiating between the sexes.

The consequences of this imbrication of sexual and racial differences for conceptualizing sex and gender difference for the individual are not intuitively clear. Given the very explicit inheritances from "race science," one might wonder how race could nonetheless seemingly disappear from the picture when looking at individuals' sex and gender. The framework for this dissolution of race into gender lies in the then-popular thesis that "ontogeny recapitulates phylogeny." As Somerville (2000) explains, this thesis sums up the assumption "that in its individual maturation, each organism proceeds through stages that are equivalent to adult forms of organisms that have preceded it in evolutionary development" (24). Racial difference and sex and gender enter here into curious shape-shifting analogizing and differentiations mapping individual and species development onto each other: "According to the logic of recapitulation, adult African Americans and white women were at the same stage as white male children and therefore represented an ancestral stage in the evolution of adult white males" (24). Recapitulation as a logic relies on interlinking different temporalities of development and presumes both a diachronic continuity and a synchronously functionally nearly absolute difference. Sometimes that means different races are assumed as contiguous, such as when present-day Blacks are posited as species ancestors of present-day whites. But species development works on a much more extended timescale than individual development, so within the theory of recapitulation, neither Blacks nor white women could as individuals ever be expected to reach the developmental heights of white males. Proof for racialized inferiority was "found" in the lack of sexual differentiation, which also meant that gender was irrelevant in relation to individual racialized subjects. Gender and sex difference obtain importance individually only within whiteness, where the white adult woman is developmentally considered equivalent to the white male child. So white male superiority is established through the inscription of both racial and gender differences. But only within whiteness does gender difference come to matter, making "man" and "woman" essentially white categories of social, psychic, and developmental difference and whiteness the medium for the duality of sex and gender.

The naturalizations of whiteness as associated with goodness, intelligence, and the most advanced evolutionary development are core to long-debunked Eurocentric civilizational narratives. Yet work remains to be done to identify and undo the far-reaching dispersion of these evolutionary biological assumptions that have served as hypotheses, heuristics, and evidence in the development of other concepts and ideas. Debunked "race science" has dropped out of view, even though it once was the medium through which sex duality was entrenched in its obviousness and importance. The importance attributed to somatic sex differences only seems obvious and inescapable once a particular metaphysics of species development and reproduction is in place. The problem here is not simply that sex differences are taken as reducible to reproductive organs. Attempts to conceptualize sex and sexual difference in relation to gender and sexuality at a distance from reproductive biology end up abetting the repression of racially coded histories if such theorizations neglect the multiple layers of how gender is produced through matrices of whiteness and historical dynamics of ungendering and hyper-sexualizing Black bodies.

Drawing on psychoanalytic theory, Hortense Spillers in "Mama's Baby, Papa's Maybe: An American Grammar Book" (1987) demonstrates powerfully the ungendering of the Black body by the violent, deep, and lasting disruption of the various layers of relationality that are required for coherent gendering in the dominant social system.[27] Spillers analyzes the interlocking effects of reducing Black bodies to property, the symbolic disruption of kinship connections by treating Black persons like animals of labor, and the inter- and intragenerational violently enforced fluidity of relationships, as all relationships among the enslaved and in the life of an enslaved person were continuously subject to radical revision at the will of the white masters.[28] In particular, kinship relationships "can be invaded at any given and arbitrary moment by the property relations" (73). Spillers points out the devastating consequences of this sustained systemic disruption. While of course deep and meaningful bonds were forged among the enslaved, nonetheless for the racialized subject, gender and kinship do not carry political and social meaning in the same way, because "gender" and "kin" have "no decisive legal or social efficacy" (75). Spillers' point is not to herald traditional gender roles, sexual positions, and kinship patterns as the ideal to pursue. Rather, her point is that for racialized subjects, gender, sex, and sexual difference were inescapably unstable and voided in their meaning. In other words, Spillers' analysis forces us to see that the symbolic, social, and legal stabilities of gender and sexual difference presuppose whiteness.

The ungendering of Blackness does not mean that there are no Black women (or men), but, as Spillers clarifies, these categories are outside the available logics of gender, which María Lugones (2007) calls the "coloniality of gender." In "Heterosexualism and the Colonial/Modern Gender System," Lugones (2007) elaborates this coloniality as "[T]he dehumanization of colonized and African-diasporic women as lacking gender, one of the marks of the human, and thus being reduced to labor and to raw sex, conceived as non-socializable sexual difference" (33). The sexual difference of the colonized is fixed as "non-socializable," which for Lugones means that it cannot appear in the social imaginary as a variation of sexual differentiation, which would unravel the monochromatic repressed colonial whiteness that stabilizes the sex binary. Remaining outside the socializable as too undifferentiated makes dehumanization possible, as Lugones argues. But this particular move through sexual difference also inscribes a seemingly non-racialized, "objective" marker for naturalizing white bodies as the standard of development. The duality of sex and investments in the stability and decisiveness of that duality are derived from, support, and carry in them a bleached history of investments in white superiority and whiteness as the civilizational norm and ideal that whiteness came to be only through European colonialism.

But how can whiteness, coloniality, and racialization as the conditions of possibility for gender and sexual difference drop out of view in psychoanalysis so easily, if they are so deeply intertwined? As Gilman (1995) and Neil Altmann (2006a, 2010) have argued, the context of antisemitism explains much of the sidelining of race, especially in early European psychoanalysis as well as in the United States after World War II.[29] Early analysts and émigré analysts were intent on avoiding the perception of psychoanalysis as "Jewish science" and hence consciously and unconsciously mostly avoided issues of race and ethnicity. The historical genealogies, however, only partially account for the difficulties of shifting our conceptual underpinnings today. Surely, some of the resistances against embracing the racial histories encoded in concepts of sex, gender, and sexual difference stem from our own unconscious investments in structural whiteness and its ordering of how our worlds work. Still, there also seems to be something genuinely confounding about why it remains so easy to arrive at perceiving sexual difference, sex, and gender as "more fundamental" for psychic development than other intensely psychically charged, unwieldy, unconscious, embodied, and eroticized experiences and structures of difference. As many theorists of intersectionality have observed, it is simply difficult to think the intertwinement of dimensions of difference in modes that reach beyond adding categories of difference or reducing a variety of categories of difference to one master category.[30] To grapple with the slipping away of race and the perceived primacy of gender, sex, and sexual difference in psychoanalysis, we need to examine which dynamics we tend to assume as privileged or self-evident sites where differentiation, its embodiments, and symbolizations take place.

One reason the perceived primacy of sexual difference is so hard to dislodge in psychoanalysis has to do with the power of the generality of the "family" and the "parental couple" as the frame for the formation and exploration of psychic and psychosexual conflicts. Alternative arrangements are by now often conceded and included, but they tend to be rendered as variations on the original structure. The "family" as the primary structure of psychosexual development, however, is also the site where whiteness is presupposed and at the same time obscured by conceiving of the "family" as a universal situation. In *Black Skin, White Masks*, Frantz Fanon ([1952] 2008) cites Jacques Lacan in pointing out that "In every case [of psychoanalytic treatment], the family is treated as the 'psychic object and circumstance'" (120).[31] Fanon observes that within the European context, the privileging of the family structure for exploring psychic formation did not raise any further questions because "In Europe the family represents the way the world reveals itself to the child. The family structure and the national structure are closely connected" (120).[32] The structural contiguity between the family and society at large is valid for the white European heterosexual bourgeois nuclear family. Centering on the family as the primary structure thus inscribes an ideal of whiteness at the heart of psychic and psychosexual development.

Half a century after Fanon, Lugones (2007) is among the theorists of color who continue to emphasize the violent inheritances attached to family as a psychological structure. Lugones writes:

> Familial unity and integration, imposed as the axes of the model of the bourgeois family in the Eurocentered world, were the counterpart of the continued disintegration of the parent–children units in the 'nonwhite' 'races,' which could be held and distributed as property not just as merchandise but as 'animals'.

(194)

Insofar as the family as a social and psychological structure gets defined primarily through sexual relationships and generational constellations, then racial, ethnic, or class specificities get cast as contingent and not defining. Consequently, the family and parent–child relationships can appear as universal and primary, while race, ethnicity, structural whiteness, and the history of the family as a social structure and ideal become, at best, secondary questions.

This kind of sidelining of race, racialization, and structural whiteness is perpetuated inside the clinic when family relationships are treated as privileged and separate from collective social and political histories.[33] Focusing on transgenerational trauma, Lynne Layton (2019) argues,

> so long as we police our psychoanalytic frame in such a way that family memory remains distinct from collective memory, from the Big History, we will not be able adequately to deal with the soul wounds of class inequities and classed racism. I believe we need to consider the possibility that what we call *depth* merely touches the surface, a surface on which the disavowals of history, our illusions, are allowed continuously to repeat themselves.
>
> (115)[34]

By calling into question the routine sidelining of collective history, Layton's (2019) critique also implicitly points us to the unevenness of how we acknowledge transgenerational trauma. Transgenerational trauma is often conceptualized primarily as what Indigenous and racialized people inherit and must cope with.[35] While transgenerational trauma is a racialized and collectivizing experience, whiteness continues to be presumed and reproduced as an empty canvass. As Fanon ([1952] 2008) observed, the experience of Blackness is exactly one of non-individuality and de-individualization: "I was responsible not only for my body but also for my race and my ancestors" (92).[36] Whiteness, in contrast, is the medium that makes individuality possible and sustains that possibility by severing the immediate equivalences and extensions between the individual and the collective that racialization produces.[37] But if we inherit psychic histories transgenerationally, and if especially violent inheritances create a long durée of ripple effects, how is it that we do not assume that white supremacy and colonialism have passed on terrible inheritances of (at best) capacities for arranging oneself with domination, oppression, and exploitation, if not capacities to actively participate in those? We might need to ask what capabilities for psychic splitting, inflicting violence, and tolerating the infliction of brutalities have been unconsciously passed along and inscribed deeply into white psyches over the centuries.[38] As a psychosocial structure, whiteness can be understood, as Harris (2019) proposes, as a "perverse pact" among white people, which is a form of "relatedness dominated by dissociation, amnesia, and disavowal" (311).[39] The immediate family as the primary context for development mediates these historical and political inheritances. As the primary frame of reference for self-formation, this structure also disperses the deep collective historical inheritances. This kind of dispersal and separation from the collective history, however, works unevenly. Individuation is primarily granted to white individuals, but whiteness is not immediately also legible as being implicated in long, inescapable collective inheritances. On the level of theoretical frameworks, privileging the family as formative thus inscribes and at the same time makes illegible whiteness as the medium and norm for psychic development and individuation.

The development of a sexed and gendered body schema and of a coherent gender identification requires seamlessness within the medium of whiteness, which, if a body does not qualify, leads to the ungendering of that body, as Spillers' analysis forcefully teaches us. Or, as Fanon ([1952] 2008) puts it, as racialization proves inescapable, the body schema breaks: "[T]he body schema, attacked in several places, collapsed, giving way to an epidermal racial schema" (92). Within the reigning system of sex, gender, and sexual difference, coherent and stable gendering requires a de-racing, which can be accomplished only to varying degrees except for the body that is not raced. "The body that is not raced" is the white body, since whiteness, as Seshadri-Crooks (1997) reminds us, works precisely by "abjection not of an identification with color per se but with *whiteness* as a color ... and with differences among humans" (152). As a psychic structure, whiteness is an investment in a fantasmatic undifferentiatedness that does not tolerate the indeterminacy of difference. Dorothy Evans Holmes (2019) suggests that whiteness resembles a "white out," both as a snowstorm in which only the dark body or object stands out as unassimilable and as liquid paper that is used to cover over impurities (367). As Jared Sexton (2003) argues, the horror of whiteness is that it cannot control itself, is unable to exist in itself, and must always fear mixing (see especially pp. 264–266). Whiteness is haunted by the horror of "impurity" and the instability of distinctions.[40] To clarify the nexus between whiteness and sex and gender, Seshadri-Crooks (2000) proposes that the investment in whiteness—as the desire for wholeness and for overcoming difference—is an attempt to overcome "the indeterminacy of the sexed subject" (7). For Seshadri-Crooks, this indeterminacy of sex and sexual difference is a given constitutive dimension. However, as we have seen in the work of Fanon, Lugones, Somerville, and Spillers, the indeterminacy of sex and sexual differences is not a given, but is itself a product of the suppressed histories of racialization and continuously elaborated through them. In other words, the haunting indeterminacy of sex and sexual difference is also a symptom of how whiteness both works and fails to varying degrees as the "fixateur" of difference and meaning for gendered and sexed bodily life.[41]

If we now circle back to Laplanche, it becomes possible to conceptualize how racialized difference and whiteness are implicated in and transmitted through our conceptions of gender and psychosexual development. Laplanche's (2007, 2011) insistence that "sex organizes gender" turns out to be particularly promising in this effort. Sex and gender, as we saw, are both sites where histories are inscribed and carried forward, but in different registers. If we follow Laplanche, sex is the register that carries a fantasmatic naturalized materiality developed over many centuries, which is marked by a duality that, as we now can see, in our time is dependent on and shaped by histories of racialized difference and whiteness. Sex organizes gender, but for the individual infant, gender, in the form of the assignment of gender, precedes the mapping and symbolization of somatic sex, which appears as natural and given because its history and alterations are not readily accessible. As Lugones emphasizes in "Gender and Universality in Colonial Methodology" (2020), a critique of the gender binary and expanding the binary to a plurality alone remains insufficient, because to date

> the critique of the binary has not been accompanied by an unveiling of the relation between colonization, race, and gender, nor by an analysis of gender as a colonial introduction of control of the humanity of the colonized, nor by an understanding that gender obscures rather than uncovers the organization of life among the colonized.
>
> (30)

To understand these deep structural inheritances and how they are transmitted both within lived experience and theoretical frameworks, I suggest that it is not sufficient to pluralize the understanding of culturally specific and divergent gender norms and experiences. Rather, in order to bring to bear on theories of psychosexual development the insights that Lugones (2020) argues are still lacking, it is helpful to examine how gender also carries suppressed and dispersed colonial and racial histories and structural whiteness through its delimitations by "sex." The dynamics of whiteness, racializations, and coloniality have shaped the ideas of and investments in sexual difference as a primary structure and in gender as a stable and authentic individual truth to be discovered. At the same time, the apparently inescapable generality of sexual difference and gender as authentic individual truth make whiteness, racializations, and coloniality appear as secondary cultural declensions of the seemingly more primary structures of sex, gender, and sexual difference.

Transgender, Whiteness, and No Easy Way Out

In *Black on Both Sides: A Racial History of Trans Identity* (2017), C. Riley Snorton takes up Fanon's and Spillers' analyses of how regimes of making Black bodies fungible in turn ungender Blackness, in order to develop the implications for transgender theory. Through tracing the ungendering and hypersexing of Black female bodies in the development of U.S. gynecology, chronicling the gender crossings utilized by enslaved individuals in their escapes, and tracking the smudged legibility of twentieth-century Black gender-non-conforming bodies,

Snorton shows that we must understand "gender as a racial arrangement" (83). Histories of Black gender indefiniteness are histories of racialized violence, but, as Snorton emphasizes, they also force us to recognize that "captive flesh figures as critical genealogy for modern transness, as chattel persons gave rise to an understanding of gender as mutable and as an amendable form of being" (57). Within racialized unfreedom, gender historically also emerged as revisable and malleable, which, as Snorton suggests, also opens up the possibility to conceive of "other ways to be trans, in which gender becomes a terrain to make space for living" (175). Snorton's insights help us see how approaching gender and transgender as questions focused on individuality and self-identity remains tightly tied to normative whiteness and cisnormativity. It seems that one task before us, then, is to explore what it would look like to honor this critical Black genealogy of expansive transness without whitewashing it and without repeating the racialized violences of ungendering and gendering.

Against this background, it may be tempting to hope that we can find in trans embodiments a way to escape from the structures of whiteness that are embedded in our existing accounts of gender formation and psychosexual development. But while trans trajectories can (and should) prompt us to analyze and wrestle with the workings of oppressive structures and histories, there is nothing inherently anti-racist and emancipatory about transgender embodiments as such. Investments in and desires for whiteness run deep. After all, "Whiteness is one hell of a drug."[42] However, questions surrounding gender prompted by trans experiences can indeed make the nexus between gender and hegemonic whiteness graspable, including how trans explorations themselves can also all too easily be used to cover over once again any fractures in the white psychic contract whenever such fractures emerge. Consequently, the following four constellations are not intended as conclusive theorizations, but more as snapshots of moments when in psychoanalysis we might start to hone our abilities to perceive and disentangle how hegemonic whiteness and cisnormativity are entangled and rear their heads around gender questions:

1   Concerns that trans people "want to have it all" or are "trying to evade sexual difference": In relation to actual gender transitions, these concerns are not actually terribly interesting, because—for every trans person—transitioning entails compromises and processes of negotiation as for any other person with a material, mortal body. Virginia Goldner (2011) pointedly asks in that light:

> [I]sn't everyone's gender a compromise formation, serving complex intrapsychic and relational agendas? All genders channel both transgression and conformity, suffering and triumph. All create psychic boundaries, make human connections, animate or deaden bodies, ward off depressive and aggressive affects and so on.
>
> (165)

But the accusations and concerns clustering around wanting "to have it all" and "evading difference" are interesting with respect to what else the envy or anxiety points to. Melanie Suchet (2011) reflects honestly and unflinchingly on running up against her own limitations in working with a transmasculine client. Suchet asks, "Perhaps I am afraid that his transitioning will rock my own gender stability. Will it open options I have never contemplated? Do I fear opening up new realms of possibility? On the other hand, I realize there is also a faint glimmer of envy; does he get to be both sexes?" (183). The tropes of "having it all" and "being done with difference" invoke the kind of fantasized accomplishing of wholeness, which, as we saw Seshadri-Crooks (2000) argue, characterizes precisely the psychic investments and promises of whiteness. It seems that in the accusation of "wanting to have it all," trans people stand accused of wanting to access, take, and occupy what whiteness claims for itself. We might then ask whose desires to evade which differences we are encountering in those concerns. Which differences need to be upheld as absolute, in order to maintain fantasies of undifferentiatedness?

2   Anxieties about trans individuals' reproductive desires and capabilities: Most strikingly, these anxieties remain legible in laws on the books well into the twenty-first century in European countries that require sterilization as a precondition for obtaining a legal sex change.[43] For instance, in Germany, the constitutional court ruled that requirement as unconstitutional in 2011. However, other stipulations of the 1981 so-called "transsexuals law" (Transsexuellengesetz) remain in effect, such as that one's legal name change, sex change, or both are automatically voided if one becomes a biological parent more than 300 days after changing one's name and/or gender marker.[44] Even in jurisdictions with more progressive laws for legally changing one's name and gender markers, difficulties arise when it comes to how biological trans parents are to be listed on children's birth certificates. As Peter Dunne (2017) elaborates, arguments insisting on recording trans parents in their gender assigned at birth claim that family law would otherwise be thrown into chaos: "The vista of a man giving birth or a woman begetting children threatens, so the argument goes, the ability of Europe's family law system to efficiently and coherently function" (561). Anxieties that the categories of "man" and "woman" would lose their meaning if both men and women could get pregnant reveal the deeply entrenched meanings and investments in these categories which, at the end of the day, rely on a crudely biologistic heteronormative reproductivity. Unsurprisingly, these concerns about the reproductive abilities of gender-non-conforming individuals stem from and continue the eugenic programs of racial purity and "cleansing" the human race from "deviants" and "degenerates," where "human" was treated as equivalent of "white."[45] In particular, the concern that the categories of "man" and "woman" may be threatened echoes late nineteenth- and early twentieth-century theories

of "sexual inverts."[46] Taking up arguments from eugenics at the time, these theories understood homosexuals as "inverts," in whom female and male aspects are mixed. These ideas have carried over into the discourse of concerns about trans people, who retain their reproductive abilities, as mixing what is properly male and properly female at the level of sex. The 2019 ruling of the UK court case denying the trans man Freddy McConnell be listed as "parent" or "father" on his child's birth certificate is remarkably revealing about how persistent the anxieties of maintaining the sex binary are.[47] The judge argued that the decisive point in the matter of birth certificates is that "there is a material difference between a person's gender and their status as a parent."[48] According to the judge, the term "mother" has been severed from its gendered connotations and only signifies the person who gave birth to the infant and must retain that meaning. It seems that there is something extremely threatening about allowing the term "father" to refer possibly to the person who gave birth and "mother" to the person who contributed the sperm.[49] Instead, according the to the logic of the court ruling, "mother" and "father" need to remain stable in designating unequivocally the *reproductive* role of the parent, regardless of the parent's gender. In other words, what is at stake here is that gender can be allowed to be revisable, but sex must remain defined in relation to reproduction, must stay clearly binary, unmixed, unadulterated, and unaltered. Yet this sex binary and its stability are also, as we know, a product of histories of "race science" and eugenics. What exactly are the concerns about gender- and sex-non-conforming bodies reproducing? What happens when sex turns out to have always also been plural? And what happens when we start to reckon with the racist histories and violences that gave us the sex binary and the foundational importance of sex differences in the first place?

3 Clinicians' refusals to affirm and explore non-binary gender trajectories in analysis: Goldner (2011) provocatively asks whether gender stasis—rather than gender in transition—might need to be regarded as "an obsessional defense, a border patrol operation" (162). In one of the few emerging psychoanalytic writings on non-binary transitions, Ann Pellegrini and Avgi Saketopoulou (2019) reflect on the challenges that non-binary individuals seem to deliver to analysts, as "[A] body not ordered around maleness or femaleness may be seen as being a de facto manifestation of psychic fragmentation." In particular, non-binary analysands asking of their analysts to use different pronouns and names are often met with resistance. Pellegrini and Saketopoulou explain:

> [T]he analyst thinks the patient is being 'too concrete' and won't keep gender hybridity where it belongs, in the realm of fantasy. But what if it is the analyst who is becoming overly concrete in narrowing her sights and refusing to join the patient in exploration?

Non-binary individuals affirm and often find pleasure in the indeterminacy of the embodiment of gender and the symbolization of sex. But more importantly, because both gender embodiment and sex symbolization are ongoing relational processes, non-binary individuals implicitly and explicitly ask of others to join them in these explorations. Since sex and gender determinacy and the sex binary are so deeply tied up with colonial civilizational histories and hegemonic whiteness, these experiences of friction around non-binary imaginaries and embodiments also mark potential inroads into exploring the sex and gender structures underwriting the white psychic contract. What exactly is being threatened by entering into and embracing gender and sex indeterminacies? Which racialized gender violences have been making non-binary bodies possible? Whose bodies never quite got to qualify as "proper"? Whose bodies were already ambiguously gendered and sexed? Whose bodies were constantly "too much"? How do norms and ideals of whiteness, youth, and thinness intersect in the ideal of permissible androgyny?[50]

4   "Trans vs. cis" as a new gender binary: Trans-antagonistic and trans-skeptical investments might be exemplary sites where entanglements with and investments in normative whiteness become graspable. However, trans-affirmative investments can equally play into the hands of the "perverse pact of whiteness" by investing in a new binary of trans and cis and thereby producing dynamics of fetishistic dissociation and identification. Gillian Straker (2004) develops this understanding of fetishism to analyze her own uncomfortable investments as a white anti-apartheid South African during the struggle against apartheid. Straker argues, "As we try to disidentify with our membership in the dominant group and move to support the minority [oppressed] group, we create the risk of using the minority group itself as a fetish" (415). In the process of what Straker terms creating a "fantasy fetish," the oppressed other gets constructed "in overly consistent, positive, and idealized terms, thereby laying the trap of the stereotype and its subtle denigration of the Other" (418). Straker takes stock of how even in their opposition to white supremacy, they often hit upon investments wherein they themselves repeated oppressive structures, because the unassailable goodness of the other reinscribed a racialized binary. Investments in trans embodiments as being entirely different from cisgender can subtend progressive desires of wanting to disown and move beyond whiteness, where trans embodiments mark out solidarity with Blackness and Indigeneity as genealogies and modes of gender mutability.

How are the ghosts of racialization, whiteness, and coloniality both shaping and haunting trans-affirmative desires? How are, for us as white people, our experiences and desires of sex and gender bound up with and shot through by desires to disown the history of whiteness? How do we reckon with other investments in the new trans vs. cis binary? As Latinx philosopher Andrea Pitts (2020) has suggested, "Transgender is exciting and white people are realizing that whiteness is boring"—and in an economy increasingly predicated on creativity, innovation, and attention, being boring is a serious liability. If the history of cisnormativity is inseparable from the history of normative whiteness, what arrays of investments animate rejections of cisnormativity?

These constellations are intentionally neither exhaustive nor resolved. There are and will be more knotted situations that will prompt and require further, maybe different, analysis and theoretical explorations. If anything, the four moments offered above stand in as provisional placeholders for generative work yet to happen to rework and expand the available narratives and conceptual frameworks for queer and trans intra- and intergenerational embodiments, kinship, intimacies, and transmissions of histories of desires, losses, dreams, pains, and pleasures.

Queer trans psychoanalysis is well suited to contribute to such affective and conceptual work by hewing to a queer trans epistemology that is less about knowing than about learning in proximity with others, how to un-know what we already know and how to know differently. Un-knowing and un-learning are taxing processes of trying to let go of what we know about ourselves in the force fields in which cisnormativity and normative whiteness are entwined. Undoing cisnormativity in its subterranean ties to whiteness may require the kind of work that Suchet ([2007] 2012) describes as the un-learning whiteness for white people. This experience involves entering into a state of melancholia that is both different and similar to David Eng and Shinhee Han's (2000) concept of racial melancholia. For the racialized individual, as Eng and Han argue, "[R]acial melancholia indicates one way that lost and socially disparaged racial others live on unconsciously in the psychic realm" (161). Conversely, as Suchet ([2007] 2012) argues, for whites racial melancholia is an experience of loss, disillusion, and horror when

> we come to own the destructiveness that is a part of Whiteness. The rewards and benefits given to Whites automatically implicates us in the acts performed to attain those privileges. There is a realization of our complicity as the beneficiaries of Whiteness. We benefit despite ourselves, despite our beliefs, values, and ideals.
>
> (206)

The process of un-learning that Suchet describes is an experience of loss of identity and of integrating what has been dissociated, of owning rather than disowning the ongoing history of whiteness. Harris (2019) concurs with Suchet but also insists that matters are more complex: "White people must go through a loss of identity. Yet, as I have to acknowledge, even the identity of colonial thief and oppressor is too necessary, too integral to be given up" (326). As Harris argues, the insight that one must work through one's attachments to whiteness is not enough, precisely because this insight still repeats the white fantasy of omnipotence by seeking to accomplish the difficult work out of one's individual powers.[51] Un-learning requires entering into the unsettling uncertainties of real intimacy, which is also what attachments to whiteness and cisnormativity defend against.

We might then conclude that queer trans psychoanalytic work—inside and outside the clinic—in part is about creating and expanding times and spaces for intimacy and proximity in relationships where we—as well as the questions and theories by which we orient ourselves—are being pushed, challenged, held, and changed. Many times in these efforts, we will cause and experience more harm, but we also stand to gain much by entering into and strengthening generative and emerging pluriform solidarities that will leave none of us unchanged. As we move away from theorizing transgender as "trapped in the wrong body" to gender and sex as malleable, as persistently relational modes of becoming, we might find that exploring gender and sex—in the psychoanalytic clinic and beyond it—provide occasions for unsettling and unclenching other and only seemingly unrelated inheritances and investments. As trans lives upend sex and gender for all of us, we perhaps stand a chance of facing and dismantling how deeply and too often illegibly sex and gender are the vessels perpetuating histories and structures of coloniality and whiteness in our lives and our theories.

Notes

1 This chapter uses capital letters for Black(ness) in accordance with the current arguments for anti-racist linguistic practices. For more detailed explanations for this practice, see, for instance, Lori Tharps (2014). Regarding pronouns, Dembroff and Wodak (2018) argue that best practice should be to use they/them pronouns to refer to authors and individuals, unless their self-identified gender makes a difference to the argument at hand.

2 For sustained work on how engaging with trans individuals requires psychoanalytic theories, training, and practice as well as analysts themselves to change and has already led to extensive reconsiderations of sex and gender, see, for instance, Sheila Cavanagh (2016, 2018), Muriel Dimen (1991), Diane Ehrensaft (2016), Patricia Gherovici (2010, 2011, 2017a, 2017b), Virginia Goldner (2003, 2011), Oren Gozlan (2008, 2015, 2018a, 2018b), Griffin Hansbury (2005, 2011, 2017a, 2017b), Adrienne Harris (2005, 2011), Hilary Offman (2017), Jack Pula (2015), Avgi Saketopoulou (2011, 2014), Gayle Salamon (2010, 2016), Melanie Suchet (2011), and Hannah Wallerstein (2017).

3 In the time that has passed since the writing of this chapter was concluded in May 2020, race and whiteness have gathered much more attention in psychoanalytic theorizing and much new work has appeared. Unfortunately, because of publishing constraints, I am unable to incorporate these important new contributions into this chapter. For analyses of the structures and dynamics of racialization, racism, and whiteness in psychoanalysis from various theoretical backgrounds since the 1990s, see, for instance, Neil Altman (2000, 2006a, 2006b, 2010), Christopher Bonovitz (2009), Daniel Butler (2019), Farhad Dalal (2006, 2013), David Eng and Shinhee Han (2000, 2006), Patricia Gherovici and Christopher Christian eds. (2018),

Forrest Hamer (2002, 2006, 2012), Adrienne Harris (2012, 2019), Dorothy Evans Holmes (1992, 1999, 2012, 2016a, 2016b, 2019), Narendra Keval (2016), Lynne Layton (2006, 2019), Kimberlyn Leary (1995, 1997a, 1997b, 2000, 2012), Lowe Frank (2006), Dionne Powell (2012, 2018), Kalpana Seshadri-Crooks (1997, 2000), Henry Smith (2006), Gillian Straker (2004), Melanie Suchet (2004, [2007] 2012), and Beverly Stoute (2017).

4 Exceptions to this situation are Avgi Saketopoulou's "Minding the Gap: Intersections between Gender, Race, and Class in Work with Gender Variant Children" (2011), which analyzes experiences and conflicts in relation to the racialization of queerness and Sheila Cavanagh's "Gender, Sexuality, and Race in the Lacanian Mirror: Urinary Segregation and the Bodily Ego" (2014), which analyzes projections of whiteness at play in the gendering and sexualizing of public space.

5 Straker (2004), Suchet (2012), and Harris (2012, 2019) vividly inhabit the urgency, difficulty, and necessity of raising and exploring these questions, and as Harris (2019) acknowledges, it is difficult to concede that one cannot work through them out of one's own abilities or in the privacy of one's own mind.

6 A dimension that adds further complexity to the issues at hand—and to which this chapter is not doing justice in any way—is the fact that racialization would need to be considered more thoroughly in relation to colonialism and settler colonialism. In "Tracing Historical Specificity: Race and the Colonial Politics of (In)Capacity" (2017), Kēhaulani Kauanui argues against ontologizing the difference between anti-Blackness and anti-Indigeneity and for grasping the dynamics of mutual implication of anti-Blackness and settler coloniality: "European colonizers racialized the colonized in specific ways that mark and reproduce (in ways that can change across time) the unequal relationships into which colonial actors initially co-opted these populations" (258). However, when considering race and racialization, it is important to keep in mind that the attempt to foreground "race as difference" to categorize Native Americans is itself a settler colonial strategy used to undermine tribal sovereignty. Moreover, inquiries such as Scott Lauria Morgensen's (2011) on settler colonialism and queerness would equally need to be part of more extensive reflections in the effort to understand further the interrelations between sex, gender, sexuality, coloniality, and racialization.

7 Lowe (2006) and Dalal (2013) similarly emphasize whiteness as a fantasy of oneness and completeness relying on splitting off and dissociating from negative aspects that get projected onto the racially othered. Suchet ([2007] 2012) also supports this analysis of whiteness, arguing that "Becoming White involves the denial of Blackness—what one is not but continues to haunt the self. Similarly, Whiteness has been viewed as an omnipotent fantasy of wholeness that attempts to avoid any feelings of lack, vulnerability, or humiliation" (201).

8 This understanding of whiteness as upholding and being upheld by fantasies of wholeness, oneness, and mastery also allows for thinking further through the convergences and mutual implications of anti-Blackness and settler coloniality within whiteness. As Ikyo Day writes in "Being or Nothingness: Indigeneity, Antiblackness, and Settler Colonial Critique" (2015),

> Indigenous peoples and slaves are not reducible to each other because settler colonialism abides by a dual logic that is originally driven to eliminate Native peoples from land and mix the land with enslaved black labor. If land is the basis of settler colonialists' relationship to Indigenous peoples, it is labor that frames that relationship with enslaved peoples.
>
> (113)

Sexuality and reproduction take on a key role, because while Blackness threatens to "contaminate" whiteness by "mixing," Indigeneity—because of the crucial relationship to the land—figures as assimilable and dilutable, and genocidally, for the coherence of whiteness needing to be diluted (Day, 2015, 113).

9   I am grateful to Rajbir Singh Judge for emphasizing the importance of Kalpana Seshadri-Crooks' work and discussing questions of psychoanalysis, whiteness, and queerness with me.

10 The role of "mixing," inheritance of racial belonging, and seeking genealogical roots are fraught issues, as, among others, Alondra Nelson (2008, 2016) has demonstrated. On Native Americanness and determining tribal belonging, see Kim TallBear (2013).

11 I am grateful to Kris Sealey for our exchanges on these questions and for helping and pushing me to think through them.

12 A similar question tends to be raised about how gender transitions differ from amputation desires. For a thoughtful negotiation of this question, see, for instance, Gherovici (2010, 12–18). Moreover, Gherovici's (2017a) comment on her own development in transgender issues is an important reminder for all of us regarding the provisionality of our positions: "Like many Lacanian analysts, I had paid too much attention to the conundrum of sex and gender, not realizing that the transgender request was aimed at the border between life and death" (552). As Gherovici explains, this revision is not so much a matter of solitary reflection, but arose from learning in response to sitting with and listening to her trans patients.

13 This kind of call for attentiveness with respect to formal academic publication sometimes gets mistaken as a call for censoring academics. The freedom of expression is vital; anyone should be free to have conversations, put their reflections into writing, and share these with their peers. When it comes to formal publication, however, we are no longer simply dealing with the freedom to speak, write, and share ideas. Rather, when it comes to publishing, questions of relationships and structures of power are also at stake, such as who and what receives institutional credentialing, what content enters formally into the scholarly record, and what values we as a community of scholars embrace in relation to our research and publication practices. Currently in the academy, publications and citations are the coin of the realm, which means whose voices get entered into the scholarly record, who gets cited, who gets read and taken up, has an impact on the shape of our institutions and curricula. Certainly, none of us can control for how we will be read. Most likely, we will even be putting things into writing which we may later wish we had not and will aim to revise. We will get things wrong, sometimes terribly so—also in print—because no pre-publication review process is infallible and then repair will be necessary. But slowing down and at least trying to hear and engage marginalized voices and communities and taking the time to build those relationships and make them a part of our work may be one step in mitigating some problems and perhaps even be a step toward transformative ameliorative practices.

14 As previously mentioned, since the completion of this chapter in May 2020, a substantial amount of work has now appeared that wrestles with race, whiteness, and coloniality as categories in psychoanalytic theory generally. In 2020, Lynne Layton's (2019) "Transgenerational Hauntings" was notable because in it race is a core theme for the analytic work in the context of a white–white dyad. When race only becomes a topic when either a patient or clinician is not white, then normative whiteness gets reaffirmed, because it works exactly by disavowing seeing itself as racialized. As Dionne Powell (2018) observes, this sidelining of race in the literature is tied to the whiteness of the profession:

> Within psychoanalysis the absence of diversity, of otherness, in those we treat, train, and teach is notable. This absence has reached a level of acceptance such

that in presentions [sic] of clinical work race for the most part is mentioned only when the patient is not white.

(1024)

Henry Smith (2006) holds that a reply "Well, race just never came up in the analysis" is not good enough:

> I would argue that it is not so much a matter of when race and racism enter the consulting room, but whether and how we notice it, for in my experience racial, ethnic, and cultural categorization are always present, even in the most apparently benign settings.

(4)

Muriel Dimen (2006) observes that psychoanalysts are generally very good at picking up on all kinds of dynamics even when the analysand does not explicitly bring them up. We might therefore ask why race falls so easily out of that purview. No analyst seems to argue that because the analyst and analysand both shared the same gender and sexual orientation, sex, gender, or sexuality "just didn't ever come up" because there was not enough of a productive difference between the analyst and analysand. Dorothy Evans Holmes (2012, 2019) suggests that often both analyst and analysand collude in avoiding dealing with race in the transference, because of its links to violent impulses and the deeply embedded cultural racism. Powell (2012) argues that race gets repressed as a topic both in analyses and in the literature, especially by whites, because of white peoples' denial of whiteness and the white fantasy that time will fix the racial wounds of the past, hence also denying the ongoing perpetuation of racial violence.

Daniel Butler (2019) adds that not only should the demographics of psychoanalysis be under scrutiny, but in order to address the structural racism in psychoanalysis, we need to understand and examine how whiteness and anti-Blackness are encoded in the setting of psychoanalysis:

> The White imaginary deposits its phantom world (i.e., the violence of slavery and settler colonialism) into the setting, and this deposit is further entrenched by projecting racist phantasies onto Black bodies. Deeply rooted, this deposit is still never total; phantoms haunt social and psychic space, dwelling in complex psychic and national topographies, and revealing how histories of structural racism are materially and corporeally lived in the present.

(148)

Some of these aspects of how the setting of psychoanalysis is raced and classed and the struggles of encountering, countering, and sometimes upending those structural violences are explored and charted in, for instance, Altman (2010) and Patricia Gherovici and Chris Christian, eds. (2018).

15 See Adrienne Harris (2019), especially pp. 327–329. Kimberlyn Leary (2012) also observes that traditionally, psychoanalysis has been considering sexuality as psychically central, while race, even if it is important for one's lived identity, is considered as a sociological issue (283). Leary (1997b) demonstrates how when issues of race are interpreted as displacements for other issues, the normative whiteness of psychoanalysis is held in place and the possibility for cultural difference narrowed or negated. In *Racist States of Mind,* Narendra Keval (2016) emphasizes the harmful effects of such practices:

> Psychoanalysis and the psychotherapies have often perceived issues to do with ethnicity or race, quite defensively, as external issues of less significance than the preoccupations with the inner world of the patient and the transference relationship, rather than seeing these attributes as integral to psychic life and

the therapeutic process. It is not an exaggeration to say that this attitude risks repeating, through a lack of engagement within the consulting room, the dynamics of splitting, marginalising, and cleansing characteristics of racist thinking.

(59)

16 Different trajectories for psychoanalytic theorizing in relation to race would have been imaginable, since there is a tradition of psychoanalytic and psychoanalytically informed scholarship that has long argued for the coevalness of race and gender, such as prominently the work of the clinician Frantz Fanon, whose *Black Skin, White Masks* was first published in French in 1952. Fanon examines the interrelations of race, gender, and coloniality and indicts the structural presupposition of the heterosexual nuclear family as European normativity for psychosexual development. Unfortunately, that analysis did not keep Fanon from drawing latently homophobic conclusions, such as that homosexuality was not a problem in the Antilles because the Oedipus complex was a European developmental structure. Given, however, the widespread and long-enduring homophobia within psychoanalysis as a profession, Fanon's brief remarks on homosexuality are very unlikely the reason for the lacking reception and incorporation of Fanon's work on race into mainstream psychoanalytic theorizing.

Within psychoanalytic feminism of the 1980s and 1990s, two major—and for quite some time underutilized—resources for dislodging the prevailing whiteness of scholarly work were Hortense Spillers' 1987 "Mama's Baby, Papa's Maybe: An American Grammar Book" and Jean Walton's 1995 "Re-Placing Race in (White) Psychoanalytic Discourse: Founding Narratives of Feminism." Spillers (1987) works with a Lacanian framework to analyze the ungendering of the Black body, in particular the Black female body. Walton (1995) returns to early twentieth-century psychoanalysis to examine how in the work of Joan Riviere the account of femininity depends on mobilizing and repressing anti-Blackness.

17 Gozlan (2018a) points out that

> [F]or Winnicott the term 'truth of the self' does not refer to the illusory coherence and sense of mastery that characterizes the ego, but to an inchoate kernel, that, like the navel of a dream, is out of reach and unsignifiable.
>
> (3)

18 Gozlan's project moves us toward understanding the difference between cis and trans as one of degree rather than quality. As Susan Stryker (2017) emphasizes, gender is a creative process of negotiation for everyone (425). Similarly, Hannah Wallerstein (2017) foregrounds the role of creativity and translational processes in trans embodiment shifting away from a focus on seeking an etiology for gender transitions in traumata or casting the trans experience as necessarily and exclusively traumatic, which of course is not to say that there may not also be aspects of trauma and loss to be addressed (426). As Gozlan (2008) and Griffin Hansbury (2017b) analyze, the alarm and concern of analysts working with trans patients are often less about the trans person's actual quandaries than the analyst's investments, anxieties, and transferences when confronted with sex and gender as ongoing negotiations and transformations. With respect to countertransference anxieties, Jack Drescher (2015) observes that often for analysts,

> [I]t is much easier to empathize with a patient whom a therapist feels was victimized by a troubled parent than to enter into the troubling subjective state of gender dysphoria, self-loathing, and shame that the patient brings into the treatment setting.
>
> (73)

19 My reading of Laplanche as offering a deeply relational and continuously dynamic understanding of gender is very much informed also by the work of Dimen (1991), who insists, "I speak of gender less as a determinate category than as something resembling a force field, that is, as a set of complex and shifting relations among multiple contrasts or differences" (335). For Dimen, gender is a "set of relations" rather than a fixed attribute of an individual.

20 For instance, Gozlan (2018a) doesn't really talk much about sex and instead their terminology of choice is the "natural body," which, as they demonstrate persuasively, is by far not as natural as it tends to be assumed.

21 The idea of sex as biologically binary has also been shown as untenable from the perspective of biology by Anne Fausto-Sterling (1999) and more recently with respect to brain science by Rebecca Jordan-Young (2011).

22 Butler (2014) writes, "[T]he communication of 'gender' provides an interpellation, a mode of interpreting the body that precedes and conditions the experience of somatic sex" (127). But as Butler has consistently argued, "somatic sex" itself is not a natural given but has a genealogy and social history of its own; see Butler (1993, 2010). Butler (1993, 2010) has focused on the importance of understanding the role of power and discursive production of "sex." My interest here is what avenues are open by considering the implications that for Laplanche, "sex" is a product of an evolutionary history that is both biological and cultural. In that regard, the timescale that Laplanche is interested in is more in line with Fausto-Sterling (1999).

23 This explicit statement only appears in the longer version of the 2007 essay, as it is published in the collection *Freud and the* Sexual: *Essays 2000–2006* (2011).

24 For an essay that attentively and innovatively explores those questions and works through their implications for psychoanalytic theorizing, see Hansbury's "The Masculine Vaginal: Working with Queer Men's Embodiment at the Transgender Edge" (2017a). Juno Roche's *Queer Sex* (2018) deals with non-binary sexuality and intimacy. The collection *Sex, Sexuality and Trans Identities* by Gary Jacobson, Jan C. Niemira, and Karalyn Violeta, eds. (2020) explicitly engages with the experiences of transgender sexuality at a variety of intersections and is directed at an audience of psychotherapists and counselors.

25 Julie Leavitt and Adrienne Harris (2020) draw on the work of Jean Laplanche and extend the understanding of enigmatic messages to include other aspects alongside sex, gender, and sexuality. This expansion is welcome and helpful. My aim in this chapter is somewhat different, since I am seeking to examine a deeper interrelation in how sex and gender as categories are already implicated in and carriers of racialized history as well.

26 Quoted in Somerville (2000, p.25). In *The Biopolitics of Feeling: Race, Sex, and Science in the Nineteenth Century* (2018), Kyla Schuller demonstrates and examines how the sex binary was marshaled in science and medicine with racializing consequences.

27 The need for layered relationality that Spillers (1987) sets out provides a keen analytic of what is needed for humanizing and humane existence and flourishing:

> This profitable 'atomizing' of the captive body provides another angle on the divided flesh: we lose any hint or suggestion of a dimension of ethics, of relatedness between human personality and its anatomical features, between one human personality and another, between human personality and cultural institutions [we might add, between human personality and the environment]. To that extent, the procedures adopted for the captive flesh demarcate total objectification, as the entire captive community becomes a living laboratory.

(68)

28 This reduction to thingness that is core to Spillers' (1987) analysis of anti-Blackness would be important to consider in relation to Iyko Day's (2015) analysis of the *terra nullius* doctrine and the dispossession of Indigenous peoples as a form of denying Indigenous peoples their corporeality (Day, 2015, 112).

29 Alfred López (2005) analyzes Freud's account of the Wolf Man case and demonstrates how Freud evades issues of race and whiteness in the countertransference. For a broader examination of the figure of the primitive in psychoanalytic theory, see Celia Brickman's *Race in Psychoanalysis: Aboriginal Populations in the Mind* (2017).

30 In *Gender Trouble* ([1990] 2010), Butler remarks on the difficulty of intersectional theorizing and its problems in aiming to describe situated identities: "The theories of feminist identity that elaborate predicates of color, sexuality, ethnicity, class, and able-bodiedness invariably close with an embarrassed 'etc.' at the end of the list" (196). The "embarrassed etc." points to what for Butler also entails a potential for feminist theorizing and political action, namely, to turn to examining and engaging with the practices and institutional dynamics through which these identities and subjectivities are produced. The difficulty, however, lies in theoretically grasping how the different dimensions interact in various circumstances at different times in history. Kyla Wazana Tompkins (2016) challenges us to consider how Spillers (1987), published three years before *Gender Trouble*, might inflect and alter Butler's articulation of "matter, performativity, abjection and regulatory normativity." In *Terrorist Assemblages* (2007), Jasbir Puar emphasizes the importance of intersectionality as a heuristic, but amends and rearticulates it with the categories of affect and assemblages to better track the dynamic entanglements of the dimensions that an intersectional analysis seeks to grasp. More recently, Jennifer C. Nash in *Black Feminism Reimagined: After Intersectionality* (2019) renews the Black feminist origins and emancipatory impulses of intersectionality against the stifling casting of intersectionality as static and dogmatic. Nash emphasizes the role of affective and intimate work and relationships that Black feminism as an intellectual and political practice entails, which includes but also exceeds intersectionality, precisely because there cannot be any fixed master category or calculus.

31 Frantz Fanon writes that Jacques Lacan's words are specifically "*le complexe, facteur concret de la psychologie familiale*," however, without providing a specific reference. Fanon is possibly referring to Lacan's "The Family Complexes" (2001). The original French edition of the article was published in 1938 under the title "La Famille" and later republished as "Les complexes familiaux dans la formation de l'individu." I am grateful to Patricia Gherovici and Manya Steinkoler for the reference to the possible origins of Fanon's citation.

32 Frantz Fanon ([1952] 2008) further details this point of continuity between the family and societal structure for the white child: "The child leaving the family environment finds the same laws, the same principles, and the same values" (121) and "The white family is the guardian of a certain structure. Society is the sum of all the families. The family is an institution, precursor of a much wider institution: i.e., the social group or nation" (127).

33 See, for instance, Dorothy Evans Holmes (2016b) on the effects of cultural trauma being artificially separated from intrafamilial and intrapsychic trauma.

34 Lynne Layton refers here to Roger Frie's (2017) "History Flows through Us: Psychoanalysis and Historical Understanding."

35 Forrest M. Hamer (2012) draws our attention to an important dimension of taking into account how gender, sexuality, and race intersect in terms of transgenerational inheritance:

> For black Americans, the presence of European ancestry beyond one or two generations is frequently evocative of associations related to rapes of enslaved

black women by the white men who owed them. It is an association that has often complicated grappling with the internal relation between African and European ancestry in general, and between self-representations as black and as white specifically.

(226)

36 Hamer (2012) proposes to understand white privilege in part exactly as this dynamic of "not having one's behavior seen as a negative reflection on or a credit to one's race" (222).

37 This repressing of deep transgenerational connections as a hallmark of whiteness also provides a further inroad for considering how anti-Blackness and settler coloniality are interrelated and structuring whiteness. The production and privileging of this kind of individuality draw on or even depend on severing and minimizing a profound connectedness to land, the environment, ancestors, future generations, and the claims that they lay on the present.

38 Harris (2012) argues for understanding whiteness as a *"psychose blanche"* in this dissociation from transgenerational transmission. See also Harris (2019).

39 For this insight, Harris (2019) draws on Ruth Stein's analysis of perversion as a structure of domination and alienation by producing a false intimacy and avoiding actual intimacy. Stein (2005) argues:

> [P]erversion is a double effort (1) to erase difference by assuming—and seductively 'demonstrating' through creating a semblance of intimacy—that one knows the other from the inside out, that people are knowable by the force of one's will; and (2) to evade intimacy by not expressing, not even contacting, a core part of oneself.
>
> (790)

Perversion on this reading is a defense structure against being entangled with others and undone by others, in order to remain in control over one's own position and to remain in power over the other.

40 Frank Lowe (2006) in "Racism as a Borderline Issue" suggests:

> Thinking of white racism as borderline phenomena helps us better understand the white's inability to make contact with the black other because it arouses immense anxiety and there is a fear of loss, of fragmentation or dissolution of self and identity.
>
> (59)

It seems easy to imagine how as a white person one might respond here by distancing oneself by wanting to reply "yes, that is true for those white supremacists." But that response too is one that resembles too much the kind of refusal of intimacy that Harris (2019) identifies as core to the "perverse pact" of whiteness—at least as long as we live in a world in which no meaningful work of abolition and reparation to undo and address anti-Blackness and settler colonialism is well underway.

41 Possibly we need to consider that other terminology may be better than "sexual difference," since sexual difference too quickly seems to invite a reduction to sex differences or sexuality. Gherovici (2017b) explains that sexual difference in Lacanian psychoanalysis actually exceeds all those meanings:

> [I]n psychoanalysis "sexual difference" is neither sex, defined by anatomical or hormonal determinations, nor gender or any socially constructed roles ascribed to men and women. Gender needs to be embodied; sex needs to be symbolized. 'Sexual difference' may exceed the notion of sexuality since it

has to do with issues of embodiment—the challenges of living in a body that is sexed and mortal.

(30)

However, the question that becomes more and more pressing is what "sexed" actually means. Might we be better served by speaking about "erotic difference" in trying to index the materiality of desire and the capacity for pleasure and pain, for giving and receiving pleasure, and for everything in between? It seems to me what is at issue is the need to develop our vocabulary and grammar for holding present an originary plurality in differentiation that at the same time is capable of making explicit historical and geographic variations and does not gloss over the violences of its own genealogies.

42 To my best knowledge, this phrase was first popularized by the anti-racist blogger Brotha Wolf in late October or early November 2012, as the following webpages indicated as of October 23, 2019: https://web.archive.org/web/20141007051623/ http://brothawolf.wordpress.com/2012/11/09/guest-post-dumb-donald-trump/ and https://abagond.wordpress.com/2012/11/08/the-southern-strategy/

43 For a review and analysis of the requirements, historical context, and argumentations supporting them, see Peter Dunne (2017) and A.J. Lowik (2018).

44 On the current legislation and the history of the sections struck down by the German constitutional court, see the information provided by the German Association for Transsexual and Intersexual Persons: https://dgti.org/tsgrecht.html

45 See Lowik (2018), Wendy Kline's (2001) *Building a Better Race: Gender, Sexuality, and Eugenics from the Turn of the Century to the Baby Boom*, and Nancy Ordover's (2003) *American Eugenics: Race, Queer Anatomy, and the Science of Nationalism*.

46 On inverts and "race science" see Melissa Stein's (2015) *Measuring Manhood: Race and the Science of Masculinity, 1830–1934*, especially the chapter "Inverts, Perverts, and Primitives: Racial Thought and the American School of Sexology" (pp. 169–215).

47 Illiana Margra (2020). "Transgender Man in U.K. Loses Appeal to Be Listed as Father." *New York Times*, April 29, 2020. https://www.nytimes.com/2020/04/29/world/europe/transgender-man-uk-mother.html (accessed May 2, 2020).

48 *The Queen v. The Registrar General for England and Wales*, [2019] EWHC 2384 (Fam). https://www.judiciary.uk/wp-content/uploads/2019/09/TT-and-YY-APPROVED-Substantive-Judgment-McF-23.9.19.pdf (accessed May 2, 2020).

49 See Lara Karaian (2013) on anxieties about "repronormativity" and unsexing reproduction.

50 On fat phobia and anti-Blackness, see Sabrina Strings' (2019) *Fearing the Black Body: The Racial Origins of Fat Phobia*.

51 Suchet ([2007] 2012) offers an important clarification to differentiate this melancholia from "white liberal guilt": "The state of melancholia is a place of loss, necessary for the reevaluation of the self through an integration of what has been dissociated" (206). While white guilt allows for nestling in that guilt and thus avoiding any substantive change, the state that Suchet describes is one that also loses that too familiar guilt and opens up onto a process of "integration of what has been dissociated," which means the histories of brutality and of benefiting from structural violence. But with Harris (2019), those of us who are white should find ourselves compelled to ask ourselves: What does it mean to integrate that which has been dissociated? What does it mean to recognize and then to lose also our identity as settler, as thief, as beneficiary of the suffering of others? If this working through is not to be another repetition of whiteness, it needs to be as much a psychic, individual, and emotional as well as communal, affective, and political process of material change.

Bibliography

Akhtar, Salman (ed.). (2012). *The African American Experience: Psychoanalytic Perspectives*, Lanham: Rowman & Littlefield.

Altman, N. (2000). "Black and White Thinking: A Psychoanalyst Reconsiders Race." *Psychoanalytic Dialogues*, 10(4), 589–605.

Altman, N. (2006a). "Whiteness." *The Psychoanalytic Quarterly*, 75(1), 45–72.

Altman, N. (2006b). "How Psychoanalysis Became White in the United States, and How That Might Change." *Psychoanalytic Perspectives*, 3(2), 65–72.

Altman, N. (2010). *The Analyst in the Inner City: Race, Class, and Culture through a Psychoanalytic Lens*, New York: Routledge.

Bettcher, T. and P. Goulimari (2017). "Theorizing Closeness: A Trans Feminist Conversation." *Angelaki*, 22(1), 49–60.

Bey, M. (2017. "The Trans*-Ness of Blackness, the Blackness of Trans*-Ness." *TSQ: Transgender Studies Quarterly* 4(2), 275–295.

Blaque, K. (2015). "Why Rachel Dolezal's Fake 'Transracial' Identity Is Nothing Like Being Trans-gender—Take It from a Black Trans Woman Who Knows." *Everyday Feminism*, June. http://everydayfeminism.com/2015/06/rachel-dolezal-not-transracial.

Bonovitz, C. (2009). "Mixed Race and the Negotiation of Racialized Selves: Developing the Capacity for Internal Conflict." *Psychoanalytic Dialogues*, 19(4), 426–441.

Brickman, C. (2017). *Race in Psychoanalysis: Aboriginal Populations in the Mind*, New York: Routledge.

Butler, D. (2019). "Racialized Bodies and the Violence of the Setting." *Studies in Gender and Sexuality*, 20(3), 146–158.

Butler, J. (1993). *Bodies That Matter: On the Discursive Limits of "Sex,"* New York: Routledge.

Butler, J. (2010). *Gender Trouble: Feminism and the Subversion of Identity* (2nd edn), New York: Routledge.

Butler, J. (2014). "Seduction, Gender, and the Drive," in *Seductions and Enigmas: Cultural Readings with Laplanche* (pp. 118–133), ed. J. Fletcher and N. Ray, London: Lawrence & Wishart.

Cavanagh, S. (2014). "Gender, Sexuality, and Race in the Lacanian Mirror: Urinary Segregation and the Bodily Ego," in *Psychoanalytic Geographies* (pp. 323–338), ed. P. Kingsbury and S. Pile, Farnham: Ashgate.

Cavanagh, S. (2016). "Transsexuality as Sinthome: Bracha L. Ettinger and the Other (Feminine) Sexual Difference." *Studies in Gender and Sexuality*, 17(1), 27–44.

Cavanagh, S. (2018). "Principles for Psychoanalytic Work with Trans Clients," in *Current Critical Debates in the Field of Transsexual Studies* (pp. 89–101), ed. O. Gozlan, New York: Routledge.

Cavanagh, S. (2019). "Queer Theory, Psychoanalysis, and the Symptom: A Lacanian Reading." *Studies in Gender and Sexuality*, 20(4), 226–230.

Dalal, F. (2006). "Racism: Processes of Detachment, Dehumanization, and Hatred." *Psychoanalytic Quarterly*, 75(1), 131–161.

Dalal, F. (2013). *Race, Color, and the Processes of Racialization: New Perspectives from Group Analysis, Psychoanalysis, and Sociology*, London: Routledge.

Day, I. (2015). "Being or Nothingness: Indigeneity, Antiblackness, and Settler Colonial Critique." *Critical Ethnic Studies*, 1(2), 102–121.

Dembroff, R. and D. Wodak (2018). "He/She/They/Ze." *Ergo: An Open Access Journal of Philosophy*, 5(14), 371–406.

Deutsche Gesellschaft für Transidentität und Intersexualität (2017). "Zur rechtlichen Situation transsexueller Menschen," December 3. https://dgti.org/tsgrecht.html.

Dimen, M. (1991). "Deconstructing Difference: Gender, Splitting, and Transitional Space." *Psychoanalytic Dialogues*, 1(3), 335–352.

Dimen, M. (2006). "Response to Roundtable: Something's Gone Missing," in *Psychoanalysis, Class, and Politics: Encounters in the Clinical Setting* (pp. 195–201), ed. L. Layton, N. C. Hollander and S. Gutwill, London: Routledge.

Drescher, J. (2015). "Gender Policing in the Clinical Setting: Discussion of Sandra Silverman's 'The Colonized Mind: Gender, Trauma, and Mentalization'." *Psychoanalytic Dialogues*, 25(1), 67–76.

Dunne, P. (2017). "Transgender Sterilisation Requirements in Europe." *Medical Law Review*, 25(4), 554–581.

Ehrensaft, D. (2016). *The Gender Creative Child: Pathways for Nurturing and Supporting Children Who Live outside Gender Boxes*, New York: The Experiment.

Ellison, T., K. Green, M. Richardson and C. Riley Snorton (2017). "We Got Issues: Toward a Black Trans*/Studies." *TSQ*, 4(2), 162–169.

Eng, D. L. and S. Han (2000). "A Dialogue on Racial Melancholia." *Psychoanalytic Dialogues*, 10(4), 667–701.

Eng, D. L. and S. Han (2006). "Desegregating Love: Transnational Adoption, Racial Reparation, and Racial Transitional Objects." *Studies in Gender and Sexuality*, 7(2), 141–172.

Fanon, F. (2008). *Black Skin, White Masks*, trans. R. Philcox, New York: Grove Press.

Fausto-Sterling, A. (1999). *Sexing the Body: Gender Politics and the Construction of Sexuality*, New York: Basic Books.

Frie, R. (2017). "History Flows through Us: Psychoanalysis and Historical Understanding." *Psychoanalysis, Self, and Context*, 12(3), 221–229.

Gherovici, P. (2010). *Please Select Your Gender: From the Invention of Hysteria to the Democratizing of Transgenderism*, New York: Routledge.

Gherovici, P. (2011). "Psychoanalysis Needs a Sex Change." *Gay & Lesbian Issues and Psychology Review* 7(1), 3–18.

Gherovici, P. (2017a). "Depathologizing Trans: From Symptom to *Sinthome*." *TSQ: Transgender Studies Quarterly*, 4(3–4), 534–555.

Gherovici, P. (2017b). *Transgender Psychoanalysis: A Lacanian Perspective on Sexual Difference*. New York: Routledge.

Gherovici, P. and C. Christian (eds) (2018). *Psychoanalysis in the Barrios: Race, Class, and the Unconscious*, New York: Routledge.

Gilman, S. L. (1985). *Difference and Pathology: Stereotypes of Sexuality, Race, and Madness*, Ithaca: Cornell University Press.

Gilman, S. L. (1995). *Freud, Race, and Gender*, Princeton: Princeton University Press.

Goldner, V. (2003). "Ironic Gender/Authentic Sex." *Studies in Gender and Sexuality*, 4(2), 113–139.

Goldner, V. (2011). "Trans: Gender in Free Fall," *Psychoanalytic Dialogues*, 21(2), 159–171.

Gozlan, O. (2008). "The Accident of Gender." *Psychoanalytic Review*, 95(4), 541–570.

Gozlan, O. (2015). *Transsexuality and the Art of Transitioning: A Lacanian Approach*, London: Routledge.

Gozlan, O. (2018a) "From Continuity to Contiguity: A Response to the Fraught Temporality of Gender." *Psychoanalytic Review* 105(1), 1–29.

Gozlan, O. (ed.) (2018b). *Current Critical Debates in the Field of Transsexual Studies: In Transition*, New York: Routledge.

Green, K. M. (2015). "'Race and Gender Are Not the Same!' Is Not a Good Response to the 'Transracial'/Transgender Question; or, We Can and Must Do Better." *The Feminist Wire*, June 14. http://www.thefeministwire.com/2015/06/race-and-gender-are-not-the-same-is-not-a-good-response-to-the-transracial-transgender-question-or-we-can-and-must-do-better/.

Green, K. M. (2016). "Troubling the Waters: Mobilizing a Trans* Analytic," in *No Tea, No Shade: New Writings in Black Queer Studies* (pp. 65–82), ed. E. Patrick Johnson, Durham: Duke UP.

Green, K. M. and M. Bey (2017). "Where Black Feminist Thought and Trans* Feminism Meet: A Conversation." *Souls*, 19(4), 438–454.

Hamer, F. M. (2002). "Guards at the Gate: Race, Resistance, and Psychic Reality." *Journal of the American Psychoanalytic Association*, 50(4), 1219–1237.

Hamer, F M. (2006). "Racism as a Transference State: Episodes of Racial Hostility in the Psychoanalytic Context." *Psychoanalytic Quarterly*, 75(1), 197–214.

Hamer, F. M. (2012). "Anti-Black Racism and the Conception of Whiteness," in *The African American Experience: Psychoanalytic Experiences* (pp. 217–227), ed. S. Akhtar. Lanham: Rowman & Littlefield.

Hansbury, Griffin. (2005). "Mourning the Loss of the Idealized Self: A Transsexual Passage." *Psychoanalytic Social Work*, 12(1), 19–35.

Hansbury, G. (2011). "King Kong & Goldilocks: Imagining Trans Masculinities through the Trans-Trans Dyad." *Psychoanalytic Dialogues*, 21(2), 210–220.

Hansbury, G. (2017a). "The Masculine Vaginal: Working with Queer Men's Embodiment at the Transgender Edge." *Journal of the American Psychoanalytic Association*, 65(6), 1009–1031.

Hansbury, G. (2017b). "Unthinkable Anxieties: Reading Transphobic Countertransferences in a Century of Psychoanalytic Writing." *TSQ: Transgender Studies Quarterly*, 4(3–4), 3.

Harris, A. (2005). *Gender as Soft Assembly*, Hillsdale: The Analytic Press.

Harris, A. (2011). "Gender as a Strange Attractor: Discussion of the Transgender Symposium." *Psychoanalytic Dialogues*, 21(2), 230–238.

Harris, A. (2012). "The House of Difference, or White Silence." *Studies in Gender and Sexuality*, 13(3), 197–216.

Harris, A. (2019). "The Perverse Pact: Racism and White Privilege." *American Imago*, 76(3), 309–333.

Holmes, D. E (1992). "Race and Transference in Psychoanalysis and Psychotherapy." *International Journal of Psychoanalysis*, 73(1), 1–11.

Holmes, D. E. (1999). "Race and Countertransference: Two 'Blind Spots' in Psychoanalytic Perception." *Journal of Applied Psychoanalytic Studies*, 1(4), 319–332.

Holmes, D. (2012). "Racial Transference Reactions in Psychoanalytic Treatment: An Update," in *The African American Experience: Psychoanalytic Perspectives* (pp. 363–376), ed. S. Akhtar, Lanham: Rowman & Littlefield.

Holmes, D. E. (2016a). "Come Hither, American Psychoanalysis: Our Complex Multicultural America Needs What We Have to Offer." *Journal of the American Psychoanalytic Association*, 64(3), 569–586.

Holmes, D. E. (2016b). "Culturally Imposed Trauma: The Sleeping Dog Has Awakened. Will Psychoanalysis Take Heed?" *Psychoanalytic Dialogues*, 26(6), 641–654.

Holmes, D. E. (2019). "Our Country 'tis of We and Them: Psychoanalytic Perspectives on Our Fractured American Identity." *American Imago*, 76(3), 359–379.

Jacobson, G., J. Niemira and V. Karalyn (eds). (2020). *Sex, Sexuality and Trans Identities: Clinical Guidance for Psychotherapists and Counselors*, London: Jessica Kingsley Publishers.

Jordan-Young, R. M. (2011). *Brain Storm: The Flaws in the Science of Sex Differences*, Cambridge: Harvard University Press.

Karaian, L. (2013). "Pregnant Men: Repronormativity, Critical Trans Theory, and the Re(conceive)ing of Sex and Pregnancy in Law." *Social and Legal Studies*, 22(2), 211–230.

Kauanui, J. K. (2017). "Tracing Historical Specificity: Race and the Colonial Politics of (In)Capacity." *American Quarterly*, 69(2), 257–265.

Keval, N. (2016). *Racist States of Mind: Understanding the Perversion of Curiosity and Concern*, London: Karnac Books.

Kline, W. (2001). *Building a Better Race: Gender, Sexuality, and Eugenics from the Turn of the Century to the Baby Boom*, Berkeley: University of California Press.

Lacan, J. (2001). "Les complexes familiaux dans la formation de l'individu: Essai d'analayse d'une fonction en psychologie," in *Autres Écrits* (pp. 23-84), Paris: Seuil.

Laplanche, J. (1999). *Essays on Otherness*, ed. J. Fletcher, trans. L. Thurston, L. Hill and P. Slotkin, London: Routledge.

Laplanche, J. and S. Fairfield (2007). "Gender, Sex, and the Sexual." *Studies in Gender and Sexuality*, 8(2), 201–219.

Laplanche, J. (2011). "Gender, Sex and the Sexual," in *Freud and the Sexual: Essays 2000–2006* (pp. 159–201), ed. J. Fletcher, trans. J. House and N. Ray, New York: International Psychoanalytic Books.

Layton, L. (2006). "Racial Identities, Racial Enactments, and Normative Unconscious Processes." *Psychoanalytic Quarterly*, 75(1), 237–270.

Layton, L. (2019) "(Trans) Generational Hauntings: Towards a Social Psychoanalysis and an Ethic of Dis-Illusionment." *Psychoanalytic Dialogues*, 29(2), 105–121.

Leary, K. (1995). "Interpreting in the Dark: Race and Ethnicity in Psychoanalytic Psychotherapy." *Psychoanalytic Psychology*, 12(1), 127–140.

Leary, K. (1997a). "Race, Self-Disclosure, and 'Forbidden Talk': Race and Ethnicity in Contemporary Clinical Practice." *Psychoanalytic Quarterly*, 66(2), 163–189.

Leary, K. (1997b). "Race in Psychoanalytic Space." *Gender and Psychoanalysis*, 2(2), 157–172.

Leary, K. (2000). "Racial Enactments in Dynamic Treatment." *Psychoanalytic Dialogues*, 10(4), 639–653.

Leary, K. (2012). "Race as an Adaptive Challenge: Working with Diversity in the Clinical Consulting Room." *Psychoanalytic Psychology*, 29(3), 279–291.

Leavitt, J. and A. Harris (2020). "Intersectionality Encountering Laplanche: Models of Otherness and the Incomprehensibility of Perpetration," in *Intersectionality and Relational Psychoanalysis: New Perspectives on Race, Gender, and Sexuality* (pp. 192–217), ed. M. Belkin and C. White, London: Routledge.

López, A. J. (2005). "The Gaze of the White Wolf: Psychoanalysis, Whiteness, and Colonial Trauma," in *Postcolonial Whiteness: A Critical Reader on Race and Empire* (pp. 155–81), ed. A. J. López, Albany: State University of New York Press.

Lowe, F. (2006). "Racism as a Borderline Issue: The Avoidance and Marginalization of Race in Psychotherapy," in *Difference: An Avoided Topic in Practice* (pp. 43–60), ed. A. Foster, A. Dickenson, B. Bishop and J. Klein, London: Karnac Books.

Lowik, A. J. (2018). "Reproducing Eugenics, Reproducing While Trans: The State Sterilization of Trans People." *Journal of GLBT Family Studies*, 14(5), 425–445.

Lugones, M. (2007). "Heterosexualism and the Colonial/Modern Gender System." *Hypatia*, 22(1), 186–209.

Lugones, M. (2020). "Gender and Universality in Colonial Methodology." *Critical Philosophy of Race*, 8(1–2), 25–47.

Magra, I. (2020). "Transgender Man in UK Loses Appeal to Be Listed as Father." *New York Times*. https://www.nytimes.com/2020/04/29/world/europe/transgender-man-uk-mother.html.

Marcus, B. and S. McNamara (2013). "'Strange and Otherwise Unaccountable Actions': Category, Conundrum, and Trans Identities." *Journal of the American Psychoanalytic Association*, 61(1), 45–66.

Morgensen Lauria, S. (2011). *Spaces between Us: Queer Settler Colonialism and Indigenous Decolonization*, Minneapolis, University of Minnesota Press.

Nash, J. C. (2018). *Black Feminism Reimagined: After Intersectionality*, Durham: Duke University Press.

Nelson, A. (2008). "Bio Science: Genetic Genealogy Testing and the Pursuit of African Ancestry." *Social Studies of Science*, 38(5), 759–783.

Nelson, A. (2016). *The Social Life of DNA: Race, Reparations, and Reconciliation after the Genome*, Boston: Beacon Press.

Offman, H. (2017). "The Queering of a Cisgender Psychoanalyst." *TSQ*, 1(3–4), 405–420.

Ordover, N. (2003). *American Eugenics: Race, Queer Anatomy, and the Science of Nationalism*, Minneapolis: University of Minnesota Press.

Pellegrini, A. and A. Saketopoulou (2019). "On Taking Sides: They/Them Pronouns, Gender and the Psychoanalyst." *Psychoanalysis Today*. http://www.psychoanalysis.today/en-GB/PT-Articles/Pellegrini167541/On-taking-sides-they-them-pronouns,-gender-and-the.aspx.

Pitts, A. (2020). "Commentary at the Session 'Framing Gender' at the Annual Meeting of the Eastern Division of the American Philosophical Association, Philadelphia, Pennsylvania, January 9, 2020.

Powell, D. R. (2012). "Psychoanalysis and African Americans: Past, Present, and Future," in *The African American Experience: Psychoanalytic Perspectives* (pp. 59–83), ed. S. Akhtar, Lanham: Aronson.

Powell, D. R. (2018). "Race, African Americans, and Psychoanalysis: Collective Silence in the Therapeutic Situation." *Journal of the American Psychoanalytic Association*, 66(6), 1021–1049.

Puar, J. (2007). *Terrorist Assemblages: Homonationalism in Queer Times*, Durham: Duke University Press.

Pula, J. (2015). "Understanding Gender through the Lens of Transgender Experience." *Psychoanalytic Inquiry*, 35(8), 809–822.

Roche, J. (2018). *Queer Sex a Trans and Non-Binary Guide to Intimacy, Pleasure and Relationships*, London: Jessica Kingsley Publishers.

Saketopoulou, A. (2011). "Minding the Gap: Intersections between Gender, Race, and Class in Work with Gender Variant Children." *Psychoanalytic Dialogues*, 21(2), 192–209.

Saketopoulou, A. (2014). "Mourning the Body as Bedrock." *Journal of the American Psychoanalytic* Association, 62(5) (October), 773–806.

Salamon, G. (2010). *Assuming a Body: Transgender and Rhetorics of Materiality*, New York: Columbia University Press.

Salamon, G. (2016). "The Meontology of Masculinity: Notes on Castration Elation." *Parallax*, 22(3), 312–322.

Sealey, K. (2018). "Transracialism and White Allyship: A Response to Rebecca Tuvel." *Philosophy Today*, 62(1), 21–29.

Seshadri-Crooks, K. (1997). "The Comedy of Domination: Psychoanalysis and the Conceit of Whiteness." *Discourse*, 19(2), 134–162.

Seshadri-Crooks, K. (2000). *Desiring Whiteness: A Lacanian Analysis of Race*, New York: Routledge.

Sexton, J. (2003). "The Consequence of Race Mixture: Racialised Barriers and the Politics of Desire." *Social Identities*, 9(2), 241–275.

Schuller, K. (2018). *The Biopolitics of Feeling: Race, Sex, and Science in the Nineteenth Century*, Durham: Duke University Press.

Smith, H. (2006). "Invisible Racism." *Psychoanalytic Quarterly*, 75(1), 3–19.

Snorton, R. C. (2017). *Black on Both Sides: A Racial History of Trans Identity*, Minneapolis: University of Minnesota Press.

Somerville, S. (2000) *Queering the Color Line: Race and the Invention of Homosexuality in American Culture*, Durham: Duke University Press.

Spillers, H. (1987). "Mama's Baby, Papa's Maybe: An American Grammar Book." *Diacritics*, 17(2): 65–81.

Stein, M. (2015). *Measuring Manhood: Race and the Science of Masculinity, 1830–1934*, Minneapolis: University of Minnesota Press.

Stein, R. (2005). "Why Perversion?: 'False Love' and the Perverse Pact." *The International Journal of Psychoanalysis*, 86(3), 775–799.

Stoute, B. J. (2017). "Race and Racism in Psychoanalytic Thought: Ghosts in Our Nursery." *The American Psychoanalyst*, 51(1), 10–29.

Straker, G. (2004) "Race for Cover: Castrated Whiteness, Perverse Consequences." *Psychoanalytic Dialogues*, 14(4), 405–422.

Strings, S. (2019). *Fearing the Black Body: The Racial Origins of Fat Phobia*, New York: NYU Press.

Stryker, S. (2017). "Transgender, Queer Theory, and Psychoanalysis," in *Clinical Encounters in Sexuality: Psychoanalytic Practice and Queer Theory* (pp. 419–426), ed. N. Giffney and E. Watson, Goleta: Punctum Books.

Suchet, M. (2004). "A Relational Encounter with Race." *Psychoanalytic Dialogues*, 14(4), 421–438.

Suchet, M. (2011). "Crossing Over." *Psychoanalytic Dialogues*, 21(2), 172–191.

Suchet, M. (2012). "Unraveling Whiteness," in *Relational Psychoanalysis, Volume 4: Expansion of Theory* (pp. 199–220), ed. L. Aron and A. Harris, London: Routledge.

TallBear, K. (2013). *Native American DNA: Tribal Belonging and the False Promise of Genetic Science*, Minneapolis: Minnesota University Press.

Tharps, L. (2014). "The Case for Black with a Capital B." *New York Times*, November 18. https://www.nytimes.com/2014/11/19/opinion/the-case-for-black-with-a-capital-b.html?gwh=E0361179FB2DC6C09F9C64D85954AAEF&gwt=pay&assetType=opinion.

Tompkins, K. W. (2016). "We Aren't Here to Learn What We Already Know." *Avidly*, September 14. http://avidly.lareviewofbooks.org/2016/09/13/we-arent-here-to-learn-what-we-know-we-already-know/.

Wallerstein, H. (2017). "Putting the 'Trans' Back in 'Truth': A Psychoanalytic Take on Gender's Authenticity." *TSQ: Transgender Studies Quarterly*, 4(3–4), 421–430.

Walton, J. (1995). "Re-Placing Race in (White) Psychoanalytic Discourse: Founding Narratives of Feminism." *Critical Inquiry*, 21(4), 775–804.

Index

Note: Page numbers followed by n denote notes.

shame, blame and 183
Shaw, Bernard 137
Shepherdson, Charles 15, 249
She Wants It 282
al-Shariati 242n3
signification, forgiveness of 183
The Silence of the Lambs (film) 249–250
Simmel, Georg 217
sinthome 125, 250–251
sinthomosexuality 119, 125, 126
Smith, Henry 311–312n14
Snorton, C. Riley 11, 290, 303–304
social bond 123
social form of personal intimacy 166
social hatred 125
social history of trans* 270
social integration 268
socialization and gender identity 9
socially unsanctioned sex 128
social media 184, 265
social norms on body 166
social order 186–187
social recognition 266
social-sexual relations, importance of
    168
social violence 63
sociogenic hysteria 62
Solanas, Valerie 281, 283, 286
Soloway, Jill 282
"Some Palaeobiological and Biopsychical
    Reflections" (Bonaparte) 97
Somerville, Siobhan 297–298
Son of Oscar Wilde (Vyvyan) 147, 149
Sophocles trilogy 210
speech and language 104
Spengler, Oswald 71
Speranza (hope) 142, 147
Spillers, Hortense 298–299, 302,
    313n16, 314n27, 315n28
Spinoza, Baruch 97
spiritual actualization 234–235
spiritual insecurity 238–239, 242n3
Spivak, Gayatri Chakravorty 225,
    227, 229
"*Sprachverwirrung*" ("Confusion of
    Tongues") 102
Spurs/Éperons (Derrida) 225
stable identity 176
Steinkoler, Manya 275n1
Stein, Ruth 316n39
Steward, Sam 51
Stoller, Robert 1, 9–10

Strachey, Alix 53n3, 79
Straker, Gillian 307
strangeness 125
Straw Dogs (Gray) 268
structural anthropology 156
Stryker, Susan 6, 268, 313n18
Studies on Hysteria (Freud) 62
subjective destitution 275
sublimation 177, 181, 183, 240
subversive multiplicity 2
Suchet, Melanie 305, 308, 310n7,
    317n51
suffering, identification with 181
suicidal behavior 128
superabundant vitality 124
superego 75, 113, 180, 192n2
surface, lamella, myth, and 106
surplus jouissance, defined 191n1
Swartz, Sally 215–216, 219, 220
Symposium (Plato) 105

tara-jinsi (transsexual) 242n1
Taylor, Anne-Christine 170n1
Télévision (Lacan) 186
Terrorist Assemblages (Puar) 263, 315n30
the Thaïs 159
Thalassa, Ferenczi's notion of *see*
    Ferenczi's notion of *Thalassa*
Thebans 208
theory of ideology 112–113
there-being 223
The Thought of Difference (Héritier) 157
Three Essays on the Theory of Sexuality
    (Freud) 5, 45, 47, 48–49, 94,
    275n2, 283
Time (magazine) 262
#Time's Up 190
Tin Dama in New Guinea 162
Tiresian myth and the Other sexual
    difference 197–210
Tóibín, Colm 119, 128–129
Tolkien, J. R. R. 264
Tompkins, Kyla Wazana 315n30
Tonga people, Polynesian 164
tongue and human language 60–62
Tort, Michel 153
trans*affirmation 275
trans*cursive enunciation 263
transcursivity 268–273, 277n12
Trans-Exclusionary Radical Feminist
    (TERF) 276n4
trans* feminine experiences 9

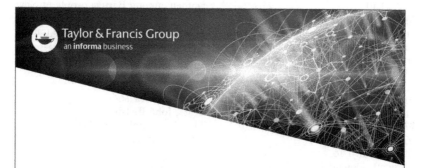